Praise for *CockroachDB: The Definitive Guide*

DoorDash has been able to use CockroachDB to forklift-migrate and scale numerous workloads without having to rewrite applications—only small index or schema changes. This definitive resource is for both new engineers and seasoned veterans who want to learn CockroachDB's internals, deployment, and capabilities. Engineers looking to build and run scalable applications using CockroachDB would do well to read this book.

—Sean Chittenden, Core Infrastructure, DoorDash

Modern distributed SQL systems bring together the best ideas of databases from the last 50 years: the relational model, strong consistency guarantees, and elastic scalability. This trinity is what modern applications need to stay in the game.

—Andy Pavlo, Associate Professor of Databases, Carnegie-Mellon University; Cofounder, OtterTune

Distributed SQL databases combine the benefits of the relational database model with native support for distributed cloud architecture. CockroachDB pairs the transactional consistency of standard SQL with elastic scalability, multiregion and multicloud deployment, and high levels of fault tolerance and availability. Developers thinking about their next-generation enterprise application requirements will find this guide very timely.

—Matt Aslett, VP & Research Director, Ventana Research

We know that sometimes (stuff) happens. And, at scale, (stuff) is always happening.

—Spencer Kimball, Cofounder, Cockroach Labs
(as mentioned in the CockroachDB: The Definitive Guide *preface)*

CockroachDB: The Definitive Guide
Distributed Data at Scale

Guy Harrison, Jesse Seldess, and Ben Darnell

Beijing · Boston · Farnham · Sebastopol · Tokyo

CockroachDB: The Definitive Guide

by Guy Harrison, Jesse Seldess, and Ben Darnell

Published by O'Reilly Media, Inc., 1005 Gravenstein Highway North, Sebastopol, CA 95472.

O'Reilly books may be purchased for educational, business, or sales promotional use. Online editions are also available for most titles (*http://oreilly.com*). For more information, contact our corporate/institutional sales department: 800-998-9938 or *corporate@oreilly.com*.

Acquisitions Editor: Andy Kwan	**Indexer:** nSight, Inc.
Development Editor: Angela Rufino	**Interior Designer:** David Futato
Production Editor: Christopher Faucher	**Cover Designer:** Karen Montgomery
Copyeditor: Stephanie English	**Illustrator:** Kate Dullea
Proofreader: Kim Cofer	

April 2022:   First Edition

Revision History for the First Edition
2022-04-08:   First Release

See *http://oreilly.com/catalog/errata.csp?isbn=9781098100247* for release details.

978-1-098-10024-7

[LSI]

Table of Contents

Part II. Developing Applications with CockroachDB

Part III. Deploying and Administering CockroachDB

Preface

Why Cockroach?

Welcome to *CockroachDB: The Definitive Guide*, and thank you for being here! With this book, we want to help you learn to build and deploy applications with CockroachDB, the distributed SQL database built for the cloud.

First, the question everyone asks: *Why the name CockroachDB?*

One immutable fact of engineering is that things break. At large enough scale, things are breaking all the time. The kinds of failures that might happen once a year on a single machine become daily occurrences when you're running hundreds of shards. A system that aspires to handle large scale must treat fault tolerance as a core responsibility. This was one of the key insights of Google's MapReduce framework. By requiring all computation to fit within a relatively restrictive framework, it became straightforward for the system to automatically rerun the necessary pieces of work after a failure.

We believe that this is how it should be: highly available replication should be the default state of a database from day one, not the result of painstaking configuration work. And looking ahead to day two (or day two hundred), the database must be able to grow along with the application so that runaway success is a cause for celebration, not panic.

When we set out to build a relational database from scratch, we wanted to bring consistency, native resilience, data locality, and massive scale to modern cloud applications. Our vision was of a system able to colonize any resource that you gave it onto the public cloud and then relentlessly optimize itself. A database that would use available space and reach equilibrium across a coordinated set of globally distributed nodes so that it would not only incorporate new resources, but—if a machine or data center or even an entire region went down—the database would simply equalize the remaining available resources.

We aimed to build a database that would be globally ubiquitous and impossible to eradicate…just like *periplaneta brunnea*, the pesky common cockroach. And so CockroachDB was born.

Building CockroachDB

CockroachDB's origin is a tale of necessity. Quite literally, Spencer Kimball, Peter Mattis, and I, Ben Darnell, set out to build the relational database that we ourselves needed.

After working together at Google, the three of us went in different directions for a while. Eventually we ended up back together (along with Spencer's brother Andy, a Microsoft SQL Server veteran) at a startup called Viewfinder, building an application for photo organization and social sharing. We, of course, hoped it would be successful, so we wanted to build for scale. After all, as Spencer says, "Sometimes shit happens. And, at scale, shit's always happening."

It turns out that, given the history of that project, we didn't do well enough to ever need massive scalability, but we wanted to plan for it from the beginning. We also didn't want to lock ourselves into a monolithic database, sharding MySQL or anything like that. We had been down that road before and knew it didn't lead where we wanted to go. This left us looking at NoSQL options as the best alternative and eventually we settled on DynamoDB.

DynamoDB ticked a lot of boxes: it's scalable, it's fast, it's predictable. It's very similar to Bigtable, which I had used as the backend for Google Reader while I was at Google. And so, on paper at least, we really liked that model. But as we got experience with it, we realized we had a couple of fundamental problems with NoSQL.

The biggest one was we found that we really needed secondary indexes. The Bigtable/DynamoDB model is really primary keys only; there's no concept of secondary indexes. To get them, we had to build our own partial implementation of transactions on top of DynamoDB, which was workable. Once we were using this system, however, we found a subsequent problem. DynamoDB on its own is very fast, predictable, and scalable—but once you start doing things that combine multiple records, as we were doing with our secondary indexes, then things got difficult.

Ultimately, we came up with a system that worked, but the layering of transactions and indexes on top of DynamoDB was inefficient, both in terms of performance and our engineering efforts.

During this time we did start talking about the idea of building a database ourselves, but Viewfinder was a startup with a small team. We decided, *You know, DynamoDB is not ideal, but it exists and we can use it today, so that's what we'll do.* But then a year or two later Square bought Viewfinder, and we found out they were struggling with sharded MySQL. We realized then, *Okay, it's not just us, this is a real database need that's not getting met.* At Square we were now in a good position to try building a system that was both inherently scalable and supported secondary indexes. So that's where the effort really started in earnest.

Spencer started on it as an open source side project on nights and weekends at first. And then he got some more contributors, and eventually it even became an official project at Square. But we knew that the real destiny of this project was to serve the entire database market, so that's when we decided to leave Square and start a company to do just that: Cockroach Labs was founded in 2015.

Next Steps

Having set out to build a database that is as indestructible as an intrusion of cockroaches, the next question was, of course, what other capabilities it would need.

We believed that the right approach was to embrace distributed transactions from the start and make them an integral part of the architecture. And while SQL is hardly anyone's idea of a perfect query language, it is the one that everyone knows, with a time-tested feature set. SQL's declarative schema management and statistics-based query optimization give operators powerful tools to manage their application's performance at runtime.

So the story of getting to CockroachDB version 1.0 was solving the new problem of scale plus transactions using SQL. The result is a globally distributed SQL database built on top of a transactional and consistent key-value (KV) store. The primary design goals are support for ACID transactions, horizontal scalability, low latency/ high availability, and survivability. CockroachDB implements a Raft consensus algorithm for consistency and aims to tolerate disk, machine, rack, and even data center failures with minimal disruption and no manual intervention.

Once we started building and deploying this, we found that the greatest interest in what we were doing came from people working with global deployments. It turns out this is something Cockroach is uniquely capable of handling, and so with version 2.0 we started building more and more features for global and geographic distribution.

It's been a long time since we launched CockroachDB 2.0 and multiregion. Since then, the biggest developments have been CockroachDB Cloud followed by CockroachDB Serverless. These fulfilled our next mission: to make data easy. Our Viewfinder startup days showed us the need for a database that can be used for projects from day one and would also grow along with it, without breaking the bank. You can self-host open source CockroachDB locally on a laptop, on a corporate dev cluster or private cloud, as well as on any public cloud infrastructure, but the price of entry is still fairly substantial. The first step toward making CockroachDB accessible was to take away the operational burden from the user, and we achieved that with our cloud-hosted, fully managed service now called CockroachDB Dedicated.

Now we have added CockroachDB Serverless to give users the low-cost or even no-cost foot in the door that you can use from the beginning, and then it scales up affordably with your usage. We are still building out serverless capabilities, but soon we will have serverless multiregion available. That will be when we can make it cheap enough for everyone to simply build multiregion by default.

What comes after that? Well, we are continuing to explore ways to use cloud native features to gain even greater efficiencies and drive down operating costs. Things like looking at the menu of various storage solutions that the clouds offer and choosing the appropriate ones for our different kinds of storage needs instead of using block storage devices for everything as we currently do. Multiregion serverless is definitely something we are building right now. First though, we have what we've been calling enterprise serverless: the ability for a company to get dedicated clusters that you then subdivide for your own private serverless-style usage. In other words, getting the operational efficiencies of serverless while still being fully isolated.

Farther along the horizon, we're looking to bring in user-defined functions and stored procedures. This is a lightning rod for discussion because people have strong opinions, but I think that when you combine user-defined functions and stored procedures with a scalable database, it gets really interesting. It can really transform the way you think about your application architecture because it lets you shift more of your logic into the database.

More speculatively? As CockroachDB's chief architect, I'd like to explore ways that you could host your entire application, just straight out of the database, using stored procedures. Even saying that out loud is going to be a bit controversial because that's the sort of thing that people tried to do back in, like, 1998 and, we admit, it didn't work well then. However, I think things have evolved to the point that now may be the right time. That's still very speculative, just something I'm thinking about and not something that is officially on the Cockroach Labs roadmap at this time. But I'd like to try to hack out some sort of prototype instead of just talking about it. Maybe now that this book is published, that will free up some time to experiment.

Why We Wrote This Book

This book aims to help you, the reader, understand the architecture and capabilities of CockroachDB as well as suitable use cases for CockroachDB. By the end of this book, you will be able to get started with CockroachDB, build effective applications on it, and, ultimately, run a cluster in production.

The chapters teach developers, architects, and DevOps teams how to build, optimize, and manage applications that run on CockroachDB. We wrote this book to give any developer, no matter how they want to work with CockroachDB, the knowledge and tools they need to do it effectively.

Who This Book Is For

Innovative developers
> *CockroachDB: The Definitive Guide* is for developers building modern applications, whether in a small startup or a large enterprise. This guide will teach developers how to build and ship apps with fewer obstacles using a powerful distributed SQL database that just works.

Architects
> *The Definitive Guide* is for modern architects delivering scalable, resilient apps across their IT ecosystem. Architects will learn how to design distributed applications to provide low latency, high availability, and faster performance.

DevOps teams
> *The Definitive Guide* is for strategic IT operators managing applications with data-intensive workloads. Operators will learn how to optimize CockroachDB's inherent abilities of scale and resilience, efficiently distributing data to meet any workload demand—wherever it's deployed.

Those already familiar with distributed systems will discover the benefits of strong data correctness and consistency guarantees as well as optimizations for delivering low-latency transactions to users anywhere in the world.

It includes specific guidance for anyone transitioning from a monolithic database (e.g., MySQL or PostgreSQL) to a distributed architecture, as well as practical examples for anyone more familiar with NoSQL systems.

How This Book Is Organized

This book contains 15 chapters divided into three sections.

- Part I, "Introduction to CockroachDB", establishes the historical context of CockroachDB, covering the evolution of databases and the emergence of distributed cloud databases. Readers cover core concepts of distributed SQL, then dive into the architecture and capabilities of CockroachDB, followed by examinations of suitable use cases for CockroachDB. Part I ends with a hands-on guide to getting started, both with a local installation and Cockroach Labs' free cloud service, and a thorough guide to CockroachDB's SQL dialect.

- Part II, "Developing Applications with CockroachDB", covers the fundamentals of CockroachDB schema design. Next, readers work through application design and implementation as well as integration with and/or migration from other databases. You will practice working with data in CockroachDB, including managing transactions, exploring change data capture, and building SQL tuning skills.

- Part III, "Deploying and Administering CockroachDB", covers the planning and execution of single and multiregion deployments. Essential topics include backup and disaster recovery; security; monitoring, administration and troubleshooting; and cluster optimization.

Conventions Used in This Book

The following typographical conventions are used in this book:

Italic
Indicates new terms, URLs, email addresses, filenames, and file extensions.

`Constant width`
Used for program listings, as well as within paragraphs to refer to program elements such as variable or function names, databases, data types, environment variables, statements, and keywords.

`Constant width bold`
Shows commands or other text that should be typed literally by the user.

`Constant width italic`
Shows text that should be replaced with user-supplied values or by values determined by context.

This element signifies a tip or suggestion.

This element signifies a general note.

This element indicates a warning or caution.

Using Code Examples

Supplemental material (code examples, exercises, etc.) is available for download at *https://github.com/cockroachdb/definitive_guide_sample_code*.

If you have a technical question or a problem using the code examples, please send email to *bookquestions@oreilly.com*.

This book is here to help you get your job done. In general, if example code is offered with this book, you may use it in your programs and documentation. You do not need to contact us for permission unless you're reproducing a significant portion of the code. For example, writing a program that uses several chunks of code from this book does not require permission. Selling or distributing examples from O'Reilly books does require permission. Answering a question by citing this book and quoting example code does not require permission. Incorporating a significant amount of example code from this book into your product's documentation does require permission.

We appreciate, but generally do not require, attribution. An attribution usually includes the title, author, publisher, and ISBN. For example: "*CockroachDB: The Definitive Guide* by Guy Harrison, Jesse Seldess, and Ben Darnell (O'Reilly). Copyright 2022 O'Reilly Media, Inc., 978-1-098-10025-4."

If you feel your use of code examples falls outside fair use or the permission given above, feel free to contact us at *permissions@oreilly.com*.

O'Reilly Online Learning

 For more than 40 years, *O'Reilly Media* has provided technology and business training, knowledge, and insight to help companies succeed.

Our unique network of experts and innovators share their knowledge and expertise through books, articles, and our online learning platform. O'Reilly's online learning platform gives you on-demand access to live training courses, in-depth learning paths, interactive coding environments, and a vast collection of text and video from O'Reilly and 200+ other publishers. For more information, visit *http://oreilly.com*.

How to Contact Us

Please address comments and questions concerning this book to the publisher:

O'Reilly Media, Inc.
1005 Gravenstein Highway North
Sebastopol, CA 95472
800-998-9938 (in the United States or Canada)
707-829-0515 (international or local)
707-829-0104 (fax)

We have a web page for this book, where we list errata, examples, and any additional information. You can access this page at *https://oreil.ly/cockroachDB-definitive-guide*.

Email *bookquestions@oreilly.com* to comment or ask technical questions about this book.

For news and information about our books and courses, visit *http://oreilly.com*.

Find us on LinkedIn: *https://linkedin.com/company/oreilly-media*.

Follow us on Twitter: *http://twitter.com/oreillymedia*.

Watch us on YouTube: *http://youtube.com/oreillymedia*.

Acknowledgments

Writing this book was a truly collaborative venture, and the authors are thankful for the many people who helped along the way, especially Andy Pavlo, Sean Chittenden, and Matt Aslett, who provided their knowledgeable opinions around Distributed SQL and CockroachDB to be shared in (and on) this book.

The authors would like to thank the vital open source community that supports and contributes to CockroachDB, as well as the many Roachers who joined Cockroach Labs to help us continually extend and improve the database. Our special thanks go to the reviewers who applied their subject matter expertise—gained from building CockroachDB—to careful technical review of each chapter. Andy Woods, Vy Ton, Piyush Singh, Liv Lobo, Abbey Russell, Keith McClellan, and Chris Ireland, all from Cockroach Labs, we are grateful for your thoughtful suggestions and keen-sighted corrections that helped improve every part of this book. We are equally grateful to external reviewers Alan Beaulieu, consultant, and software engineer and machine learning specialist Patrick Deziel from Rotational Labs, LLC. We would also like to thank Jessica Edwards for shepherding the process from day one, and Michelle Gienow for then taking over and helping us cross the finish line.

We'd like to thank the team from O'Reilly whose consistent diligence and professionalism kept us on track and ensured we created a high-quality and useful book. Thanks especially to Angela Rufino, Andy Kwan, and Sharon Cordesse: it really was a pleasure to work with you. Additional thanks to the production team: Christopher Faucher, our production editor; Stephanie English, the copyeditor; Kim Cofer, proofreader; Johnna VanHoose Dinse, our indexer; and Kate Dullea, the interior illustrator.

Guy Harrison

I'd like to thank all the folks at O'Reilly and CockroachDB who collaborated on the book, and particularly Ben and Jesse for giving me the opportunity to work with them to write this guide. As the "old man" of the team, I've been writing books on database technology for more than 20 years, and the opportunity to work at the cutting edge of modern database technology was really exciting. I'd, of course, most especially like to thank my wonderful wife, Jenny, who makes every day a good day, and who tolerated my distraction and absence during this project.

Jesse Seldess

I would like to thank everyone who has been part of the Cockroach Labs Documentation team over the years. Great docs make for self-sufficient and happy users, and I've been fortunate to work with dedicated, talented writers producing world-class docs that users can trust and rely on for their day-to-day work. Many, many thanks to Guy Harrison as well; your extensive database and development experience took this project to new levels, and your productive writing approach kept us in constructive discussion and on track. Finally, love and appreciation to my wife, Leonie, and kids, Selma and Paz, for helping me find space and clarity to do my part in this book, all my work at Cockroach Labs, and so much more.

Ben Darnell

I would like to thank Spencer Kimball and Peter Mattis for being colleagues, cofounders, and true collaborators in creating CockroachDB. It's been quite a journey so far, and putting this guide together was a constant reminder of just how far we have come since we first came up with the crazy idea of building our own distributed database. Enormous thanks also to Guy Harrison, whose deep existing database knowledge paired with his diligence in learning Cockroach just as deeply contributed immeasurably to the scope and thoroughness of the book. I also wish to thank Brandi Evans for making it possible for me to find time to step away to work on this project. Most of all, I want to thank my wife, Juliet Moser, for her support and patience throughout the evenings and weekends it took to produce this book, as well as the many other reasons I am grateful for her.

## PART I

Introduction to CockroachDB

## CHAPTER 1

Introduction to CockroachDB

CockroachDB is a distributed, transactional, relational, cloud native SQL database system. That's quite a mouthful! But in short, CockroachDB leverages both the strengths of the previous generation of relational database systems—strong consistency, the power of SQL, and the relational data model—and the strengths of modern distributed cloud principles. The result is a database system that is broadly compatible with other SQL-based transactional databases but delivers much greater scalability and availability.

In this chapter, we'll review the history of database management systems (DBMSs) and discover how CockroachDB exploits technology advances of the last few decades to deliver on its ambitious goals.

A Brief History of Databases

Data storage and data processing are the "killer apps" of human civilization. Verbal language gave us an enormous advantage in cooperating as a community. Still, it was only when we developed data storage—e.g., written language—that each generation could build on the lessons of preceding generations.

The earliest written records—dating back almost 10,000 years—are agricultural accounting records. These cuneiform records, recorded on clay tablets (Figure 1-1), serve the same purpose as the databases that support modern accounting systems.

Information storage technologies over thousands of years progressed slowly. The use of cheap, portable, and reasonably durable paper media organized in libraries and cabinets represented best practices for almost a millennia.

Figure 1-1. Cuneiform tablet circa 3000 BC (Source: Wikipedia (https://cockroa.ch/3AFZ9eY))

The emergence of digital data processing has truly resulted in an information revolution. Within a single human life span, digital information systems have resulted in exponential growth in the volume and rate of information storage. Today, the vast bulk of human information is stored in digital formats, much of it within database systems.

Pre-Relational Databases

The first digital computers had negligible storage capacity and were used primarily for computation—for instance, generating ballistic tables, decrypting codes, and performing scientific calculations. However, as magnetic tape and disks became mainstream in the 1950s, it became increasingly possible to use computers to store and process volumes of information that would be unwieldy by other means.

Early applications used simple flat files for data storage. But it soon became obvious that the complexities of reliably and efficiently dealing with large amounts of data required specialized and dedicated software platforms—and these became the first data systems.

Early database systems ran within monolithic mainframe computers, which also were responsible for the application code. The applications were tightly coupled with the database systems and processed data directly using procedural language directives. By the 1970s, two models of database systems were vying for dominance—the *network* and *hierarchical* models. These models were represented by the major databases of the day, *IMS* (Information Management System) and *IDMS* (Integrated Database Management System).

These systems were great advances on their predecessors but had significant drawbacks. Queries needed to be anticipated in advance of implementation, and only record-at-a-time processing was supported. Even the simplest report required programming resources to implement, and all IT departments suffered from a huge backlog of reporting requests.

The Relational Model

Probably no one has had more influence over database technology than Edgar Codd (whatever Larry Ellison might think). Codd was a "programming mathematician"— what we might today call a data scientist—who had worked at IBM on and off since 1949. In 1970, Codd wrote his seminal paper, "A Relational Model of Data for Large Shared Data Banks" (*https://cockroa.ch/3LICx1M*). This paper outlined what Codd saw as fundamental issues in the design of existing database systems:

- Existing database systems merged physical and logical representations of data in a way that often complicated requests for data and created difficulties in satisfying requests that were not anticipated during database design.
- There was no formal standard for data representation. As a mathematician, Codd was familiar with theoretical models for representing data—he believed these principles should be applied to database systems.
- Existing database systems were too hard to use. Only programmers were able to retrieve data from these systems, and the process of retrieving data was needlessly complex. Codd felt that there needed to be an easy-access method for data retrieval.

Codd's relational model described a means of logically representing data that was independent of the underlying storage mechanism. It required a *query language* that could be used to answer any question that could be satisfied by the data.

The relational model defines the fundamental building blocks of a relational database:

- *Tuples* are a set of *attribute* values. Attributes are named scalar (single-dimensional) values. A tuple can be thought of as an individual "record" or "row."

- A *relation* is a collection of distinct tuples of the same form. A relation represents a two-dimensional data set with a fixed number of attributes and an arbitrary number of tuples. A table in a database is an example of a relation.

- *Constraints* enforce consistency and define relationships between tuples.

- Various *operations* are defined, such as joins, projections, and unions. Operations on relations always return relations. For instance, when you join two relations, the result is itself a relation.

- A *key* consists of one or more attributes that can be used to identify a tuple. There can be more than one key, and a key can consist of multiple attributes.

The relational model furthermore defined a series of "normal forms" that represent reducing levels of redundancy in the model. A relation is in *third normal form* if all the data in each tuple is dependent on the entire primary key of that tuple and on no other attributes. We generally remember this by the adage, "The key, the whole key, and nothing but the key (so help me, Codd)."

Third normal form generally represents the starting point for the construction of an efficient and performant data model. We will come back to third normal form in Chapter 5. Figure 1-2 illustrates data in third normal form.

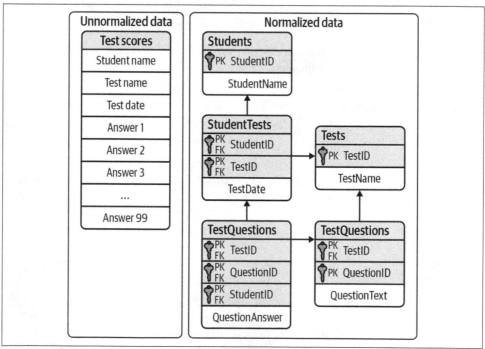

Figure 1-2. Data represented in a relational "third normal form" structure

Implementing the Relational Model

The relational model served as the foundation for the familiar structures present in all relational databases today. Tuples are represented as *rows* and relations as *tables*.

A table is a relation that has been given physical storage. The underlying storage may take different forms. In addition to the physical representation of the data, indexing and clustering schemes were introduced to facilitate efficient data processing and implement constraints.

Indexes and clustered storage were not a part of the relational model, but they were incorporated in relational databases to transparently enhance query performance without changing the types of queries that could be performed. Thus, the logical representation of the data as presented to the application was independent of the underlying physical model.

Indeed, in some relational implementations, a table might be implemented by multiple indexed structures, allowing different access paths to the data.

Transactions

A transaction is a logical unit of work that must succeed or fail as a unit. Transactions predated the relational model, but in pre-relational systems, transactions were often the responsibility of the application layer. In Codd's relational model, the database took formal responsibility for transactional processing.[1] In Codd's formulation, a relational system would provide explicit support for commencing a transaction and either committing or aborting that transaction.

The use of transactions to maintain consistency in application data was also used internally to maintain consistency between the various physical structures that represented tables. For instance, when a table is represented in multiple indexes, all of those indexes must be kept synchronized in a transactional manner.

Codd's relational model did not define all the aspects of transactional behavior that became common to most relational database systems. In 1981 Jim Gray articulated the core principles of transaction processing that we still use today. These principles later became known as *ACID*—atomic, consistent, isolated and durable—transactions.

As Gray put it, "A transaction is a transformation of state which has the properties of *atomicity* (all or nothing), *durability* (effects survive failures) and *consistency* (a correct transformation)." The principle of *isolation*—added in a later revision—

---

1 From "Rule 5" in Codd's 12 rules, which were published in the early '80s.

required that one transaction should not be able to see the effects of other in-progress transactions.

Perfect isolation between transactions—*serializable* isolation—creates some restrictions on concurrent data processing. Many databases adopted lower levels of isolation or allowed applications to choose from various isolation levels. These implications will be discussed further in Chapter 2.

The SQL Language

Codd specified that a relational system should support a "database sublanguage" to navigate and modify relational data. He proposed the Alpha language in 1971, which influenced the QUEL language designed by the creators of Ingres—an early relational database system developed at the University of California, which influenced the open source PostgreSQL database.

Meanwhile, researchers at IBM were developing System R, a prototype DBMS based on Codd's relational model. They developed the SEQUEL language as the data sublanguage for the project. SEQUEL eventually was renamed SQL and was adopted in commercial IBM databases, including IBM DB2.

Oracle chose SQL as the query language for its pioneering Oracle relational database management system (RDBMS), and by the end of the 1970s, SQL had won out over QUEL as the relational query language and became an ANSI (American National Standards Institute) standard language in 1986.

SQL needs very little introduction. Today, it's one of the most widely used computer languages in the world. We will devote Chapter 4 to the CockroachDB SQL implementation. However, it's worth noting that the relative ease of use that SQL provided expanded the audience of database users dramatically. No longer did you need to be a highly experienced database programmer to retrieve data from a database: SQL could be taught to casual users of databases, such as analysts and statisticians. It's fair to say that SQL brought databases within reach of business users.

The RDBMS Hegemony

The combination of the relational model, SQL language, and ACID transactions became the dominant model for new database systems from the early 1980s through the early 2000s. These systems became known generically as RDBMS.

The RDBMS came into prevalence around the same time as a seismic paradigm shift in application architectures. The world of mainframe applications was giving way to the *client/server* model. In the client/server model, application code ran on microcomputers (PCs) while the database ran on a minicomputer, increasingly running the Unix OS. During the migration to client/server, mainframe-based pre-relational databases were largely abandoned in favor of the new breed of RDBMSs.

By the end of the 20th century, the RDBMS reigned supreme. The leading commercial databases of the day—Oracle, Sybase, SQL Server, Informix, and DB2—competed on performance, functionality, or price, but all were virtually identical in their adoption of the relational model, SQL, and ACID transactions. As open source software grew in popularity, open source relational database management systems such as MySQL and PostgreSQL gained significant and growing traction.

Enter the Internet

Around the turn of the 21st century, an even more important shift in application architectures occurred. That shift was, of course, the internet. Initially, internet applications ran on a software stack not dissimilar to a client/server application. A single large server hosted the application's database, while application code ran on a "middle tier" server and end users interacted with the application through web browsers.

In the early days of the internet, this architecture sufficed—though often just barely. The monolithic database servers were often a performance bottleneck, and although standby databases were routinely deployed, a database failure was one of the most common causes of application failure.

As the web grew, the limitations of the centralized RDBMS became untenable. The emerging "web 2.0" social network and ecommerce sites had two characteristics that were increasingly difficult to support:

- These systems had a global or near-global scale. Users in multiple continents needed simultaneous access to the application.
- Any level of downtime was undesirable. The old model of "weekend upgrades" was no longer acceptable. There was no maintenance window that did not involve significant business disruption.

All parties agreed that the monolithic single database system would have to give way if the demands of the new breed of internet applications were to be realized. It became recognized that a very significant and potentially immovable obstacle stood in the way: *CAP theorem*. CAP—or Brewer's (*https://cockroa.ch/3KbklgD*)—theorem states that you can only have at most two of three desirable characteristics in a distributed system (illustrated in Figure 1-3):

Consistency
   Every user sees the same view of the database state.

Availability
   The database remains available unless all elements of the distributed system fail.

Partition tolerance

> The system runs in an environment in which a network partition might divide the distributed system in two, or if two nodes in the network cannot communicate. A partition-tolerant system will continue to operate despite an arbitrary number of messages being dropped (or delayed) by the network between nodes.

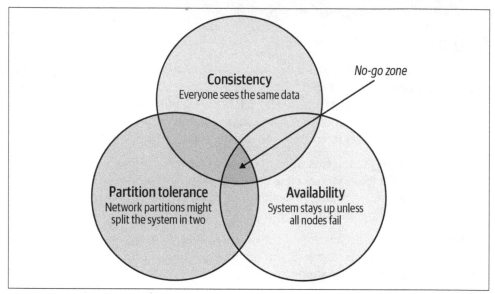

Figure 1-3. CAP theorem states that a system cannot support all three properties of consistency, availability, and partition tolerance

For instance, consider the case of a global ecommerce system with users in North America and Europe. If the network between the two continents fails (a network partition), then you must choose one of the following outcomes:

- Users in Europe and North America may see different versions of the database: *sacrificing consistency*.

- One of the two regions needs to shut down (or go read-only): *sacrificing availability*.

Clustered RDBMSs at that time would generally sacrifice availability. For instance, in Oracle's Real Application Clusters (RAC) clustered database, a network partition between nodes would cause all nodes in one of the partitions to shut down.

Internet pioneers such as Amazon, however, believed that availability was more important than strict consistency. Amazon developed a database system—*Dynamo*—that implemented "*eventual consistency*." In the event of a partition, all zones would continue to have access to the system, but when the partition was resolved, inconsistencies would be reconciled—possibly losing data in the process.

The NoSQL Movement

Between 2008 and 2010, dozens of new database systems emerged, all of which abandoned the three pillars of the RDBMS: the relational data model, SQL language, and ACID transactions. Some of these new systems—Cassandra, Riak, Project Voldemort, and HBase, for example—were directly influenced by nonrelational technologies developed at Amazon and Google.

Many of these systems were essentially "schema-free"—supporting or even requiring no specific structure for the data they stored. In particular, in key-value databases, an arbitrary key provides programmatic access to an arbitrary structured "value." The database knows nothing about what is in this value. From the database's view, the value is just a set of unstructured bits. Other nonrelational systems represented data in semi-tabular formats or as JSON (JavaScript Object Notation) documents. However, none of these new databases implemented the principles of the relational model.

These systems were initially referred to as distributed nonrelational database systems (DNRDBMSs), but—because they did not include the SQL language—rapidly became known by the far catchier term "NoSQL" databases.

NoSQL was always a questionable term. It defined what the class of systems discarded, rather than their unique distinguishing features. Nevertheless, "NoSQL" stuck, and in the following decade, NoSQL databases such as Cassandra, DynamoDB, and MongoDB became established as a distinct and important segment of the database landscape.

The Emergence of Distributed SQL

The challenges of implementing distributed transactions at a web scale, more than anything else, led to the schism in modern database management systems. With the rise of global applications with extremely high uptime requirements, it became unthinkable to sacrifice availability for perfect consistency. Almost in unison, the leading web 2.0 companies such as Amazon, Google, and Facebook introduced new database services that were only "eventually" or "weakly" consistent but globally and highly available, and the open source community responded with databases based on these principles.

However, NoSQL databases had their own severe limitations. The SQL language was widely understood and was the basis for almost all business intelligence tools. NoSQL databases found that they had to offer some SQL compatibility, and so many added some SQL-like dialect—leading to the redefinition of NoSQL as "not only SQL." In many cases, these SQL implementations were query-only and intended only to support business intelligence features. In other cases, a SQL-like language supported transactional processing but provided only the most limited subset of SQL functionality.

However, the problems caused by weakened consistency were harder to ignore. Consistency and correctness in data are often nonnegotiable for mission-critical applications. While in some circumstances—social media, for instance—it might be acceptable for different users to see slightly different views of the same topic, in other contexts—such as logistics—any inconsistency is unacceptable. Advanced non-relational databases adopted tunable consistency and sophisticated conflict resolution algorithms to mitigate data inconsistency. However, any database that abandons strict consistency must accept scenarios in which data can be lost or corrupted during the reconciliation of network partitions or from ambiguously timed competing transactions.

Google pioneered many of the technologies behind important open source NoSQL systems. For instance, the Google File System and MapReduce technologies led directly to Apache Hadoop, and Google Bigtable led to Apache HBase. As such, Google was well aware of the limitations of these new data stores.

The Spanner project was initiated as an attempt to build a distributed database, similar to Google's existing Bigtable system, that could support both strong consistency and high availability.

Spanner benefited from Google's highly redundant network, which reduced the probability of network-based availability issues, but the really novel feature of Spanner was its *TrueTime* system. TrueTime explicitly models the uncertainty of time measurement in a distributed system so that it can be incorporated into the transaction protocol. Distributed databases go to a lot of effort to return consistent information from replicas maintained across the system. Locks are the primary mechanism to prevent inconsistent information from being created in the database, while snapshots are the primary mechanism for returning consistent information. Queries don't see changes to data that occur while they are executing because they read from a consistent "snapshot" of data. Maintaining snapshots in distributed databases can be tricky: usually, there's a large amount of inter-node communication required to create agreement on the ordering of transactions and queries. Clock information provided by TrueTime enables the use of snapshots with minimal communication between nodes.

Google Spanner further optimizes the snapshot mechanism by using GPS receivers and atomic clocks installed in each data center. GPS provides an externally validated timestamp while the atomic clock provides high-resolution time between GPS "fixes." The result is that every Spanner server across the world has almost the same clock time. This allows Spanner to order transactions and queries precisely without requiring excessive inter-node communication or delays due to excessive clock uncertainty.

Spanner is highly dependent on Google's redundant network and specialized server hardware. Spanner can't operate independently of the Google network.

The initial version of Spanner pushed the boundaries of the CAP theorem as far as technology allowed. It represented a distributed database system in which consistency was guaranteed, availability maximized, and network partitions avoided as much as possible. Over time, Google added relational features to the data model of Spanner as well as SQL language support. By 2017, Spanner had evolved to a distributed database that supported all three pillars of the RDBMS: the SQL language, relational data model, and ACID transactions.

The Advent of CockroachDB

With Spanner, Google persuasively demonstrated the utility of a highly consistent distributed database. However, Spanner was tightly coupled to the Google Cloud Platform (GCP) and—at least initially—not publicly available.

There was an obvious need for the technologies pioneered by Spanner to be made more widely available. In 2015, a trio of Google alumni—Spencer Kimball, Peter Mattis, and Ben Darnell—founded Cockroach Labs with the intention of creating an open source, geo-scalable, ACID-compliant database.

Spencer, Peter, and Ben chose the name "CockroachDB" in honor of the humble cockroach, which, it is told, is so resilient that it would survive even a nuclear war (Figure 1-4).

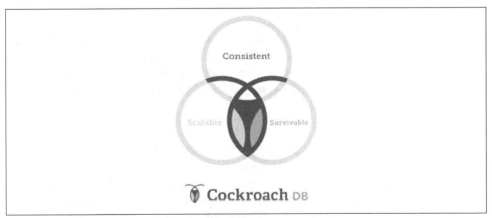

Figure 1-4. The original CockroachDB logo

CockroachDB Design Goals

CockroachDB was designed to support the following attributes:

Scalability

The CockroachDB distributed architecture allows a cluster to scale seamlessly as workload increases or decreases. Nodes can be added to a cluster without any manual rebalancing, and performance will scale predictably as the number of nodes increases.

High availability

A CockroachDB cluster has no single point of failure. CockroachDB can continue operating if a node, zone, or region fails without compromising availability.

Consistency

CockroachDB provides the highest practical level of transactional isolation and consistency. Transactions operate independently of each other and, once committed, transactions are guaranteed to be durable and visible to all sessions.

Performance

The CockroachDB architecture is designed to support low-latency and high-throughput transactional workloads. Every effort has been made to adopt database best practices with regard to indexing, caching, and other database optimization strategies.

Geo-partitioning

CockroachDB allows data to be physically located in specific localities to enhance performance for "localized" applications and to respect data sovereignty requirements.

Compatibility

CockroachDB implements ANSI-standard SQL and is wire-protocol compatible with PostgreSQL. This means that the majority of database drivers and frameworks that work with PostgreSQL will also work with CockroachDB. Many PostgreSQL applications can be ported to CockroachDB without requiring significant coding changes.

Portability

CockroachDB is offered as a fully managed database service, which in many cases is the easiest and most cost-effective deployment mode. But it's also capable of running on pretty much any platform you can imagine, from a developer's laptop to a massive cloud deployment. The CockroachDB architecture is very well aligned with containerized deployment options, and in particular, with Kubernetes. CockroachDB provides a Kubernetes operator that eliminates much of the complexity involved in a Kubernetes deployment.

You may be thinking, "This thing can do everything!" However, it's worth pointing out that CockroachDB was not intended to be all things to all people. In particular:

CockroachDB prioritizes consistency over availability

We saw earlier how the CAP theorem states that you have to choose either consistency or availability when faced with a network partition. Unlike "eventually" consistent databases such as DynamoDB or Cassandra, CockroachDB guarantees consistency at all costs. This means that there are circumstances in which a CockroachDB node will refuse to service requests if it is cut off from its peers. A Cassandra node in similar circumstances might accept a request even if there is a chance that the data in the request will later have to be discarded.

The CockroachDB architecture prioritizes transactional workloads

CockroachDB includes the SQL constructs for issuing aggregations and the SQL 2003 analytic "windowing" functions, and CockroachDB is certainly capable of integrating with popular business intelligence tools such as Tableau. There's no specific reason why CockroachDB could not be used for analytic applications. However, the unique features of CockroachDB are targeted more at transactional workloads. For analytic-only workloads that do not require transactions, other database platforms might provide better performance.

It's important to remember that while CockroachDB was inspired by Spanner, it is in no way a "Spanner clone." The CockroachDB team has leveraged many of the Spanner team's concepts but has diverged from Spanner in several important ways.

First, Spanner was designed to run on very specific hardware. Spanner nodes have access to an atomic clock and GPS device, allowing incredibly accurate timestamps. CockroachDB is designed to run well on commodity hardware and within containerized environments (such as Kubernetes) and therefore cannot rely on atomic clock synchronization. As we will see in Chapter 2, CockroachDB does rely on decent clock synchronization between nodes but is far more tolerant of clock skew than Spanner. As a result, CockroachDB can run anywhere, including any cloud provider or on-premise data center (and one CockroachDB cluster can even span multiple cloud environments).

Second, while the distributed storage engine of CockroachDB is inspired by Spanner, the SQL engine and APIs are designed to be PostgreSQL compatible. PostgreSQL is one of the most implemented RDBMSs today and is supported by an extensive ecosystem of drivers and frameworks. The "wire protocol" of CockroachDB is completely compatible with PostgreSQL, which means that any driver that works with PostgreSQL will work with CockroachDB. At the SQL language layer, there will always be differences between PostgreSQL and CockroachDB because of differences in the underlying storage and transaction models. However, most commonly used SQL syntax is shared between the two databases.

Third, CockroachDB has evolved to satisfy the needs of its community and has introduced many features never envisaged by the Spanner project. Today, CockroachDB is a thriving database platform whose connection to Spanner is only of historical interest.

CockroachDB Releases

The first production release of CockroachDB appeared in May 2017. This release introduced the core capabilities of the distributed transactional SQL databases, albeit with some limitations of performance and scale. Version 2.0—released in 2018— included new partitioning features for geographically-distributed deployments, support for JSON data, and massive improvements in performance.

In 2019, CockroachDB courageously leaped from version 2 to version 19! This was not because of 17 failed versions between 2 and 19 but instead reflects a change in numbering strategy to associate each release with its release year rather than designating releases as "major" or "minor".

Some highlights of past releases include:

- Version 19.1 (April 2019) introduced security features such as encryption at rest and LDAP (Lightweight Directory Access Protocol) integration, the change data capture facility described in Chapter 7, and multiregion optimizations.
- Version 19.2 (November 2019) introduced the Parallel Commits transaction protocol and other performance improvements.
- Version 20.1 (May 2020) introduced many SQL features including `ALTER PRIMARY KEY`, `SELECT FOR UPDATE`, nested transactions, and temporary tables.
- Version 20.2 (November 2020) added support for spatial data types, new transaction detail pages in the DB console, and made the distributed `BACKUP` and `RESTORE` functionality available for free.
- Version 21.1 (May 2021) simplified the use of multiregion functionality and expanded logging configuration options.
- Version 21.2 (November 2021) introduced bounded staleness reads and numerous stability and performance improvements including an admission control system to prevent overloading the cluster

CockroachDB in Action

CockroachDB has gained strong and growing traction in a crowded database market. Users who have been constrained by the scalability of traditional relational databases such as PostgreSQL and MySQL are attracted by the greater scalability of CockroachDB. Those who have been using distributed NoSQL solutions such as Cassandra are attracted by the greater transactional consistency and SQL compatibility offered by CockroachDB. And those who are transforming toward modern containerized and cloud native architectures appreciate the cloud and container readiness of the platform.

Today, CockroachDB can boast of significant adoption at scale across multiple industries. Let's look at a few of these case studies.[2]

CockroachDB at DevSisters

DevSisters is a South Korean–based game development company responsible for games such as the mobile phone game *Cookie Run: Kingdom*. Originally, DevSisters used Couchbase for its persistence layer but was challenged by issues relating to transactional integrity and scalability. When looking for a new database solution, DevSister's requirements included scalability, transactional consistency, and support for very high throughput.

DevSisters considered Amazon Aurora and DynamoDB as well as CockroachDB, but in the end, chose CockroachDB. Sungyoon Jeong from the DevOps team says, "It would have been impossible to scale this game on MySQL or Aurora. We experienced more than six times the workload size we anticipated, and CockroachDB was able to scale with us throughout this journey."

CockroachDB at DoorDash

DoorDash is a local commerce platform that connects consumers with their favorite businesses across the United States, Canada, Australia, Japan, and Germany. Today, DoorDash has created more than 160 CockroachDB clusters for its developers for various customer-facing, backend analytics, and internal workloads.

The DoorDash team likes that CockroachDB scales horizontally, speaks SQL and has Postgres wire compatibility, and handles heavy reads/writes without impacting performance. CockroachDB's resilient architecture and live schema changes are also a huge bonus for the team. "DoorDash has been able to use CockroachDB to forklift-migrate and scale numerous workloads without having to rewrite applications—only small index or schema changes," says Sean Chittenden, engineering lead for the Core Infrastructure team at DoorDash.

CockroachDB at Bose

Bose is a world leading consumer technology company particularly well known as a provider of high-fidelity audio equipment.

---

2 Cockroach Labs maintains a growing list of CockroachDB case studies (*https://cockroa.ch/3u6vHwZ*).

Bose's customer base spans the globe, and Bose aims to provide those customers with best-in-class cloud-based support solutions.

Bose has embraced modern, microservices-based software architecture. The backbone of the Bose platform is Kubernetes, which allows applications access to low-level services—containerized computation—and to higher-level services such Elasticsearch, Kafka, and Redis. CockroachDB became the foundation of the database platform for this containerized microservice platform.

Aside from the resiliency and scalability of CockroachDB, CockroachDB's ability to be hosted within a Kubernetes environment was decisive.

By running CockroachDB in a Kubernetes environment, Bose has empowered developers by providing a self-service, database-on-demand capability. Developers can spin up CockroachDB clusters for development or testing simply and quickly within a Kubernetes environment. In production, CockroachDB running with Kubernetes provides full-stack scalability, redundancy, and high availability.

Summary

In this chapter, we've placed CockroachDB in a historical context and introduced the goals and capabilities of the CockroachDB database.

The RDBMSs that emerged in the 1970s and 1980s were a triumph of software engineering that powered software applications from client/server through to the early internet. But the demands of globally scalable, always available internet applications were inconsistent with the monolithic, strictly consistent RDBMS architectures of the day. Consequently, a variety of NoSQL distributed, "eventually consistent" systems emerged around 2010 to support the needs of a new generation of internal applications.

While these NoSQL solutions have their advantages, they are a step backward for many or most applications. The inability to guarantee data correctness and the loss of the highly familiar and productive SQL language was a regression in many respects. CockroachDB was designed as a highly consistent and highly available SQL-based transactional database that provides a better compromise between availability and consistency—prioritizing consistency above all but providing very high availability.

CockroachDB is a highly available, transactionally consistent SQL database compatible with existing development frameworks and with increasingly important containerized deployment models and cloud architectures. CockroachDB has been deployed at scale across a wide range of verticals and circumstances.

In the next chapter, we'll examine the architecture of CockroachDB and see exactly how it achieves its ambitious design goals.

## CHAPTER 2

CockroachDB Architecture

The architecture of a software system defines the high-level design decisions that enable the goals of that system. As you may recall from Chapter 1, the goals of CockroachDB are to provide a scalable, highly available, highly performant, strongly consistent, geo-distributed, SQL-powered relational database system capable of running across a wide variety of hardware platforms. The architecture of CockroachDB is aligned to those objectives.

Feel Free to Skip Ahead!

The CockroachDB architecture is sophisticated: it incorporates decades of database engineering best practice designs together with several unique innovations. However, CockroachDB doesn't require that you understand its internals to get things done. If you're in a hurry to get started with CockroachDB, you can skip forward to the next chapter and return to this chapter later as necessary. We will, however, assume you are broadly familiar with the key concepts in this chapter when we consider advanced topics later in the book. Those key concepts are summarized over the next few pages and elaborated on in the remainder of the chapter.

There are multiple ways of looking at the CockroachDB architecture. At the cluster level, a CockroachDB deployment consists of one or more shared-nothing, leaderless nodes that collaborate to present a single logical view of the distributed database system. Within each node, we can observe the CockroachDB architecture as a series of layers that provide essential database services, including SQL processing, transaction processing, replication, distribution, and storage.

In this chapter, we'll endeavor to give you a comprehensive overview of the CockroachDB architecture. The aim of the chapter is to provide you with the fundamental concepts that will help you make sensible decisions regarding schema design, performance optimization, cluster deployment, and other topics.

The CockroachDB Cluster Architecture

From a distance, a CockroachDB deployment consists of one or more database server processes. Each server has its own dedicated storage—the familiar "shared-nothing" database cluster pattern. The nodes in a CockroachDB cluster are symmetrical—there are no "special" or "primary" nodes. This storage is often directly attached to the machine on which the CockroachDB server runs, though it's also possible for that data to be physically located on a shared storage subsystem. Data is distributed across the cluster based on *key ranges*. Each range is replicated to at least three members of the cluster.

Database clients—applications, administrative consoles, the CockroachDB shell, and so on—connect to a CockroachDB server within the cluster.

The communications between a database server and database client occur over the PostgreSQL *wire protocol* format. This protocol describes how SQL requests and responses are transmitted between a PostgreSQL client and a PostgreSQL server. Because CockroachDB uses the PostgreSQL wire protocol, any PostgreSQL driver can be used to communicate with a CockroachDB server. In a more complex deployment, one or more *load balancer* processes will be responsible for ensuring that these connections are evenly and sensibly distributed across nodes. The load balancer will connect the client with one of the nodes within the cluster, which will become the *gateway server* for the connection.

The client request might involve reading and writing data to a single node or to multiple nodes within the cluster. For any given range of key-values, a *leaseholder node* will be responsible for controlling reads and writes to that range. The leaseholder is also usually the *Raft leader*, which has the responsibility to make sure that replicas of the data are maintained correctly.

Figure 2-1 illustrates some of these concepts. A database client connects to a load balancer (1) that serves as a proxy for the CockroachDB cluster. The load balancer directs requests to an available CockroachDB node (2). This node becomes the gateway node for this connection. The request requires data in range 4, so the gateway node communicates with the leaseholder node for this range (3), which returns data to the gateway, which in turn returns the required data to the database client (4).

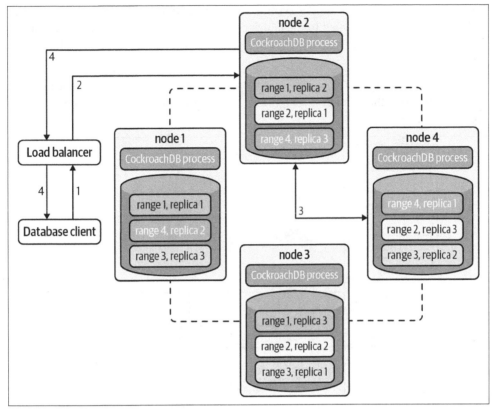

Figure 2-1. CockroachDB cluster architecture

This architecture distributes load evenly across the nodes of the cluster. Gateway duties are distributed evenly across the nodes of the cluster by the load balancer; leaseholder duties are similarly distributed by ranges across all the nodes.

If a query requires data from multiple ranges or where data must be changed (and therefore replicated), the workflow involves more steps.

Ranges and Replicas

We'll examine the nuances of CockroachDB distribution and replication later in this chapter. For now, there are a few concepts we need to understand.

Under the hood, data in a CockroachDB table is organized in a *key-value* (KV) storage system. The key for the KV store is the table's primary key. The value in the KV store is a binary representation of the values for all the columns in that row.

Indexes are also stored in the KV system. In the case of a non-unique index, the key is the index key concatenated to the table's primary key. In the case of a unique index, the key is the index key, with the primary key appearing as the corresponding value for that key.

Ranges store contiguous spans of key-values. Ranges are analogous to *shards* or *shard chunks* in other databases. Figure 2-2 illustrates how a "dogs" table might be segmented into ranges.

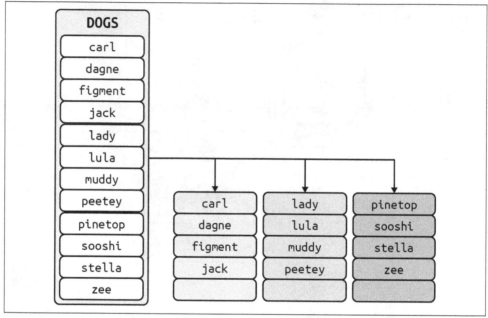

Figure 2-2. Ranges

As mentioned earlier, *leases* are granted to a node giving it responsibility for managing reads and writes to a range. The node holding the lease is known as the *leaseholder*. The same node is generally also the *Raft leader*, which is responsible for ensuring that replicas of the node are correctly maintained across multiple nodes.

The CockroachDB Software Stack

Each CockroachDB node runs a copy of the CockroachDB software, which is a single multithreaded process. From the OS perspective, the CockroachDB process might seem like a closed box, but internally it is organized into multiple logical layers, as shown in Figure 2-3.

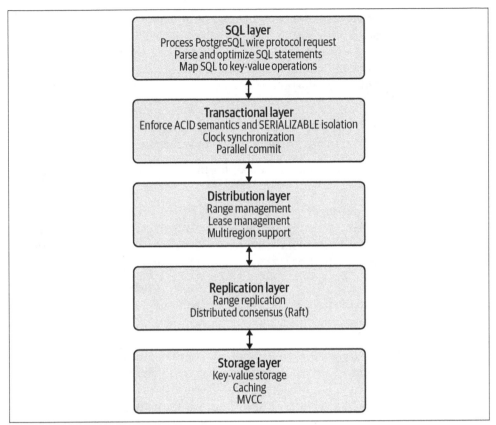

Figure 2-3. CockroachDB software layers

We'll discuss each of these layers in turn as we proceed through the chapter.

The CockroachDB SQL Layer

The SQL layer is the part of the CockroachDB software stack that is responsible for handling SQL requests. Because CockroachDB is a SQL database, you would be forgiven for thinking that the SQL layer does pretty much everything. However, the core responsibility of the SQL layer is actually to turn SQL requests into requests that can be serviced by the KV subsystem. Other layers handle transactions, distribution, and replication of ranges and physical storage to disk.

The SQL layer receives requests from database clients over the PostgreSQL wire protocol. A database client is any program that uses a database driver to communicate with the server. It includes the CockroachDB command-line SQL processor, GUI tools such as DBeaver or Tableau, or applications written in Java, Go, Node.js, Python, or any other language that has a compatible driver.

The PostgreSQL wire protocol describes the format of network packets that are used to send requests and receive results from a database client and server. The wire protocol lays on top of a transport medium such as TCP/IP or Unix-style sockets. The use of the PostgreSQL wire protocol allows CockroachDB to take advantage of the large ecosystem of compatible language drivers and tools that support the PostgreSQL database.

The SQL layer parses the SQL request, checking it for syntactical accuracy and ensuring that the connection has privileges to perform the requested task.

CockroachDB then creates an execution plan for the SQL statement and proceeds to *optimize* that plan.

SQL is a declarative language: you define the data you want, not how to get it. Although the nonprocedural nature of SQL results in improvements in programmer productivity, the database server must support a set of sophisticated algorithms to determine the optimal method of executing the SQL. These algorithms are collectively referred to as *the optimizer*.

For almost all SQL statements, there will be more than one way for CockroachDB to retrieve the rows required. For instance, given a SQL with JOIN and WHERE clauses, there may be multiple join orders and multiple access paths (table scans, index lookups, etc.) available to retrieve data. It's the goal of the optimizer to determine the best access path. CockroachDB's SQL optimizer has some unique features relating to its distributed architecture, but broadly speaking, the cost-based optimizer is similar to that found in other SQL databases such as Oracle or PostgreSQL.

The optimizer uses both heuristics—rules—and cost-based algorithms to perform its work.

The first stage of the SQL optimization process is to transform the SQL into a normalized form suitable for further optimization. This transformation removes any redundancies in the SQL statement and performs rule-based transformations to improve performance. The transformation takes into account the distribution of data for the table, adding predicates to direct parts of the queries to specific ranges or adding predicates that allow the use of indexed retrieval paths.

The optimization of the SQL statement proceeds in two stages: expansion and ranking. The SQL statement is transformed into an initial plan. Then the optimizer expands that plan into a set of equivalent candidate plans that involve alternative execution paths such as join orders or indexes. The optimizer then ranks the plans by calculating the relative cost of each operation, leveraging statistics that supply the size and distribution of data within each table. The plan with the lowest cost is then selected.

CockroachDB also supports a *vectorized execution* engine that can speed up the processing of batches of data. This engine translates data from a row-oriented format (where sets of data contain data from the same row) to a column-oriented format (where every set of data contains information from the same column).

We'll return to the optimizer in Chapter 8 when we look in detail at SQL tuning.

From SQL to Key-Values

As we mentioned earlier, CockroachDB data ends up stored in a key-value storage system that is distributed across multiple nodes in ranges. We'll look at the details of this storage system toward the end of the chapter, but since the outputs of the SQL layer are, in fact, KV operations, the mapping of data from tables and indexes to KV representation is part of the SQL layer. The output of the SQL layer are KV operations.

This translation means that only the SQL layer needs to be concerned with SQL syntax—all the subsequent layers are blissfully unaware of the SQL language.

Tables as Represented in the KV Store

Each entry in the KV store has a key based on the following structure:

```
/<tableID>/<indexID>/<IndexKeyValues>/<ColumnFamily>
```

We'll discuss column families in the next section. By default, all columns are included in a single default column family.

For a base table, the default `indexID` is "primary."

Figure 2-4 shows a simplified version of this mapping, omitting the column family identifier. 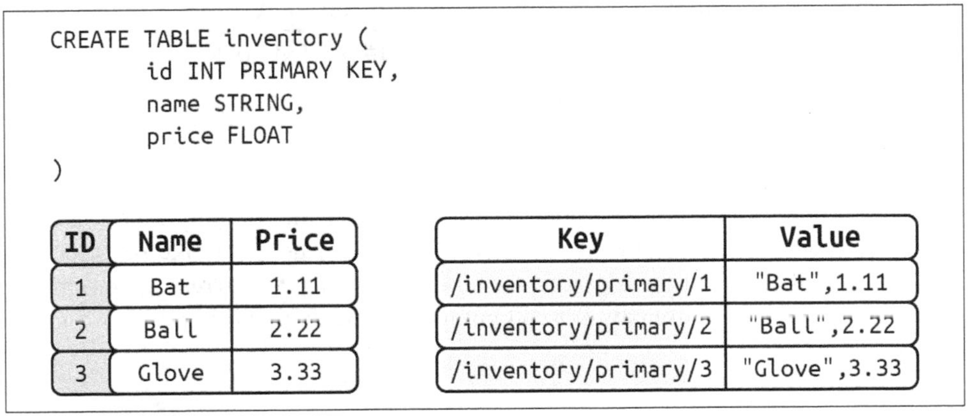

```
CREATE TABLE inventory (
       id INT PRIMARY KEY,
       name STRING,
       price FLOAT
)
```

ID	Name	Price
1	Bat	1.11
2	Ball	2.22
3	Glove	3.33

Key	Value
/inventory/primary/1	"Bat",1.11
/inventory/primary/2	"Ball",2.22
/inventory/primary/3	"Glove",3.33

Figure 2-4. KV to column mappings

Figure 2-4 shows the table name and index name ("primary") as text, but within the KV store, these are represented as compact table and index identifiers.

Column Families

In the preceding example, all the columns for a table are aggregated in the value section of a single KV entry. However, it's possible to direct CockroachDB to store groups of columns in separate KV entries using column families. Each column family in a table will be allocated its own KV entry. Figure 2-5 illustrates this concept—if a table has two column families, then each row in the table will be represented by two KV entries.

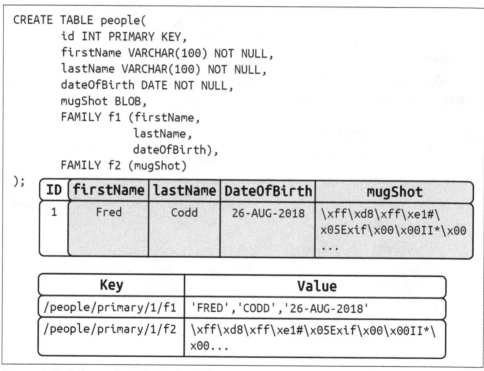

Figure 2-5. Column families in the KV store

Column families can have a number of advantages. If infrequently accessed large columns are separated, then they will not be retrieved during row lookups, which can improve the efficiency of the KV store cache. Furthermore, concurrent operations on columns in separate column families will not interfere with each other.

Indexes in the KV Store

Indexes are represented by a similar KV structure. For instance, the representation of a non-unique index is shown in Figure 2-6.

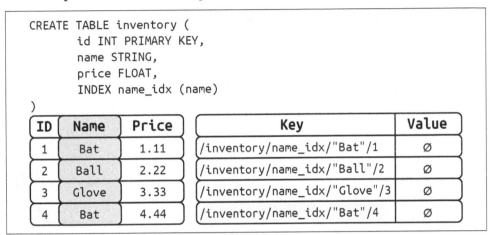

Figure 2-6. Non-unique index KV store representation

The key for a non-unique index includes the table and index name, the key-value, and the primary key-value. For a non-unique index, there is no "value" by default.

For a unique index, the KV value defaults to the value of the primary key. So, if name was unique in the inventory table used in previous examples, a unique index on name is represented in Figure 2-7.

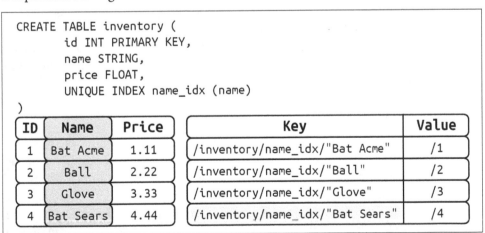

Figure 2-7. Unique index KV store representation

Inverted Indexes

CockroachDB columns can be defined as arrays or JSON documents. We'll discuss this in detail in Chapter 4.

Inverted indexes allow indexed searches into values included in these arrays or JSON documents. In this case, the key-values include the JSON path and value together with the primary key, as shown in Figure 2-8.

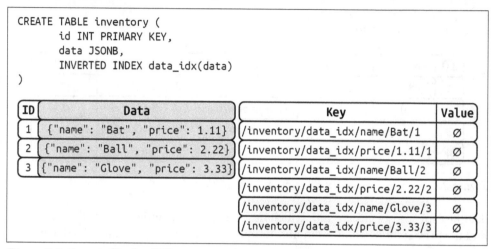

Figure 2-8. Inverted index KV representation

Inverted indexes are also used on spatial data.

Inverted indexes can be larger and more expensive to maintain than other indexes because a single JSON document in a row will generate one index entry for each unique attribute. For complex JSON documents, this might result in dozens of index entries for each document. We'll also discuss this further—and consider some alternatives—in Chapter 8.

The STORING Clause

The STORING clause of CREATE INDEX allows us to add additional columns to the value portion of the KV index structure. These additional columns can streamline a query that contains a projection (e.g., a SELECT list) that includes only those columns and the index keys. For instance, in Figure 2-9, we see a non-unique index on name and DateOfBirth that uses the STORING clause to add the phone number to the KV value. Queries that seek to find the phone number using name and date of birth can now be resolved by the index alone without reference to the base table.

```
CREATE TABLE people(
        id INT PRIMARY KEY,
        firstName VARCHAR(100) NOT NULL,
        lastName VARCHAR(100) NOT NULL,
        dateOfBirth DATE NOT NULL,
        phoneNumber int not null,
        otherColumns blob,,
        INDEX (firstName,lastName,dateOfBirth) STORING (phoneNumber)
);
```

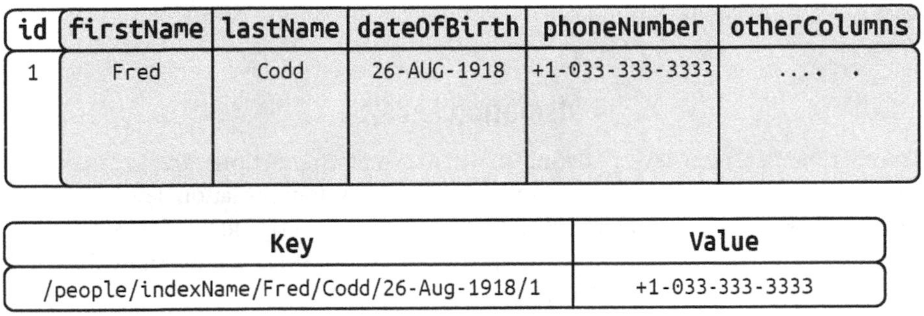

id	firstName	lastName	dateOfBirth	phoneNumber	otherColumns
1	Fred	Codd	26-AUG-1918	+1-033-333-3333	.... .

Key	Value
/people/indexName/Fred/Codd/26-Aug-1918/1	+1-033-333-3333

Figure 2-9. STORING clause of CREATE INDEX

Table Definitions and Schema Changes

The schema definitions for tables (and their associated indexes) are stored in a special keyspace called a *table descriptor*. For performance reasons, table descriptors are replicated on every node. The table descriptor is used to parse and optimize SQL and to correctly construct KV operations for a table.

CockroachDB supports online schema changes using ALTER TABLE, CREATE INDEX, and other commands. The schema is changed in discrete stages that allow the new schema to be rolled out while the previous version is still in use. Schema changes run as background tasks.

The node initiating the schema change will acquire a write lease on the relevant table descriptor. Nodes that are performing data manipulation language (DML) on a table will have a lease on the relevant table descriptor. When the node holding the write lease modifies the definition, it is broadcast to all nodes in the cluster that will—when it becomes possible—release their lease on the old schema.

The schema change may involve changes to table data (removing or adding columns) and/or creating new index structures. When all of the instances of the table are stored according to the requirements of the new schema, then all nodes will switch over to the new schema and will allow reads and writes of the table using the new schema.

The CockroachDB Transaction Layer

The transaction layer is responsible for maintaining the atomicity of transactions by ensuring that all operations in a transaction are committed or aborted.

Additionally, the transaction layer maintains serializable isolation between transactions—which means that transactions are completely isolated from the effects of other transactions. Although multiple transactions may be in progress at the same time, the experience of each transaction is as if the transactions were run one at a time—the *serializable* isolation level.

Isolation Levels

Transaction "isolation levels" define to what extent transactions are isolated from the effects of other transactions. ANSI SQL defines four isolation levels that are, from weakest to strongest: READ UNCOMMITTED, READ COMMITTED, REPEATABLE READ, and SERIALIZABLE. Additionally, an isolation level of SNAPSHOT is used by many databases as an alternative "strong" isolation level.

In some databases, users may choose a lower level of isolation to achieve improved concurrency at the expense of consistency.

However, CockroachDB supports only the serializable level of isolation. This means that CockroachDB transactions must exhibit absolute independence from all other transactions. The results of a set of concurrent transactions must be the same as if they had all been performed one after the other.

The transaction layer processes KV operations generated by the SQL layer. A transaction consists of multiple KV operations, some of which may be the result of a single SQL statement. In addition to updating table entries, index entries must also be updated. Maintaining perfect consistency under all circumstances involves multiple sophisticated algorithms, not all of which can be covered in this chapter. For comprehensive information, you may wish to consult the CockroachDB 2020 SIGMOD paper (*https://cockroa.ch/3rKVaJX*), which covers many of these principles in more detail.

MVCC Principles

Like most transactional database systems, CockroachDB implements the multiversion concurrency control (MVCC) pattern. MVCC allows readers to obtain a consistent view of information, even while that information is being modified. Without MVCC, consistent reads of a data item need to block (typically using a "read lock") simultaneous writes of that item and vice versa. With MVCC, readers can obtain a consistent view of information even while the information is being modified by a concurrent transaction.

Figure 2-10 illustrates the basic principles of MVCC. At time t1, session s1 reads from row r2 and accesses version v1 of that row (1). At timestamp t2, another database session, s2, updates the row (2), creating version v2 of that row (3). At t3, session s1 reads the row again, but—because s2 has not yet committed its change—continues to read from version v1 (4). After s2 commits (5), session s1 issues another select and now reads from the new v2 version of the row (6).

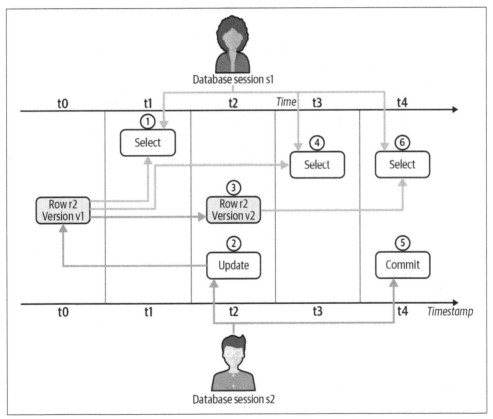

Figure 2-10. MVCC

The CockroachDB implementation limits the ability of transactions to read from previous versions. For instance, if a read transaction commences after a write transaction has begun, it may not be able to read the original version of the row because it might be inconsistent with other data already read or that will be read later in the transaction. This may result in the read transaction "blocking" until the write transaction commits or aborts.

We'll see later on how the storage engine implements MVCC, but for now, the important concept is that multiple versions of any row are maintained by the system, and transactions can determine which version of the row to read depending on their timestamp and the timestamp of any concurrent transactions.

Transaction Workflow

Distributed transactions must proceed in multiple stages. Simplistically, each node in the distributed system must lay the groundwork for the transaction and the transaction will be finalized only if all nodes report that the transaction can be performed.

Figure 2-11 illustrates a highly simplified flow of transaction preparation. In this case, a two-statement transaction is sent to the CockroachDB gateway node (1). The first statement involves a change to range 2, so that request is sent to the leaseholder for that range (2), which creates a new tentative version of the row and propagates changes to replica nodes (3 and 4). The second statement affects range 4, so the transaction coordinator sends that request to the appropriate leaseholder (5), which is also propagated (6 and 7). When all changes have correctly propagated, the transaction completes, and the client is notified of success (8).

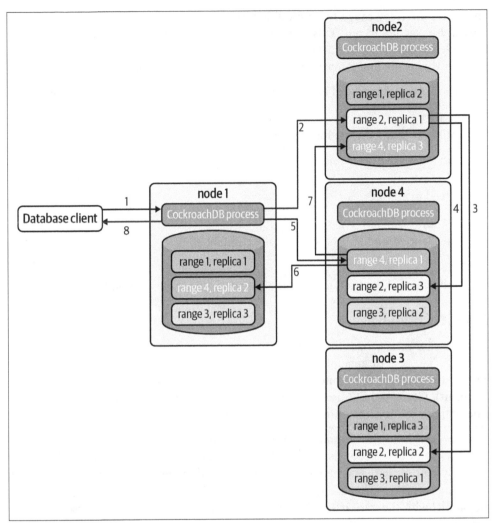

Figure 2-11. Basic transaction flow

Write Intents

During the initial stages of transaction processing, when it is not yet known whether the transaction will succeed, the leaseholder writes tentative modifications to modified values known as *write intents*. Write intents are specially constructed MVCC-compliant versions of the records, which are marked as provisional. They serve both as tentative transaction outcomes and as locks that prevent any concurrent attempts to update the same record.

Inside the first key range to be modified by the transaction, CockroachDB writes a special *transaction record*. This records the definitive status of the transaction. In the example shown in Figure 2-11, this transaction record would be stored in range 2 because that is the first range to be modified in the transaction.

This transaction record will record the transaction state as one of the following:

PENDING
> Indicates that the write intent's transaction is still in progress.

STAGING
> All transaction writes have been performed, but the transaction is not yet guaranteed to commit.

COMMITTED
> The transaction has been successfully completed.

ABORTED
> Indicates that the transaction was aborted and its values should be discarded.

Parallel Commits

In a distributed database, the number of network round trips is often the dominant factor in latency. In general, committing a distributed transaction requires at least two round trips (indeed, one of the classic algorithms for this is called Two-Phase Commit). CockroachDB uses an innovative protocol called *Parallel Commits* to hide one of these round trips from the latency as perceived by the client.

The key insight behind Parallel Commits is that the gateway can return success to the client as soon as it becomes impossible for the transaction to abort, even if it is not yet fully committed. The remaining work can be done after returning as long as its outcome is certain. This is done by transitioning the transaction to the STAGING state in parallel with the transaction's last round of writes. The keys of all of these writes are recorded in the transaction record. A STAGING transaction must be committed if and only if all of those writes succeed.

Usually, the gateway learns the status of these writes as soon as they are complete and returns control to the client before beginning the final resolution of the transaction in the background. If the gateway fails, the next node to encounter the STAGING transaction record is responsible for querying the status of each write and determining whether the transaction must be committed or aborted (but because the transaction record and each write intent have been written durably, the outcome is guaranteed to be the same whether the transaction is resolved by its original gateway or by another node).

Note that any locks held by the transaction are not released until after this resolution process has been completed. Therefore, the duration of a transaction from the perspective of another transaction waiting for its locks is still at least two round trips (just as in Two-Phase Commit). However, from the point of view of the session issuing the transaction, the elapsed time is significantly reduced.

Transaction Cleanup

As discussed in the previous section, a COMMIT operation "flips a switch" in the transaction record to mark the transaction as committed, minimizing any delays that would otherwise occur when a transaction is committed. After the transaction has reached the COMMIT stage, then it will asynchronously resolve the write intents by modifying them into normal MVCC records representing the new record values.

However, as with any asynchronous operation, there may be a delay in performing this cleanup. Furthermore, since a committed write intent looks the same as a pending write intent, transactions that encounter a write intent record when reading a key will need to determine if the write intent is committed.

If another transaction encounters a write intent that has not yet been cleaned up by the transaction coordinator, then it can perform the write intent cleanup by checking the transaction record. The write intent contains a pointer to the transaction records, which can reveal if the transaction is committed.

Overview of Transaction Flow

Figure 2-12 illustrates the flow of a successful two-statement transaction. A client issues an UPDATE statement (1). This creates a transaction coordinator that maintains a transaction record in PENDING state. Write intent commands are issued to the leaseholder for the range concerned (2). The leaseholder writes the intent markers to its copy of the data. It returns success to the transaction coordinator without waiting for the replica's intents to be acknowledged.

Subsequent modifications in the transaction are processed in the same manner.

The client issues a COMMIT (3). The transaction coordinator marks the transaction status as STAGING. When all write intents are confirmed, the initiating client is advised of success, and then the transaction status is set to COMMITTED (4).

After a successful commit, the transaction coordinator resolves the write intents in affected ranges, which become normal MVCC records (5). At this point, the transaction has released all its locks, and other transactions on the same records are free to proceed.

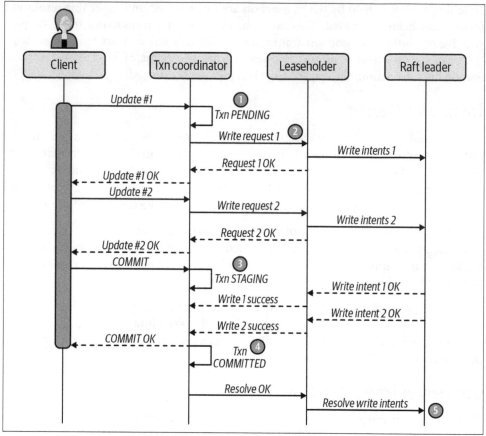

Figure 2-12. Transaction sequence

Figure 2-12 is highly simplified but can still be a little hard to unpack. There are two main takeaways from the diagram:

- Most operations respond in two stages; we can proceed to the next step after the first response and need to resolve everything only at the end of the commit.

- The latency for the client doesn't include all of the cleanup operations. The UPDATE operations return before all the write intents are propagated, and the COMMIT returns before all the write intents are resolved. Hopefully, this removes a lot of the overhead of distributed database management from application response time.

Read/Write Conflicts

So far, we've looked at the processing of successful transactions. It would be great if all transactions succeeded, but in all but the most trivial scenarios, concurrent transactions create conflicts that must be resolved.

The most obvious case is when two transactions attempt to update the same record. There cannot be two write intents active against the same key, so either one of the transactions will wait for the other to complete, or one of the transactions will be aborted. If the transactions are of the same priority, then the second transaction—the one that has not yet created a write intent—will wait. However, if the second transaction has a higher priority, then the original transaction will be aborted and will have to retry.

Transaction priorities can be adjusted with the SET TRANSACTION statement—see Chapter 6.

The TxnWaitQueue object tracks the transactions that are waiting and the transactions that they are waiting on. This structure is maintained within the Raft leader of the range associated with the transaction. When a transaction commits or aborts, the TxnWaitQueue is updated, and any waiting transactions are notified.

A *deadlock* can occur if two transactions are both waiting on write intents created by the other transaction. In this case, one of the transactions will be randomly aborted. We'll discuss this in more detail in Chapter 6.

Transaction conflicts can also occur between readers and writers. If a reader encounters an uncommitted write intent that has a lower (e.g., earlier) timestamp than the consistent read timestamp for the read, then a consistent read cannot be completed. This can happen if a modification occurs between the time a read transaction starts and the time it attempts to read the key concerned. In this case, the read will need to wait until the write either commits or aborts.

These "blocked reads" can be avoided in the following circumstances:

- If the read has a high priority, CockroachDB may "push" the lower-priority write's timestamp to a higher value, allowing the read to complete. The "pushed" transaction may need to restart if the push invalidates any previous work in the transaction.

- Stale reads that use AS OF SYSTEM TIME will not block (as long as the transaction does not exceed the specified staleness). We'll discuss AS OF SYSTEM TIME a bit later in this chapter.

- In multiregion configurations—which we'll describe in detail in Chapter 11—
  GLOBAL tables use a modified transaction protocol in which reads are not blocked
  by writes.

Many transaction conflicts are managed automatically, and while these have performance implications, they don't impact functionality or code design. However, there
are multiple scenarios in which an application may need to handle an aborted transaction. We'll look at these scenarios and discuss best practices for transaction retries
in Chapter 6.

Clock Synchronization and Clock Skew

You may have noticed in previous sections that CockroachDB must compare timestamps of operations frequently to determine if a transaction is in conflict. Simplistically, we might imagine that every node in the system can agree on the time of
each operation and make these comparisons easily. In reality, every system is likely
to have a slightly different system clock time, and this discrepancy is likely to be
greater the more geographically distributed a system is. The difference in clock times
is referred to as *clock skew*. Consequently, in widely distributed systems with very
high transaction rates, getting nodes to agree on the exact sequence of transactions
is problematic. As you might remember, Spanner attacked this problem by using
specialized hardware—atomic clocks and GPS—to reduce the inconsistency between
system clocks. As a result, Spanner can keep the clock skew within 7 ms and simply
adds a 7 ms sleep to every transaction to ensure that no transactions complete out of
order.

Since CockroachDB must run reliably on generic hardware, it synchronizes time
using the venerable and ubiquitous internet Network Time Protocol (NTP). NTP
produces accurate timestamps but nowhere near as accurate as Spanner's GPS and
atomic clocks.

By default, CockroachDB will tolerate a clock skew as high as 500 ms. Adding
half a second to every transaction in the Spanner manner would be untenable, so
CockroachDB takes a different approach for dealing with transactions that appear
within the 500 ms uncertainty interval. Put simply, while Spanner always waits after
writes, CockroachDB sometimes retries reads.

If a reader can't say for certain whether a value being read was committed before the
read transaction started, then it pushes its own provisional timestamp just above the
timestamp of the uncertain value. Transactions reading constantly updated data from
many nodes may be forced to restart multiple times, though never for longer than the
uncertainty interval, nor more than once per node.

The CockroachDB time synchronization strategy allows CockroachDB to deliver true serializable consistency. However, there are still some anomalies that can occur. Two transactions that operate on unrelated key-values that still have some real-world sequencing dependency might appear to be committed in reverse order—the *causal reverse* anomaly. This is not a violation of serializable isolation because the transactions are not actually logically dependent. Nevertheless, it is possible in CockroachDB for transactions to have timestamps that do not reflect their real-world ordering.

The CockroachDB Distribution Layer

Logically, a table is represented in CockroachDB as a monolithic KV structure, in which the key is a concatenation of the primary keys of the table, and the value is a concatenation of all of the remaining columns in the table. We introduced this structure back in Figure 2-2.

The distribution layer breaks this monolithic structure into contiguous chunks of approximately 512 MB. The 512 MB chunk size is sized to keep the number of ranges per node manageable. The distribution layer keeps data distributed evenly across the cluster while simultaneously presenting a unified and consolidated view of that data to the applications that need it.

Meta Ranges

The distribution of ranges is stored in global keyspaces `meta1` and `meta2`. `meta1` can be thought of as a "range of ranges" lookup, which then allows a node to find the location of the node holding the `meta2` record, which in turn points to the nodes holding copies of every range within the "range of ranges." Figure 2-13 illustrates this two-level lookup structure.

Node 1 needs to get data for the key "HarrisonGuy." It looks in its copy of `meta1`, which tells it that node2 contains the `meta2` information for the range G–M. It accesses the `meta2` data concerned from node 2, which indicates that node4 is the leaseholder for the range G–I, and therefore the leaseholder for the range concerned.

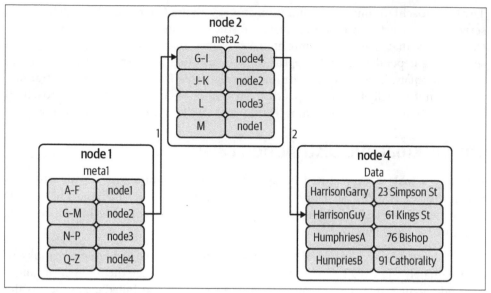

Figure 2-13. Meta ranges

Gossip

CockroachDB uses the *gossip* protocol to share ephemeral information between nodes. Gossip is a widely used protocol in distributed systems in which nodes propagate information virally through the network.

Gossip maintains an eventually consistent KV map maintained on all the CockroachDB nodes. It is used primarily for bootstrapping: it contains a "meta0" record that tells the cluster where the `meta1` range can be found, as well as mappings from the node IDs stored in meta records to network addresses. Gossip is also used for certain operations that do not require strong consistency, such as maintaining information about the available storage space on each node for rebalancing purposes.

Leaseholders

The leaseholder is the CockroachDB node responsible for serving reads and coordinating writes for a specific range of keys. We discussed some of the responsibilities of the leaseholder in "The CockroachDB Transaction Layer" on page 30. When a transaction coordinator or gateway node wants to initiate a read or write against a range, it finds that range's leaseholder (using the meta ranges structure discussed in the previous section) and forwards the request to the leaseholder.

Leaseholders are assigned using the Raft protocol, which we will discuss in "The CockroachDB Replication Layer" on page 43.

Range Splits

CockroachDB will attempt to keep a range at less than 512 MB. When a range exceeds that size, the range will be split into two smaller contiguous ranges.

Ranges can also be split if they exceed a load threshold. If the parameter kv.range_split.by_load_enabled is true and the number of queries per second to the range exceeds the value of kv.range_split.load_qps_threshold, then a range may be split even if it is below the normal size threshold for range splitting. Other factors will determine if a split actually occurs, including whether the resulting split would actually split the load between the two new ranges and the impact on queries that might now have to span the new ranges.

When splitting based on load, the two new ranges might not be of equal sizes. By default, the range will be split at the point at which the load on the two new ranges will be roughly equal. Figure 2-14 illustrates a basic range split when an insert causes a range to exceed the 512 MB threshold. Two ranges are created as a consequence.

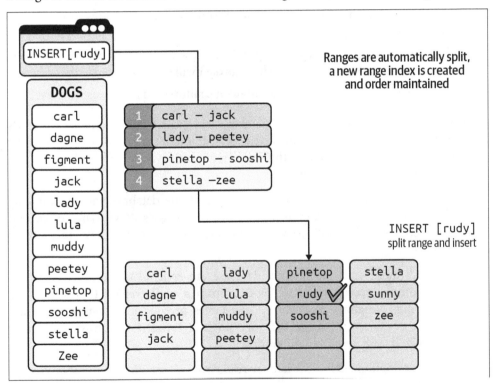

Figure 2-14. Range splits

Ranges can also be split manually using the SPLIT AT clause of the ALTER TABLE and ALTER INDEX statements.

Ranges can be merged as well. If DELETE statements remove data from ranges and the range falls below a size threshold, CockroachDB may merge the range with a neighboring range.

Multiregion Distribution

Geo-partitioning is a special feature of CockroachDB Enterprise that allows data to be located within a specific geographic region. This might be desirable from a performance point of view—reducing latencies for queries from a region about that region—or from a data sovereignty perspective—keeping data within a specific geographic region for legal or regulatory reasons. CockroachDB supports a multiregion configuration that controls how data should be distributed across regions. The following core concepts are relevant:

- *Cluster regions* are geographic regions that a user specifies at node start time.
- *Regions* may have multiple zones.
- Databases within the cluster are assigned to one or more regions: one of these regions is the *primary* region.
- Tables within a database may have specific *locality rules* (global, regional by table, regional by row), which determine how its data will be distributed across zones.
- *Survival goals* dictate how many simultaneous failures a database can survive.

With the *zone-level survival goal*, the database will remain fully available for reads and writes, even if a zone goes down. However, the database may not remain fully available if multiple zones fail in the same region. Surviving zone failures is the default setting for multiregion databases.

The *region-level survival goal* has the property that the database will remain fully available for reads and writes, even if an entire region goes down. This, of course, means that copies of data will need to be maintained in other regions, magnifying write time.

By default, all tables in a multiregion database are *regional tables*—that is, CockroachDB optimizes access to the table's data from a single region (by default, the database's primary region). *Regional by row* tables provide low-latency reads and writes for one or more rows of a table from a single region. Different rows in the table can be optimized for access from different regions.

Global tables are optimized for low-latency reads from all regions.

The CockroachDB Replication Layer

High availability requires that data not be lost or made unavailable should a node fail. This, of course, requires that multiple copies of data be maintained.

The two most commonly used high-availability designs are:

- *Active-passive*, in which a single node is a "primary" or "active" node whose changes are propagated to passive "secondary" or "passive" nodes.
- *Active-active*, in which all nodes run identical services. Typically, active-active database systems are of the "eventually consistent" variety. Since there is no "primary," conflicting updates can be processed by different nodes. These will need to be resolved, possibly by discarding one of the conflicting updates.

CockroachDB implements a *distributed consensus* mechanism that is called multi-active. Like active-active, all replicas can handle traffic, but for an update to be accepted, it must be confirmed by a majority of voting replicas.

Not all replicas necessarily get a vote. Nonvoting replicas are useful in globally distributed systems since they allow for low latency reads in remote regions without requiring that region to participate in consensus during writes. This concept is discussed in more detail in Chapter 11.

This architecture ensures that there is no data loss in the event of a node failure, and the system remains available, providing at least a majority of nodes remain active.

CockroachDB implements replication at the range level: each range is replicated independently of other ranges. At any given moment, a single node is responsible for changes to a single node, but there is no overall "primary" node within the cluster.

Raft

CockroachDB employs the widely used *Raft protocol (https://cockroa.ch/3x1fR8y)* as its distributed consensus mechanism. In CockroachDB, each range is a distinct Raft group—the consensus for each range is determined independently of other ranges.

In Raft and in most distributed consensus mechanisms, we need a minimum of three nodes. This is because a majority of nodes (a quorum) must always agree on the state. In the event of a network partition, only the side of the partition with the majority of nodes can continue.

In a Raft group, one of the nodes is elected as leader by a majority of nodes in the group. The other nodes are known as followers. The Raft leader controls changes to the Raft group.

Changes sent to the Raft leader are written to its *Raft log* and propagated to the followers. When a majority of nodes accept the change, then the change is committed by the leader. Note that in CockroachDB, each range has its own Raft log because every range is replicated separately.

Leader elections occur regularly or may be triggered when a node fails to receive a heartbeat message from the leader. In the latter case, a follower who cannot communicate with the leader will declare itself a candidate and initiate an election. Raft includes a set of safety rules that prevent any data loss during the election process. In particular, a candidate cannot win an election unless its log contains all committed entries.

Nodes that are temporarily disconnected from the cluster can be sent to relevant sections of the Raft log to resynchronize or—if necessary—a point-in-time snapshot of the state followed by a catch-up via Raft logs.

Raft and Leaseholders

The CockroachDB leaseholder and the Raft leader responsibilities serve similar purposes. The leaseholder controls access to a range for the purposes of transactional integrity and isolation, while the Raft leader controls access to a range for the purposes of replication and data safety.

The leaseholder is the only node that can propose writes to the Raft leader. CockroachDB will attempt to elect a leaseholder who is also the Raft leader so that these communications can be streamlined. The leaseholder serves all writes and most reads, so it is able to maintain the in-memory data structures necessary to mediate read/write conflicts for the transaction layer.

Closed Timestamps and Follower Reads

Periodically the leaseholder will "close" a timestamp in the recent past, which guarantees that no new writes with lower timestamps will be accepted.

This mechanism also allows for *follower reads*. Normally, reads have to be serviced by a replica's leaseholder. This can be slow since the leaseholder may be geographically distant from the gateway node that is issuing the query. A follower read is a read taken from the closest replica, regardless of the replica's leaseholder status. This can result in much better latency in geo-distributed, multiregion deployments.

If a query uses the AS OF SYSTEM TIME clause, then the gatekeeper forwards the request to the closest node that contains a replica of the data—whether it be a follower or the leaseholder. The timestamp provided in the query (i.e., the AS OF SYSTEM TIME value) must be less than or equal to the node's closed timestamp. This allows followers to service consistent reads in the recent past (i.e., several seconds ago).

Global tables in a multiregion database use a special variation of the transaction protocol called *nonblocking transactions* that is optimized for reads (from any replica) at the expense of writes. Writes to tables in this mode are assigned timestamps in the future, and timestamps in the future may be closed. This makes it possible for followers to serve consistent reads at the present time.

The CockroachDB Storage Layer

We touched upon the logical structure of the KV store earlier in the chapter when we discussed the store. However, we have not yet looked at the physical implementation of the KV storage engine.

As of CockroachDB version 20, CockroachDB uses the PebbleDB storage engine—an open source KV store inspired by the LevelDB and RocksDB storage engines. PebbleDB is primarily maintained by the CockroachDB team and is optimized specifically for CockroachDB use cases. Older versions of CockroachDB use the RocksDB storage engine.

Let's look under the hood of the PebbleDB storage engine so that we can fully appreciate how CockroachDB stores and manipulates data at its foundational layer.

Log-Structured Merge Trees

PebbleDB implements the log-structured merge (LSM) tree architecture. LSM is a widely implemented and battle-tested architecture that seeks to optimize storage and support extremely high insert rates, while still supporting efficient random read access.

The simplest possible LSM tree consists of two indexed "trees:"

- An in-memory tree that is the recipient of all new record inserts—the *MemTable*.
- A number of on-disk trees represent copies of in-memory trees that have been flushed to disk. These are referred to as *sorted strings tables* (SSTables).

SSTables exist at multiple levels, numbered L0 to L6 (L6 is also called the base level). L0 contains an unordered set of SSTables, each of which is simply a copy of an in-memory MemTable that has been flushed to disk. Periodically, SSTables are compacted into larger consolidated stores in the lower levels. In levels other than L0, SSTables are ordered and nonoverlapping so that only one SSTable per level could possibly hold a given key.

SSTables are internally sorted and indexed, so lookups within an SSTable are fast.

The basic LSM architecture ensures that writes are always fast since they primarily operate at memory speed, although there is often also a sequential *write-ahead log*

(WAL) on disk. The transfer to on-disk SSTables is also fast since it occurs in append-only batches using fast sequential writes. Reads occur either from the in-memory tree or from the disk tree; in either case, reads are facilitated by an index and are relatively swift.

Of course, if a node fails while data is in the in-memory store, then it could be lost. For this reason, database implementations of the LSM pattern include a WAL that persists transactions to disk. The WAL is written via fast sequential writes.

Figure 2-15 illustrates LSM writes. Writes from higher CockroachDB layers are first applied to the WAL (1) and then to the MemTable (2). Once the MemTable reaches a certain size, it is flushed to disk to create a new SSTable (3). Once the flush completes, WAL records may be purged (4). Multiple SSTables are routinely merged (compacted) into larger SSTables (5).

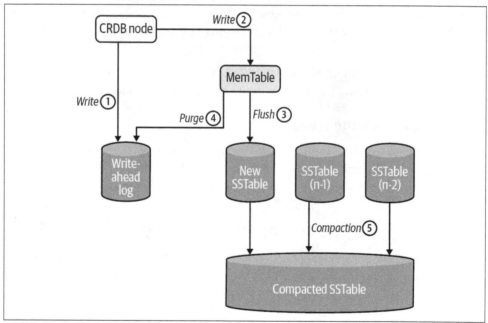

Figure 2-15. LSM writes

The compaction process results in multiple "levels"—Level 0 (L0) contains the uncompacted data. Each compaction creates a file at a deeper level—up to 7 levels (L0–L6) are typical.

SSTables and Bloom Filters

Each SSTable is indexed. However, there may be many SSTables on disk, and this creates a multiplier effect on index lookups because we might theoretically have to examine every index for every SSTable to find our desired row.

To reduce the overhead of multiple index lookups, *Bloom filters* are used to reduce the number of lookups that must be performed. A Bloom filter is a compact and quick-to-maintain structure that can quickly tell you if a given SSTable "might" contain a value. CockroachDB uses Bloom filters to quickly determine which SSTables have a version of a key. Bloom filters are compact enough to fit in memory and are quick to navigate. However, to achieve this compression, Bloom filters are "fuzzy" and may return false positives. If you get a positive result from a Bloom filter, it means only that the file *may* contain the value. However, the Bloom filter will never incorrectly advise you that a value is not present. So, if a Bloom filter tells us that a key is not included in a specific SSTable, then we can safely omit that SSTable from our lookup.

Figure 2-16 shows the read pattern for an LSM. A database request first reads from the MemTable (1). If the required value is not found, it will consult the Bloom filters for all SSTables in L0 (2). If the Bloom filter indicates that no matching value is present, it will examine the SSTable in each subsequent level that covers the given key (3). If the Bloom filter indicates a matching key-value may be present in the SSTable, then the process will use the SSTable index (4) to search for the value within the SSTable (5). Once a matching value is found, no older SSTables need to be examined.

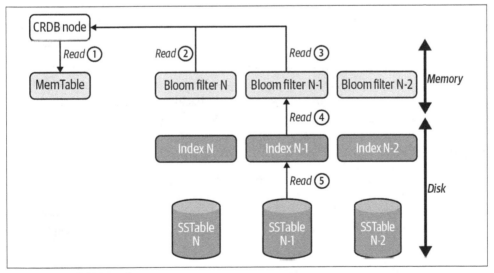

Figure 2-16. LSM reads

Deletes and Updates

SSTables are immutable—once the MemTable is flushed to disk and becomes an SSTable, no further modifications to the SSTable can be performed. If a value is modified repeatedly over a period of time, the modifications will build up across multiple SSTables. When retrieving a value, the system will read SSTables from youngest to oldest to find the most recent value for a key. Therefore, to update a value, we only need to insert the new value since the older values will not be examined when a newer version exists.

Deletions are implemented by writing tombstone markers into the MemTable, which eventually propagate to SSTables. Once a tombstone marker for a row is encountered, the system stops examining older entries and reports "not found" to the application.

As SSTables multiply, read performance and storage will degrade as the number of Bloom filters, indexes, and obsolete values increases. During compaction, rows that are fragmented across multiple SSTables will be consolidated and deleted rows removed. Tombstones are retained until they are compacted to the base level L6.

MultiVersion Concurrency Control

We introduced MVCC as a logical element of the transaction layer in "MVCC Principles" on page 31.

CockroachDB encodes the MVCC timestamp into each key so that multiple MVCC versions of a key are stored as distinct keys within PebbleDB. However, the Bloom filters that we introduced previously exclude the MVCC timestamp so that a query does not need to know the exact timestamp to look up a record.

CockroachDB removes records older than the configuration variable `gc.ttlseconds`, but will not remove any records covered by *protected timestamps*. Protected timestamps are created by long-running jobs such as backups, which need to be able to obtain a consistent view of data.

The Block Cache

PebbleDB implements a block cache providing fast access to frequently accessed data items. This block cache is separate from the in-memory indexes, Bloom filters, and MemTables. The block cache operates on a least recently used (LRU) basis—when a new data entry is added to the cache, the entry that was least recently accessed will be evicted from the cache.

Reading from the block cache bypasses the need to scan multiple SSTables and associated Bloom filters. We'll speak more about the cache in Chapter 14 when we discuss cluster optimization.

Summary

In this chapter, we've tried to give you an overview of the essential architectural elements of CockroachDB.

Although having a strong grasp of the CockroachDB architecture is advantageous when performing advanced systems optimization or configuration, it's by no means a prerequisite for working with a CockroachDB system. CockroachDB includes many sophisticated design elements, but its internal complexity is not reflected in its UI—you can happily develop a CockroachDB application without mastering the architectural concepts in this chapter.

At a cluster level, a CockroachDB deployment consists of three or more symmetrical nodes, each of which carries a complete copy of the CockroachDB software stack and each of which can service any database client requests. Data in a CockroachDB table is broken up into ranges of 512 MB in size and distributed across the nodes of the cluster. Each range is replicated at least three times.

The CockroachDB software stack consists of five major layers:

- The SQL layer accepts SQL requests in the PostgreSQL wire protocol. It parses and optimizes the SQL requests and translates the requests into KV operations that can be processed by lower layers.

- The transaction layer is responsible for ensuring ACID transactions and serializable isolation. It ensures that transactions see a consistent view of data and that modifications occur as if they had been executed one at a time.

- The distribution layer is responsible for the partitioning of data into ranges and the distribution of those ranges across the cluster. It is responsible for managing Range leases and assigning leaseholders.

- The replication layer ensures that data is correctly replicated across the cluster to allow high availability in the event of a node failure. It implements a distributed consensus mechanism to ensure that all nodes agree on the current state of any data item.

- The storage layer is responsible for the persistence of data to local disk and the processing of low-level queries and updates on that data.

In the next chapter, we'll gleefully abandon the complexities and sophisticated CockroachDB architecture and focus on the far simpler task of getting started with the CockroachDB system.

Getting Started

CockroachDB has a sophisticated and modern architecture and is designed for global scale. However, that complexity and scalability don't imply a steep learning curve or barrier to entry. In this chapter, we'll help you get started with a CockroachDB installation and introduce you to the basics of working with a CockroachDB system.

Installation

CockroachDB can be installed on virtually any flavor of desktop OS within a few minutes. Alternatively, you can create a free CockroachDB Serverless database or run CockroachDB within a Docker container or Kubernetes cluster.

Installing CockroachDB Software

In most scenarios, you'll want to have the CockroachDB software installed on your desktop computer, so let's start with that. You'll find a full list of CockroachDB binaries at *https://www.cockroachlabs.com/docs/releases*. From there, you can pick your OS and download the most recent version or pick a previous version.

The instructions that follow worked as of the time of writing, but installation can change with each release, so make sure you consult the CockroachDB website for the most up-to-date instructions.

Installation on macOS

If you have the brew package manager installed, then that is probably the easiest way to get started installing CockroachDB on Mac. In fact, even if you don't have brew installed, it's probably easier to install it and then install CockroachDB than to install CockroachDB manually.

To install brew, issue the following command from a terminal window:

```
/bin/bash -c \
   "$(curl -fsSL https://raw.githubusercontent.com/Homebrew/install/HEAD/install.sh
```

Once brew is installed, you can install CockroachDB with the following command:

```
guyharrison@macos ~ % brew install cockroachdb/tap/cockroach
==> Tapping cockroachdb/tap
Cloning into '/usr/local/Homebrew/Library/Taps/cockroachdb/homebrew-tap'...
 …
==> Installing cockroach from cockroachdb/tap
….
To have launchd start cockroachdb/tap/cockroach now and restart at login:
  brew services start cockroachdb/tap/cockroach
Or, if you don't want/need a background service you can just run:
  cockroach start-single-node --insecure
==> Summary
 usr/local/Cellar/cockroach/20.2.7: 134 files, 184.8MB, built in 8 sec
```

One of the great things about brew is that it sets up CockroachDB as a service, so you can issue `brew services start cockroach` to start a background instance of CockroachDB. However, if you don't want to use brew, then you can download the CockroachDB binary directly and copy the binary into your path. Review the releases documentation (*https://cockroa.ch/3j1bUbQ*) to determine the path for the release you want, then use `curl` or `wget` to copy and decompress that release.

```
% curl https://binaries.cockroachdb.com/cockroach-v21.2.3.darwin-10.9-amd64.tgz \
   | tar -xJ
   % Total    % Received % Xferd  Average Speed   Time    Time     Time  Current
                                   Dload  Upload   Total   Spent    Left  Speed
   100 49.1M  100 49.1M    0       0   15.5M      0  0:00:03  0:00:03 --:--:-- 15.5M
```

You can then copy the binary into your path so you can execute Cockroach commands from any directory:

```
sudo cp -R cockroach-v21.2.3.darwin-10.9-amd64/* /usr/local/bin
```

Once you've installed CockroachDB either manually or via brew run the `cockroach`
`demo` command to start a demo instance and confirm that it is running:

```
% cockroach demo
#
# Welcome to the CockroachDB demo database!
#
# You are connected to a temporary, in-memory CockroachDB cluster of 1 node.
#
# This demo session will attempt to enable enterprise features
# by acquiring a temporary license from Cockroach Labs in the background.
# To disable this behavior, set the environment variable
# COCKROACH_SKIP_ENABLING_DIAGNOSTIC_REPORTING=true.
#
# Enter \? for a brief introduction.
#
demo@127.0.0.1:26257/movr> show databases;
  database_name | owner | primary_region | regions | survival_goal
----------------+-------+----------------+---------+---------------
  defaultdb     | root  | NULL           | {}      | NULL
  movr          | demo  | NULL           | {}      | NULL
  postgres      | root  | NULL           | {}      | NULL
  system        | node  | NULL           | {}      | NULL
(4 rows)

Time: 2ms total (execution 1ms / network 0ms)
```

Installation on Linux

To perform a basic installation on Linux, find the latest release (*https://cockroa.ch/3DChScP*) (or a specific version you're interested in), and download and unpack it. Of course, you can use `curl` or `wget` to obtain the tarball once you have determined its path:

```
$ wget https://binaries.cockroachdb.com/cockroach-v21.2.3.linux-amd64.tgz

2021-12-23 11:00:41 (24.7 MB/s) - 'cockroach-v21.2.3.linux-amd64.tgz' saved

$ tar zxvf cockroach-v21.2.3.linux-amd64.tgz
cockroach-v21.2.3.linux-amd64/cockroach
cockroach-v21.2.3.linux-amd64/lib/libgeos.so
cockroach-v21.2.3.linux-amd64/lib/libgeos_c.so

$ sudo cp -r cockroach-v21.2.3.linux-amd64/* /usr/local/bin
```

Once installed, run the cockroach demo command to start a temporary local instance of CockroachDB and verify the installation:

```
$ cockroach demo
#
# Welcome to the CockroachDB demo database!
#
# You are connected to a temporary, in-memory CockroachDB cluster of 1 node.
#
…
#
# Enter \? for a brief introduction.
#
root@127.0.0.1:44913/movr> show databases;
  database_name | owner
----------------+--------
  defaultdb     | root
  movr          | root
  postgres      | root
  system        | node
(4 rows)

Time: 1ms total (execution 1ms / network 0ms)

root@127.0.0.1:44913/movr>
```

For a completely manual installation like this, you may have to install geo-spatial libraries manually if you want to use geo-spatial features. See the CockroachDB documentation (*https://cockroa.ch/33OAFEb*) for more details.

Installation on Microsoft Windows

Microsoft Windows is not a fully supported platform for running a CockroachDB server. However, Windows is completely supported for CockroachDB clients and the server runs well enough for experimentation and most development.

Find the link for the release (*https://cockroa.ch/3ukrENL*) you'd like to download. Once downloaded, unzip the archive into a directory and add the subdirectory containing the *cockroach.exe* file to your path. Alternatively, you can download the file directly from a PowerShell prompt. Instructions for doing so can be found on the CockroachDB documentation site (*https://cockroa.ch/3nWawds*).

CockroachDB URLs

When connecting to a CockroachDB cluster, we need to identify the location and credentials with which we wish to connect. When connecting to a local server using cockroach demo or cockroach sql, the CockroachDB client will default to a local server on the default port, but as we will see, more complex installations require quite a bit more information.

The most common way to connect is to use a PostgreSQL-compatible URL. This URL is of the following format:

```
postgresql://[user[:passwd]]@[host][:port]/[db][?parameters...]
```

The simplest possible URL for a local cluster running without authentication would look something like this:

```
$ cockroach sql --url 'postgres://root@localhost:26257?sslmode=disable'
#
# Welcome to the CockroachDB SQL shell.
# All statements must be terminated by a semicolon.
# To exit, type: \q.
#
# Cluster ID: 072189bb-3970-4f37-afe4-55bc37cdf76e
#
# Enter \? for a brief introduction.
#
root@localhost:26257/defaultdb>
```

This is equivalent to running the command cockroach sql – insecure.

The beauty of the URL is that it can be accepted by most PostgreSQL-compatible programs or drivers. For instance, if we have the PostgreSQL client installed, we can use it to connect to CockroachDB:

```
$ psql 'postgres://root@localhost:26257?sslmode=disable'
psql (13.2, server 9.5.0)
Type "help" for help.

root=#
```

Creating a CockroachDB Serverless Instance

The cockroach demo command is a handy way to play around with the CockroachDB server, but the easiest way to get a fully functional CockroachDB server with persistent storage is to take advantage of the free CockroachDB Serverless database service. This service grants you access to a fully functional multitenant cloud service with 5 GB of storage.

CockroachDB Serverless has a number of advantages compared with a desktop deployment:

- It's automatically configured for high availability and backup. You don't have to worry about losing your data in the event of a hard drive failure on your desktop.
- It's fully secured using encryption at rest and in transit.
- It's available from anywhere, so it can be used for team development purposes.
- It's well-suited for starter projects and evaluating CockroachDB. To create a CockroachDB Serverless cluster, navigate to the signup page (*https://cockroa.ch/38sTXkv*) and select the CockroachDB Serverless option, as shown in Figure 3-1.

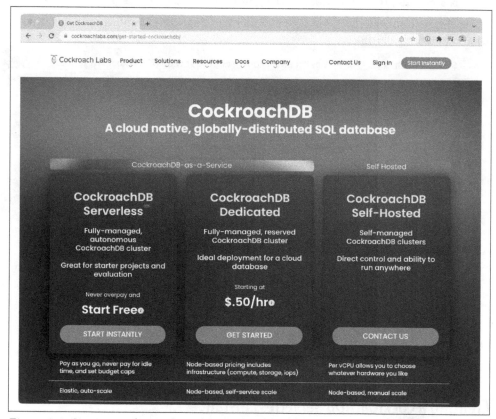

Figure 3-1. Signing up for CockroachDB Serverless

After entering your details and validating your email address, you'll be given the option to create your free cluster, as shown in Figure 3-2.

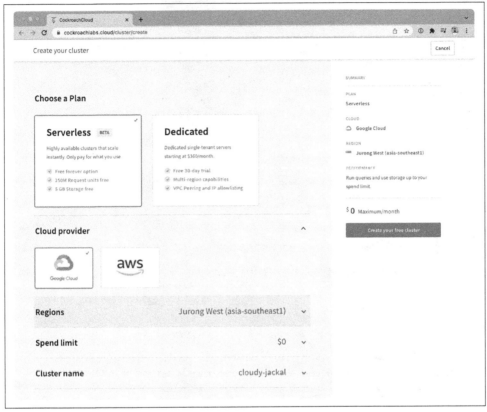

Figure 3-2. Creating a free CockroachDB Serverless database

Once the database is created, you'll be given instructions similar to those in Figure 3-3, which you can follow to connect to your server.

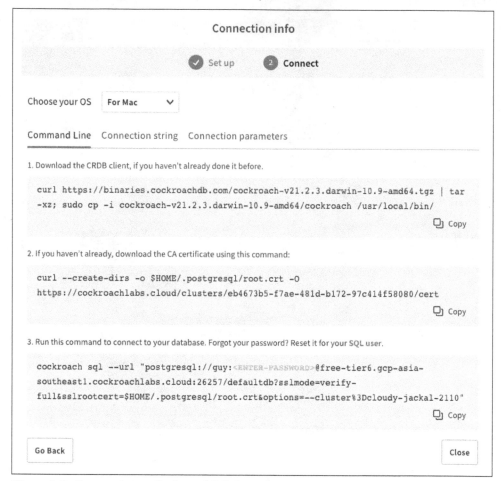

Figure 3-3. *Connecting to CockroachDB Serverless*

Assuming you have already downloaded the CockroachDB binary, issue the `curl` command from step 2 to copy the necessary certificates to the desktop, then the `cockroach sql` command from step 3 to connect to the database:

```
$ curl -create-dirs -o $HOME/.postgresql/root.crt -O \
    https://cockroachlabs.cloud/clusters/eb4673b5-f7ae-481d-b172-97c414f58080/cert

  % Total    % Received % Xferd  Average Speed   Time    Time     Time  Current
                                 Dload  Upload   Total   Spent    Left  Speed
100  2728    0  2728    0     0   5250      0 --:--:-- --:--:-- --:--:--  5317

$   cockroach sql -url "postgresql://guy:xxxxxxxxxx@free-tier6.gcp-asia-
```

```
southeast1.cockroachlabs.cloud:26257/defaultdb?sslmode=verify-
full&sslrootcert=$HOME/.postgresql/root.crt&options=
--cluster%3Dcloudy-jackal-2110"
#
# Welcome to the CockroachDB SQL shell.
# All statements must be terminated by a semicolon.
# To exit, type: \q.
#
# Cluster ID: 45851b67-5277-4795-aab9-390c70a78786
warning: cannot show server execution timings: unexpected column found
#
# Enter \? For a brief introduction.
#
guy@free-tier6.gcp-asia-southeast1/defaultdb> show databases;

  database_name | owner | primary_region | regions | survival_goal
----------------+-------+----------------+---------+---------------
  defaultdb     | root  | NULL           | {}      | NULL
  postgres      | root  | NULL           | {}      | NULL
  system        | node  | NULL           | {}      | NULL
(3 rows)

Time: 123ms
CockroachDB
CockroachDBCockroachDB
```

CockroachDB Serverless Cloud Passwords

Note that the password in the connection string is *not* the password you provided to connect to your CockroachDB Serverless account. Your CockroachDB Serverless account might be associated with many databases, each of which has its own password. The password shown in the connection dialog in Figure 3-3 will be shown only if you hover over the REVEAL_PASSWORD link and will be shown only at this point in the database creation. It's up to you to save that password and keep it safe. If you forget your password, you can reset it by going to the SQL Users page.

Starting a Local Single-Node Server

As we've seen previously, you can use the cockroach demo command to start a temporary demo cluster, and we can quickly create a free CockroachDB Serverless cluster. If you want to start a single-node CockroachDB server with persistent storage on your own hardware, you can use the cockroach start-single-node command:

```
$ cockroach start-single-node --insecure --listen-addr=localhost
*
* WARNING: ALL SECURITY CONTROLS HAVE BEEN DISABLED!
*
* This mode is intended for non-production testing only.
```

```
*
* In this mode:
* - Your cluster is open to any client that can access any
    of your IP addresses.
* - Intruders with access to your machine or network can observe
    client/server traffic.
* - Intruders can log in without password and read or write any
    data in the cluster.
* - Intruders can consume all your server's resources and cause unavailability.
*
*
* INFO: To start a secure server without mandating TLS for clients,
* consider --accept-sql-without-tls instead. For other options, see:
*
* - https://go.crdb.dev/issue-v/53404/v20.2
* - https://www.cockroachlabs.com/docs/v20.2/secure-a-cluster.html
*
```

This will start a single-node CockroachDB cluster with no security. To connect to this
server, we can use the cockroach sql command with the default connection string:

```
$ cockroach sql --insecure
#
# Welcome to the CockroachDB SQL shell.
# All statements must be terminated by a semicolon.
# To exit, type: \q.
#
# Cluster ID: 848d8b85-4000-484a-b4ad-8f2c76c68221
#
# Enter \? for a brief introduction.
#
root@:26257/defaultdb> show databases;
  database_name | owner | primary_region | regions | survival_goal
----------------+-------+----------------+---------+---------------
  defaultdb     | root  | NULL           | {}      | NULL
  postgres      | root  | NULL           | {}      | NULL
  system        | node  | NULL           | {}      | NULL
(3 rows)

Time: 3ms total (execution 3ms / network 0ms)

root@:26257/defaultdb>
```

Insecure Mode

The use of the --insecure flag is convenient for quickly starting a CockroachDB
cluster, but it's absolutely not appropriate for a production system. Please see Chapter 10 for instructions on setting up a properly secured production system.

Starting Up CockroachDB in a Docker Container

If you have Docker, you can quickly start a CockroachDB single-node instance inside a Docker container. You'll need a persistent volume for data, so let's create that first:

```
$ docker volume create crdb1
```

Then, we invoke `docker run` to pull and start the latest CockroachDB Docker image and start the server in single-node, insecure mode:

```
$ docker run -d \
> --name=crdb1 \
> --hostname=crdb1 \
> -p 26257:26257 -p 8080:8080 \
> -v "crdb1:/cockroach/cockroach-data" \
> cockroachdb/cockroach:latest start-single-node \
> --insecure \
>
Unable to find image 'cockroachdb/cockroach:latest' locally
latest: Pulling from cockroachdb/cockroach
a591faa84ab0: Pull complete
…
6913e7a5719….914b1aafe8
```

The output of the `docker run` command is the container identifier for the CockroachDB container. Using that `containerId`, we can connect to that container using the `cockroach sql` command:

```
$ docker exec -it 6913e7a5719….914b1aafe8 \
    cockroach sql --insecure
#
# Welcome to the CockroachDB SQL shell.
# All statements must be terminated by a semicolon.
# To exit, type: \q.
#
# Cluster ID: 8fcbb9bb-ec7c-40dc-afe0-90306c87f5d7
#
# Enter \? for a brief introduction.
#
root@:26257/defaultdb> show databases;
  database_name | owner | primary_region | regions | survival_goal
----------------+-------+----------------+---------+----------------
    defaultdb   | root  | NULL           | {}      | NULL
    postgres    | root  | NULL           | {}      | NULL
    system      | node  | NULL           | {}      | NULL
(3 rows)

Time: 4ms total (execution 3ms / network 1ms)
```

We don't need to have the CockroachDB software installed on our local host to connect using the preceding method because we're using the CockroachDB client installed within the Docker container. However, since we've forwarded port 26257 from the Docker container, we can attach from the desktop using the default connection:

```
$  ~ cockroach sql --insecure
#
# Welcome to the CockroachDB SQL shell.
# All statements must be terminated by a semicolon.
# To exit, type: \q.
#
# Cluster ID: d070609f-58a7-4aea-aa27-92bc4a1e5406
#
# Enter \? for a brief introduction.
#
root@:26257/defaultdb>
```

Note that this port forwarding can work only if there's not already a CockroachDB server listening on that port.

Starting Up a Secure Server

In the previous examples, we've used the --insecure flag to start the server without needing to configure secure communications. This is a quick way to set up a test server but is catastrophically dangerous for anything that contains valuable data.

We'll cover CockroachDB security in depth within Chapter 13, but for now, to set up a secure server, we need to create security certificates to encrypt the communications channel and authenticate the client and server.

The following commands create the certificates. The certificate authority key will be held in my-safe-directory; the certificates themselves will be held in the certs directory:

```
$ mkdir certs my-safe-directory

$ # CA certificate and keypair

$ cockroach cert create-ca \
>     --certs-dir=certs \
>     --ca-key=my-safe-directory/ca.key


$ # certificate and keypair for localhost
$ cockroach cert create-node localhost `hostname` --certs-dir=certs \
>     --ca-key=my-safe-directory/ca.key

$ # certificate for the root user
$ cockroach cert create-client root \
>     --certs-dir=certs \
>     --ca-key=my-safe-directory/ca.key
```

We can now start the server and specify the directory containing the certificates:

```
$ # start single node
$ cockroach start-single-node --certs-dir=certs \
  --listen-addr=localhost
```

Now, when connecting, we must specify the certificates directory. If we're connecting from a remote host, then we would need to copy the certificates to that host.

```
$ cockroach sql --certs-dir=certs
#
# Welcome to the CockroachDB SQL shell.
# All statements must be terminated by a semicolon.
# To exit, type: \q.
#
# Cluster ID: f908d29e-1fb6-40b8-9e1f-a2a0a3763603
#
# Enter \? for a brief introduction.
#
root@:26257/defaultdb>
```

Certificates Directory

On Linux or macOS systems, CockroachDB will look for certificates in the *~/.cockroach-certs* directory. If your certificates are placed there, then you won't need to specify the --certs-dir argument. However, if you have multiple CockroachDB servers, then you may need to maintain distinct certificates for each, possibly in their own directories.

Shutting Down the Server

If the server has been started with the --background flag, then we shut down the server using a kill signal. For instance, killall can be used to issue a kill command to all cockroach commands currently running:

```
$ killall cockroach

initiating graceful shutdown of server
server drained and shutdown completed
```

To kill a specific server, identify its process ID and then issue the kill command specifying the process ID:

```
$ ps -ef |grep cockroach
ubuntu     13911       1 10 10:16 pts/0    00:00:43 cockroach
     start-single-node --insecure --listen-addr=localhost

$ kill 13911
$ initiating graceful shutdown of server
server drained and shutdown completed
```

Remote Connection

In the previous examples, we've connected to a server running on the same host as our client. This is pretty unusual in the real world, where we would normally be connecting to a server on another machine. Typically, we'd specify the URL parameter to identify the server concerned. For instance, to connect to a server on the mubuntu server on the default port, we could issue the following command:

```
$ cockroach sql --certs-dir=certs --url postgresql://root@mubuntu:26257/defaultdb
#
# Welcome to the CockroachDB SQL shell.
# All statements must be terminated by a semicolon.
# To exit, type: \q.
#
# Cluster ID: f908d29e-1fb6-40b8-9e1f-a2a0a3763603
#
# Enter \? for a brief introduction.
#
root@mubuntu:26257/defaultdb>
```

Creating a Kubernetes Cluster

In the previous examples, we've created single-node clusters and connected to a free CockroachDB Serverless database that is a shared region of a multitenant cluster. If you want to start with a dedicated multinode cluster, then the easiest way is to install a CockroachDB cluster in a Kubernetes environment using the CockroachDB Kubernetes operator.

Kubernetes is an increasingly ubiquitous framework that coordinates—orchestrates—the management of the components of a distributed system. The CockroachDB Kubernetes operator contains the configuration and utilities that allow CockroachDB to be deployed in Kubernetes.

We'll come back to production deployment options for Kubernetes later in the book. For now, we will deploy CockroachDB in a Kubernetes minikube cluster, which implements a local Kubernetes cluster on a desktop system.

For this example, we are using a minikube cluster running on macOS with 6 CPUs and 12 GB of memory. You can start such a cluster with the following command:

```
~ minikube start --memory=12G --cpus=6
😄 minikube v1.18.1 on Darwin 12.1
```

The first step is to deploy the operator, and its manifest:

```
$ kubectl apply -f https://cockroa.ch/crdbclusters_yaml

customresourcedefinition.apiextensions.k8s.io/crdbclusters.crdb.cockroachlabs.com
created
```

```
$ kubectl apply -f https://cockroa.ch/operator_yaml

clusterrole.rbac.authorization.k8s.io/cockroach-database-role created
serviceaccount/cockroach-database-sa created
clusterrolebinding.rbac.authorization.k8s.io/cockroach-database-rolebinding
created
role.rbac.authorization.k8s.io/cockroach-operator-role created
clusterrolebinding.rbac.authorization.k8s.io/cockroach-operator-rolebinding
created
clusterrole.rbac.authorization.k8s.io/cockroach-operator-role created
serviceaccount/cockroach-operator-sa created
rolebinding.rbac.authorization.k8s.io/cockroach-operator-default created
deployment.apps/cockroach-operator created
```

Once this is done, a kubectl `get pods` command should show the CockroachDB Kubernetes operator running inside the cluster:

```
$ kubectl config set-context --current --namespace=cockroach-operator-system
$ kubectl get pods
NAME                                 READY   STATUS             RESTARTS   AGE
cockroach-operator-84bf588dbb-65m8k  0/1     ContainerCreating  0          9s
```

We then retrieve the example configuration file that is included in the operator's repository:

```
$ curl -O https://cockroa.ch/example_yaml -o example.yaml

  % Total    % Received % Xferd  Average Speed   Time    Time     Time  Current
                                 Dload  Upload   Total   Spent    Left  Speed
100  1098  100  1098    0     0   3399      0 --:--:-- --:--:-- --:--:--  3399
```

This file contains definitions for the cluster to be configured, such as the number of nodes to be created and the memory and CPU required by each node. The configuration is tilted toward a production deployment, so you might want to trim down the requirements. For instance, in the following code we see that the default configuration file specifies a 60 GB storage requirement. We might want to change this to a lower value for a simple test system (or increase it for a bigger deployment):

```
apiVersion: crdb.cockroachlabs.com/v1alpha1
kind: CrdbCluster
metadata:
  name: cockroachdb
spec:
  dataStore:
    pvc:
      spec:
        accessModes:
          - ReadWriteOnce
        resources:
          requests:
            storage: "60Gi"
        volumeMode: Filesystem
```

You could edit other elements of the configuration file, such as the number of nodes to be created or the version of CockroachDB to be used.

We now apply the configuration file to the operator, which will perform the necessary tasks to create the cluster:

```
$ kubectl apply -f example.yaml
crdbcluster.crdb.cockroachlabs.com/cockroachdb created
```

The cluster creation process can take some time. We'll know it's complete when a `kubectl get pods` command shows all nodes in `Running` state:

```
$ kubectl get pods
NAME                                      READY   STATUS    RESTARTS   AGE
cockroach-operator-84bf588dbb-65m8k       1/1     Running   0          6m59s
cockroachdb-0                             1/1     Running   0          87s
cockroachdb-1                             1/1     Running   0          71s
cockroachdb-2                             1/1     Running   0          57s
```

We can connect to the cluster by invoking the `cockroach sql` command from within any of the CockroachDB nodes. For instance, here we connect to `cockroachdb-2` and connect to the cluster:

```
$ kubectl exec -it cockroachdb-2 -- ./cockroach sql --certs-dir cockroach-certs
#
# Welcome to the CockroachDB SQL shell.
# All statements must be terminated by a semicolon.
# To exit, type: \q.
#
# Cluster ID: cb78255b-befa-4447-9fa8-c06b7a353564
#
# Enter \? for a brief introduction.
#
  database_name | owner | primary_region | regions | survival_goal
----------------+-------+----------------+---------+----------------
  defaultdb     | root  | NULL           | {}      | NULL
  postgres      | root  | NULL           | {}      | NULL
  system        | node  | NULL           | {}      | NULL
(3 rows)

Time: 7ms total (execution 6ms / network 1ms)
```

Connecting to the cluster using this method requires a high level of access to the cluster. In a production environment, we would set up a load balancer to securely handle incoming requests to the cluster. We'll look at these sorts of configurations in Chapter 10.

Using a GUI Client

While some are more than happy to use only a command-line client to interact with a database, some of us prefer a GUI. Many GUI applications for PostgreSQL exist, and most of these will work with CockroachDB. However, DBeaver Community edition (*https://dbeaver.io*) is a free database GUI that has dedicated support for CockroachDB. Figure 3-4 shows the DBeaver GUI client.

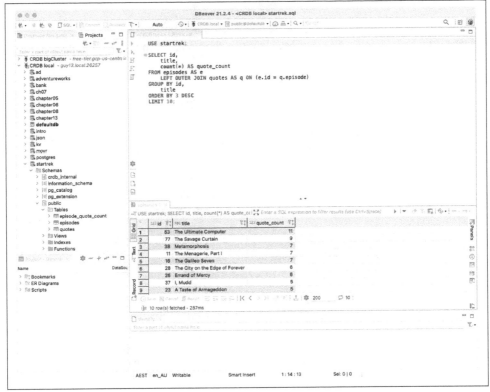

Figure 3-4. The DBeaver GUI

The CockroachDB documentation has some further information about using DBEaver (*https://cockroa.ch/3DHtScT*).

Exploring CockroachDB

Now that we've got access to a CockroachDB cluster and have the client ready to connect, let's take CockroachDB for a drive! In the following examples, we are using a local cluster—the connection strings may be different if you are using a Serverless instance.

Adding Some Data

As folks say in Australia, "A database without data is like a pub with no beer!" Let's get some data into the database so that we have something to look at.

The CockroachDB software includes a number of demonstration databases that you can quickly add to your CockroachDB installation. In some cases, these databases are prepopulated with data; in other cases, you create the schemas and then add data afterward.

To initialize the schemas, we use the `cockroach workload init [schema]` command. To run a workload against the schema, we use the `cockroach workload run [schema]` command.

The schemas include:

bank
> Models a set of accounts with currency balances. After initializing the schema, use `workload run` to generate a workload against the database.

intro
> A simple single-table database.

kv
> A simple KV schema. After initializing the schema, use `run` to generate a workload that will be evenly distributed across the cluster.

movr
> A schema for a fictional ride-sharing application. This schema can be used with the `workload run` command to generate load against the databases.

startrek
> A Star Trek database, with two tables, `episodes` and `quotes`.

tpcc
> A transaction processing schema for the TPC-C standard benchmark. This schema can be used with the `workload run` command to generate load against the databases.

ycsb
> The Yahoo Cloud Serving Benchmark schema. This schema can be used with the `workload run` command to generate load against the databases.

For the `intro` and `startrek` databases, we create the tables and data using the `workload init` command. For instance, in the following example, we create the `startrek` schema and look at some data:

```
$ cockroach workload init startrek \
      'postgres://root@localhost:26257?sslmode=disable
I210501 04:29:29.694340 1   imported episodes (0s, 79 rows)
I210501 04:29:29.898945 1   imported quotes (0s, 200 rows)
$ cockroach sql --insecure
#
```

```
# Welcome to the CockroachDB SQL shell.
# All statements must be terminated by a semicolon.
# To exit, type: \q.
#
#
# Enter \? for a brief introduction.
#
root@:26257/defaultdb> show databases;

   database_name | owner | primary_region | regions | survival_goal
  ---------------+-------+----------------+---------+---------------
   defaultdb     | root  | NULL           | {}      | NULL
   postgres      | root  | NULL           | {}      | NULL
   startrek      | root  | NULL           | {}      | NULL
   system        | node  | NULL           | {}      | NULL
(4 rows)


Time: 3ms total (execution 3ms / network 1ms)


root@:26257/defaultdb> use startrek;
SET


Time: 1ms total (execution 0ms / network 0ms)


root@:26257/startrek> show tables;

   schema_name | table_name | type  | owner | estimated_row_count | locality
  -------------+------------+-------+-------+---------------------+----------
   public      | episodes   | table | root  |                   0 | NULL
   public      | quotes     | table | root  |                   0 | NULL
(2 rows)


Time: 24ms total (execution 24ms / network 0ms)


root@:26257/startrek> select * from episodes limit 1;
   id | season | num |    title     | stardate
  ----+--------+-----+--------------+----------
    1 |      1 |   1 | The Man Trap | 1531.1
(1 row)


Time: 1ms total (execution 1ms / network 0ms)
```

In this example, we create the bank schema:

```
$ cockroach workload init bank \
     'postgres://root@localhost:26257?sslmode=disable'
I210501 04:31:41.214008 1 imported bank (0s, 1000 rows)
I210501 04:31:41.221478 1 starting 9 splits
```

And then run a workload simulation for 60 seconds:

```
$ cockroach workload run bank 'postgres://root@localhost:26257?sslmode=disable' \
     --duration 60s
I210501 04:33:52.340852 1   creating load generator...
```

```
I210501 04:33:52.344074 1   creating load generator... done (took 3.220303ms)
_elapsed_ops/sec(inst)___ops/sec(cum)__p50(ms)__p95(ms)_pMax(ms)
     1.0s        187.3         187.9      16.8     48.2    121.6 transfer
     2.0s        295.0         241.5      11.0     31.5     79.7 transfer
     3.0s        260.9         248.0      13.1     37.7     83.9 transfer
     4.0s        203.1         236.7      17.8     39.8     79.7 <snip>

_elapsed____ops(total)___ops/sec(cum)__avg(ms)__p50(ms)__p99(ms)_pMax(ms
    60.0s        14230         237.2      16.9     13.6     65.0    192.9
```

The run command is primarily meant to generate data for load testing purposes but is useful to generate data for query purposes as well.

Databases and Tables

As we've seen already, data in a CockroachDB deployment is organized into specific namespaces called databases. Database is a fairly loosely used and overloaded term—it's quite common for a CockroachDB cluster to be referred to as a database or for a database within a cluster to be referred to as a schema. However, in CockroachDB, as in most other SQL databases, a database cluster contains one or more databases. Within a database, one or more schemas may be defined, though it's common for each database to contain only one schema.

We can list the databases in the cluster using the show databases command:

```
root@:26257/defaultdb> show databases;
  database_name | owner | primary_region | regions | survival_goal
----------------+-------+----------------+---------+---------------
  bank          | root  | NULL           | {}      | NULL
  defaultdb     | root  | NULL           | {}      | NULL
  postgres      | root  | NULL           | {}      | NULL
  startrek      | root  | NULL           | {}      | NULL
  system        | node  | NULL           | {}      | NULL
(5 rows)
```

We can set our current database with the use command:

```
root@:26257/defaultdb> use startrek;
SET

Time: 1ms total (execution 0ms / network 0ms)
```

We list tables within a database with the show tables command:

```
root@:26257/startrek> show tables;
  schema_name | table_name | type  | owner | estimated_row_count | locality
--------------+------------+-------+-------+---------------------+----------
  public      | episodes   | table | root  |                  79 | NULL
  public      | quotes     | table | root  |                 200 | NULL
(2 rows)

Time: 16ms total (execution 16ms / network 0ms)
```

We can describe a table using the \d command:

```
root@:26257/startrek> \d quotes;
  column_name | data_type | is_nullable | column_default |        indices
--------------+-----------+-------------+----------------+-----------------------
  quote       | STRING    | true        | NULL           | {primary}
  characters  | STRING    | true        | NULL           | {primary}
  stardate    | DECIMAL   | true        | NULL           | {primary}
  episode     | INT8      | true        | NULL           | {primary,quotes_epis
  rowid       | INT8      | false       | unique_rowid() | {primary,quotes_epis
(5 rows)

Time: 13ms total (execution 12ms / network 1ms)
```

Issuing SQL

From the CockroachDB client, we can issue any SQL commands for which we are authorized.

Here we connect to the Star Trek sample database and issue a query to find the episodes with the most quotes:

```
root@localhost:26257/defaultdb> USE startrek;

SELECT id,
    title,
    count(*) AS quote_count
FROM episodes AS e
    LEFT OUTER JOIN quotes AS q ON (e.id = q.episode)
GROUP BY id,
    title
ORDER BY 3 DESC
LIMIT 10;
SET

Time: 1ms total (execution 0ms / network 1ms)

  id |                title                | quote_count
-----+-------------------------------------+--------------
  53 | The Ultimate Computer               |      11
  77 | The Savage Curtain                  |       9
  11 | The Menagerie, Part I               |       7
  38 | Metamorphosis                       |       7
  16 | The Galileo Seven                   |       7
  28 | The City on the Edge of Forever     |       6
  26 | Errand of Mercy                     |       6
  24 | This Side of Paradise               |       5
  23 | A Taste of Armageddon               |       5
  37 | I, Mudd                             |       5
(10 rows)

Time: 5ms total (execution 3ms / network 1ms)
```

The DB Console

The CockroachDB server exposes a web-based client that shows the status of the cluster and useful performance metrics. The web server is usually exposed on port 8080, though this can be changed using the `--http-addr` setting when starting the server. Figure 3-5 shows an example of the DB Console, in this case from the Kubernetes cluster that we started earlier in this chapter (we forwarded port 8080 from one of the pods in the cluster).

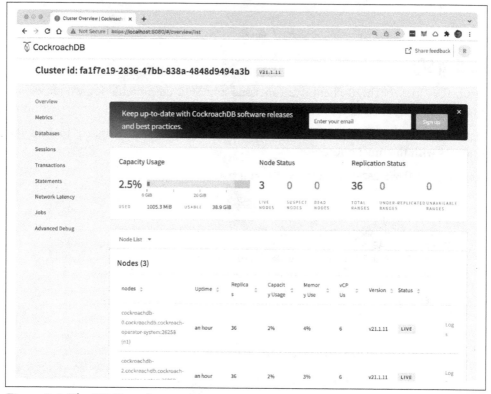

Figure 3-5. The DB Console

Working with Programming Languages

Working with the CockroachDB shell is useful for experimentation, but eventually, most databases interact with application code written in languages such as JavaScript, Java, Go, or Python.

Because CockroachDB is wire-compatible with Postgres, most Postgres-compatible drivers will work with CockroachDB. Indeed, there are no CockroachDB-specific drivers on the market because the Postgres drivers work so well. In this section, we'll get you up to speed with "hello world" programs in Java, GoLang, Python, and JavaScript that connect to and query a CockroachDB cluster. A full list of supported languages can be found in the CockroachDB online documentation (*https://cockroa.ch/3j6S8fb*).

Connecting to CockroachDB from Node.js

Server-side JavaScript using the Node.js platform is an increasingly popular choice for application development because it allows the same JavaScript language to be used for both frontend web presentation code and server-side application logic.

Assuming that you have Node.js and the Node package manager (npm) installed, we'll use the `node-postgres` driver to connect to CockroachDB. We can install this driver with the following command:

```
npm install pg
```

Once pg is installed, then the following example should connect to any CockroachDB database using a connection URI:

```
// Example of connecting to CockroachDB using Node.js

const CrClient = require('pg').Client; //load pg client

async function main() {
    try {
        // Check parameters
        if (process.argv.length != 3) {
            console.log('Usage: node helloWorld.js CONNECTION_URI');
            process.exit(1);
        }
        // Establish a connection using the command line URI
        const connectionString = process.argv[2];
        const crClient = new CrClient(connectionString);
        await crClient.connect();

        // Issue a SELECT
        const data = await crClient.query(
            `SELECT CONCAT('Hello from CockroachDB at ',
                        CAST (NOW() as STRING)) as hello`
        );
        // Print out the error message
        console.log(data.rows[0].hello);
    } catch (error) {
        console.log(error.stack);
    }
    // Exit
    process.exit(0);
}

main();
```

This program expects the connection string to be provided as the first argument to the program. The process.argv array contains the full command line including "node" and "helloWorld.js", so the URI actually shows up as the third element in the array.

We then attempt to establish a connection using that connection string, then issue a SELECT statement that retrieves the time as known to the server.

Here we connect to a CockroachDB Serverless cluster:

```
$ node helloWorld.js "postgresql://jesse:xxxxxxxxxxxx
free-tier4.aws-us-west-2.cockroachlabs.cloud:26257/defaultdb?
sslmode=verify-full&sslrootcert=$HOME/.postgresql/root.crt&
options=--cluster%3Dalert-dingo-2030"

Hello from CockroachDB at 2021-05-02 00:17:40.835834+00:00
```

And here we connect to a local CockroachDB running in insecure mode:

```
$ node helloWorld.js 'postgres://root@localhost:26257?sslmode=disable'
Hello from CockroachDB at 2021-05-02 00:32:39.125419+00:00
```

Connecting to CockroachDB from Java

Java is the workhorse of millions of applications across all industries and contexts.

In this example, we will use the official PostgresSQL JDBC driver to connect to a CockroachDB server.

Download the Java Database Connectivity (JDBC) driver (*https://cockroa.ch/3DHucID*) and place it in your class path or configure it as a dependency in your IDE.

The following program accepts a URL, username, and password as arguments on the command line and connects to the CockroachDB cluster concerned, and issues a SELECT statement:

```
package helloCRDB;

import java.sql.Connection;
import java.sql.DriverManager;
import java.sql.ResultSet;
import java.sql.Statement;

public class HelloCRDB {
  public static void main(String[] args) {
      Connection cdb = null;
      try {
            Class.forName("org.postgresql.Driver");
            String connectionURL="jdbc:"+args[0];
            String userName=args[1];
            String passWord=args[2];
```

```java
            cdb = DriverManager.getConnection(connectionURL,userName,passWord);
            Statement stmt = cdb.createStatement();
            ResultSet rs = stmt
                .executeQuery("SELECT CONCAT('Hello from CockroachDB at',"
                            + "CAST (NOW() as STRING)) AS hello");
            rs.next();
            System.out.println(rs.getString("hello"));

        } catch (Exception e) {
            e.printStackTrace();
            System.err.println(e.getClass().getName() + ": " + e.getMessage());
            System.exit(0);
        }
    }
}
```

If we want to connect to the CockroachDB Serverless cluster we created earlier, we issue the following command:[1]

```
$ java -m helloCRDB/helloCRDB.HelloCRDB
 postgresql://free-tier6.gcp-asia-southeast1.cockroachlabs.cloud:26257/defaultdb
 ?sslmode=verify-full&sslrootcert=/Users/guyharrison/CockroachDBCockroachDBKeys/
cc-ca.crt&options=--cluster=grumpy-orca-56 \
 guy xxxxxxxxxxxx


Hello from CockroachDB at 2021-05-05 15:39:07.667438+10:00
```

And here we connect to a local CockroachDB cluster in insecure mode:

```
$ java  -m helloCRDB/helloCRDB.HelloCRDB postgresql://localhost:26257/
?sslmode=disable root ''

Hello from CockroachDB at 2021-05-05 15:38:56.691009+10:00
```

Connecting to CockroachDB from Python

Python is a widely used scripting language as well as the tool of choice for many data scientists and data wranglers. In this example, we'll use the psycopg python-postgresql package to connect to CockroachDB.

To install the psycopg package, issue the following command:

```
$ pip3 install psycopg2

Collecting psycopg2
  Using cached psycopg2-2.8.6.tar.gz (383 kB)
Building wheels for collected packages: psycopg2
```

---

1 Note that the URL is slightly different from the ones used for other languages. The Java Postgres driver does not support embedding the username and password in the URL, so we need to pass them separately.

```
  Building wheel for psycopg2 (setup.py) ... done
  Created wheel for psycopg2: filename=psycopg2-2.8.6-cp39-...
  Stored in directory: /Users/guyharrison/Li...
Successfully built psycopg2
Installing collected packages: psycopg2
Successfully installed psycopg2-2.8.6
```

Now the following short program will connect to CockroachDB using a URL provided on the command line and issue a SELECT statement:

```
#!/usr/bin/env python3

import psycopg2
import sys

def main():

  if ((len(sys.argv)) !=2):
    sys.exit("Error:No URL provided on command line")
  uri=sys.argv[1]

  conn = psycopg2.connect(uri)
  with conn.cursor() as cur:
    cur.execute("""SELECT CONCAT('Hello from CockroachDB at ',
                CAST (NOW() as STRING))""")
    data=cur.fetchone()
    print("%s" % data[0])

main()
```

Here we connect to the CockroachDB Serverless database we established earlier in the chapter:[2]

```
$ python helloCockroachDB.py \
 'postgres://guy:xxxxxx@free-tier6.gcp-asia-
southeast1.cockroachlabs.cloud:26257/defaultdb?sslmode=verify-
full&sslrootcert=/Users/guyharrison/CockroachDBCockroachDBKeys/
cc-ca.crt&options=--cluster%3dgrumpy-orca-56'

Hello from CockroachDB at 2021-05-02 02:39:55.859734+00:00
```

And here we connect to a local CockroachDB cluster running in insecure mode:

```
$ python helloCockroachDB.py 'postgres://root@localhost:26257?sslmode=disable'
Hello from CockroachDB at 2021-05-02 02:33:00.755359+00:00
```

---

2 Note that because of limitations in the psycopg2 driver, we need to replace the final "=" in the URL with "%3d." Instead of cluster=grumpy-orca-56, we use cluster%3dgrumpy-orca-56.

Connecting to CockroachDB from Go

The Go language is one of the fastest-growing programming languages, and it offers high performance, modern programming paradigms, and a low footprint. Much of the CockroachDB database platform is written in Go, so Go is a great choice for CockroachDB development.

In this example, we're going to use the pgx PostgreSQL driver for Go to connect to the CockroachDB Serverless cluster we created earlier. First, we need to install the driver:

```
$ go env -w GO111MODULE=auto
$ go get github.com/jackc/pgx
```

This short program connects to CockroachDB using the URL provided on the command line, and issues a SELECT statement:

```go
package main

import (
        "context"
        "fmt"
        "os"
        "github.com/jackc/pgx"
)

func main() {
        uri := "postgresql://root@localhost:26257/bank?ssl=disabled"
        conn, err := pgx.Connect(context.Background(), uri)
        if err != nil {
                fmt.Fprintf(os.Stderr,
                        "Unable to connect to database: %v\n", err)
                os.Exit(1)
        }
        var text string
        err = conn.QueryRow(context.Background(),
                `SELECT CONCAT('Hello from CockroachDB at ',
                    CAST (NOW() as STRING))`).Scan(&text)
        if err != nil {
                fmt.Fprintf(os.Stderr, "QueryRow failed: %v\n", err)
                os.Exit(1)
        }

        fmt.Println(text)
}
```

Here, we connect to a CockroachDB Serverless cluster:

```
$ go run helloCockroachDB.go \
   "postgres://guy:xxxxxxx@free-tier6.gcp-asia-
southeast1.cockroachlabs.cloud:26257/defaultdb?sslmode=verify-
full&sslrootcert=$HOME/CockroachDBCockroachDBKeys/
cc-ca.crt&options=--cluster=grumpy-orca-56"

Hello from CockroachDB at 2021-05-02 02:24:13.930662+00:00
```

And here we run the program to connect to a local CockroachDB cluster in insecure mode:

```
$ go run helloCockroach.go 'postgres://root@localhost:26257?sslmode=disable'
Hello from CockroachDB at 2021-05-02 02:21:59.179171+00:00
```

Summary

In this chapter, we've shown you how to install CockroachDB software on a local computer, how to create a CockroachDB cluster in a variety of configurations, and how to work with CockroachDB from the command line or a programming language.

It's easy to install CockroachDB software on a desktop and, in most cases, necessary if you want to work with a CockroachDB server from the command line. You can also install CockroachDB software using Docker or Kubernetes.

While a single-node test server can be a useful tool for learning CockroachDB, the CockroachDB Serverless cloud option offers a free 5 GB server that provides backup and security. You can also install CockroachDB in a Kubernetes cluster to experiment with a full cluster in a local environment.

Because CockroachDB is PostgreSQL-compatible, you can use any Postgres-compatible driver to connect to CockroachDB. We also provided simple examples of connecting to CockroachDB using the PostgreSQL drivers for Java, Python, Go, and Node.js.

CockroachDB SQL

The language of CockroachDB is SQL. While there are some command-line utilities, all interactions between an application and the database are mediated by SQL language commands.

SQL is a rich language with a long history—we touched upon some of that history in Chapter 1. A full definition of all SQL language features would require a book in its own right and would be almost instantly out of date because the SQL language evolves with each release.

Therefore, this chapter aims to provide you with a broad overview of the SQL language used in CockroachDB without attempting to be a complete reference. We'll take a task-oriented approach to SQL, covering the most common SQL language tasks with particular reference to unique features of the CockroachDB SQL implementation.

As we described in Chapter 1, SQL is a *declarative* language. SQL statements represent logical requests for queries and data manipulation operations without specifying how the database should implement those requests.

A complete reference for the CockroachDB SQL language can be found in the CockroachDB documentation set (*https://cockroa.ch/3DC6MV0*). A broader review of the SQL language can be found in the O'Reilly book *SQL in a Nutshell*.

Some of the examples in this chapter use the MovR sample data set in this chapter to illustrate various SQL language features. We showed how to install sample data in Chapter 2.

SQL Language Compatibility

CockroachDB is broadly compatible with the PostgreSQL implementation of the SQL:2016 standard. The SQL:2016 standard contains a number of independent modules, and no major database implements all of the standards. However, the PostgreSQL implementation of SQL is arguably as close to "standard" as exists in the database community.

CockroachDB varies from PostgreSQL in a couple of areas:

- CockroachDB does not currently support stored procedures, events, or triggers. In PostgreSQL, these stored procedures are written in the PL/pgSQL language and allow for the execution of program logic within the database server, either on-demand or in response to some triggering event.
- CockroachDB does not currently support user-defined functions.
- CockroachDB does not support PostgreSQL XML functions.
- CockroachDB does not support PostgreSQL full-text indexes and functions.

Querying Data with SELECT

Although we need to create and populate tables before querying them, it's logical to start with the SELECT statement since many features of the SELECT statement appear in other types of SQL—subqueries in UPDATEs, for instance—and for data scientists and analysts, the SELECT statement is often the only SQL statement they ever need to learn.

The SELECT statement (Figure 4-1) is the workhorse of relational queries and has a complex and rich syntax. The CockroachDB SELECT statement implements the standard features of the standard SELECT, with just a few CockroachDB-specific features.

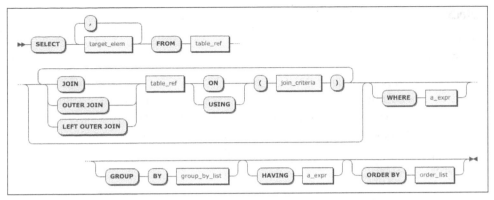

Figure 4-1. SELECT statement

In the following sections, we'll examine each of the major elements of the SELECT statement as well as the functions and operators that can be included in it.

The SELECT List

A simple SQL statement consists of nothing but a SELECT statement together with scalar expressions (e.g., expressions that return a single value). For instance:

```
SELECT CONCAT('Hello from CockroachDB at ',
              CAST (NOW() as STRING)) as hello;
```

The SELECT list includes a comma-separated list of expressions that can contain combinations of constants, functions, and operators. The CockroachDB SQL language supports all the familiar SQL operators. A complete list of functions and operators can be found in the CockroachDB documentation set (*https://cockroa.ch/3uObifc*).

The FROM Clause

The FROM clause is the primary method of attaching table data to the SELECT statement. In its most simple incarnation, all rows and columns from a table can be fetched via a full table scan:

```
SELECT * FROM rides;
```

Table names may be aliased using the AS clause or simply by following the table name with an alias. That alias can then be used anywhere in the query to refer to the table. Column names can also be aliased. For instance, the following are all equivalent:

```
SELECT name FROM users;
SELECT u.name FROM users u;
SELECT users.name FROM users;
SELECT users.name AS user_name FROM users;
SELECT u.name FROM users AS u;
```

JOINS

Joins allow the results from two or more tables to be merged based on some common column values.

The INNER JOIN is the default JOIN operation. In this join, rows from one table are joined to rows from another table based on some common ("key") values. Rows that have no match in both tables are not included in the results. For instance, the following query links vehicle and ride information in the movr database:

```
SELECT v.id,v.ext,r.start_time, r.start_address
  FROM vehicles v
  INNER JOIN rides r
    ON (r.vehicle_id=v.id);
```

Note that a vehicle that had not been involved in a ride would not be included in the result set.

The ON clause specifies the conditions that join the two tables—in the previous query, the columns vehicle_id in the rider table were matched with the id column in the vehicles table. If the JOIN is on an identically named column in both tables, then the USING clause provides a handy shortcut. Here we join users and user_ride_counts using the common name column:[1]

```
SELECT *
  FROM users u
  JOIN user_ride_counts urc
  USING (name);
```

The OUTER JOIN allows rows to be included even if they have no match in the other table. Rows that are not found in the OUTER JOIN table are represented by NULL values. LEFT and RIGHT determine which table may have missing values. For instance, the following query prints all the users in the users table, even if some are not associated with a promo code:

```
SELECT u.name , upc.code
  FROM users u
  LEFT OUTER JOIN user_promo_codes upc
    ON (u.id=upc.user_id);
```

The RIGHT OUTER JOIN reverses the default (LEFT) OUTER JOIN. So, this query is identical to the previous query because the users table is now the "right" table in the join:

```
SELECT DISTINCT u.name , upc.code
  FROM user_promo_codes upc
```

---

1 Note that user_ride_counts is not defined in the default rides schema. It is defined as SELECT u.name, COUNT(u.name) AS rides FROM "users" AS u JOIN "rides" AS r ON (u.id=r.rider_id) GROUP BY u.name.

```
RIGHT OUTER JOIN users u
  ON (u.id=upc.user_id);
```

Anti-Joins

It is often required to select all rows from a table that do not have a matching row in some other result set. This is called an anti-join, and while there is no SQL syntax for this concept, it is typically implemented using a subquery and the IN or EXISTS clause. The following example illustrates an anti-join using the EXISTS and IN operators.

Each example selects users who are not also employees:

```
SELECT *
  FROM users
 WHERE id NOT IN
       (SELECT id FROM employees);
```

This query returns the same results but using a correlated subquery (we'll discuss subqueries in more detail in an upcoming section):

```
SELECT *
  FROM users u
 WHERE NOT EXISTS
       (SELECT id
          FROM employees e
         WHERE e.id=u.id);
```

Cross Joins

CROSS JOIN indicates that every row in the left table should be joined to every row in the right table. Usually, this is a recipe for disaster unless one of the tables has only one row or is a laterally correlated subquery (see "Correlated Subquery" on page 85).

Set Operations

SQL implements a number of operations that deal directly with result sets. These operations, collectively referred to as "set operations," allow result sets to be concatenated, subtracted, or overlaid.

The most common of these operations is the UNION operator, which returns the sum of two result sets. By default, duplicates in each result set are eliminated. By contrast, the UNION ALL operation will return the sum of the two result sets, including any duplicates. The following example returns a list of customers and employees. Employees who are also customers will be listed only once:

```
SELECT name, address
  FROM customers
 UNION
```

```
SELECT name,address
  FROM employees;
```

INTERSECT returns those rows that are in both result sets. This query returns customers who are also employees:

```
SELECT name, address
  FROM customers
 INTERSECT
SELECT name,address
  FROM employees;
```

EXCEPT returns rows in the first result set that are not present in the second. This query returns customers who are not also employees:

```
SELECT name, address
  FROM customers
 EXCEPT
SELECT name,address
  FROM employees;
```

All set operations require that the component queries return the same number of columns and that those columns are of a compatible data type.

Group Operations

Aggregate operations allow for summary information to be generated, typically upon groupings of rows. Rows can be grouped using the GROUP BY operator. If this is done, the select list must consist only of columns contained within the GROUP BY clause and aggregate functions.

The most common aggregate functions are shown in Table 4-1.

Table 4-1. Aggregate functions

AVG	Calculate the average value for the group.
COUNT	Return the number of rows in the group.
MAX	Return the maximum value in the group.
MIN	Return the minimum value in the group.
STDDEV	Return the standard deviation for the group.
SUM	Return the total of all values for the group.

The following example generates summary ride information for each city:

```
SELECT u.city,SUM(urc.rides),AVG(urc.rides),max(urc.rides)
  FROM users u
  JOIN user_ride_counts urc
 USING (name)
 GROUP BY u.city;
```

Subqueries

A subquery is a SELECT statement that occurs within another SQL statement. Such a "nested" SELECT statement can be used in a wide variety of SQL contexts, including SELECT, DELETE, UPDATE, and INSERT statements.

The following statement uses a subquery to count the number of rides that share the maximum ride length:

```
SELECT COUNT(*) FROM rides
  WHERE (end_time-start_time)=
        (SELECT MAX(end_time-start_time) FROM rides );
```

Subqueries may also be used in the FROM clause wherever a table or view definition could appear. This query generates a result that compares each ride with the average ride duration for the city:

```
SELECT id, city,(end_time-start_time) ride_duration, avg_ride_duration
  FROM rides
  JOIN (SELECT city,
               AVG(end_time-start_time) avg_ride_duration
          FROM rides
         GROUP BY city)
  USING(city) ;
```

Correlated Subquery

A correlated subquery is one in which the subquery refers to values in the parent query or operation. The subquery returns a potentially different result for each row in the parent result set. We saw an example of a correlated subquery when performing an "anti-join" earlier in the chapter.

```
SELECT *
   FROM users u
  WHERE NOT EXISTS
        (SELECT id
           FROM employees e
          WHERE e.id=u.id);
```

Subqueries can often be used to perform an operation that is functionally equivalent to a join. In many cases, the query optimizer will transform these statements to joins to streamline the optimization process.

Lateral Subquery

When a subquery is used in a join, the LATERAL keyword indicates that the subquery may access columns generated in preceding FROM table expressions. For instance, in the following query, the LATERAL keyword allows the subquery to access columns from the users table:

```
SELECT name, address, start_time
FROM users CROSS JOIN
     LATERAL (SELECT *
              FROM rides
              WHERE rides.start_address = users.address ) r;
```

This example is a bit contrived, and clearly, we could construct a simple JOIN that performed this query more naturally. Where LATERAL joins really shine is in allowing subqueries to access computed columns in other subqueries within a FROM clause. Andy Woods' CockroachDB blog post (*https://cockroa.ch/3DFUpXW*) describes a more serious example of lateral subqueries.

The WHERE Clause

The WHERE clause is common to SELECT, UPDATE, and DELETE statements. It specifies a set of logical conditions that must evaluate to true for all rows to be returned or processed by the SQL statement concerned.

Common Table Expressions

SQL statements with a lot of subqueries can be hard to read and maintain, especially if the same subquery is needed in multiple contexts within the query. For this reason, SQL supports *Common Table Expressions* using the WITH clause. Figure 4-2 shows the syntax of a Common Table Expression.

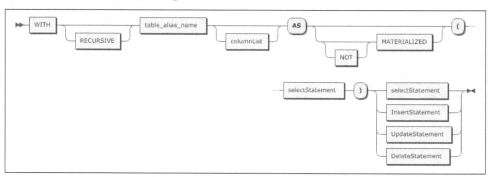

Figure 4-2. Common Table Expression

In its simplest form, a Common Table Expression is simply a named query block that can be applied wherever a table expression can be used. For instance, here we use the WITH clause to create a Common Table Expression, riderRevenue, then refer to it in the FROM clause of the main query:

```
WITH riderRevenue AS (
        SELECT u.id, SUM(r.revenue) AS sumRevenue
          FROM rides r JOIN "users" u
          ON (r.rider_id=u.id)
```

```
        GROUP BY u.id)
SELECT * FROM "users" u2
        JOIN riderRevenue rr USING (id)
ORDER BY sumrevenue DESC;
```

The RECURSIVE clause allows the Common Table Expression to refer to itself, potentially allowing for a query to return an arbitrarily high (or even infinite) set of results. For instance, if the employees table contained a manager_id column that referred to the manager's row in the same table, then we could print a hierarchy of employees and managers as follows:

```
WITH RECURSIVE employeeMgr AS (
    SELECT id,manager_id, name , NULL AS manager_name, 1 AS level
      FROM employees managers
     WHERE manager_id IS NULL
    UNION ALL
    SELECT subordinates.id,subordinates.manager_id,
           subordinates.name, managers.name ,managers.LEVEL+1
      FROM employeeMgr managers
      JOIN employees subordinates
        ON (subordinates.manager_id=managers.id)
)
SELECT * FROM employeeMgr;
```

The MATERIALIZED clause forces CockroachDB to store the results of the Common Table Expression as a temporary table rather than re-executing it on each occurrence. This can be useful if the Common Table Expression is referenced multiple times in the query.

ORDER BY

The ORDER BY clause allows query results to be returned in sorted order. Figure 4-3 shows the ORDER BY syntax.

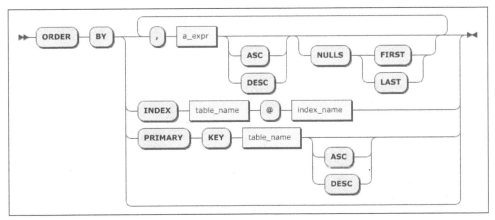

Figure 4-3. ORDER BY

In the simplest form, ORDER BY takes one or more column expressions or column numbers from the SELECT list.

In this example, we sort by column numbers:

```
SELECT city,start_time, (end_time-start_time) duration
   FROM rides r
   ORDER BY 1,3 DESC;
```

And in this case, by column expressions:

```
SELECT city,start_time, (end_time-start_time) duration
   FROM rides r
   ORDER BY city,(end_time-start_time) DESC;
```

You can also order by an index. In the following example, rows will be ordered by city and start_time, since those are the columns specified in the index:

```
CREATE INDEX rides_start_time ON rides (city ,start_time);

SELECT city,start_time, (end_time-start_time) duration
   FROM rides
   ORDER BY INDEX rides@rides_start_time;
```

The use of ORDER BY INDEX guarantees that the index will be used to directly return rows in sorted order, rather than having to perform a sort operation on the rows after they are retrieved. See Chapter 8 for more advice on optimizing statements that contain an ORDER BY.

Window Functions

Window functions are functions that operate over a subset—a "window" of the complete set of the results. Figure 4-4 shows the syntax of a window function.

Figure 4-4. Window function syntax

PARTITION BY and ORDER BY create a sort of "virtual table" that the function works with. For instance, this query lists the top 10 rides in terms of revenue, with the percentage of the total revenue and city revenue displayed:

```
SELECT city, r.start_time ,revenue,
       revenue*100/SUM(revenue) OVER () AS pct_total_revenue,
       revenue*100/SUM(revenue) OVER (PARTITION BY city) AS pct_city_revenue
   FROM rides r
   ORDER BY 5 DESC
   LIMIT 10;
```

There are some aggregation functions that are specific to windowing functions. RANK() ranks the existing row within the relevant window, and DENSE_RANK() does the same while allowing no "missing" ranks. LEAD and LAG provide access to functions in adjacent partitions.

For instance, this query returns the top 10 rides, with each ride's overall rank and rank within the city displayed:

```
SELECT city, r.start_time ,revenue,
       RANK() OVER
           (ORDER BY revenue DESC) AS total_revenue_rank,
       RANK() OVER
             (PARTITION BY city ORDER BY revenue DESC) AS city_revenue_rank
  FROM rides r
ORDER BY revenue DESC
LIMIT 10;
```

Other SELECT Clauses

The LIMIT clause limits the number of rows returned by a SELECT while the OFFSET clause "jumps ahead" a certain number of rows. This can be handy to paginate through a result set though it is almost always more efficient to use a filter condition to navigate to the next subset of results because otherwise, each request will need to reread and discard an increasing number of rows.

CockroachDB Arrays

The ARRAY type allows a column to be defined as a one-dimensional array of elements, each of which shares a common data type. We'll talk about arrays in the context of data modeling in the next chapter. Although they can be useful, they are strictly speaking a violation of the relational model and should be used carefully.

An ARRAY variable is defined by adding "[]" or the word "ARRAY" to the data type of a column. For instance:

```
CREATE TABLE arrayTable (arrayColumn STRING[]);
CREATE TABLE anotherTable (integerArray INT ARRAY);
```

The ARRAY function allows us to insert multiple items into the ARRAY:

```
INSERT INTO arrayTable VALUES (ARRAY['sky', 'road', 'car']);
SELECT * FROM arrayTable;

    arraycolumn
-------------------
  {sky,road,car}
```

We can access an individual element of an array with the following familiar array element notation:

```
SELECT arrayColumn[2] FROM arrayTable;
  arraycolumn
---------------
  road
```

The @> operator can be used to find arrays that contain one or more elements:

```
SELECT * FROM arrayTable WHERE arrayColumn @>ARRAY['road'];
  arraycolumn
------------------
  {sky,road,car}
```

We can add elements to an existing array using the array_append function and remove elements using array_remove:

```
UPDATE  arrayTable
   SET arrayColumn=array_append(arrayColumn,'cat')
  WHERE arrayColumn @>ARRAY['car']
 RETURNING arrayColumn;

     arraycolumn
----------------------
  {sky,road,car,cat}

UPDATE  arrayTable
   SET arrayColumn=array_remove(arrayColumn,'car')
  WHERE arrayColumn @>ARRAY['car']
  RETURNING arrayColumn;

  arraycolumn
------------------
  {sky,road,cat}
```

Finally, the unnest function transforms an array into a tabular result—one row for each element of the array. This can be used to "join" the contents of an array with data held in relational form elsewhere in the database. We show an example of this in the next chapter:

```
SELECT unnest(arrayColumn)
   FROM ((("queries", "arrays", startref="qarys")))arrayTable;

  unnest
----------
  sky
  road
  cat
```

Working with JSON

The `JSONB` data type allows us to store JSON documents into a column, and Cockroach DB provides operators and functions to help us work with JSON.

For these examples, we've created a table with a primary key `customerid` and all data in a `JSONB` column, `jsondata`. We can use the `jsonb_pretty` function to retrieve the JSON in a nicely formatted manner:

```
SELECT jsonb_pretty(jsondata)
  FROM customersjson WHERE customerid=1;
```

```
                     jsonb_pretty
------------------------------------------------------------
  {
      "Address": "1913 Hanoi Way",
      "City": "Sasebo",
      "Country": "Japan",
      "District": "Nagasaki",
      "FirstName": "MARY",
      "LastName": "Smith",
      "Phone": 886780309,
      "_id": "5a0518aa5a4e1c8bf9a53761",
      "dateOfBirth": "1982-02-20T13:00:00.000Z",
      "dob": "1982-02-20T13:00:00.000Z",
      "randValue": 0.47025846594884335,
      "views": [
          {
              "filmId": 611,
              "title": "MUSKETEERS WAIT",
              "viewDate": "2013-03-02T05:26:17.645Z"
          },
          {
              "filmId": 308,
              "title": "FERRIS MOTHER",
              "viewDate": "2015-07-05T20:06:58.891Z"
          },
          {
              "filmId": 159,
              "title": "CLOSER BANG",
              "viewDate": "2012-08-04T19:31:51.698Z"
          },
          /* Some data removed */
      ]
  }
```

Each JSON document contains some top-level attributes and a nested array of documents that contains details of films that they have streamed.

We can reference specific JSON attributes in the SELECT clause using the -> operator:

```
SELECT jsondata->'City' AS City
 FROM customersjson WHERE customerid=1;

   city
------------
 "Sasebo"
```

The ->> operator is similar but returns the data formatted as text, not JSON.

If we want to search inside a JSONB column, we can use the @> operator:

```
SELECT COUNT(*) FROM customersjson
 WHERE jsondata @> '{"City": "London"}';

  count
---------
    3
```

We can get the same result using the ->> operator:

```
SELECT COUNT(*) FROM customersjson
 WHERE jsondata->>'City' = 'London';

  count
---------
    3
```

The ->> and @> operators can have different performance characteristics. In particular, ->> might exploit an inverted index where @> would use a table scan.

We can interrogate the structure of the JSON document using the jsonb_each and jsonb_object_keys functions. jsonb_each returns one row per attribute in the JSON document, while jsonb_object_keys returns just the attribute keys. This is useful if you don't know what is stored inside the JSONB column.

jsonb_array_elements returns one row for each element in a JSON array. For instance, here we expand out the views array for a specific customer, counting the number of movies that they have seen:

```
SELECT COUNT(jsonb_array_elements(jsondata->'views'))
  FROM customersjson
 WHERE customerid =1;

  count
---------
     37
(1 row)
```

Summary of SELECT

The SELECT statement is probably the most widely used statement in database programming and offers a wide range of functionality. Even after decades of working in the field, the three of us don't know every nuance of SELECT functionality. However, here we've tried to provide you with the most important aspects of the language. For more depth, view the CockroachDB documentation set (*https://cockroa.ch/3v07BTY*).

Although some database professionals use SELECT almost exclusively, the majority will be creating and manipulating data as well. In the following sections, we'll look at the language features that support those activities.

Creating Tables and Indexes

In a relational database, data can be added only to predefined tables. These tables are created by the CREATE TABLE statement. Indexes can be created to enforce unique constraints or to provide a fast access path to the data. Indexes can be defined within the CREATE TABLE statement or by a separate CREATE INDEX statement.

The structure of a database schema forms a critical constraint on database performance and also on the maintainability and utility of the database. We'll discuss the key considerations for database design in Chapter 5. For now, let's create a few simple tables.

We use CREATE TABLE to create a table within a database. Figure 4-5 provides a simplified syntax for the CREATE TABLE statement.

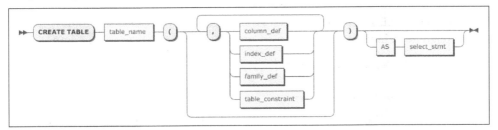

Figure 4-5. CREATE TABLE statement

A simple CREATE TABLE is shown in the next example. It creates a table, mytable, with a single column, mycolumn. The mycolumn column can store only integer values:

```
CREATE TABLE mytable
(
    mycolumn int
);
```

The CREATE TABLE statement must define the columns that occur within the table and can optionally define indexes, column families, constraints, and partitions associated with the table. For instance, the CREATE TABLE statement for the rides table in the movr database would look something like this:

```
CREATE TABLE public.rides (
        id UUID NOT NULL,
        city VARCHAR NOT NULL,
        vehicle_city VARCHAR NULL,
        rider_id UUID NULL,
        vehicle_id UUID NULL,
        start_address VARCHAR NULL,
        end_address VARCHAR NULL,
        start_time TIMESTAMP NULL,
        end_time TIMESTAMP NULL,
        revenue DECIMAL(10,2) NULL,
        CONSTRAINT "primary" PRIMARY KEY (city ASC, id ASC),
        CONSTRAINT fk_city_ref_users
            FOREIGN KEY (city, rider_id)
            REFERENCES public.users(city, id),
        CONSTRAINT fk_vehicle_city_ref_vehicles
            FOREIGN KEY (vehicle_city, vehicle_id)
            REFERENCES public.vehicles(city, id),
        INDEX rides_auto_index_fk_city_ref_users
            (city ASC, rider_id ASC),
        INDEX rides_auto_index_fk_vehicle_city_ref_vehicles
            (vehicle_city ASC, vehicle_id ASC),
        CONSTRAINT check_vehicle_city_city
            CHECK (vehicle_city = city)
);
```

This CREATE TABLE statement specified additional columns, their nullability, primary and foreign keys, indexes, and constraints upon table values.

The relevant clauses in Figure 4-5 are listed in Table 4-2.

Table 4-2. CREATE TABLE options

column_def	The definition of a column. This includes the column name, data type, and nullability. Constraints specific to the column can also be included here, though it's better practice to list all constraints separately.
index_def	Definition of an index to be created on the table. Same as CREATE INDEX but without the leading CREATE verb.
table_constraint	A constraint on the table, such as PRIMARY KEY, FOREIGN KEY, or CHECK. See "Constraints" on page 98 for constraint syntax.
family_def	Assigns columns to a column family. See Chapter 2 for more information about column families.

Let's now look at each of these CREATE TABLE options.

Column Definitions

A column definition consists of a column name, data type, nullability status, default value, and possibly column-level constraint definitions. At a minimum, the name and data type must be specified. Figure 4-6 shows the syntax for a column definition.

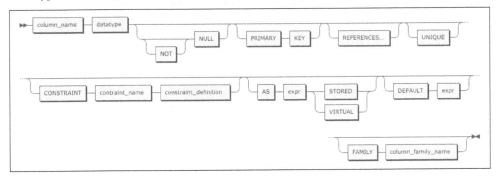

Figure 4-6. Column definition

Although constraints may be specified directly against column definitions, they may also be independently listed below the column definitions. Many practitioners prefer to list the constraints separately in this manner because it allows all constraints, including multicolumn constraints, to be located together.

Computed Columns

CockroachDB allows tables to include *computed columns* that in some other databases would require a view definition:

```
column_name AS expression [STORED|VIRTUAL]
```

A VIRTUAL computed column is evaluated whenever it is referenced. A STORED expression is stored in the database when created and need not always be recomputed.

For instance, this table definition has the firstName and lastName concatenated into a fullName column:

```
CREATE TABLE people
(
    id INT PRIMARY KEY,
    firstName VARCHAR NOT NULL,
    lastName VARCHAR NOT NULL,
    dateOfBirth DATE NOT NULL,
    fullName STRING AS (CONCAT(firstName,' ',lastName) ) STORED

);
```

Computed columns cannot be context-dependent. That is, the computed value must not change over time or be otherwise nondeterministic. For instance, the computed column in the following example would not work since the `age` column would be static rather than recalculated every time. While it might be nice to stop aging in real life, we probably want the `age` column to increase as time goes on.

```
CREATE TABLE people
(
    id INT PRIMARY KEY,
    firstName VARCHAR NOT NULL,
    lastName VARCHAR NOT NULL,
    dateOfBirth timestamp NOT NULL,
    fullName STRING AS (CONCAT(firstName,' ',lastName) ) STORED,
    age int AS (now()-dateOfBirth) STORED
);
```

Data Types

The base CockroachDB data types (*https://cockroa.ch/3LOXXu4*) are shown in Table 4-3.

Table 4-3. CockroachDB data types

Type	Description	Example
ARRAY	A 1-dimensional, 1-indexed, homogeneous array of any nonarray data type.	{"sky","road","car"}
BIT	A string of binary digits (bits).	B'10010101'
BOOL	A Boolean value.	true
BYTES	A string of binary characters.	b'\141\061\142\062\143\063'
COLLATE	The COLLATE feature lets you sort STRING values according to language- and country-specific rules, known as collations.	*a1b2c3* COLLATE en
DATE	A date.	DATE *2016-01-25*
ENUM	New in v20.2: A user-defined data type comprised of a set of static values.	ENUM (*club, diamond, heart, spade*)
DECIMAL	An exact, fixed-point number.	1.2345
FLOAT	A 64-bit, inexact, floating-point number.	3.141592653589793
INET	An IPv4 or IPv6 address.	192.168.0.1
INT	A signed integer, up to 64 bits.	12345
INTERVAL	A span of time.	INTERVAL *2h30m30s*
JSONB	JSON data.	{"first_name": "Lola", "last_name": "Dog", "location": "NYC", "online" : true, "friends" : 547}
SERIAL	A pseudotype that creates unique ascending numbers.	148591304110702593
STRING	A string of Unicode characters.	*a1b2c3*

Type	Description	Example
TIME TIMETZ	TIME stores a time of day in UTC. TIMETZ converts TIME values with a specified time zone offset from UTC.	TIME *01:23:45.123456* TIMETZ *01:23:45.123456-5:00*
TIME STAMP TIME STAMPTZ	TIMESTAMP stores a date and time pairing in UTC. TIMESTAMPTZ converts TIMESTAMP values with a specified time zone offset from UTC.	TIMESTAMP *2016-01-25 10:10:10* TIMESTAMPTZ *2016-01-25 10:10:10-05:00*
UUID	A 128-bit hexadecimal value.	7f9c24e8-3b12-4fef-91e0-56a2d5a246ec

Note that other data type names may be aliased against these CockroachDB base types. For instance, the PostgreSQL types BIGINT and SMALLINT are aliased against the CockroachDB type INT.

In CockroachDB, data types may be cast—or converted—by appending the data type to an expression using "::". For instance:

```
SELECT revenue::int FROM rides;
```

The CAST function can also be used to convert data types and is more broadly compatible with other databases and SQL standards. For instance:

```
SELECT CAST(revenue AS int) FROM rides;
```

Primary Keys

As we know, a primary key uniquely defines a row within a table. In CockroachDB, a primary key is mandatory because all tables are distributed across the cluster based on the ranges of their primary key. If you don't specify a primary key, a key will be automatically generated for you.

It's common practice in other databases to define an autogenerating primary key using clauses such as AUTOINCREMENT. The generation of primary keys in distributed databases is a significant issue because it's the primary key that is used to distribute data across nodes in the cluster. We'll discuss the options for primary key generation in the next chapter, but for now, we'll simply note that you can generate randomized primary key-values using the UUID data type with the gen_random_uuid() function as the default value:

```
CREATE TABLE people (
        id UUID NOT NULL DEFAULT gen_random_uuid(),
        firstName VARCHAR NOT NULL,
        lastName VARCHAR NOT NULL,
        dateOfBirth DATE NOT NULL
    );
```

This pattern is considered best practice to ensure even distribution of keys across the cluster. Other options for autogenerating primary keys will be discussed in Chapter 5.

Constraints

The CONSTRAINT clause specifies conditions that must be satisfied by all rows within a table. In some circumstances, the CONSTRAINT keyword may be omitted, for instance, when defining a column constraint or specific constraint types such as PRIMARY KEY or FOREIGN KEY. Figure 4-7 shows the general form of a constraint definition.

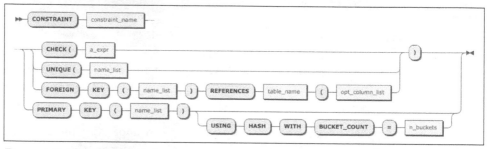

Figure 4-7. CONSTRAINT statement

A UNIQUE constraint requires that all values for the column or column_list be unique.

PRIMARY KEY implements a set of columns that must be unique and which can also be the subject of a FOREIGN KEY constraint in another table. Both PRIMARY KEY and UNIQUE constraints require the creation of an implicit index. If desired, the physical storage characteristics of the index can be specified in the USING clause. The options of the USING INDEX clause have the same usages as in the CREATE INDEX statement.

NOT NULL indicates that the column in question may not be NULL. This option is only available for column constraints, but the same effect can be obtained with a table CHECK constraint.

CHECK defines an expression that must evaluate to true for every row in the table. We'll discuss best practices for creating constraints in Chapter 5.

Sensible use of constraints can help ensure data quality and can provide the database with a certain degree of self-documentation. However, some constraints have significant performance implications; we'll discuss these implications in Chapter 5.

Indexes

Indexes can be created by the CREATE INDEX statement or an INDEX definition can be included within the CREATE TABLE statement.

We talked a lot about indexes in Chapter 2, and we'll keep discussing indexes in the schema design and performance tuning chapters (Chapters 5 and 8, respectively). Effective indexing is one of the most important success factors for a performance CockroachDB implementation.

Figure 4-8 illustrates a simplistic syntax for the CockroachDB `CREATE INDEX` statement.

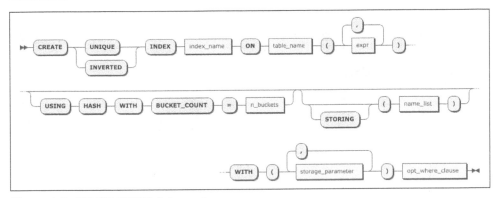

Figure 4-8. CREATE INDEX statement

We looked at the internals of CockroachDB indexes in Chapter 2. From a performance point of view, CockroachDB indexes behave much as indexes in other databases—providing a fast access method for locating rows with a particular set of nonprimary key-values. For instance, if we simply want to locate a row with a specific name and date of birth, we might create the following multicolumn index:

```
CREATE INDEX people_namedob_ix ON people
  (lastName,firstName,dateOfBirth);
```

If we wanted to further ensure that no two rows could have the same value for name and date of birth, we might create a unique index:

```
CREATE UNIQUE INDEX people_namedob_ix ON people
  (lastName,firstName,dateOfBirth);
```

The `STORING` clause allows us to store additional data in the index, which can allow us to satisfy queries using the index alone. For instance, this index can satisfy queries that retrieve phone numbers for a given name and date of birth:

```
CREATE UNIQUE INDEX people_namedob_ix ON people
  (lastName,firstName,dateOfBirth) STORING (phoneNumber);
```

Inverted indexes

An inverted index can be used to index the elements within an array or the attributes within a JSON document. We looked at the internals of inverted indexes in Chapter 2. Inverted indexes can also be used for spatial data.

For example, suppose our `people` table used a JSON document to store the attributes for a person:

```
CREATE TABLE people
( id UUID NOT NULL DEFAULT gen_random_uuid(),
  personData JSONB );

INSERT INTO people (personData)
VALUES('{
        "firstName":"Guy",
        "lastName":"Harrison",
        "dob":"21-Jun-1960",
        "phone":"0419533988",
        "photo":"eyJhbGciOiJIUzI1NiIsI..."
    }');
```

We might create an inverted index as follows:

```
CREATE INVERTED INDEX people_inv_idx ON
people(personData);
```

Which would support queries into the JSON document such as this:

```
SELECT *
FROM people
WHERE personData @> '{"phone":"0419533988"}';
```

Bear in mind that inverted indexes index every attribute in the JSON document, not just those that you want to search on. This potentially results in a very large index. Therefore, you might find it more useful to create a calculated column on the JSON attribute and then index on that computed column:

```
ALTER TABLE people ADD phone STRING AS (personData->>'phone') VIRTUAL;

CREATE INDEX people_phone_idx ON people(phone);
```

Hash-sharded indexes

If you're working with a table that must be indexed on sequential keys, you should use hash-sharded indexes. Hash-sharded indexes distribute sequential traffic uniformly across ranges, eliminating single-range hotspots and improving write performance on sequentially keyed indexes at a small cost to read performance:

```
CREATE TABLE people
( id INT PRIMARY KEY,
  firstName VARCHAR NOT NULL,
  lastName VARCHAR NOT NULL,
  dateOfBirth timestamp NOT NULL,
  phoneNumber VARCHAR NOT NULL,
  serialNo SERIAL ,
  INDEX serialNo_idx (serialNo) USING HASH WITH BUCKET_COUNT=4);
```

We'll discuss hash-sharded indexes—as well as other more advanced indexing top-ics—in more detail in the next section.

CREATE TABLE AS SELECT

The AS SELECT clause of CREATE TABLE allows us to create a new table that has the data and attributes of a SQL SELECT statement. Columns, constraints, and indexes can be specified for an existing table but must align with the data types and number of columns returned by the SELECT statement. For instance, here we create a table based on a JOIN and aggregate of two tables in the movr database:

```
CREATE TABLE user_ride_counts AS
SELECT u.name, COUNT(u.name) AS rides
  FROM "users" AS u JOIN "rides" AS r
    ON (u.id=r.rider_id)
 GROUP BY u.name;
```

Note that while CREATE TABLE AS SELECT can be used to create summary tables and the like, CREATE MATERIALIZED VIEW offers a more functional alternative.

Altering Tables

The ALTER TABLE statement allows table columns or constraints to be added, modi-fied, renamed, or removed, as well as allowing for constraint validation and partition-ing. Figure 4-9 shows the syntax.

Altering table structures online is not something to be undertaken lightly, although CockroachDB provides highly advanced mechanisms for propagating such changes (*https://cockroa.ch/3J1A6Wh*) without impacting availability and with minimal impact on performance. We'll discuss the procedures for online schema changes in later chapters.

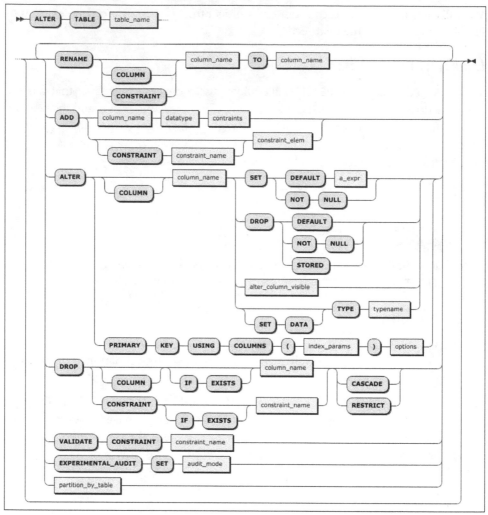

Figure 4-9. ALTER TABLE statement

Dropping Tables

Tables can be dropped using the DROP TABLE statement. Figure 4-10 shows the syntax.

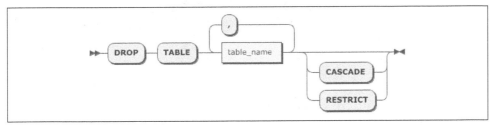

Figure 4-10. DROP TABLE statement

More than one table can be removed with a single DROP TABLE statement. The CAS CADE keyword causes dependent objects such as views or foreign key constraints to be dropped as well. RESTRICT—the default—has the opposite effect; if there are any dependent objects, then the table will not be dropped.

DROP CASCADE and Foreign Keys

DROP TABLE...CASCADE will drop any foreign key constraints that reference the table but will not drop the tables or rows that contain those foreign keys. The end result will be "dangling" references in these tables.

Because of this incompleteness, and because it can be hard to be certain exactly what CASCADE will do, it's usually better to manually remove all dependencies on a table before dropping it.

Views

A standard view is a query definition stored in the database that defines a virtual table. This virtual table can be referenced the same way as a regular table. Common Table Expressions can be thought of as a way of creating a temporary view for a single SQL statement. If you had a Common Table Expression that you wanted to share among SQL statements, then a view would be a logical solution.

A materialized view stores the results of the view definition into the database so that the view need not be re-executed whenever encountered. This improves performance but may result in stale results. If you think of a view as a stored query, then a materialized view can be thought of as a stored result.

Figure 4-11 shows the syntax of the CREATE VIEW statement.

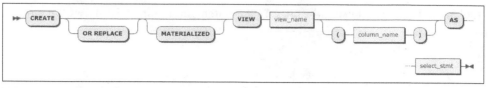

Figure 4-11. CREATE VIEW statement

The REFRESH MATERIALIZED VIEW statement can be used to refresh the data underlying a materialized view.

Inserting Data

We can load data into a new table using the CREATE TABLE AS SELECT statement discussed earlier, using the INSERT statement inside a program or from the command-line shell, or by loading external data using the IMPORT statement. There are also non-SQL utilities that insert data—we'll look at these in Chapter 7.

The venerable INSERT statement adds data to an existing table. Figure 4-12 illustrates a simplified syntax for the INSERT statement.

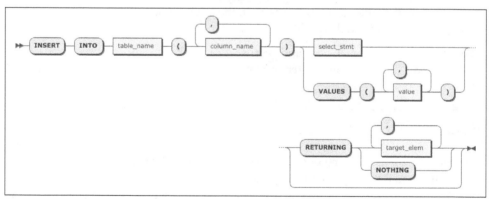

Figure 4-12. INSERT statement

INSERT takes either a set of values or a SELECT statement. For instance, in the following example, we insert a single row into the people table:

```
INSERT INTO people (firstName, lastName, dateOfBirth)
VALUES('Guy', 'Harrison', '21-JUN-1960');
```

The VALUES clause of the INSERT statement can accept array values, inserting more than one row in a single execution:

```
INSERT INTO people (firstName, lastName, dateOfBirth)
VALUES ('Guy', 'Harrison', '21-JUN-1960'),
       ('Michael', 'Harrison', '19-APR-1994'),
       ('Oriana', 'Harrison', '18-JUN-2020');
```

There are alternative ways to insert batches in the various program language drivers, and we'll show some examples in Chapter 7.

A SELECT statement can be specified as the source of the inserted data:

```
INSERT INTO people (firstName, lastName, dateOfBirth)
SELECT firstName, lastName, dateOfBirth
  FROM peopleStagingData;
```

The RETURNING clause allows the data inserted to be returned to the user. The data returned will include not just the variables that were inserted but any autogenerated data. For instance, in this case, we INSERT data without specifying an ID value and have the ID values that were created returned to us:

```
INSERT INTO people (firstName, lastName, dateOfBirth)
VALUES ('Guy', 'Harrison', '21-JUN-1960'),
       ('Michael', 'Harrison', '19-APR-1994'),
       ('Oriana', 'Harrison', '18-JUN-2020')
  RETURNING id;
```

The ON CONFLICT clause allows you to control what happens if an INSERT violates a uniqueness constraint. Figure 4-13 shows the syntax.

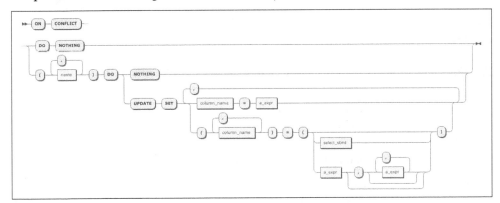

Figure 4-13. ON CONFLICT clause

Without an ON CONFLICT clause, a uniqueness constraint violation will cause the entire INSERT statement to abort. DO NOTHING allows the INSERT statement as a whole to succeed but ignores any inserts that violate the uniqueness clause. The DO UPDATE clause allows you to specify an UPDATE statement that executes instead of the INSERT. The DO UPDATE functionality is similar in functionality to the UPSERT statement discussed later in this chapter.

UPDATE

The UPDATE statement changes existing data in a table. Figure 4-14 shows a simplified syntax for the UPDATE statement.

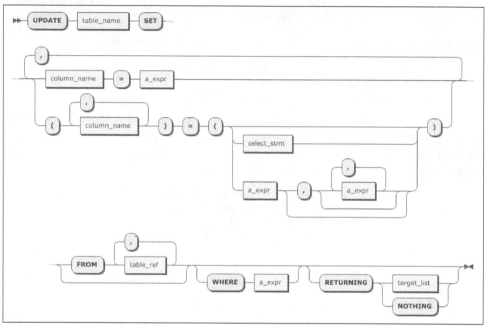

Figure 4-14. UPDATE statement

An UPDATE statement can specify static values as in the following example:

```
UPDATE users
  SET address = '201 E Randolph St',
         city='amsterdam'
  WHERE name='Maria Weber';
```

Alternatively, the values may be an expression referencing existing values:

```
UPDATE user_promo_codes
  SET usage_count=usage_count+1
  WHERE user_id='297fcb80-b67a-4c8b-bf9f-72c404f97fe8';
```

Or the UPDATE can use a subquery to obtain the values:

```
UPDATE rides SET (revenue, start_address) =
  (SELECT revenue, end_address FROM rides
    WHERE id = '94fdf3b6-45a1-4800-8000-000000000123')
  WHERE id = '851eb851-eb85-4000-8000-000000000104';
```

The RETURNING clause can be used to view the modified columns. This is particularly useful if a column is being updated by a function, and we want to return the modified value to the application:

```
UPDATE user_promo_codes
   SET usage_count=usage_count+1
  WHERE user_id='297fcb80-b67a-4c8b-bf9f-72c404f97fe8'
 RETURNING (usage_count);
```

UPSERT

UPSERT can insert new data and update existing data in a table in a single operation. If the input data does not violate any uniqueness constraints, it is inserted. If an input matches an existing primary key, then the values of that row are updated.

In CockroachDB, the ON CONFLICT clause of INSERT provides a similar—though more flexible—mechanism. When this flexibility is not needed, UPSERT is likely to be faster than a similar INSERT...ON CONFLICT DO UPDATE statement.

Figure 4-15 shows the syntax of the UPSERT statement.

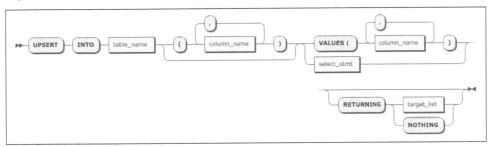

Figure 4-15. UPSERT statement

The UPSERT compares the primary key-value of each row provided. If the primary key is not found in the existing table, then a new row is created. Otherwise, the existing row is updated with the new values provided.

The RETURNING clause can be used to return a list of updated or inserted rows.

In this example, the primary key of user_promo_codes is (city, user_id, code). If a user already has an entry for that combination in the table, then that row is updated with a user_count of 0. Otherwise, a new row with those values is created.

```
UPSERT INTO user_promo_codes
  (user_id,city,code,timestamp,usage_count)
SELECT id,city,'NewPromo',now(),0
  FROM "users";
```

DELETE

DELETE allows data to be removed from a table. Figure 4-16 shows a simplified syntax for the DELETE statement.

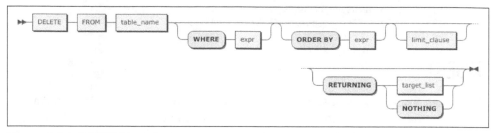

Figure 4-16. DELETE statement

Most of the time, a DELETE statement accepts a WHERE clause and not much else. For instance, here we delete a single row in the people table:

```
DELETE FROM people
  WHERE firstName='Guy'
    AND lastName='Harrison';
```

The RETURNING clause can return details of the rows that were removed. For instance:

```
DELETE FROM user_promo_codes
  WHERE code='NewPromo'
RETURNING(user_id);
```

You can also include an ORDER BY and LIMIT clause to perform batch deletes in an incremental fashion. For instance, you can construct a DELETE statement to remove the oldest 1,000 rows. See the CockroachDB documentation (*https://cock roa.ch/3x4LnTg*) for more information.

TRUNCATE

TRUNCATE provides a quick mechanism for removing all rows from a table. Internally, it is implemented as a DROP TABLE followed by a CREATE TABLE. TRUNCATE is not transactional—you cannot ROLLBACK a TRUNCATE.

IMPORT/IMPORT INTO

The IMPORT statement imports the following types of data into CockroachDB:

- Avro
- Comma Separated Values (CSV)/Tab Separated Values (TSV)
- Postgres dump files

- MySQL dump files
- CockroachDB dump files

IMPORT creates a new table, while IMPORT INTO allows an import into an existing table.

The files to be imported should exist either in a cloud storage bucket—Google Cloud Storage, Amazon S3, or Azure Blob storage—from an HTTP address or from the local filesystem ("nodelocal").

We'll discuss the various options for loading data into CockroachDB in Chapter 7. However, for now, let's create a new table customers from a CSV file:

```
IMPORT INTO TABLE customers (
        id INT PRIMARY KEY,
        name STRING,
        INDEX name_idx (name)
);
CSV DATA ('nodelocal://1/customers.csv');
        job_id       |  status  | fra | rows | index_entries | bytes
---------------------+----------+-----+------+---------------+--------
  659162639684534273 | succeeded |  1  |  1  |             1 |    47
(1 row)

Time: 934ms total (execution 933ms / network 1ms)
```

For a single-node demo cluster, the nodelocal location will be somewhat dependent on your installation but will often be in an extern directory beneath the CockroachDB installation directory.

Transactional Statements

We talked a lot about CockroachDB transactions in Chapter 2, so review that chapter if you need a refresher on how CockroachDB transactions work. From the SQL language point of view, CockroachDB supports the standard SQL transactional control statements.

BEGIN Transaction

The BEGIN statement commences a transaction and sets its properties. Figure 4-17 shows the syntax.

PRIORITY sets the transaction priority. In the event of a conflict, HIGH priority transactions are less likely to be retried.

READ ONLY specifies that the transaction is read-only and will not modify data.

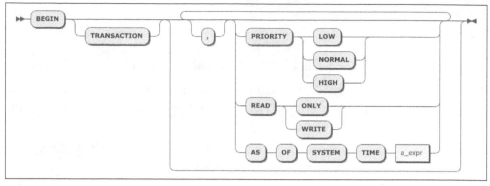

Figure 4-17. BEGIN transaction

AS OF SYSTEM TIME allows a READ ONLY transaction to view data from a snapshot of database history. We'll come back to this in a few pages.

SAVEPOINT

SAVEPOINT creates a named rollback point that can be used as the target of a ROLLBACK statement. This allows a portion of a transaction to be discarded without discarding all of the transaction's work. See the ROLLBACK section for more details.

COMMIT

The COMMIT statement commits the current transactions, making changes permanent.

Note that some transactions may require client-side intervention to handle retry scenarios. These patterns will be explored in Chapter 6.

ROLLBACK

ROLLBACK aborts the current transaction. Optionally, we can ROLLBACK to a savepoint, which rolls back only the statements issued after the SAVEPOINT.

For instance, in the following example, the insert of the misspelled number *tree* is rolled back and corrected without abandoning the transaction as a whole:

```
BEGIN ;

INSERT INTO numbers VALUES(1,'one');
INSERT INTO numbers VALUES(2,'two');
SAVEPOINT two;

INSERT INTO numbers VALUES(3,'tree');
ROLLBACK TO SAVEPOINT two;
```

```
INSERT INTO numbers VALUES(3,'three');
COMMIT;
```

SELECT FOR UPDATE

The FOR UPDATE clause of a SELECT statement locks the rows returned by a query, ensuring that they cannot be modified by another transaction between the time they are read and when the transaction ends. This is typically used to implement the pessimistic locking pattern that we'll discuss in Chapter 6.

A FOR UPDATE query should be executed within a transaction. Otherwise, the locks are released on completion of the SELECT statement.

A FOR UPDATE issued within a transaction will, by default, block other FOR UPDATE statements on the same rows or other transactions that seek to update those rows from completing until a COMMIT or ROLLBACK is issued. However, if a higher-priority transaction attempts to update the rows or attempts to issue a FOR UPDATE, then the lower-priority transaction will be aborted and will need to retry.

We'll discuss the mechanics of transaction retries in Chapter 6.

Figure 4-18 illustrates two FOR UPDATE statements executing concurrently. The first FOR UPDATE holds locks on the affected rows, preventing the second session from obtaining those locks until the first session completes its transaction.

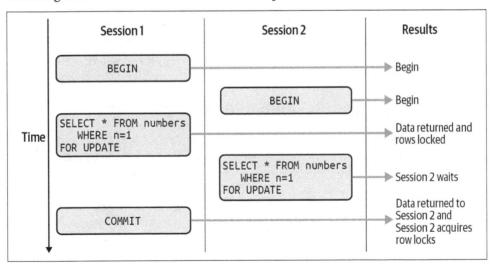

Figure 4-18. FOR UPDATE clause behavior

AS OF SYSTEM TIME

The AS OF SYSTEM TIME clause can be applied to SELECT and BEGIN TRANSACTION statements as well as in BACKUP and RESTORE operations. AS OF SYSTEM TIME specifies that a SELECT statement or all the statements in a READ ONLY transaction should execute on a snapshot of the database at that system time. These snapshots are made available by the MVCC architecture described in Chapter 2.

The time can be specified as an offset, or an absolute timestamp, as in the following two examples:

```
SELECT * FROM rides r
   AS OF SYSTEM TIME '-1d';

SELECT * FROM rides r
   AS OF SYSTEM TIME '2021-5-22 18:02:52.0+00:00';
```

The time specified cannot be older in seconds than the replication zone configuration parameter ttlseconds, which controls the maximum age of MVCC snapshots.

It is also possible to specify *bounded* stale reads using the with_max_staleness argument:

```
SELECT * FROM rides r
   AS OF SYSTEM TIME with_max_staleness('10s')
 WHERE city='amsterdam'
   AND id='aaaae297-396d-4800-8000-0000000208d6';
```

Bounded stale reads can be used to optimize performance in distributed deployments by allowing CockroachDB to satisfy the read from local replicas that may contain slightly stale data. We'll return to bounded stale reads in Chapter 11.

Other Data Definition Language Targets

So far, we've looked at SQL to create, alter, and manipulate data in tables and indexes. These objects represent the core of database functionality in CockroachDB, as in other SQL databases. However, the CockroachDB Data Definition Language (DDL) provides support for a large variety of other, less frequently utilized objects. A full reference for all these objects would take more space than we have available here—see the CockroachDB documentation (*https://cockroa.ch/3DC6MV0*) for a complete list of CockroachDB SQL.

Table 4-4 lists some of the other objects that can be manipulated in CREATE, ALTER, and DROP statements.

Table 4-4. Other CockroachDB schema objects

Object	Description
Database	A database is a namespace within a CockroachDB cluster containing schemas, tables, indexes, and other objects. Databases are typically used to separate objects that have distinct application responsibilities or security policies.
Schema	A schema is a collection of tables and indexes that belong to the same relational model. In most databases, tables are created in the PUBLIC schema by default.
Sequence	Sequences are often used to create primary key-values; however, in CockroachDB, there are often better alternatives. See Chapter 5 for more guidance on primary key generation.
Role	A role is used to group database and schema privileges, which can then be granted to users as a unit. See Chapter 12 for more details on CockroachDB security practices.
Type	In CockroachDB, a type is an enumerated set of values that can be applied to a column in a CREATE or ALTER TABLE statement.
User	A user is an account that can be used to log in to the database and can be assigned specific privileges. See Chapter 12 for more details on CockroachDB security practices.
Statistics	Statistics consist of information about the data within a specified table that the SQL optimizer uses to work out the best possible execution plan for a SQL statement. See Chapter 8 for more information on query tuning.
changefeed	A changefeed streams row-level changes for nominated tables to a client program. See Chapter 7 for more information on changefeed implementation.
Schedule	A schedule controls the periodic execution of backups. See Chapter 11 for guidance on backup policies.

Administrative Commands

CockroachDB supports commands to maintain authentication of users and their authority to perform database operations. It also has a job scheduler that can be used to schedule backup and restore operations as well as scheduled schema changes. Other commands support the maintenance of the cluster topology.

These commands are generally tightly coupled with specific administrative operations, which we'll discuss in subsequent chapters, so we'll refrain from defining them in detail here. You can always see the definitions for them in the CockroachDB documentation (https://cockroa.ch/3DC6MV0). Table 4-5 summarizes the most significant of these commands.

Table 4-5. CockroachDB administrative commands

Command	Description
CANCEL JOB	Cancel long-running jobs such as backups, schema changes, or statistics collections.
CANCEL QUERY	Cancel a currently running query.
CANCEL SESSION	Cancel and disconnect a currently connected session.
CONFIGURE ZONE	CONFIGURE ZONE can be used to modify replication zones for tables, databases, ranges, or partitions. See Chapter 10 for more information on zone configuration.

Command	Description
SET CLUSTER SETTING	Change a cluster configuration parameter.
EXPLAIN	Show an execution plan for a SQL statement. We'll look at EXPLAIN in detail in Chapter 8.
EXPORT	Dump SQL output to CSV files.
SHOW/CANCEL/PAUSE JOBS	Manage background jobs—imports, backups, schema changes, etc.—in the database.
SET LOCALITY	Change the locality of a table in a multiregion database. See Chapter 10 for more information.
SET TRACING	Enable tracing for a session. We'll discuss this in Chapter 8.
SHOW RANGES	Show how a table, index, or database is segmented into ranges. See Chapter 2 for a discussion on how CockroachDB splits data into ranges.
SPLIT AT	Force a range split at the specified row in a table or index.
BACKUP	Create a consistent backup for a table or database. See Chapter 11 for guidance on backups and high availability.
SHOW STATISTICS	Show optimizer statistics for a table.
SHOW TRACE FOR SESSION	Show tracing information for a session as created by the SET TRACING command.
SHOW TRANSACTIONS	Show currently running transactions
SHOW SESSION	Show sessions on the local node or across the cluster.

The Information Schema

The *information schema* is a special schema in each database that contains metadata about the other objects in the database—it is named INFORMATION_SCHEMA in Cock-roachDB. You can use the information schema to discover the names and types of objects in the database. For instance, you can use the information schema to list all the objects in the information_schema schema:

```
SELECT * FROM information_schema."tables"
  WHERE table_schema='information_schema';
```

Or you can use information_schema to show the columns in a table:

```
SELECT column_name,data_type, is_nullable,column_default
  FROM information_schema.COLUMNS WHERE TABLE_NAME='customers';
```

The information schema is particularly useful when writing applications against an unknown data model. For instance, GUI tools such as DBeaver use the information schema to populate the database tree and display information about tables and indexes.

The information schema is defined by ANSI standards and implemented by many relational databases. CockroachDB also includes some internal tables specific to the CockroachDB system in the crdb_internal schema. Information about these tables can be found in the CockroachDB documentation (*https://cockroa.ch/3797wF3*).

Summary

In this chapter, we've reviewed the basics of the SQL language for creating, querying, and modifying data within the CockroachDB database.

A full definition of all syntax elements of CockroachDB SQL would take an entire book, so we've focused primarily on the core features of the SQL language with some emphasis on CockroachDB-specific features. For detailed syntax and for details of CockroachDB administrative commands, see the CockroachDB online documentation.

SQL is the language of CockroachDB, so of course we'll continue to elaborate on the CockroachDB SQL language as we delve deeper into the world of CockroachDB.

Developing Applications with CockroachDB

CockroachDB Schema Design

A sound data model is the foundation of a highly performant and maintainable application. In this chapter, we'll review the fundamentals of relational schema design, with a particular focus on aspects of schema design that bear on distributed database operations and on advanced CockroachDB features such as column families and JSON binary (JSONB) support. We'll cover the creation of tables, indexes, and other schema objects that support a well-designed CockroachDB application.

Although CockroachDB supports mechanisms for efficiently altering schemas online, schema changes to production applications are nevertheless high-impact changes, typically involving coordinated changes to application code and production database configuration. If done poorly, there's the risk of loss of application functionality, availability, or performance. Therefore, although it's quite possible to alter CockroachDB schemas in production, it's far better to get the schema right during application design.

Relational database design is a big topic and has been the subject of many books and continuing debate. We don't want to try to cover advanced design principles here, nor do we want to engage in any debates about the purity of various design patterns. Most database models are a compromise between the mathematical purity of the relational model and the practicalities imposed by the physical database system. Therefore, in this chapter, we'll attempt to briefly cover only the theoretical side of the relational model while diving quite deep into the practicalities of designing a model that will work well with a CockroachDB implementation.

Logical Data Modeling

Application data models are commonly created in two phases. Establishing the logical data model involves modeling the information that will be stored and processed by the application and ensuring that all necessary data is correctly, completely, and unambiguously represented. The logical data model is then mapped to a physical data model. The physical data model describes the tables, indexes, and views that are created in the DBMS.

The logical data model typically satisfies only the functional requirements of the application. The physical data model must also satisfy nonfunctional requirements, particularly performance requirements.

In practice, these two phases are often blurred together, especially in agile and other iterative development environments. Nevertheless, whether done explicitly or not, there is definitely a difference between the analysis required to determine *what* data an application might process and *how* that data is best represented in a specific database system.

We introduced some of the core concepts of the relational model in Chapter 1. Theoretically, during logical data modeling, we deal with relations, tuples, and attributes, while in physical design, we deal with tables, rows, and columns. However, outside of academia, these distinctions are often ignored, and in practice, it's commonplace to develop a logical model using the language of tables and columns.

Mea Culpa

Relational data modeling has generated an immense volume of research and debate over the past four decades. It's almost impossible to say anything sensible about relational data modeling without oversimplification or misrepresentation.

This is a book about CockroachDB, not about relational theory, so we have tried to avoid getting bogged down in debates about the correct way to perform relational design. Our purpose here is to provide enough quick background on relational modeling to allow for us to sensibly talk about CockroachDB-specific physical design principles.

If you want to further explore relational theory and design, there are many excellent books dedicated to the topic.[1]

---

1 For instance, *Database Design and Relational Theory* by C. J. Date (O'Reilly).

Normalization

A normalized data model is one in which any data redundancy has been eliminated and in which all data is completely identifiable by primary and foreign keys. Although the normalized data model is rarely the final destination from a performance point of view, the normalized data model is almost always the best initial representation of a schema because it minimizes redundancy and ambiguity.

The relational theory defines multiple "levels" of normalization. The third normal form is the generally accepted standard of an adequately normalized data model.

In the third normal form, every attribute (column) in a tuple (row) is dependent on the entire primary key of that tuple only and not on any other attribute or key. We sometimes remember this as, "The key, the whole key, and nothing but the key." For example, consider the data shown in Figure 5-1.

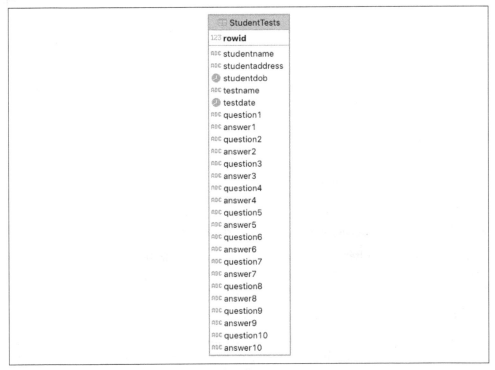

Figure 5-1. Student test data (denormalized)

Even if we created a primary key on **studentname**, **testname**, and **testdate**, we would still be a long way from the third normal form. Attributes such as **studentdob** are dependent only on part of the key (**studentname**), and the repeating "answer" columns are dependent on a nonkey attribute (the corresponding question).

A normalized version of this data is shown in Figure 5-2. Students take tests, and tests have questions, and students answer those questions. All attributes in each relation are now fully dependent on the primary keys for that relation.

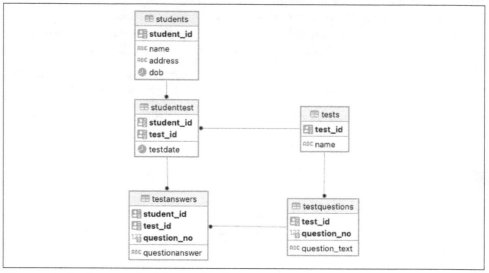

Figure 5-2. Student test data (normalized)

Don't Go Too Far

You'll generally recognize a well-normalized data model by the absence of any redundant information. For instance, in Figure 5-2, you'll notice that student names, test names, question texts, etc., are never repeated across multiple entries. There is one and only one entry for each attribute. The only thing that is repeated in a well-normalized model should be foreign key references.

That being said, it's often a mistake to take the normalization process too far. In a real-world database, each new table in the model adds complexity to program code and overhead in joining information during data retrieval.

For example, from time to time we see addresses "normalized" as in Figure 5-3.

There's nothing theoretically wrong with this model. Two students could share an apartment, and the relationships between cities, states, and countries are very real. We could even throw continent, solar system, and galaxy entities into the model without violating the third normal form.

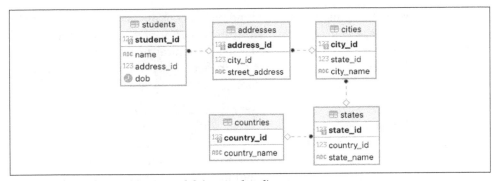

Figure 5-3. Student address model (normalized)

However, in practice, this model will require a five-way JOIN whenever a student's address needs to be retrieved. Because this is a pretty common operation, the cost of the JOIN across the life of the application will be high. It's probably better just to leave the address fully embedded in the students table, as shown in Figure 5-2.

Purists will definitely argue that this sort of denormalization should be performed in the physical data modeling stage. It's also worth noting that there may be good reasons for having a city or state table in a production system—each might be associated with specific attributes of relevance. But we'd suggest that you be pragmatic when contemplating such extended relationships. There's a lot of wasted effort in modeling logical relationships that are inevitably going to be collapsed in the physical design phase.

Primary Key Choices

In CockroachDB, the choice of primary keys is critical to performance because it is the primary key that will determine the distribution of data across the nodes in the system. We'll talk extensively about this in the Physical Design section.

However, even from the logical modeling point of view, there are some factors to consider.

The third normal form requires that each relation have a primary key. Yet, it does not specify whether that key should be natural or artificial. A *natural key* is one constructed from unique attributes that normally occur within the entity. An *artificial key* is one that contains no meaningful column information and which exists only to uniquely identify the row. There is a continual debate within the database community regarding the merits of "artificial" primary keys versus the "natural" key.

CockroachDB will create an artificial key automatically if an explicit key is not provided.

In general, we're of the opinion that most fundamental entities should use an artificial key. Artificial keys are generally superior from a performance point of view and eliminate some of the overhead involved when a natural primary key is changed. Furthermore, in CockroachDB, the use of an artificial key provides us with methods for ensuring an even distribution of keys throughout the cluster.

For example, suppose we decided that a user's email address could serve as a primary key. The email address is unique to the user, so it's a perfectly valid key. However, users can change their email addresses. If that happens, then the update to the users' data will require not just an update in place to the row but also a relocation of the data within the cluster. Any foreign keys pointing to the email address key will also have to be updated and will also have to be relocated.

Special-Purpose Designs

For any given set of data, there usually exists more than one way to create a nearly correct relational model. Within the universe of possible models, there exist some patterns that are particularly applicable to certain workloads. Two of the most common are:

Data warehousing designs
> These models, such as the *star* and *snowflake* schemas, have a large central "fact" table with foreign keys to multiple "dimension" tables. CockroachDB is not primarily intended as a data warehousing database, so these models are not typical of a CockroachDB deployment.

Time-series designs
> In these models, the time of origin of data is part of each data element's key and data accumulates primarily as continual inserts. We'll briefly consider some of the considerations for time-series in the next section.

Physical Design

Physical design involves modifying the logical design to improve its performance, compatibility with the target database, or maintainability.

Not all "relational" databases implement relational features in the same way, and many have extensions to the relational model that can be useful. Therefore, a logical to physical mapping depends heavily on the characteristics of the target database.

Other changes are driven by workload considerations. For instance, if a table is only ever accessed in a JOIN with another table, we might replicate some columns from the second table into the first to avoid the join.

The other primary physical design drivers are the capabilities and performance characteristics of the database engine. For instance, in CockroachDB, ascending primary keys cause hotspots on certain nodes and should be avoided, while in a nondistributed SQL database such as PostgreSQL, ascending keys are fine.

In the following sections, we'll discuss the various logical to physical translations that apply when implementing a model on CockroachDB.

Entities to Tables

The major output of the logical design process are entities, attributes, and keys. To convert the logical model to a physical model, we need to convert entities to tables and attributes to columns.

Depending on your logical model, this conversion may be close to a one-to-one mapping. However, be aware that in some cases, a single entity may map to multiple tables or vice versa. For instance, we might decide that the logical model shown in Figure 5-3 should be collapsed to a single table, folding all address attributes into the student table. Or we might collapse the addresses entity into students and collapse states and countries into cities.

In some cases, a logical model may include *subtypes* in which an entity is defined that includes multiple "types" of tuples. For instance, a person entity might be defined as shown in Figure 5-4.

Figure 5-4. Logical model with subtypes

People can be customers or employees (or both). So should there be a single person table, a `customer` and an `employee` table, or even three tables: a `person` table with attributes common to customers and employees and a `customer` table and an `employee` tables with attributes unique to each type?

The answer depends on your workload and performance requirements. Each of the previous solutions has a performance advantage for a certain class of query; you'll need to think through the operations that are most important to your application. However, the solution that we've seen most often is the two-table model (`customers` and `employees`).

Attributes to Columns

When mapping attributes to columns, we're mainly concerned with selecting the best data type for the column and defining its nullability correctly.

Null values are an important concept in relational databases—they distinguish between data that has a known value and data that is unknown or missing. Three-valued logic—TRUE/FALSE/NULL—is at the heart of SQL operations, such as WHERE.

In some systems, the use of NULLs in indexed columns is discouraged, and it is recommended to use NOT NULL with a DEFAULT value. This is because, in some databases (PostgreSQL, for instance), NULL values are not included in indexes. However, CockroachDB does store NULL values in indexes, and you can use an index to evaluate an IS NULL condition within a WHERE clause.

CockroachDB data types generally map easily to logical data types. Consider the following:

- All these CockroachDB string data types are equivalent: TEXT, CHAR, VARCHAR, CHARACTER VARYING and STRING.

- All of the integer data types—INT, INT2, INT4, INT8, BIGINT, SMALLINT, etc.—are stored in the same manner in the database. A BIGINT and a SMALLINT consume the same storage (providing they hold the same value). The types serve to constrain only the ranges of values that can be stored. The INT type can hold any allowable integer value (a 64-bit signed integer).

- Similarly, FLOAT, FLOAT4, FLOAT8, and REAL data types all store 64-bit signed floating-point numbers.

- DECIMAL stores exact fixed-point numbers and should be used when it's important to preserve precision, such as for monetary values.

- BYTES, BYTEA, and BLOB store binary strings of variable length. The data is stored in line with other row data, and therefore, this data type is not suitable for very large objects (a maximum of 1 MB is suggested).

- `TIME` stores a time value in UTC, while `TIMETZ` stores a time value with a time zone offset from UTZ. `TIMESTAMP` and `TIMESTAMPZ` are similar but include both date and time in the value.

We'll discuss some of the other CockroachDB data types—such as `ARRAY`s and `JSON`—later in the chapter.

Primary Key Design

We've touched upon the importance of properly defining CockroachDB primary keys in preceding chapters; now it's time to get serious about this important topic.

The primary key of a table is used to distribute the ranges of that table's data across the cluster. If the primary key-value is monotonically increasing, then all new data will go into a new range and will be sent to a specific node in the cluster. Most likely, this node will become a hotspot and limit the insert throughput for the cluster. This becomes particularly significant as your cluster grows—adding new nodes to a cluster may fail to result in higher throughput.

The same phenomenon can be encountered in a time-series database in which the primary key is prefixed with a timestamp. All "new" data will hit a single node, and your cluster scalability will be compromised.

For instance, consider this implementation of the `ORDERS` table:

```
CREATE SEQUENCE order_seq;

CREATE TABLE orders  (
        salesorderid INT NOT NULL PRIMARY KEY DEFAULT nextval('order_seq'),
        orderdate DATE NOT NULL DEFAULT now() ,
        duedate DATE NOT NULL,
        shipdate DATE NULL,
        customerid INT NOT NULL,
        salespersonid INT NULL,
        totaldue DECIMAL NULL
    );
```

The `orders_seq` sequence generator generates numbers that are guaranteed to be incrementing and—most of the time—without gaps.[2] Since every value of `ORDERID` is one higher than the preceding value, new orders will be inserted into a single range that will be located on a single node. Consequently, that node will bear the burden of all `INSERT` operations. As new ranges are created, the responsibility of handling inserts will shift to new nodes, but at any given point in time, just a single node will be handling all of the inserts.

---

2 Sequence generators are provided mainly for compatibility with other databases and are not recommended for most CockroachDB applications.

Figure 5-5 illustrates this problem: because ranges are ordered by keys, workloads with sequential keys will cause all traffic to hit one of the boundaries of a range.

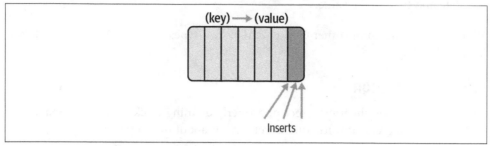

Figure 5-5. Sequential keys can create hotspots

In the next few sections, we'll look at ways of avoiding this primary key "hotspot" antipattern.

UUID-based primary keys

If your application doesn't need primary key values to be continuously increasing, then a universal unique identifier (UUID) primary key is the recommended solution.

A UUID is a value that is guaranteed to be unique across all systems. A UUID combines host-specific data, random numbers, and timestamp data to generate an identifier that will be unique across systems and times.

The gen_random_uuid() function generates UUIDs and can be used as the default value for a primary key, as in the following example:

```
CREATE TABLE orders (
        orderid uuid NOT NULL PRIMARY KEY DEFAULT gen_random_uuid(),
        orderdate DATE NOT NULL DEFAULT now() ,
        duedate DATE NOT NULL,
        shipdate DATE NULL,
        customerid INT NOT NULL,
        salespersonid INT NULL,
        totaldue DECIMAL NULL
    );
```

UUIDs are unique, selective, and guaranteed to be evenly distributed across all nodes of a cluster. They are, therefore, the preferred mechanism for CockroachDB primary keys.

The SERIAL Data Type

In PostgreSQL, the SERIAL data type is typically used to create autoincrementing key-values. It's a handy alternative to creating a sequence, as shown in an earlier example.

However, in CockroachDB, the SERIAL data type by default generates unique identifiers using the unique_rowid() function. unique_rowid() generates unique numbers that combine nodeid and timestamp. Although the numbers are generally ascending, the order is not absolutely guaranteed, so large gaps will occur and "hotspots" are still possible.

You can change the behavior of SERIAL to a more PostgreSQL-compatible behavior using the session variable serial_normalization. However, as with PostgreSQL, gaps in sequence numbers generated in this manner may still occur, and the performance overhead is significant. The CockroachDB team recommends against using SERIAL data types unless compatibility with PostgreSQL is required.

Avoiding hotspots with a composite key

It may be that your application really requires a monotonically increasing key-value. One way to avoid a hotspot, in this case, is to create a composite primary key that leads with a nonmonotonically increasing value. For instance, in this implementation, the customerid is prefixed to the order number in the primary key:

```
CREATE TABLE orders  (
        orderid INT NOT NULL DEFAULT nextval('order_seq'),
        orderdate DATE NOT NULL DEFAULT now() ,
        duedate DATE NOT NULL,
        shipdate DATE NULL,
        customerid INT NOT NULL,
        salespersonid INT NULL,
        totaldue DECIMAL NULL,
        PRIMARY KEY  (customerid,orderid)
);
```

This implementation tends to send orders for a specific customer into the same ranges, but sequential orders from multiple customers should be distributed across the cluster.

There may be some upside in "clustering" customer data this way, but the clear downside is that we now need to know the customer ID when searching for an order. We've probably all experienced the irritation of having to provide both a customer identifier *and* an order identifier to a sales associate, so this downside is potentially significant. Of course, we could create a secondary index just on orderid, but then we'd create a secondary index with a hotspot.

What we need is a way to index monotonically increasing key-values without creating unscalable insert hotspots. The solution is *hash-sharded indexes*.

Hash-sharded primary keys

Hash-sharded indexes add a hashed value to the prefix of a primary key. These hash values are unique but nonsequential. Consequently, if the primary key of a table is based on a hash-sharded index, then its values will be distributed evenly across all the ranges in the cluster. The result should be (statistically) a perfect distribution of writes across nodes.

At the time of writing, hash-sharded indexes required the experimen tal_enable_hash_sharded_indexes configuration variable be set to on. So to create a hash-sharded primary key, we would use this syntax:

```
SET experimental_enable_hash_sharded_indexes=on;

CREATE TABLE orders  (
        orderid INT NOT NULL DEFAULT nextval('order_seq'),
        orderdate DATE NOT NULL DEFAULT now() ,
        duedate DATE NOT NULL,
        shipdate DATE NULL,
        customerid INT NOT NULL,
        salespersonid INT NULL,
        totaldue DECIMAL NULL ,
        PRIMARY KEY (orderid) USING HASH WITH BUCKET_COUNT=6
);
```

The hash sharding is transparent to the application: you'll never see the hashed values, and all filters against existing primary keys will work as normal. However, the new index cannot be used to find ranges of primary keys or to sort the output by primary key. For instance, with a traditional primary key, the following query would be resolved efficiently by a range scan of the primary key index:

```
SELECT * FROM orders
 WHERE ORDERID>0
 ORDER BY ORDERID;
```

With a hash-sharded index, scan and sort operations would be required, although the optimizer may be able to perform multiple short scans on hash buckets rather than one full scan.

The WITH BUCKET_COUNT clause determines how many "shards" of the index are created. Setting the number of buckets to twice the number of nodes in the cluster is a sensible default.

Gaps in Sequential Keys

Although sequences provide for guaranteed ascending key-values, they cannot guarantee that there will be no missing values in the ordered sequence. For performance reasons, sequence number increments are not within the scope of an application transaction. Therefore, if a transaction issues a ROLLBACK after a sequence number is consumed, that number is lost. To achieve anything like scalable distributed performance, you would use the CACHE option to give each node its own unique set of ranges—which will result in keys being inserted out of order across nodes. Furthermore, cached sequence numbers may be lost on a cluster restart.

If an application needs absolutely gap-free numbers ("no missing orders," for instance), then the application will need to implement its own sequence-generating logic. Balancing performance and functionality, in this case, is not trivial—we'll look at this more in Chapter 6.

Ordering of primary key attributes

For a multicolumn primary key, the order of attributes has significant implications for performance. You should follow the guidelines for composite indexes, which we'll outline later in the chapter. Generally, the more often a column is used independently of other columns, the more you'll want to place that column first in the primary key. Likewise, the appearance of primary key columns in ORDER BY clauses should also influence the sequencing.

Summary of primary key performance

We've spent a fair bit of time on primary key mechanisms in CockroachDB for a good reason. The effect on scalability can be dramatic, and practices that worked fine in traditional monolithic SQL databases can backfire in CockroachDB.

Figure 5-6 shows just how significant these effects can be. We see that insert throughput is severely diminished when SERIAL or sequence-generated keys are used. UUIDs are preferred, but if you need ascending primary keys, then a hash-sharded primary key index is recommended.

The data in Figure 5-6 came from a nine-node CockroachDB Cloud cluster. The performance penalty from ascending primary keys is proportional to the size of the cluster; the more nodes in the cluster, the larger the relative penalty. So your mileage may vary depending on your cluster size.

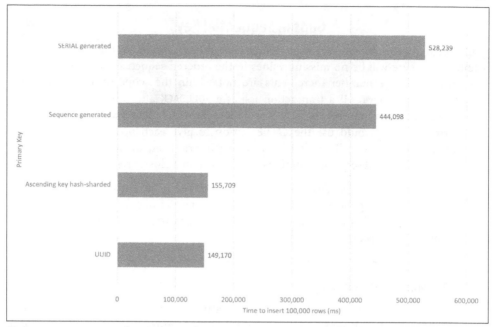

Figure 5-6. Insert performance with various primary key schemes

It's possible to greatly improve the performance of sequences by creating them with the CACHE option. This avoids the blocking wait involved in acquiring the "next" sequence number. However, in a distributed system like CockroachDB, using CACHE defeats the purpose of the sequence generator. Because each node in the cluster has its own cache, sequence numbers will be generated out of order across the cluster as a whole.

Foreign Key Constraints

Foreign key constraints help ensure data integrity and provide internal documentation of the data model, which can be leveraged by query generators and diagramming tools. However, during DML operations—particularly inserts—the validity of the foreign key must be checked by performing primary key lookups on the referenced table. These lookups can significantly increase the overhead of the operations and reduce throughput.

For the table that includes the foreign key constraint, this shows up mostly in insert performance since it is somewhat unusual for a foreign key to be updated, and the foreign key references do not need to be validated during deletes.

For the tables that are referenced within the foreign key constraint (e.g., the "parent" table), the overhead is felt most critically during deletes, where all child tables must be checked for "dangling" references.

The ON DELETE CASCADE clause of a CONSTRAINT definition will automatically delete any child rows during the delete of a parent row. ON UPDATE CASCADE has a similar effect when a primary key is updated (which in most applications is a rare event).

Because of the overhead of foreign key constraints, it is not unusual for them to be removed in a production system. They may be left enabled only in test and development environments to catch any data anomalies.

Denormalization

One of the outcomes in the development of a normalized data model is the removal of redundancies in data representation. In a well-normalized model, a data element is represented in just one place within the model. This eliminates the possibility of inconsistent information within the database.

Denormalization is the process of reintroducing redundant, repeating, or otherwise nonnormalized structures into the physical model—almost always with the intention of improving performance.

Denormalizing data is a common practice and one that you should not feel guilty about. However, do remember that denormalization has potential downsides:

Denormalized data can create inconsistencies
> These might be transitory (waiting for a materialized view to refresh) or permanent (a derived value is not updated due to a program error). You need to be sure that you have robust mechanisms in place to preserve data integrity.

Denormalization has a performance overhead
> Although denormalization exists to improve performance, most denormalizations have overhead. Typically, you improve query performance at the expense of DML performance. Make sure you understand and accept these trade-offs.

The best types of denormalizations are those that can be maintained by the database system automatically and transparently. For instance, in some databases, you might be tempted to vertically partition a table so that you can separate frequently accessed and rarely accessed columns. In CockroachDB, column families—introduced in Chapter 2—provide this capability without the need to change application code—we'll discuss column families in more detail in "Vertical Partitioning" on page 135.

Replicating Columns to Avoid Joins

JOIN operations magnify the overhead of retrieving data. Over-enthusiastic normalization can often result in even the most trivial SELECT operations requiring multitable joins. For instance, consider the partial schema shown in Figure 5-7.

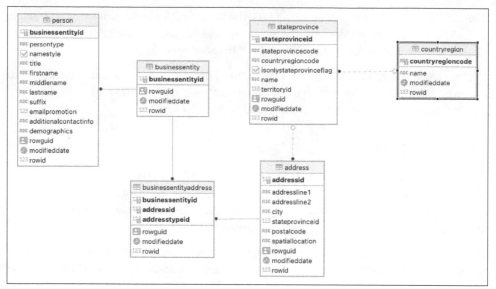

Figure 5-7. Overnormalized address data model

To retrieve the address for a person (something we presumably do a lot), we need a five-table join:

```
SELECT p.firstname,p.lastname, a.addressline1,a.city, s2.name,c2.name
  FROM person p
  JOIN businessentityaddress b3 ON (b3.businessentityid=p.businessentityid)
  JOIN address a ON (b3.addressid=a.addressid)
  JOIN stateprovince s2 ON (s2.stateprovinceid=a.stateprovinceid)
  JOIN countryregion c2 ON (c2.countryregioncode=s2.countryregioncode)
 WHERE p.businessentityid =1
```

Because this JOIN follows primary key-values, it's going to be reasonably efficient, but it's still clearly going to involve five times as many lookup operations as would occur if all the columns were in the base table. So the solution is obvious: replicate the address directly into the person table. When a person's address changes, you may need to perform two UPDATEs (one to address, one to person), but you will not have to perform a five-way JOIN every time you want an address.

As with many design decisions, there are many options between the two extremes. Suppose you want to preserve the multiple-address-per-person design of Figure 5-7. You could still consider collapsing the state and country tables into the address table to reduce the number of tables involved in the join.

Summary Tables

A summary table typically contains aggregated information that is expensive to compute on the fly. For instance, in the MovR application, we might have a dashboard that shows revenue trends by city based on the following query:

```
SELECT CAST(r.start_time AS date) AS ride_date,u.city,SUM(r.revenue)
  FROM rides r
  JOIN users u ON (u.id=r.rider_id)
  GROUP BY 1,2;
```

Because revenue for previous days rarely changes, it's wasteful to continually reissue this expensive query every time the dashboard requests it. Instead, we create a summary table from this data and reload the data at regular intervals (perhaps once an hour).

We can create such a summary table manually, but *materialized views* exist for this very purpose. We'd create a materialized view as follows:

```
CREATE MATERIALIZED VIEW ride_revenue_by_date_city AS
  SELECT cast(r.start_time AS date) AS ride_date,u.city,SUM(r.revenue)
  FROM rides r
  JOIN users u ON (u.id=r.rider_id)
  GROUP BY 1,2;
```

The resulting table is far smaller than the source tables, and we can manually refresh it whenever we like. One of the advantages of a materialized view is that we can also update it whenever we like with the REFRESH command:

```
REFRESH MATERIALIZED VIEW ride_revenue_by_date_city;
```

Vertical Partitioning

Vertical partitioning involves breaking up a table into multiple tables, each of which contains a different set of rows. This is typically done to reduce the amount of work that needs to be completed when updating a row and can also reduce the conflicts that occur when two columns are subject to high concurrent update activity.

For instance, consider an Internet of Things (IoT) application in which a city's current temperature and air pressure are updated multiple times a second by weather sensor devices across the city:

```
CREATE TABLE cityWeather (
        city_id uuid NOT NULL PRIMARY KEY DEFAULT gen_random_uuid(),
        city_name varchar NOT NULL,
        currentTemp float NOT NULL,
        currentAirPressure float NOT NULL);
```

The temperature values and air pressure readings come from different systems, and we're concerned that they will cause transaction conflicts when they attempt to change the same row simultaneously. We could partition the table into two tables to avoid this conflict:

```
CREATE TABLE cityTemp (
        city_id uuid NOT NULL PRIMARY KEY DEFAULT gen_random_uuid(),
        city_name varchar NOT NULL,
        currentTemp float NOT NULL);

CREATE TABLE cityPressure (
        city_id uuid NOT NULL PRIMARY KEY DEFAULT gen_random_uuid(),
        city_name varchar NOT NULL,
        currentTemp float NOT NULL,
        currentAirPressure float NOT NULL);
```

However, CockroachDB column families provide a solution that does not require us to modify our data model. As discussed in Chapter 2, column families allow groups of columns to be stored separately in the storage layer. We simply add each measurement to its own family:

```
CREATE TABLE cityWeather (
        city_id uuid NOT NULL PRIMARY KEY DEFAULT gen_random_uuid(),
        city_name varchar NOT NULL,
        currentTemp float NOT NULL,
        currentAirPressure float NOT NULL,
        FAMILY f1 (city_id,city_name),
        FAMILY f2 (currentTemp),
        FAMILY f3 (currentAirPressure)
);
```

Horizontal Partitioning

Horizontal partitioning (usually just referred to as partitioning) allows a table or index to be comprised of multiple segments. Some examples are:

- Queries can read only the partitions that contain relevant data, reducing the number of logical reads required for a particular query. This technique—known as partition elimination—is particularly suitable for queries that read too great a portion of the table to be able to leverage an index but still do not need to read the entire table.

- By splitting tables and indexes into multiple segments, parallel processing can be significantly improved since operations can be performed on partitions concurrently.

The CockroachDB Enterprise edition does support explicit table partitioning using syntax familiar to those who have used other enterprise databases such as Oracle.

However, CockroachDB's multiregion capabilities eliminate many of the possible motivations for explicitly partitioning tables. *Regional by row tables* are effectively transparently partitioned in such a way as to optimize access to those rows from a particular region. In other databases, explicit partitioning might be required to realize this goal. We'll look at multiregion topologies in Chapter 10.

Repeating Groups

The relational model abhors repeating groups because, in any such repeating group, the attributes are not fully dependent on the primary key alone. For instance, an array element is identified by the primary key and the array index.

However, it can be extremely tedious to perform joins to retrieve small groups of data elements of the same type. For example, at the beginning of the chapter (see Figure 5-2), we defined a `testAnswers` entity that contains one row for each answer on a test. If a test has 100 questions, we need to access 100 rows to see all the results.

The `array` type provides an alternative mechanism. CockroachDB arrays are one-dimensional collections of data of the same data type. For instance, we could store the answers to the test in such an array:

```
CREATE TABLE  studentTest (
        student_id uuid NOT NULL ,
        test_id uuid NOT NULL,
        testDate date NOT NULL,
        testAnswers varchar[] NOT NULL
    );
```

We can set the results in a single update as follows:

```
UPDATE studentTest s
   SET testAnswers=array['a','b','c','d']
 WHERE student_id='2fdaadf5-ff3e-45c4-bc92-cc0d566e1ad9'
   AND test_id='dca69ac4-6c53-4efb-8c7e-bca9f412e2ee';
```

Now we need to access only a single row to get all the test results, which is a significant reduction in overhead.

Array data types do have some downsides—the query syntax is awkward, and it can be hard to perform analytic queries. For instance, finding the sum or average of all elements in an array is not directly supported.

Inverted indexes allow us to directly, efficiently retrieve data from an array data type: we'll elaborate on inverted indexes later in the chapter.

JSON Document Models

The biggest challenge to relational databases over the past decade has come from "document databases" such as MongoDB and Couchbase. These databases store all data in the form of JSON documents. JSON documents are self-describing, so there doesn't need to be a formal implementation of a schema in the DBMS. One simply retrieves the JSON from the database and examines the JSON to decode the structure.

Without entering into any sort of religious debate about the obvious heresy involved in abandoning the relational model in favor of JSON documents, it's worth pointing out that document databases do offer significant conveniences for the developer:

- Modern object-oriented programming practices involve the creation of complex "objects" that have an internal structure that allows for nesting and repeating groups. These program objects are typically highly denormalized and, when stored in an RDBMS, must be unpacked. Object-oriented programmers used to say, "A relational database is like a garage that forces you to take your car apart and store the pieces in little drawers." In contrast, a document database allows the objects to be stored directly.

- JSON allows for the data model to evolve dynamically. For instance, an application can store responses from IoT devices over a REST interface without having a preconceived notion of how those responses are structured.

- Modern DevOps practices involve continuous integration in which the entire application can be built directly from code and tested upon any significant change. RDBMS makes this difficult because a code change and a database change will need to be coordinated—ALTER TABLE statements and code commits need to be synchronously applied. Document databases avoid this issue.

If these document database advantages are attractive to you, then you'll probably be drawn to the idea of storing all or some of your data in a JSONB data type.

JSON objects are self-describing and can contain nested JSON objects and arrays. It's commonplace in document databases to embed child data within parent objects to avoid the need to perform joins. For instance, a house rental database might include all of the attributes of a property within a nested array:

```
{
    "_id": "10006546",
    "listing_url": "https://www.airbnb.com/rooms/10006546",
    "name": "Ribeira Charming Duplex",
    "summary": "Fantastic duplex apartment with three bedrooms,
located in the historic area of Porto, Ribeira (Cube)...",
    "amenities": [
        "TV",
        "Cable TV",
```

```
            "Wifi",
            "Kitchen",
            "Paid parking off premises",
            "Waterfront"
        ],
        "images": {
            "thumbnail_url": "",
            "medium_url": "",
            "picture_url": "https://a0.muscache.com/im/p/9b.jpg?aki_policy=large",
            "xl_picture_url": ""
        },
        "host": {
            "host_id": "51399391",
            "host_url": "https://www.airbnb.com/users/show/51399391",
        }
    }
```

JSON Document Antipatterns

In CockroachDB, implementing *one-to-many relationships* in JSON documents is inadvisable. Because the JSON data is stored inline within the row data within the underlying KV store, CockroachDB recommends that you keep the size of the JSON documents fairly small—under 1 MB.

For instance, in the video streaming JSON model that we introduced in the previous chapter, we embedded all the films that a customer had viewed within a JSON array. Given all the video streaming that has been going on lately, it's quite likely that, at least for some users, the 1 MB limit would be exceeded.

Indexing JSON Attributes

As mentioned in previous chapters, you can create inverted indexes on JSONB columns. These inverted indexes allow you to search for attribute value matches within the JSON object. Inverted indexes are easy to create and guarantee that you'll have indexed access to attributes within the JSON object without having to anticipate in advance what those attributes might be.

However, inverted indexes index every attribute in the JSON object and so can have many more entries in the index than rows in the table—with possible impacts on storage and index maintenance overhead. An alternative is to create computed columns on the JSONB attributes and create an index on those attributes. In this case, you'll need to know which attributes might need an index lookup, but your indexes will remain relatively compact.

So let's say we have decided to store our customer details as a JSONB document. The basic customer details look like this:

```
{ "Address" : "1913 Hanoi Way",
      "City" : "Sasebo",
      "Country" : "Japan",
      "District" : "Nagasaki",
      "FirstName" : "Mary",
      "LastName" : "Smith",
      "Phone" : "886780309",
      "dob" :  "1982-02-20T13:00:00Z",
   "likes": ["Dinosaurs","Dogs","People"] }
```

We know that we want to search on `LastName`, `FirstName`, and we also know we want to have a foreign key out to an existing `cities` table. Our `CREATE TABLE` might look like this:

```
CREATE TABLE people (
      personId UUID PRIMARY KEY NOT NULL default gen_random_uuid(),
      cityId UUID ,
      personData JSONB,
      FirstName STRING AS (personData->>'FirstName') VIRTUAL,
      LastName STRING AS (personData->>'LastName') VIRTUAL,
      FOREIGN KEY (cityId) REFERENCES cities(cityid),
      INDEX  (LastName,Firstname)
);
```

This design allows us to perform index searches on `LastName` and `FirstName`, and to retrieve those attributes from the `JSONB` document without the awkward JSON dereferencing syntax that we introduced in the last chapter. We can, however, add attributes without needing to issue an `ALTER TABLE` statement, and programmers can load the `personData` JSON data directly into a JSON object in their application code.

Using JSON or Arrays to Avoid Joins

We said before that one-to-many relationships should not be modeled in `JSONB` columns. The same is true of `array` columns. We want to avoid storing more data in these columns than the KV store can process in a single operation.

However, it can be quite effective to model *one-to-few relationships* in `JSONB` or `arrays`. For instance, consider the Student Tests schema we modeled way back in Figure 5-2. We know that there can be at most only a couple of hundred questions in a test. In the normalized solution, we always have to `JOIN` tables to get the answers for a specific test:

```
SELECT s.student_id,s.test_id,question_no,questionanswer
  FROM studentTest s
  JOIN testAnswers t on(t.student_id=s.student_id AND t.test_id=s.test_id)
 WHERE s.student_id=?
   AND s.test_id=?;
```

We know that there can be only a couple of hundred questions in a test, and the answers can at most be only a few KB. Being sure that the 1 MB limit will not be exceeded, we could collapse the test answers into a JSON document:

```
CREATE TABLE  studentTest (
        student_id uuid NOT NULL ,
        test_id uuid NOT NULL,
        testDate date NOT NULL,
        answers JSONB
);

INSERT INTO studentTest (student_id,test_id,testDate,answers)
 VALUES ('2fdaadf5-ff3e-45c4-bc92-cc0d566e1ad9',
        'dca69ac4-6c53-4efb-8c7e-bca9f412e2ee',
         now(),
        '{"answers":[
                        {"questionNumber":1,"Answer":5},
                        {"questionNumber":2,"Answer":25},
                        {"questionNumber":3,"Answer":58},
                        {"questionNumber":4,"Answer":3425},
                        {"questionNumber":5,"Answer":432},
                        {"questionNumber":6,"Answer":0},
                        {"questionNumber":7,"Answer":673}
                ]}');
```

We can also use `arrays` or JSON repeating groups to avoid joins where there is a *many-to-few relationship* between two tables. For instance, consider the relationship between students and classes as shown in Figure 5-8.

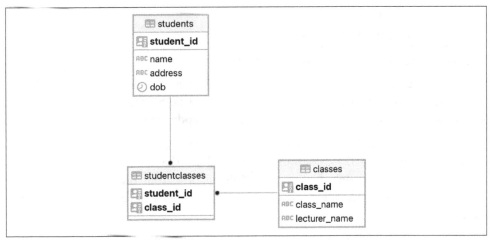

Figure 5-8. Students and classes

Whenever we want to get a list of a student's classes, we're forced to perform a three-way join:

```
SELECT class_name FROM students
  JOIN studentClasses USING(student_id)
  JOIN classes USING(class_id)
  WHERE student_id='000390a6-4e1d-4bc1-aad7-66b645131d54';
```

The table `studentClasses` exists only to `JOIN` the `students` and `classes` tables—it contains no independent information.

We could instead store foreign keys for all the classes in an `array` type:

```
ALTER TABLE students ADD COLUMN classes UUID[];

UPDATE students s SET classes= (
      SELECT array_agg(class_id)
        FROM studentClasses sc
      WHERE s.student_id=sc.student_id);
```

The `array_agg` function takes all the columns in a result set and converts them to an array. In the prior example, we copied all the `class_id` values for each student into the `classes` array.

Now when we want to get the classes for a particular student, we can "unnest" the array and `JOIN` the resulting `class_id` values directly to the `classes` table:

```
WITH students_classes AS (
        SELECT student_id , UNNEST(classes) class_id
          FROM students
)
SELECT class_name FROM classes
  JOIN students_classes USING(class_id)
  WHERE student_id='000390a6-4e1d-4bc1-aad7-66b645131d54';
```

This might all seem to be a bit convoluted, but in a high-performance workload, reducing a three-way `JOIN` to a two-way `JOIN` might be necessary to achieve performance objectives, even if it complicates application code a little.

Of course, we can avoid the joins altogether if we embed all the information about a student's classes into a `JSONB` column, just as we did earlier for test answers. However, that array solution doesn't duplicate any information from the `classes` table into the `students` table, so if the name of a class changes, we have only one update to perform.

Do bear in mind that by embedding foreign keys this way, we lose the capability of defining `FOREIGN KEY` constraints and create some opportunities for data inconsistencies. Furthermore, with this solution, it is difficult to find all students for a given class because we would have to unpack the array of classes for every student.

Indexes

An index is a database object that provides a fast path to specific data within a table.

We looked at the structure of indexes in Chapter 2. You might recall that in CockroachDB, indexes and tables share a common fundamental storage structure. A base table is essentially a relation indexed by the primary key. Secondary indexes are also relations but are indexed by the index key, with the column values representing the primary key-values associated with that secondary key.

Indexes exist to optimize performance and enforce uniqueness. Indexes can generally be added to a system without requiring any change to application code, so compared with other options for physical implementation, they are fairly easy to modify. Creating an optimal set of indexes is one of the most important factors in ensuring optimal database performance.

Index Selectivity

The *selectivity* of a column or group of columns is a common measure of the usefulness of an index on those columns. Columns or indexes are selective if they have a large number of unique values and few duplicate values. For instance, a Date_of_birth column will be quite selective, while a Gender column will not be at all selective.

Selective indexes are more efficient than nonselective indexes because they point more directly to specific values. The CockroachDB optimizer will determine the selectivity of the various indexes available to it and will generally try to use the most selective index.

Index Break-Even Point

When you want to look up just a few things in a textbook, you go to the index. When you want to assimilate all or most of the content, you bypass the index and go directly to the text. It's the same with database indexes—we generally want to use them only when we are retrieving a relatively small amount of a table's data.

A noncovering index—one that includes the filter conditions but not all the columns in the SELECT list—is generally effective only when we are retrieving a small percentage of a table's data. Beyond that, the overhead of going backward and forward from index to base table will be slower than simply reading all the rows in the table.

The optimizer will attempt to determine how much data is being accessed and choose an index or a table scan as appropriate. However, you don't want to create an index that will never be used, so it's important to understand the cut-off point between an index and a table scan.

However, when we create a covering index using the STORING clause, the situation is very different; in this case, the index can outperform the table access even if large proportions of data are accessed. It is true that adding columns to the index using the STORING clause will increase the overhead of index maintenance, but most of the time, the improvement in query performance will be greater than the increase in write overhead.

For instance, let's say we have time-series data where a measurement (say a temperature) was recorded every minute over the past year. The application is often asked to determine the average measurement over some recent time period. The query looks something like this:

```
SELECT AVG(measurement)
  FROM timeseries_data
 WHERE measurement_timestamp >
   ((date '20220101')- INTERVAL '$dayFilter days');
```

The variable $dayFilter can take low or high values. We can create a noncovering index on the table as follows:

```
CREATE INDEX timeseries_timestamp_i1
    ON timeseries_data(measurement_timestamp);
```

However, this index will be effective only when the number of days selected is very small—probably less than a week. Alternatively, we could create a covering index that includes the measurement column:

```
CREATE INDEX timeseries_covering
    ON timeseries_data(measurement_timestamp) STORING (measurement);
```

This index can be used effectively for any span of data—from one day to the entire year's data.

Figure 5-9 compares the performance of an index scan with a table scan against the number of days of data being retrieved. The table scan must do the same amount of work regardless of the amount of data being processed, while an index scan increases in overhead the larger the amount of data being processed. For a noncovering index, a table scan is better if there's more than about a week's worth of data retrieved (about 2% of the total data). However, a covering index can perform well even if we are retrieving all of the table's data.

There are a few lessons to be drawn from Figure 5-9:

- The optimizer switches from an index scan to table scan when the amount of data hits about 10% to 15% of the total. The optimizer is a sophisticated piece of software, but it isn't magic, and it can't always work out which access path is better. In some circumstances, creating a noncovering index will actually degrade performance.

- A covering index is far superior in performance to a noncovering index and can be used effectively even if all or most of the table is being accessed. Whenever possible, use a covering index.

- Remember that in CockroachDB, indexes and tables have the same storage format: a covering index is not just a fast access mechanism—it's also a compact representation of a subset of table columns that can be scanned far faster than the base table.

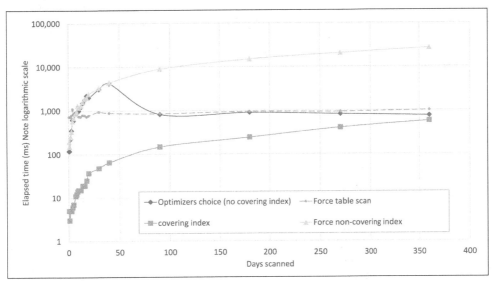

Figure 5-9. Comparison of table scan versus index scan performance

We'll come back to index performance and tuning queries in Chapter 8.

Index Overhead

Although indexes can dramatically improve read performance, they do reduce the performance of write operations. All of a table's indexes must normally be updated when a row is inserted or deleted, and an index must also be amended when an update changes any column that appears in the index.

It is, therefore, important that all our indexes contribute to query performance since these indexes will otherwise needlessly degrade write performance. In particular, you should be especially careful when creating indexes on frequently updated columns. A row can be inserted or deleted only once but may be updated many times. Indexes on heavily updated columns or on tables that have a very high insert/delete rate will therefore exact a particularly high cost. Figure 5-10 illustrates the overhead on write performance that occurs as more indexes are added to a table.

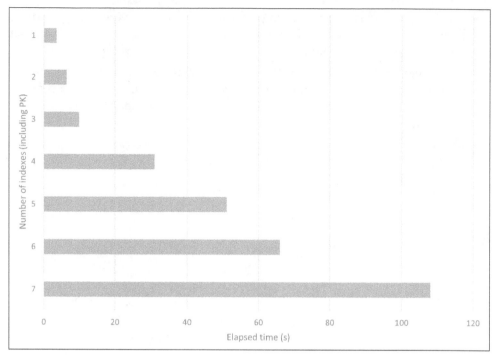

Figure 5-10. Index overhead—time to insert 120,000 rows

Note that you can't improve performance by removing the primary key index. If an explicit primary key index does not exist, CockroachDB will create an artificial primary key for you.

Composite Indexes

A composite index is simply an index created from more than one column. The advantage of a composite key is that it is often more selective than a single key index. The combination of columns will point to a smaller number of rows than indexes composed of the individual columns.

For instance, if we know that we frequently perform searches on `firstname` and `lastname`, then it makes sense to create an index on both of those columns:

```
CREATE INDEX flname_idx ON person (lastname,firstname);
```

Such an index will be far more effective than an index on `lastname` alone or separate indexes on `lastname` and `firstname`. We'll provide some performance comparisons for composite indexes a bit later in the chapter.

If a composite index could be used only when all of its keys appeared in the `WHERE` clause, then you would have to create a lot of composite indexes—as many as you had distinct combinations of columns in the WHERE clause. Luckily, a composite index can be used effectively, provided any of the initial or "leading" columns are used. Leading columns are those that are specified earliest in the index definition.

So, for instance, the index on (lastname, firstname) that we just created can optimize this query:

```
SELECT * FROM person WHERE lastname='Wood';
```

But not this query:

```
SELECT * FROM person WHERE firstname='John' ;
```

Covering Indexes

A covering index is one that is capable of satisfying a query without reference to the base table. For instance, in the following query:

```
SELECT phonenumber
  FROM people
 WHERE lastname='Smith'
   AND firstname='Samantha'
   AND state='California' ;
```

an index on lastname, firstname, state, and phonenumber would not only be able to *find* the data requested but would also be able to *return* the phonenumber. Only a single index access—and no base table read—would be needed.

In CockroachDB, we can use the STORING clause to store data elements that we might use in the SELECT clause but not in the WHERE clause. This provides a more efficient mechanism for implementing a covering index. So for the previous query, this index would be optimal:

```
CREATE INDEX people_lastfirststatephone_ix ON people
    (lastname,firstname,state)
      STORING (phonenumber);
```

Of course, we could also create a covering index without the STORING clause simply by adding the column to the index. For example:

```
CREATE INDEX people_lastfirststatephone_ix ON people
    (lastname,firstname,state,phonenumber);
```

This index could then be used to satisfy queries that included the phone number in the WHERE clause and, therefore, will often be superior. However, STORING does have some advantages. Some data types (such as JSON and arrays) can't be indexed, but all data types can be stored. Other data types take up more space when indexed than when stored (this is most severe for collated strings). If you know you don't need to query by a column, it may be more efficient to store it instead of indexing it.

Composite and Covering Index Performance

Figure 5-11 illustrates the performance advantages offered by composite and covering indexes. The chart shows the number of KV store options necessary to satisfy this query under various indexing scenarios:

```
SELECT phonenumber
  FROM people
 WHERE lastname='Smith'
   AND firstname='Samantha'
   AND state='California' ;
```

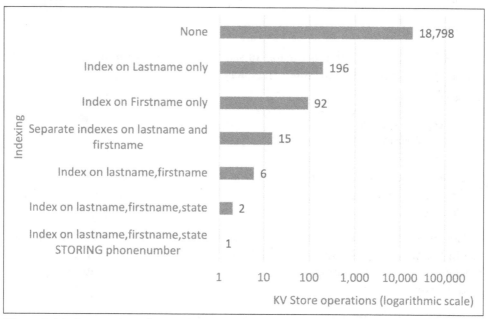

Figure 5-11. Composite index performance

Figure 5-11 shows that without indexing, the query requires 18,798 KV operations—we have to read every row in the table. Single indexes on lastname or firstname improve the performance somewhat, and having both a lastname and firstname index is better than just having either of the two indexes alone.

However, it's not until we use a composite index that we see truly efficient indexing. Only six KV reads are needed if we have an index on lastname and firstname, and only two KV operations are needed for an index on lastname, firstname, and state. If we STORE the phonenumber in the index, then only a single KV operation is needed.

Guidelines for Composite Indexes

As we saw earlier, the performance improvements from indexes don't come without a cost—each index adds overhead to DML operations, so we can't usually create every possible index that we might like.

The best strategy is to create composite indexes that cover the broadest possible ranges of queries. A composite index can be used if any of its leading columns are included in a WHERE clause, so the ordering of columns in composite indexes is important.

The following guidelines might help when deciding which indexes to create:

- Create composite indexes for columns that appear together in the WHERE clause.
- If columns sometimes appear on their own in a WHERE clause, place them at the start of the index.
- The more *selective* a column is, the more useful it will be at the leading end of the index.
- A composite index is more useful if it also supports queries where not all columns are specified. For instance, lastname, firstname is more useful than firstname, lastname because queries against only lastname are more likely to occur than queries against only firstname.

Indexes and Null Values

In many relational databases, null values are not included in indexes, and consequently, in these systems, it is often recommended not to use null values if you might want to search for those values. However, in CockroachDB, null values are included in indexes and can be found using an index in the normal way.

Inverted Indexes

We discussed inverted indexes in Chapter 2 and earlier in this chapter in "JSON Document Models" on page 138. An inverted index creates an index for all elements in an array and for all attributes in a JSONB column. As useful and flexible as these inverted indexes may be, they are expensive from a storage and maintenance point of view. We recommend, whenever possible, creating a computed column from the JSONB attribute concerned and indexing on that column.

Partial Indexes

A partial index can be created on only a subset of rows in the table. A partial index is created by adding a WHERE clause to the CREATE INDEX statement.

Partial indexes can have a lower maintenance overhead, require less storage in the database, and be more efficient for suitable queries. They are, therefore, a very useful type of index.

The key limitation with a partial index is that it can be used only when CockroachDB can be certain that the partial index contains all the necessary entries to satisfy the query. In practice, this means that a partial index is normally used to optimize queries that contain the same WHERE clause filter condition that was included in the index definition.

Sort-Optimizing Indexes

Indexes can be used to optimize ORDER BY operations in certain circumstances. When CockroachDB is asked to return data in sorted order, it must retrieve all the rows to be sorted and perform a sort operation on those rows before returning any of the data. However, if an index exists on the ORDER BY columns, then CockroachDB can read the index and retrieve the rows directly from the index in sorted order.

Using the index to retrieve data in sorted order is usually only worthwhile if you are optimizing for some small number of "top" rows. If you read the entire table in sorted order from the index, then you'll be reading all the index entries as well as all the table entries, and the total number of I/O operations will be excessive. However, if you are just getting the first "page" of data or a "top 10," then the index will be much faster since you never have to read the rest of the table rows at all.

However, if the index contains all the columns you need in the output—either because it indexes all those columns or is using STORING on the others—then you get the best of both worlds—you can retrieve all rows efficiently in sorted order.

Figure 5-12 illustrates the effect of an index to optimize a sort like this:

```
SELECT *
  FROM orderdetails
  ORDER BY modifieddate;
```

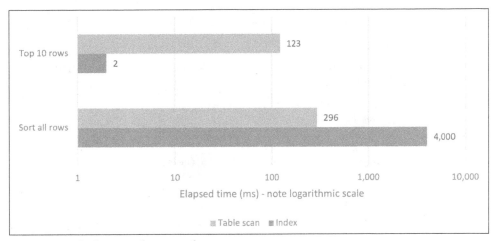

Figure 5-12. Indexes and sort performance

When a `LIMIT` clause was added to the query, the index reduced execution time from 123 ms to just 2 ms—a fantastic improvement. However, if we force CockroachDB to use the index to retrieve all rows (something it won't do by default), then execution time will increase from 296 ms to 4,000 ms.

Expression Indexes

Expression indexes allow us to create an index on an expression rather than a column name. It's similar in effect to creating a `COMPUTED` column and then creating an index on that column.

For instance, we could create an index on a lowercased version of the user's name:

```
CREATE INDEX lower_users_ix ON users (LOWER(name))
```

Such an index would be able to optimize queries that ignored case by using the `LOWER` function in the query:

```
SELECT *
  FROM users
 WHERE name=LOWER('Guy');
```

Spatial Indexes

A spatial index is a special type of inverted index that supports operations on the `GEOMETRY` and `GEOGRAPHY` two-dimensional spatial data types.

Spatial indexing is a complex topic, and we aim only to introduce you to some key concepts here. For more details, consult the CockroachDB documentation set (*https://cockroa.ch/3LzUm2E*).

To create a spatial index, we add the `USING GIST(geom)` clause:

```
CREATE INDEX geom_idx_1 ON some_spatial_table USING GIST(geom);
```

We can further fine-tune the index using various spatial index tuning parameters (*https://cockroa.ch/3r0ABcY*):

```
CREATE INDEX geom_idx_1 ON geo_table1 USING GIST(geom)
WITH (s2_level_mod=3);
CREATE INDEX geom_idx_2 ON geo_table2 USING GIST(geom)
WITH (geometry_min_x=0, s2_max_level=15)
CREATE INDEX geom_idx_3 ON geo_table3 USING GIST(geom)
WITH (s2_max_level=10)
CREATE INDEX geom_idx_4 ON geo_table4 USING GIST(geom)
WITH (geometry_min_x=0, s2_max_level=15);
```

We don't recommend that you change these default tuning parameters; the default values will generally provide the best performance.

Hash-Sharded Indexes

Earlier in this chapter, we showed how in a distributed database, monotonically increasing primary keys can lead to "hotspots" in a distributed database. We recommended using hash-sharded indexes as a way of avoiding such an issue for monotonically increasing primary keys.

These sorts of hotspots don't occur just in primary keys. Any indexed column that is monotonically increasing might end up with all new values in a single range, thus creating a scalability and throughput issue.

If you have indexed columns where the value is constantly increasing (timestamps are a good example) and you want to avoid such an insert hotspot, then you should consider hash-sharding the index. The syntax is the same as for the primary key example we showed in "Hash-sharded primary keys" on page 130. For instance, to create a hash-sharded index on the `modifieddate` column, we might do the following:

```
SET experimental_enable_hash_sharded_indexes=on;

CREATE INDEX orderdetails_hash_ix
    ON orderdetails(modifieddate)
  USING HASH WITH BUCKET_COUNT=6;
```

Note that while CockroachDB might not optimize a sort with a hash-sharded index, it still might provide good enough performance for a "top 10" type of query. We can force the use of the hash-sharded index to perform an `ORDER BY` using an *index hint* (more on this in Chapter 8):

```
SELECT *
  FROM orderdetails@orderdetails_hash_ix
 ORDER BY modifieddate LIMIT 10;
```

CockroachDB will retrieve the top 10 from each "bucket" and amalgamate the results on the gateway node. The result might still be a marked improvement over a full scan.

Measuring Index Effectiveness

Having created an index, we'd like to be sure that it is being used to optimize our query and discover exactly how much benefit we have achieved. We can do this using the EXPLAIN and EXPLAIN ANALYZE commands.

EXPLAIN reveals to us the CockroachDB optimizer "plan" for a SQL statement. We'll dig into EXPLAIN in detail in Chapter 8, but for now, let's just quickly see how EXPLAIN works to reveal your query's performance characteristics.

EXPLAIN reveals the optimizer's plan for resolving a query. For instance, if we created an index on people and wanted to see if the query would use it, we could issue the following command:

```
EXPLAIN
SELECT phonenumber
  FROM people
 WHERE lastname='Smith'
   AND firstname='Samantha'
   AND state='California';
                                      info
-------------------------------------------------------------------------
  distribution: local
  vectorized: true

  • filter
  | estimated row count: 63
  | filter: state = 'California'
  |
  └── • index join
      | estimated row count: 5
      | table: people@primary
      |
      └── • scan
            estimated row count: 5 (0.02% of the table;)
            table: people@people_lastfirst_ix
            spans: [/'Smith'/'Samantha'-/'Smith'/'Samantha']
```

We can see that the people_lastfirst_ix will be used to resolve the query.

However, in some cases, we might still not be sure if the index improved execution time. If we use EXPLAIN analyze, then CockroachDB will execute the operation and will report on the amount of I/O and other operations that occurred:

```
EXPLAIN analyze
SELECT phonenumber
  FROM people
 WHERE lastname='Smith'
```

```
    AND firstname='Samantha'
    AND state='California';

                                    info
----------------------------------------------------------------------
  planning time: 2ms
  execution time: 4ms
  distribution: local
  vectorized: true
  rows read from KV: 6 (598 B)
  cumulative time spent in KV: 3ms
  maximum memory usage: 30 KiB
  network usage: 0 B (0 messages)

  • filter
  | cluster nodes: n1
  | actual row count: 1
  | estimated row count: 63
  | filter: state = 'California'
  |
  └── • index join
      | cluster nodes: n1
      | actual row count: 3
      | KV rows read: 3
      | KV bytes read: 430 B
      | estimated row count: 5
      | table: people@primary
      |
      └── • scan
          cluster nodes: n1
          actual row count: 3
          KV rows read: 3
          KV bytes read: 168 B
          estimated row count: 5 (0.02% of the table)
          table: people@people_lastfirst_ix
          spans: [/'Smith'/'Samantha'-/'Smith'/'Samantha']
```

EXPLAIN has some additional advanced features that we'll learn about in Chapter 8. However, you can see how easy it is to use EXPLAIN to simply determine index utilization and effectiveness.

Summary

In this chapter, we looked at design principles for a CockroachDB database schema. A sound data model is an essential foundation for a performant and maintainable CockroachDB database.

Database modeling typically proceeds in two stages: logical modeling followed by physical modeling. The aim of the logical modeling phase is to identify the data required for application functionality. The physical modeling phase attempts to construct a data model that can meet functional requirements together with performance and availability requirements. The physical model should almost never be a direct copy of the logical model.

Database design for a distributed SQL database like CockroachDB creates some unique challenges when compared with a traditional monolithic database. In particular, primary keys should be constructed so that new rows are distributed equitably across the nodes in the cluster. The UUID data type can achieve this, but if an ascending primary key is required, then using hash-sharded primary key indexes is indicated.

We also looked at indexing choices for a CockroachDB database design. Creating the least number of composite indexes to support common filter conditions is our objective. We may also want to create some indexes to support sort operations.

Now that we've learned how to create a data model, we are in a position to start writing application code. We've already introduced CockroachDB SQL: in the next chapter, we'll see how to use CockroachDB SQL in application development frameworks.

Application Design and Implementation

Like all databases, CockroachDB responds to requests from application code. How an application requests and uses data has a huge bearing on application performance and scalability. In this chapter, we'll review how an application should work with CockroachDB, including best practices for coding CockroachDB requests and transactional models.

Because CockroachDB is PostgreSQL wire protocol–compatible, any language that supports PostgresSQL can be used with CockroachDB. And in general, the programming idioms and best practices of PostgreSQL apply to CockroachDB. However, because of the distributed nature of CockroachDB, there are some differences in programming styles between CockroachDB and PostgreSQL.

Although you can work with CockroachDB using pretty much any programming language in common use, in this chapter, we'll constrain our discussion to four languages: Go, Java, Python, and JavaScript.

Previously, we showed how to install language drivers for each of these languages. Please refer back to Chapter 3 for instructions on driver installation, or refer to the CockroachDB documentation (*https://cockroa.ch/3Kpm8ik*) for more detailed guidelines, including guidance on how to install drivers for other languages or for alternative drivers.

CockroachDB Programming

CockroachDB is broadly compatible with the universe of SQL relational databases and particularly compatible with PostgreSQL. However, there are a few unique programming idioms specific to CockroachDB as a result of its distributed nature and transactional consistency model.

In the following sections, we'll review both the general principles involved in coding an application against a CockroachDB server and look at some issues specific to CockroachDB.

Performing CRUD Operations

We provided basic "Hello world" examples for each language back in Chapter 3. Let's extend those examples to perform some nontrivial "CRUD" operations—Create, Read, Update, Delete.

Programming drivers differ in terms of vocabulary, but they generally adopt a similar grammar. The fundamental operations in a database program are:

- The driver establishes a *connection* object representing a connection to the database server. In this chapter, we'll be creating individual connections, but applications will often use a *connection pool* to manage multiple reusable connections instead.

- The connection object is used to execute SQL statements.

- Some statements return *result sets* that can be used to iterate through tabular output returned by SELECT statements, DML statements that include a RETURNING clause, and some other statements that return results.

Here we see this basic pattern in Java:

```java
package chapter06c;

import java.sql.Connection;
import java.sql.DriverManager;
import java.sql.ResultSet;
import java.sql.Statement;

public class example1 {

  public static void main(String[] args) {
    try {
      Class.forName("org.postgresql.Driver");
      String connectionURL = "jdbc:" + args[0];
      String userName = args[1];
      String passWord = args[2];

      Connection connection = DriverManager.getConnection(
          connectionURL, userName, passWord);
      Statement stmt = connection.createStatement();
      stmt.execute("DROP TABLE IF EXISTS names");
      stmt.execute("CREATE TABLE names (name String PRIMARY KEY NOT NULL)");
      stmt.execute("INSERT INTO names (name) VALUES('Ben'),('Jesse'),('Guy')");

      ResultSet results = stmt.executeQuery("SELECT name FROM names");
```

```
      while (results.next()) {
        System.out.println(results.getString(1));

      }
      results.close();
      stmt.close();
      connection.close();

    } catch (Exception e) {
      e.printStackTrace();
      System.exit(0);
    }
  }
}
```

We create a single *connection* object and a single *statement* object, then use the statement to execute multiple SQL commands. When we execute a query, we create a *ResultSet* object that we can use to iterate through results. Finally, we close all these objects.

Note that we can retrieve column values from the ResultSet object by position or by name—in the example, we provided the column position, but we could have also specified the column name.

What follows is similar logic for Python. The cursor() method of the connection object creates a cursor object that can be used to execute a statement or navigate through a result set:

```python
import psycopg2
import sys

def main():

  if ((len(sys.argv)) !=2):
    sys.exit("Error:No URL provided on command line")
  uri=sys.argv[1]

  connection = psycopg2.connect(uri)
  cursor=connection.cursor()
  cursor.execute("DROP TABLE IF EXISTS names")
  cursor.execute("""CREATE TABLE names
                (name String PRIMARY KEY NOT NULL)""")
  cursor.execute("""INSERT INTO names (name)
                VALUES('Ben'),('Jesse'),('Guy')""")
  cursor.execute("SELECT name FROM names")
  for row in cursor:
    print(row[0])
  cursor.close()
  connection.close()

main()
```

Here we do the same thing in a Node.js JavaScript program:

```javascript
const CrClient = require('pg').Client;

async function main() {
    try {
        if (process.argv.length != 3) {
            console.log(`Usage: node ${process.argv[1]} CONNECTION_URI`);
            process.exit(1);
        }

        const connection = new CrClient(process.argv[2]);
        await connection.connect();

        await connection.query('DROP TABLE IF EXISTS names');
        await connection.query(`CREATE TABLE names
                                (name String PRIMARY KEY NOT NULL)`);
        await connection.query(`INSERT INTO names (name)
                                VALUES('Ben'),('Jesse'),('Guy')`);

        const data = await connection.query('SELECT name from names');
        data.rows.forEach((row) => {
            console.log(row.name);
        });
    } catch (error) {
        console.error(error.stack);
    }
    process.exit(0);
}

main();
```

We've used the "async/await" style for handling asynchronous database requests. You can also use callbacks or promises if that is your programming style. The node-postgres driver documentation (*https://cockroa.ch/3j1GSjY*) contains examples of using each of these programming styles.

Finally, let's look at how we'd perform the same task in Go:

```go
package main

import (
        "context"
        "fmt"
        "os"

        "github.com/jackc/pgx"
)

func main() {
        if len(os.Args) < 2 {
                fmt.Fprintln(os.Stderr, "Missing URL argument")
                os.Exit(1)
```

```
        }
        uri := os.Args[1]
        conn, err := pgx.Connect(context.Background(), uri)
        if err != nil {
                fmt.Fprintf(os.Stderr, "CockroachDB error: %v\n", err)
        }
        execSQL(*conn, "DROP TABLE IF EXISTS names")
        execSQL(*conn, "CREATE TABLE names (name String PRIMARY KEY NOT NULL)")
        execSQL(*conn, "INSERT INTO names(name) VALUES('Ben'),('Jesse'),('Guy')")

        rows, err := conn.Query(context.Background(), "SELECT name FROM names")
        if err != nil {
                fmt.Fprintf(os.Stderr, "CockroachDB error: %v\n", err)
        }
        defer rows.Close()
        for rows.Next() {
                var name string
                err = rows.Scan(&name)
                fmt.Println(name)
        }
}

func execSQL(conn pgx.Conn, sql string) {
        result, err := conn.Exec(context.Background(), sql)
        if err != nil {
                fmt.Fprintf(os.Stderr, "CockroachDB error: %v\n", err)
                os.Exit(1)
        }
        fmt.Fprintf(os.Stdout, "%v rows affected\n", result.RowsAffected())
}
```

We created the execSQL function in the Go example to modularize the repetitive error checking involved in the initial SQL statements, though in production code, we would perform error checking independently for each query.

Connection Pools

It's often good practice to create small reusable routines to perform small tasks. If the service requires database access, then it might seem natural to supply each of these small routines with a dedicated connection. This has a clear advantage over a single shared connection because it allows for concurrent requests. For instance, imagine that we have a simple web service that we call whenever a new ride is commenced in our Uber-busting ride-sharing app.

We might code the database logic for it as follows:

```
async function newRide(city, riderId, vehicleId, startAddress) {
    const connection = new pg.Client(connectionString);
    await connection.connect();
    const sql = `INSERT INTO movr.rides
    (id, city,rider_id,vehicle_id,start_address,start_time)
    VALUES(gen_random_uuid(), $1,$2,$3,$4,now())`;
    await connection.query(sql, [city, riderId, vehicleId, startAddress]);
    await connection.end();
}
```

We don't want to single-thread these requests, so we've given each call its own connection. Unfortunately, creating a connection has a nontrivial overhead. When the database access is simple, the time taken to create and dispose of the connection might dominate overall response time. But we can't run every request through the same connection because that would restrict concurrent queries.

The solution is to use *connection pools*. A connection pool is a set of connections that the application can reuse. You avoid the overhead of constantly creating and destroying connections, and you can control the maximum amount of concurrency hitting the database.

In Node.js, we'd create the pool as follows:

```
const pool = new pg.Pool({
    connectionString,
    max: 40
});
```

We now can change our routine so that it gets connections from the pool:

```
async function newRidePool(city, riderId, vehicleId, startAddress) {
    const connection = await pool.connect();
    const sql = `INSERT INTO movr.rides
                (id, city,rider_id,vehicle_id,start_address,start_time)
                VALUES(gen_random_uuid(), $1,$2,$3,$4,now())`;
    await connection.query(sql, [city, riderId, vehicleId, startAddress]);
    await connection.release();
}
```

Figure 6-1 illustrates how the two approaches compare for performance. With 40 concurrent requests, a connection pool implementation outperformed the unique connection approach by about 700%. The benefit you get from connection pools will vary depending on the amount of work performed in each connection and the amount of concurrent activity that the application issues. However, it's almost always advisable to use a connection pool instead of a single connection used by all threads or allocating each thread with its own transitory connection.

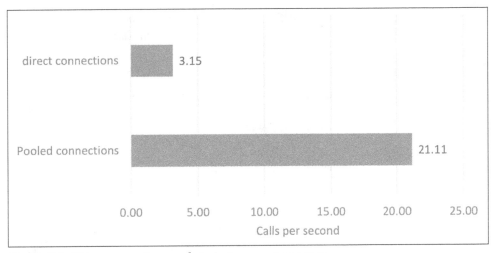

Figure 6-1. Using connection pools to improve concurrency

Connections in the pool can be broken by cluster topology changes or network inter-
ruptions. It may be advisable to configure "keep alive" settings to periodically recheck
the connections. See the CockroachDB documentation (*https://cockroa.ch/3Jch9jA*)
for further details.

Connection Pools and Blocked Connections

Most connection pool implementations will block requests for new connections if
all the pooled connections are in use. Therefore, it's important to configure a sufficient number of connections in the pool for the anticipated concurrency. The CockroachDB documentation (*https://cockroa.ch/3DDo3NC*) suggests configuring four
connections for every core in the entire cluster. For instance, if you have a three-node
cluster with eight cores in each node, you might configure $3 \times 8 \times 4 = 96$ connections.
However, this is just a guideline—the optimal number will depend heavily on the
duration of each connection and the amount of idle time each connection experiences
as the application performs nondatabase tasks.

Bear in mind that the number of connections you determine should be shared across
all of the connection pools that you have configured. So, for example, if you have
calculated an ideal number of connections as 96, and you have four application
servers, then each of these applications servers should have 24 connections (96 / 4).

It's also critically important to release connections when not in use. For instance, in
the Node.js example, the `connection.release()` statement at the end of our function
is vital.

In Java, there are a variety of connection pool options (*https://cockroa.ch/3uOgUWO*). Here's an example using the Hikari framework (*https://cockroa.ch/3LwwKfw*):

```java
import com.zaxxer.hikari.*;
import java.sql.*;

public class ConnectionPoolDemo {

  public static void main(String[] args) {
    try {
      Class.forName("org.postgresql.Driver");
      String connectionURL = "jdbc:" + args[0];
      String userName = args[1];
      String passWord = args[2];

      HikariConfig config = new HikariConfig();
      config.setJdbcUrl(connectionURL);
      config.setUsername(userName);
      config.setPassword(passWord);
      config.addDataSourceProperty("ssl", "true");
      config.addDataSourceProperty("sslMode", "require");
      config.addDataSourceProperty("reWriteBatchedInserts", "true");
      config.setAutoCommit(false);
      config.setMaximumPoolSize(40);
      config.setIdleTimeout(3000);

      HikariDataSource hikariPool = new HikariDataSource(config);
```

This example creates a connection pool with 40 connections using arguments passed in on the command line. Once the pool is created, a connection can be obtained from the pool as follows:

```java
Connection connection = hikariPool.getConnection();
```

In the Go `pgx` driver, we can use the pgxpool package to create and use a connection pool:

```go
ctx := context.Background()
config, err := pgxpool.ParseConfig(uri)
config.MaxConns = 40
pool, err := pgxpool.ConnectConfig(ctx, config)
defer pool.Close()
```

We can acquire a connection from the pool as follows:

```go
connection, err := pool.Acquire(ctx)
```

The Python driver `psycopg2` includes a built-in connection pool that we can easily configure as follows:

```python
import psycopg2
from psycopg2 import pool

def main():
```

```
if ((len(sys.argv)) !=2):
   sys.exit("Error:No URL provided on command line")
uri=sys.argv[1]

pool= psycopg2.pool.ThreadedConnectionPool(10, 40, uri)
# min connection=10, max=40
```

And we can connect to the pool as follows:

```
connection = pool.getconn()
```

Prepared and Parameterized Statements

Most SQL operations are parameterized—the same statement is run multiple times with different input parameters. For instance, we might have a lookup program that retrieves rider names for a specified ride ID as follows:

```
SELECT u.name FROM movr.rides r
  JOIN movr.users u ON (r.rider_id=u.id)
  WHERE r.id='ffc3c373-63ec-43fe-98ff-311f29424d8b'
```

We would, of course, execute this SQL many times, each time specifying a different value for the ride ID.

When coding a generic lookup function, it seems natural enough to append the parameter to the SQL statement using string concatenation. For example, in Java, we might be tempted to do something like this:

```
private static String getRiderName(String riderId) throws SQLException {
Statement stmt = connection.createStatement();
       String sql = " SELECT u.name FROM movr.rides r "
                     + "  JOIN movr.users u ON (r.rider_id=u.id) "
                     + "  WHERE r.id='"
                 + riderId + "'";
       ResultSet rs = stmt.executeQuery(sql);
       rs.next();
       return (rs.getString("name"));
       }
```

However, as natural as this might seem, it represents an extremely poor practice that has both performance and security downsides.

Most significantly, this code is vulnerable to *SQL injection*. For instance, imagine the application could somehow be persuaded to pass the following string to the function:

```
riderName = getRiderName(
"ffc3c373-63ec-43fe-98ff-311f29424d8b' UNION
 select credit_card from movr.users order by 1,name 'n");
```

The resulting SQL statement would become:

```
SELECT u.name FROM movr.rides r
  JOIN movr.users u ON (r.rider_id=u.id)
  WHERE r.id='ffc3c373-63ec-43fe-98ff-311f29424d8b'
  UNION select credit_card from movr.users order by 1,name
```

And the function would now return credit card numbers as well as rider names.

Of course, the application should prevent such a string from being entered at the UI layer, but creating the vulnerability in the database code is poor practice.

The solution is to use *prepared* or *parameterized* statements. As in the preceding Java example, we would declare a `preparedStatement` as follows:

```
getRiderStmt = connection.prepareStatement(
    "SELECT u.name FROM movr.rides r "
+ " JOIN movr.users u ON (r.rider_id=u.id) "
+ " WHERE r.id=?");
```

The "?" indicates a placeholder for a parameter (sometimes called a *bind variable*). We can call the prepared statement by setting the parameter and executing the statement:

```
getRiderStmt.setString(1, riderId);
ResultSet rs = getRiderStmt.executeQuery();
rs.next();
return (rs.getString("name"));
```

As well as avoiding SQL injection, `preparedStatements` generally execute faster because CockroachDB can more easily recognize the SQL as one that has already been parsed and can avoid some of the overhead involved with examining what would otherwise appear to be a brand new statement.

Formally "preparing" statements is a Java practice. In other languages, it's sufficient to simply call a SQL statement with placeholders and provide the values in the call. For instance, in JavaScript:

```
const sql = `SELECT u.name FROM movr.rides r
                JOIN movr.users u ON (r.rider_id=u.id)
                WHERE r.id=$1`;
const results = await connection.query(sql,
['ffc3c373-63ec-43fe-98ff-311f29424d8b']);
console.log(results.rows[0].name);
```

In Python:

```
sql = """SELECT u.name FROM movr.rides r
            JOIN movr.users u ON (r.rider_id=u.id)
            WHERE r.id=%s"""
cursor.execute(sql,('ffc3c373-63ec-43fe-98ff-311f29424d8b',))
row=cursor.fetchone()
print(row[0])
```

And in Go:

```
sql := `SELECT u.name FROM movr.rides r
         JOIN movr.users u ON (r.rider_id=u.id)
         WHERE r.id=$1`
rows, err := conn.Query(ctx, sql, "ffc3c373-63ec-43fe-98ff-311f29424d8b")
rows.Next()
var name string
err = rows.Scan(&name)
fmt.Println(name)
```

Batch Inserts

It's common for an application to insert multiple rows of data in a single logical operation.

When you have an array of values to insert, it can seem natural to simply insert the values in a loop, as in this Python example:

```
for value in arrayValues:
    cursor.execute("INSERT INTO insertTestP1(id,x,y) VALUES ($1,$2,$3)",value)
```

It's inefficient to insert large amounts of data one at a time—each insert will require a network round trip, and there may be transactional implications if we want all of the rows committed in a single transaction (because the single row inserts will take longer, the chance of a transaction conflict and subsequent retries will be magnified).

SQL allows multiple VALUES to be included in a single operation, such as:

```
INSERT INTO insertTest(id,x,y)
VALUES (3,'x',1) ,
       (4,'y',2) ,
       (5,'x',5)
```

So we could, if necessary, dynamically construct an INSERT statement to insert an array of data in a single operation. For instance, in Python, the following code will generate and execute an INSERT statement to insert an array of arbitrary length:

```
sql="INSERT INTO insertTestP(id,x,y) VALUES"
valueCount=0
for value in arrayValues:
    if valueCount>0:
        sql=sql+","
    sql=sql+"(%d,'%s',%d)" % value
    valueCount+=1
cursor.execute(sql)
```

Note that this formulation is vulnerable to SQL injection. In the psycopg2 extras package, there is an execute_values extras helper function that simplifies the coding required and reduces the change of SQL injection:

```
from psycopg2 import extras

<snip>

extras.execute_values(cursor,
  "INSERT INTO insertTestP1(id,x,y) VALUES %s",
  arrayValues)
```

The performance improvements obtained with batch inserts are dramatic. Figure 6-2 illustrates the improvement.

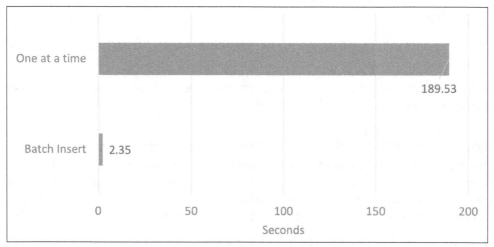

Figure 6-2. Improvement obtained by inserting rows in an array

JDBC includes addBatch and executeBatch methods that allow you to prepare inserts one at a time and then submit all the inserted values in a single operation. This avoids the need to concatenate a huge VALUES list and allows us to use formal parameters.

Here's an example of the addBatch and executeBatch methods:

```
String sql="INSERT INTO insertTest(id,x,y) VALUES (?,?,?)";
PreparedStatement InsertStmt = connection.prepareStatement(sql);

for (int arrayIdx = 1; arrayIdx < arrayCount; arrayIdx++) {
    InsertStmt.setInt(1, idArray.get(arrayIdx));
    InsertStmt.setString(2, xArray.get(arrayIdx));
    InsertStmt.setInt(3, yArray.get(arrayIdx));
    InsertStmt.addBatch();
    }

InsertStmt.executeBatch();
```

We use setInt and setString methods to supply values to the prepared statement as usual, but instead of executing, we use addBatch to add them to the batch of rows to be inserted. When we are ready, we call `executeBatch` to add all the rows in a single operation.

The JDBC `addBatch` method has minimal effect unless the `reWriteBatchedInserts` poperty is set to true. You can set `reWriteBatchedInserts` when establishing a connection:

```
Class.forName("org.postgresql.Driver");
String connectionURL = "jdbc:" + args[0];
String userName = args[1];
String passWord = args[2];
Properties props = new Properties();
props.setProperty("user", userName);
props.setProperty("password", passWord);
props.setProperty("reWriteBatchedInserts", "true");

Connection connection = DriverManager.getConnection(connectionURL, props);
```

The Node.js library does not include any direct support for batch inserts. However, we can use the *pg-format* package to create SQL statements that contain multiple VALUES from an array:

```
const pg = require('pg');
const format = require('pg-format');

async function main() {
    const connection = new pg.Client(connectionString);

    const sql = format('INSERT INTO insertTestP2(id,x,y) VALUES  %L,
arrayData);

    await connection.query(sql);
```

The Go `pgx` library does not currently support bulk inserts directly. You would need to construct dynamic SQL with multiple VALUES entries, as shown earlier for Python. However, some users have written helper functions to expedite dynamic SQL generation for bulk inserts (*https://cockroa.ch/3uXoyyl*).

Pagination of Results

Some applications need to return data in batches. For instance, an online application might want to return lists of information in pages—similar to the pages of results that you might get from a Google search.

From a syntactic point of view, most of the drivers allow you to scroll through rows one at a time. However, in many cases, you are still bringing the entire result set into program memory before retrieving the first row. For example, the Python psycopg2 driver provides methods access to the entire result set (`fetchall()`), a selection of rows (`fetchmany()`), or a single row (`fetchone()`). However, regardless of the method called, the entire result set is always transferred from the database to the application.

The Java JDBC driver supports client-side cursors that allow for data to be efficiently pulled from the database in batches. The size of the batches is controlled by the `setFetchSize()` method of the `Statement` object. By default, `fetchSize` is set to 0, which results in *all* the rows being pulled into the application before the first row can be processed.

We can adjust the `fetchSize` if we want to pull only a few rows in each batch as follows:[1]

```
Statement stmt = connection.createStatement();
stmt.setFetchSize(100);
 results = stmt
     .executeQuery("SELECT post_timestamp, summary "
                 + "  FROM blog_posts "
                 + "  ORDER BY post_timestamp DESC ");
 for (int ri = 0; ri < 10; ri++) {
   if (results.next())
     System.out.println(results.getString("SUMMARY"));
 }
```

You don't have to change your loop logic when you change `setFetchSize()`, but under the hood, the PostgreSQL driver will pull rows in batches of `setFetchSize()` size. Figure 6-3 shows that this can be very effective if we want to optimize for fetching the first few rows.

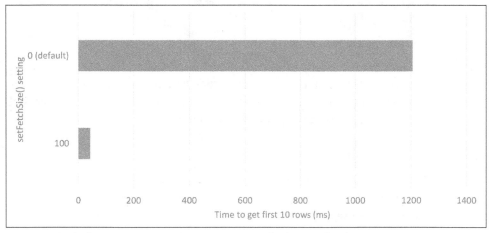

Figure 6-3. Reducing `setFetchSize` to improve fetch time for first rows

---

1 Note that the `setFetchSize()` call has no effect if `setAutoCommit` is set to `true`.

In Java, the `fetchSize` parameter gives us an adequate solution for pagination. However, the other drivers either do not support effective client-side cursors or do so in a way that results in some unnatural coding styles.

The recommended language-independent pattern for navigating pages of data is referred to as "KeySet pagination." However, before considering this technique, let's look at a "natural" solution that has very poor performance characteristics.

Let's suppose that we are returning pages of blog posts from the following query:

```
SELECT post_timestamp, summary
  FROM blog_posts ORDER BY post_timestamp DESC
```

We have a covering index on `POST_TIMESTAMP`, and this index stores the `summary` column, so we can retrieve rows efficiently in order. We want to create some code to display blog posts in order of posting, with a certain number of posts per "page."

SQL supports `OFFSET` and `LIMIT` functions, allowing us to jump ahead and to limit the number of rows returned. This might seem an ideal solution for pagination; we can use the `OFFSET` to jump to the page we want and `LIMIT` to restrict the number of results to just that page. In Python, we might code this as follows:

```
def getPage(startIndex,nEntries):
  // Don't do this!
  cursor=connection.cursor()
  sql="""SELECT post_timestamp, summary
          FROM blog_posts ORDER BY post_timestamp DESC
        OFFSET %s LIMIT %s"""
  cursor.execute(sql,(startIndex,nEntries))
  return cursor.fetchall()
```

The problem with this approach is that `OFFSET` requires us to process all of the data up to and including the first row of interest. So, for instance, if we specify an offset of one million, we have to retrieve and discard all the data prior to the one-millionth row. Each page will take longer to retrieve than the last.

The correct method is to move through the result set in key order so that we can efficiently retrieve the rows using index ranges. Of course, this approach absolutely requires that we have an index on the `WHERE` clause condition, and ideally, this index should be a covering index that includes the `SELECT` list columns as well. So our Python method would look like this:

```
def getPageKeySet(startTimeStamp,nEntries):
  cursor=connection.cursor()
  sql="""SELECT post_timestamp, summary
          FROM blog_posts
          WHERE post_timestamp< %s
          ORDER BY post_timestamp DESC
          LIMIT %s"""
```

```
    cursor.execute(sql,(startTimeStamp,nEntries))
    return cursor.fetchall()
```

We would need to track the oldest blog timestamp from each page retrieved and forward that to the next invocation of the method.

In some circumstances, it might be important to ensure that the pages of data are consistent. Since each invocation of the method occurs at a different time, each "page" of data will reflect the database at a different time. If this is a concern, then AS OF SYSTEM TIME can be used to ensure that each page of data reflects the state of the database as of a specific time:

```
def getPageKeySetST(startTimeStamp,nEntries,systemTime):
    cursor=connection.cursor()
    sql="""SELECT post_timestamp, summary
            FROM blog_posts
            AS OF SYSTEM TIME %s
            WHERE post_timestamp< %s
            ORDER BY post_timestamp DESC
            LIMIT %s
            """
    cursor.execute(sql,(systemTime,startTimeStamp,nEntries))
    return cursor.fetchall()
```

Figure 6-4 illustrates how the use of OFFSET and LIMIT results in increasing overhead as we retrieve each page of information. In contrast, the KeySet pagination pattern returns each page in the same amount of time.

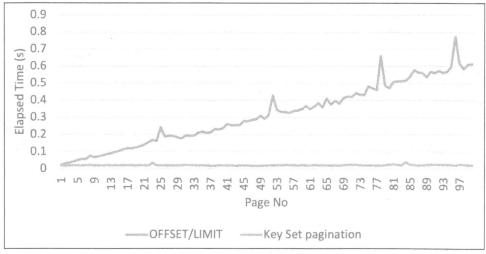

Figure 6-4. KeySet pagination provides better scalability than OFFSET/LIMIT

Projections

In relational database parlance, "projection" refers to the selection of a subset of columns from a table (or *attributes* from an *entity*). In practice, a projection is represented by the list of columns in a SELECT clause.

While SELECT accepts a wildcard projection (*), this should almost never be used in production code because it results in unnecessary transport of columns from the database to the application. Using * can seem like a handy programming shortcut, but it can have severe performance penalties when processing large result sets. Furthermore, it can cause errors if the structure of the table is changed.

For instance, let's say we are retrieving a list of user IDs and blog post dates to populate a dashboard or to perform some other real-time diagnostic. The following code might seem acceptable:

```
ResultSet results = stmt.executeQuery(
    "SELECT * FROM blog_posts");
while (results.next()) {
  java.sql.Timestamp postTimestamp =
      results.getTimestamp("POST_TIMESTAMP");
  Integer userid = results.getInt("USERID");
  plotPost(userid, postTimestamp);

}
```

However, a couple of coding seconds saved in omitting the column names costs the application dearly. Every time this code is executed, it retrieves not only the user ID and timestamp but also the potentially very large blog post text. As a result, each network packet can hold less data, and the number of network round trips is magnified. If we add a projection:

```
    results = stmt.executeQuery(
  "SELECT userid,post_timestamp FROM blog_posts");
```

then elapsed time is reduced dramatically. Figure 6-5 illustrates the elapsed time savings for a 10-million row result set from a remote cluster.

Of course, the absolute time saved will depend on the total row size versus the size of the projection and the network latency between the application and the server. Furthermore, this degradation only kicks in when we pull more rows from the database than can fit in a single network packet. For single-row retrievals, the overhead is negligible.

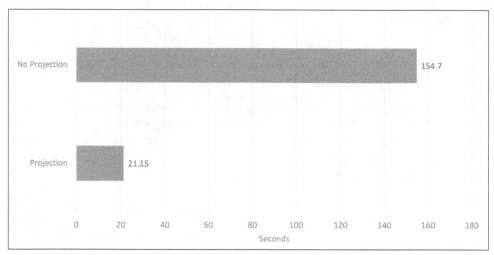

Figure 6-5. Improvement obtained by adding a projection to a query

Client-Side Caching

The best way to optimize a database request is to not send it at all. No matter how carefully we optimize the database—adding indexes, memory, fast disks, etc.—database requests are blocking operations that can never be made as fast as local computation. For most applications, database accesses are the slowest operations performed and the most critical component of application response time.

One of the most effective ways of avoiding unnecessary database calls is to cache frequently accessed static data in application code. Avoid asking the database repeatedly for the same data unless there's a chance that the data will change.

For instance, let's say that we have a function to return a user's name given a `userId`:

```
func getUserName(userId string) string {
    conn, err := pool.Acquire(context.Background())
    defer conn.Release()
    if err != nil {
        fmt.Fprintf(os.Stderr, "CockroachDB error: %v\n", err)
    }
    sql := `SELECT name FROM movr.users WHERE id=$1`
    rows, err := conn.Query(context.Background(), sql, userId)
    defer rows.Close()
    if err != nil {
        fmt.Fprintf(os.Stderr, "CockroachDB error: %v\n", err)
    }
    if !rows.Next() {
        return "Invalid userId"
    } else {
        var name string
        rows.Scan(&name)
```

```
        return (name)
    }
}
```

It's relatively simple to extend this function with a client-side cache. We just need to declare and initialize a map structure:

```
var userCache map[string]string

userCache = make(map[string]string)
```

Now in our function, we check this map to see if we can find the user's name. Only if the name does not exist in the cache do we go to the database:

```
func getCachedUserName(userId string) string {

    name, nameFound := userCache[userId]
    if !nameFound {
        conn, err := pool.Acquire(context.Background())
        defer conn.Release()
        if err != nil {
            fmt.Fprintf(os.Stderr, "CockroachDB error: %v\n", err)
        }
        fmt.Println("cache miss")
        sql := `SELECT name FROM movr.users WHERE id=$1`
        rows, err := conn.Query(context.Background(), sql, userId)
        defer rows.Close()
        if err != nil {
            fmt.Fprintf(os.Stderr, "CockroachDB error: %v\n", err)
        }
        if !rows.Next() {
            return "Invalid userId"
        } else {
            rows.Scan(&name)
            userCache[userId] = name
        }
    }
    return (name)
}
```

The performance improvements obtained by not going to the database are greater than any tuning of the database accesses themselves since we can never make a database access a zero-cost activity. However, bear in mind the following:

- Caches consume memory on the client program. In many environments, memory is abundant, and the tables considered for caching are relatively small. However, for large tables and memory-constrained environments, the implementation of a caching strategy could actually degrade performance by contributing to memory shortages in the application layer or client.

- If the table being cached is updated during program execution, then the changes may not be reflected in your cache unless you implement some sophisticated synchronization mechanism. For this reason, local caching is best performed on static tables.

Managing Transactions

Transactions provide an important mechanism for ensuring that related modifications succeed or fail as a unit. We discussed the internals of CockroachDB transactions back in Chapter 2.

The basics of programming transactions are common across a wide variety of SQL databases and even some non-SQL systems. A transaction is commenced with a BEGIN statement. Multiple SQL statements are executed within the transaction scope, and then all the changes are made permanent with the COMMIT statement. If an error is encountered during the transaction, all of the transaction's work can be abandoned with a ROLLBACK statement.

Example 6-1 shows a relatively simple transaction—implemented in Node.js Java-Script—that transfers money from one account to another, after first checking that there are sufficient funds.

Example 6-1. Example of a simple transaction

```
try {
    await connection.query('BEGIN TRANSACTION');
    // Check for sufficient funds
    const results = await connection.query(
        'SELECT balance FROM accounts WHERE id=$1',
        [fromId]
    );
    const fromBalance = results.rows[0].balance;
    if (fromBalance < transferAmt) {
        throw Error('Insufficient funds');
    }
    // Transfer the money
    await connection.query(`UPDATE accounts SET balance=balance-$1
                            WHERE id=$2`,
        [transferAmt, fromId]);
    await connection.query(`UPDATE accounts SET balance=balance+$1
                            WHERE id=$2`,
        [transferAmt, toId]);
    await connection.query('COMMIT');
    success = true;
} catch (error) {
    console.error(error.message);
    connection.query('ROLLBACK');
    success = false;
}
```

If you run this code in parallel, you'll find that some percentage of the transactions fail with an error something like this:

```
restart transaction: TransactionRetryWithProtoRefreshError:
WriteTooOldError: write at timestamp 16412
```

Transaction Retry Errors

In databases that default to lower levels of transaction isolation (PostgreSQL, for instance), this transaction would almost always succeed, perhaps failing only if there was a database outage. However, in `SERIALIZABLE` transaction isolation (which is the default in CockroachDB and an option in other databases), there is a good chance of transaction failure. If a concurrent transaction modifies the same table row between the time our transaction commences and the time we attempt to modify that row, then we will encounter a `TransactionRetryWithProtoRefreshError: WriteTooOldError` (we'll call this a *transaction retry* error for the sake of brevity).

Types of Transaction Retry Errors

The `WriteTooOldError` type of transaction retry is one of a family of errors—including `RETRY_SERIALIZABLE` and others that indicate that a retry can and probably should be attempted. While the various errors have different—and sometimes quite complex—underlying causes,[2] they all issue the same 40001 error code.

Figure 6-6 illustrates a possible sequence of events in two concurrent transactions that would lead to a transaction retry error.

The chance of receiving a transaction retry error depends on the chance of two transactions colliding on the same row. In one test, the percentage of retries varied from fewer than 1% if there were 10,000 distinct accounts involved to more than 75% when there were just 10 accounts.[3]

However, whatever the probability of encountering a transaction retry error, the possibility exists, and your application code should be able to cope with these expected error scenarios.

---

2 See the Cockroach documentation (*https://cockroa.ch/3u5fzeX*) for a complete discussion.

3 The simulation ran 100 concurrent threads randomly executing a transaction 10 times per second.

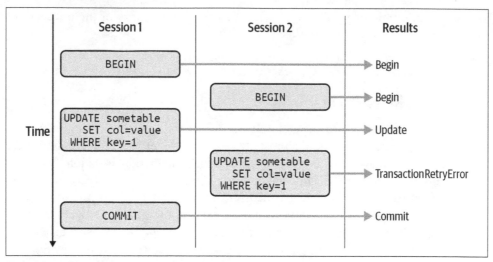

Figure 6-6. Transaction retry error scenario

Implementing Transaction Retries

The relatively obvious way to handle retry errors is to do exactly what the error code suggests—retry the transaction. When the transaction retry error is encountered, issue a ROLLBACK command to discard the work done so far in the transaction and try the transaction again. In Example 6-2, we add some logic to the Node.js method in Example 6-1 to retry the transaction when necessary.

Example 6-2. Transaction logic with retry handler

```
let retryCount = 0;
let transactionEnd = false;
while (!transactionEnd) {
    if (retryCount++ >= maxRetries) {
        throw Error('Maximum retry count exceeded');
    }
    try {
        await connection.query('BEGIN TRANSACTION');
        // Check for sufficient funds
        const results = await connection.query(
            'SELECT balance FROM accounts where id=$1',
            [fromId]
        );
        const fromBalance = results.rows[0].balance;
        if (fromBalance < transferAmt) {
            throw Error('Insufficient funds');
        }
        // Transfer the money
        await connection.query(
```

```
            `UPDATE accounts SET balance=balance-$1
                WHERE id=$2`,
            [transferAmt, fromId]
        );
        await connection.query(
            `UPDATE accounts SET balance=balance+$1
                WHERE id=$2`,
            [transferAmt, toId]
        );
        await connection.query('COMMIT');
        success = true;
        console.log('success');
    } catch (error) {
        if (error.code == '40001') { // Transaction retry error
            console.log(error.code, retryCount);
            connection.query('ROLLBACK');
            // Exponential backoff
            const sleepTime = (2 ** retryCount) * 100
                + Math.ceil(Math.random() * 100);
            await sleep(sleepTime);
        } else {
            console.log('aborted ', error.message);
            transactionEnd = true;
        }
    }
  }
 }
}
```

If this method encounters an error 40001—the retry transaction code—it issues a
ROLLBACK, waits for a short time, and then tries the transaction again.

In this implementation, the sleep time increases exponentially as the number of
retries increases. This is done to avoid a situation in which transactions "thrash"
on a resource. This exponential backoff strategy tends to reduce the load on a busy
system, but it can result in some high transaction waits for "unlucky" transactions.
Furthermore, when we retry transactions, there is no guarantee that updates will
succeed in the order in which they are originally submitted. Transactions that are
submitted first may succeed only after transactions that are submitted at a later time
commit.

Automatic Transaction Retries

The logic shown in the previous section can be implemented in any language.[4]
However, some drivers implement this logic for you transparently:

4 See the Cockroach documentation (*https://cockroa.ch/3uQ1Tny*) for a generic implementation.

- If a single statement that returns less than 16 KB of output (a single UPDATE, for instance, with no RETURNS clause) encounters a 40001, then CockroachDB will automatically retry the statement with no intervention required on your part. This logic applies to both implicit transactions (without a BEGIN statement) and explicit transactions with only a single statement. The retries will continue indefinitely unless the session variable statement_timeout is specified.

- The Go DBTools library includes a transaction retry handler for Go transactions. You pass a set of operations to the transaction handler, which will automatically retry transactions with a configurable retry limit and delay (*https://cockroa.ch/ 3x3F8PM*). The cockroach-go (*https://cockroa.ch/3K7HXmw*) project contains similar helper functions maintained by the CockroachDB team.

- Many object-relational mapping frameworks—SQLAlchemy for Python, for instance—will automatically retry transactions for you transparently. See the CockroachDB documentation (*https://cockroa.ch/3r3D0DL*) for further details.

Why Can't CockroachDB Handle All Transaction Retries?

Coding for transaction retries can seem tedious and since CockroachDB retries transactions automatically in some circumstances, why can't CockroachDB handle *all* retries automatically?

The short answer is that in many circumstances CockroachDB cannot determine the logical connection between different statements in a transaction. For instance, in Example 6-1, CockroachDB cannot know how the SELECT statement before the UPDATEs might affect the UPDATE logic. Only when the transaction is completely unambiguous—which only really happens when there's just a single statement in the transaction—can CockroachDB safely perform a retry.

Avoiding Transaction Retry Errors with FOR UPDATE

Performing transaction retries has some significant downsides. First, they are wasteful since work in the transaction that is done before the retry is discarded. Second, they introduce a delay in transaction processing that is unpredictable or even unnecessary. It's hard to know how long to sleep between transaction retries, and exponential backoffs can lead to some extreme waits. Finally, transaction retries result in nondeterministic behaviors. Transactions will not necessarily be applied to the database in the order in which they are submitted by the application, and even under identical workloads, differences in outcomes will be observed.

The alternative to the transaction retry approach is to "lock" the rows required at the beginning of the transaction with a FOR UPDATE statement. FOR UPDATE is a blocking statement, and once it returns, your transaction has the update rights over the rows concerned.

Here's our sample code with the FOR UPDATE logic:

```
try {
    await connection.query('BEGIN TRANSACTION');
    // Check for sufficient funds (and lock row)
    const results = await connection.query(
        `SELECT balance FROM accounts where id=$1
            FOR UPDATE`,
        [fromId]
    );
    const fromBalance = results.rows[0].balance;
    if (fromBalance < transferAmt) {
        throw Error('Insufficient funds');
    }
    // Lock second row
    await connection.query(
        `SELECT balance FROM accounts where id=$1
            FOR UPDATE`,
        [toId]
    );
    // Transfer the money
    await connection.query(
        `UPDATE accounts SET balance=balance-$1
            WHERE id=$2`,
        [transferAmt, fromId]
    );
    await connection.query(
        `UPDATE accounts SET balance=balance+$1
            WHERE id=$2`,
        [transferAmt, toId]
    );
    await connection.query('COMMIT');
    success = true;
    console.log('success');
} catch (error) {
    console.error(error.message);
    connection.query('ROLLBACK');
    success = false;
} }
```

By locking the ACCOUNTS rows with FOR UPDATE before actually issuing UPDATE statements, we avoid any chance of a transaction retry being issued. However, in a production implementation, it is probably advisable to include a transaction retry error handler in any transaction, even one that attempts to avoid a retry using FOR UPDATE because retry errors can still occur due to clock synchronization or other issues. For instance, the preceding code is vulnerable to a deadlock condition if simultaneous transfers between two accounts in opposite directions collide—we'll look more at deadlocks in a couple of pages.

Reducing Contention by Eliminating Hot Rows

The most significant cause of transaction retries is contention for a small number of "hot" rows.

Hot rows are those that are frequently changed by multiple database sessions.

Hot rows often indicate design flaws in the data model. For instance, if we decided to maintain running totals of account transfers per day, we might end up updating a single row after every transaction.

The use of embedded arrays or JSON data types can also create these sorts of issues. For example, it might seem convenient to maintain an array of measurements in a JSON document:

```
SELECT * FROM latest_measurements;

    "measurements": [{
            "locationid": "8a90ec6e-370a-4f90-bdc7-2f4bcdd381c2",
            "measurement": "32.6933968058154"
    }, {
            "locationid": "ccc240a0-3322-4a02-9538-23e0d98a39e5",
            "measurement": "1.1379426982748297"
    }, {
            "locationid": "15f41b26-f1a7-4d35-a88b-9f6bce022c7b",
            "measurement": "39.21261847039683"

    }, <snip>
    {
            "locationid": "f9b422d5-e9fd-44e7-8db3-35a243e45a95",
            "measurement": "25.66958037632363"
```

```
        }, {
            "locationid": "abdd31e7-b553-4798-896d-be492b11dbf1",
            "measurement": "41.09557231178944"
        }
    ]
}
```

This design might result in quick retrieval time but has now created a super hotspot. Keeping every location in its own row would be superior. Remember—denormalization should generally serve the goal of improving performance; beware of denormalizations that actually reduce throughput.

Reducing Transaction Elapsed Time

The longer a transaction runs, the greater the chance of contention with another transaction. Therefore, you should always move any time-consuming application logic—and certainly any human intervention—outside of the transaction. The code between the BEGIN and COMMIT (or ROLLBACK) statements should include only code critical to the transaction itself. For instance, the following is a variation on the transaction originally introduced in Example 6-1:

```
await connection.query('BEGIN TRANSACTION');
// Check for sufficient funds (and lock row)
const results = await connection.query(
    `SELECT balance FROM accounts where id=$1
        FOR UPDATE`,
    [fromId]
);
const fromBalance = results.rows[0].balance;
if (fromBalance < transferAmt) {
    throw Error('Insufficient funds');
}
// Lock second row
await connection.query(
    `SELECT balance FROM accounts where id=$1
        FOR UPDATE`,
    [toId]
);

// Perform anti-money laundering check
await performAMLCheckViaRESTCall(txnDetails);

// Transfer the money
await connection.query(
    `UPDATE accounts SET balance=balance-$1
        WHERE id=$2`,
    [transferAmt, fromId]
);
await connection.query(
    `UPDATE accounts SET balance=balance+$1
        WHERE id=$2`,
```

```
        [transferAmt, toId]
    );
    await connection.query('COMMIT');
```

The `performAMLCheckViaRESTCall()` performs an anti-money-laundering (AML) check via a REST call—which might take a few seconds in the worst-case scenario. We issued this call after issuing a `FOR UPDATE` statement. While this might make sense from a logical point of view (not checking with the AML authorities until we are sure the transaction will go through), the extra duration of the `FOR UPDATE` locks will reduce throughput significantly. It would be better from a performance point of view to perform the AML check before commencing the transaction.

A similar effect can occur in retry logic. If unnecessary time-consuming statements occur within a transaction with retry logic, then the chance of a retry is increased with a consequent decrease in throughput.

Reordering Statements

The ordering of DML statements within a transaction can have a big impact on contention. Generally, the statement most likely to involve contention should be placed first in the transaction sequence. Placing the contentious statement first has several good implications:

- CockroachDB can automatically retry the first statement in a transaction transparently, without requiring explicit handling.
- If the transaction fails, it will fail before the execution of other statements. The execution and rollback of these other statements will involve overhead on the server.

In Figure 6-6, moving the `UPDATE` of location ahead of the insert into `measurements` eliminated explicit retries completely (though there would still have been transparent, automatic retries). In one benchmark, average transaction time was reduced by about 35%. Although the impact of the reordering statement will vary from case to case, in general, moving the most contentious statements earlier in the transaction sequence will be worthwhile.

Time Travel Queries

If a transaction attempts to read data that has a higher timestamp than the transaction start time, then a retry error will occur. For read operations, we can avoid these errors by using `AS OF SYSTEM TIME`.

This can be particularly important for read-only transactions in which you want consistent results from multiple `SELECT` statements but don't need these results to be completely up-to-date with respect to the system time. You can include the `AS OF`

SYSTEM TIME in a SELECT statement or in a BEGIN statement. If included in the BEGIN statement, then the transaction is a read-only transaction with read consistency as of the timestamp provided.

For instance, here, we read from rides and user_ride_counts consistently. Without the AS OF SYSTEM TIME clause, a concurrent write to rides or user_ride_counts might cause the transaction to fail.

```
cursor.execute('ROLLBACK')
cursor.execute("BEGIN AS OF SYSTEM TIME '-10s'" )
top10cities=cursor.execute('''SELECT city,count(*)
                              FROM movr.rides GROUP BY city
                              ORDER BY 2 DESC LIMIT 10''')
top10users=cursor.execute('''SELECT name, rides
                             FROM movr.user_ride_counts
                             ORDER BY  rides DESC LIMIT 10''')
cursor.execute('COMMIT')
```

Ambiguous Transactions Errors

In a distributed system, some errors can have ambiguous results. For example, if you receive a connection closed error while processing a COMMIT statement, you cannot tell whether the transaction was successfully committed or not. These errors are possible in any database, but CockroachDB is somewhat more likely to produce them than other databases because ambiguous results can be caused by failures between the nodes of a cluster. These errors are reported with the PostgreSQL error code 40003(statement_completion_unknown).

Ambiguous errors can be caused by nodes crashing, network failures, or timeouts. Note that ambiguity is possible for only the last statement of a transaction (COMMIT or RELEASE SAVEPOINT) or for statements outside a transaction. If a connection drops during a transaction that has not yet tried to commit, the transaction will definitely be aborted.

In general, you should handle ambiguous errors the same way as connection closed errors. If your transaction is idempotent—capable of being executed multiple times with the same result—it's safe to retry it on ambiguous errors. UPSERT operations are typically idempotent (providing there are no dynamically allocated column values), and other transactions can be written to be idempotent by verifying the expected state before performing any writes. Increment operations such as UPDATE my_table SET x=x+1 WHERE id=$1 are typical examples of operations that cannot easily be made idempotent. For a detailed discussion of idempotency keys, see @brandur's blog post (*https://cockroa.ch/3JeOtqo*).

If your transaction is not idempotent, then you should decide to retry based on whether it would be better for your application to apply the transaction twice or return an error to the user.

Deadlocks

Transaction retry errors can also occur with FOR UPDATE if two sessions lock resources wanted by the other. For instance, in Figure 6-7, we see that two sessions have each locked resources wanted by the other. Session 1 has a lock on id=1 and wants to lock id=2. Session 2 has a lock on id=2 and wants to lock id=1. This situation can never resolve, so CockroachDB will terminate one of the sessions, which will have to retry the transaction.

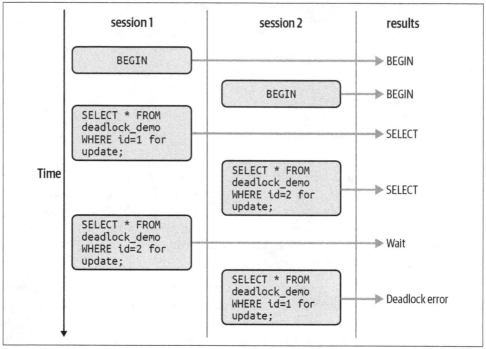

Figure 6-7. Deadlocks occur when two sessions each lock a resource wanted by the other

Deadlocks are rare and can be made more unlikely if transactions always lock resources in a specific order. However, it's hard to be completely sure that a deadlock will never occur in a complex application. The solution is to ensure that all critical transactions have retry logic.

If the transactions in a deadlock scenario have different priorities, CockroachDB allows the transaction with higher priority to abort the other, which must then retry. If the transactions have the same priority, one is selected randomly to abort.

Transaction Priorities

Transactions can be associated with priorities, and—in the event of a conflict—a higher-priority transaction will be favored over a lower-priority transaction. Adjusting transaction priorities can ensure that critical transactions don't get blocked by lower-priority work. However, these decisions should be made very deliberately. It's possible for lower-priority transactions to be deferred indefinitely on a busy system, which might be more undesirable than a delay for the high-priority workload.

Transaction priorities can be set using the SET TRANSACTION command. By default, all transactions have the NORMAL priority.

Summary of Transaction Approaches

We've looked at a lot of transaction execution patterns, and you may be feeling that the "correct" way to program a CockroachDB transaction is not clear. Fair enough—there is indeed more than one way to do it. However, the following guidelines are generally applicable:

- Your critical transactions should include some form of retry logic. Even if you avoid retry errors using every technique we have explored, there's still a chance of a retry error due to contention on internal resources.

- Transactions should be kept as short in scope and duration as possible. Any statement that is not needed within the transaction should be moved out of scope.

- The DML most likely to cause a conflict should be placed first in the transaction.

- If preserving order in the queue is important, use the FOR UPDATE statement to lock resources before modifying them. This pessimistic locking pattern will not always be faster, but it will tend to ensure that transactions get processed in the order in which they are received.

- For read-only transactions, consider performing "time travel" queries with AS OF SYSTEM TIME to avoid transaction retries.

- When possible, batching all the SQL statements in the transaction into a single request can improve performance and simplify retry logic. Be mindful of the possibility of SQL injection in these batched routines.

Working with ORM Frameworks

Object-relational mapping (ORM) frameworks automate the mapping of program objects to relational structures and reduce or eliminate the need to use SQL language instructions in program code.

ORMs are popular because they reduce code complexity and relieve the developer from the need to manually determine the way in which object-oriented program artifacts map to relational tables. On the other hand, ORMs sometimes reduce the flexibility provided by a relational database and can result in less-than-optimal performance.

Since the ORM layer is on top of the SQL layer and since the CockroachDB SQL layer is PostgreSQL-compatible, most PostgreSQL ORMs will work with CockroachDB without modification. In some cases, the CockroachDB team has worked with the ORM maintainer to ensure compatibility with CockroachDB. You can see a list of supported ORMs in the CockroachDB documentation (*https://cockroa.ch/3j6S8fb*), together with instructions on installing any necessary CockroachDB prerequisites.

Table 6-1 summarizes some of the ORM framework options for CockroachDB.

Table 6-1. Object-relational mapping systems for CockroachDB

Go	Java	Python	JavaScript
GORM	Hibernate	SQLAlchemy	Sequelize
	jOOQ	Django	TypeORM
		PonyORM	
		peewee	

We don't have space to explore all the options for using the various ORMs, and there are plenty of examples within the CockroachDB documentation. But let's review the essential workflow using one of the original ORMs: Hibernate for Java.

The code in this section is borrowed from the CockroachDB Hibernate example on GitHub (*https://cockroa.ch/3u7kGLP*).

The Hibernate configuration is stored in an XML file and tells Hibernate how to connect to the backend database and which SQL language dialect to use. The following configuration file tells Hibernate to use the PostgreSQL driver and provides the connection URL, username, and password:

```
<hibernate-configuration>
    <session-factory>
        <!-- Database connection settings -->
        <property name="hibernate.connection.driver_class">
org.postgresql.Driver</property>
        <property name="hibernate.dialect">
org.hibernate.dialect.CockroachDB201Dialect</property>
        <property name="hibernate.connection.url">
jdbc:postgresql://localhost:26257/bank?ssl=true&amp;sslmode=require</property>
        <property name="hibernate.connection.username">maxroach</property>
        <property name="hibernate.connection.password">password</property>
        <property name="hibernate.hbm2ddl.auto">create-drop</property>
```

```
        </session-factory>
    </hibernate-configuration>
```

Note the property `hibernate.dialect` is set to `org.hibernate.dialect.Cock roachDB201Dialect`; this should correspond to the version of CockroachDB being connected to.

In the user code, we create classes that map to database tables and methods within those classes that define operations that can be performed on those tables. For example, here we create an `Accounts` class. Annotations tell Hibernate that this class will map to the `ACCOUNTS` table:

```java
@Entity
@Table(name = "accounts")
public static class Account {
    @Id
    @Column(name = "id")
    public long id;
    public long getId() {
        return id;
    }
    @Column(name = "balance")
    public BigDecimal balance;
    public BigDecimal getBalance() {
        return balance;
    }
    public void setBalance(BigDecimal newBalance) {
        this.balance = newBalance;
    }
    // Convenience constructor.
    public Account(int id, int balance) {
        this.id = id;
        this.balance = BigDecimal.valueOf(balance);
    }
    // Hibernate needs a default constructor to create model objects.
    public Account() {
    }
}
```

We can now write functions that manipulate the database by using these Hibernate methods without executing SQL code:

```java
private static Function<Session, BigDecimal> transferFunds
  (long fromId, long toId, BigDecimal amount) throws JDBCException {
    Function<Session, BigDecimal> f = s -> {
        BigDecimal rv = new BigDecimal(0);
        try {
            Account fromAccount = (Account) s.get(Account.class, fromId);
            Account toAccount = (Account) s.get(Account.class, toId);
            if (!(amount.compareTo(fromAccount.getBalance()) > 0)) {
                fromAccount.balance = fromAccount.balance.subtract(amount);
                toAccount.balance = toAccount.balance.add(amount);
```

```
                s.save(fromAccount);
                s.save(toAccount);
                rv = amount;
                System.out.printf(
                        "APP: transferFunds(%d, %d, %.2f) --> %.2f\n",
                        fromId, toId, amount, rv);
            }
        } catch (JDBCException e) {
            throw e;
        }
        return rv;
    };
    return f;
}
```

This code is fairly standard Hibernate code that would work on almost any SQL database. However, as we've seen, CockroachDB does have some unique transactional behaviors, and these may need to be accounted for in a nontrivial application. In the Java Hibernate example, the CockroachDB team defined a runTransaction method. It takes as its argument a function containing commands that might trigger a retry Transaction error. The method retries the transaction using the exponential backoff strategy shown in Figure 6-6:

```
private static BigDecimal runTransaction(
                Session session,
                Function<Session, BigDecimal> fn) {
    BigDecimal rv = new BigDecimal(0);
    int attemptCount = 0;
    while (attemptCount < MAX_ATTEMPT_COUNT) {
        attemptCount++;
        if (attemptCount > 1) {
            System.out.printf(
                "APP: Entering retry loop again, iteration %d\n",
                attemptCount);
        }
        Transaction txn = session.beginTransaction();
        System.out.printf("APP: BEGIN;\n");
        if (attemptCount == MAX_ATTEMPT_COUNT) {
            String err = String.format("hit max of %s attempts, aborting",
                MAX_ATTEMPT_COUNT);
            throw new RuntimeException(err);
        }
        try {
            rv = fn.apply(session);
            if (!rv.equals(-1)) {
                txn.commit();
                System.out.printf("APP: COMMIT;\n");
                break;
            }
        } catch (JDBCException e) {
            if (RETRY_SQL_STATE.equals(e.getSQLState())) {
```

```
                // Exponential backoff
                System.out.printf("APP: retryable exception occurred:\n sql
   state = [%s]\n     message = [%s]\n    retry counter = %s\n", e.getSQLState(),
   e.getMessage(), attemptCount);
                System.out.printf("APP: ROLLBACK;\n");
                txn.rollback();
                int sleepMillis = (int) (Math.pow(2, attemptCount) * 100) +
                    RAND.nextInt(100);
                System.out.printf("APP: Hit 40001 transaction retry error,
   sleeping %s milliseconds\n", sleepMillis);
                try {
                    Thread.sleep(sleepMillis);
                } catch (InterruptedException ignored) {
                    // no-op
                }
                rv = BigDecimal.valueOf(-1);
            } else {
                throw e;
            }
        }
    }
    return rv;
}
```

Different ORM frameworks have different approaches to configuration and coding, but the general practices are similar. Table 6-2 summarizes your options.

Table 6-2. Options for retrying transactions in ORMs

Language/ORM	Retry transaction procedure
SQLAlchemy	Use the `sqlalchemy_cockroachdb.run_transaction()` method
Django (*https://cockroa.ch/3NLktWo*)	Define a transaction retry loop in the decorator function
PonyORM (*https://cockroa.ch/3uTz8WT*)	Provide the retry option for the `db_session` decorator
GORM (*https://cockroa.ch/3x3sdgE*)	Wrap the function call in `crdbgorm.ExecuteTx()`
Java (*https://cockroa.ch/3u6MGz5*)	Use the `runTransaction()` method

Summary

In this chapter, we covered topics relating to application development with CockroachDB.

Because CockroachDB is highly compatible with PostgreSQL and somewhat compatible with many other SQL databases, the basics of software development in CockroachDB are not unique. Best practices for software development include the use of connection pools, bulk processing, minimizing network traffic, and avoiding unnecessary database requests.

The CockroachDB serializable consistency model is stricter than many other SQL databases, and that, together with the higher possibility of conflicts in a distributed database, does lead to the possibility of transactional conflicts. There are two major patterns for dealing with these conflicts—retrying transactions (optimistic transactions) or locking data with FOR UPDATE before modification (pessimistic transactions). Both patterns are valid, but regardless of which pattern you use, transaction retry logic is recommended.

Application Migration and Integration

As a thoroughly modern database system, CockroachDB is a perfect choice for new application development. However, it's also a good choice for the modernization of existing applications. Many applications built on the last generation of relational database systems are now facing limitations that can sensibly be addressed only by a migration to a distributed architecture. In many cases, a distributed SQL-based system such as CockroachDB is the most attractive migration target because it does not—unlike distributed NoSQL systems—require a complete rework of the application's data model or code base. In this chapter, we'll explain how to move data from existing databases into CockroachDB.

Moving data into CockroachDB is just one part of the story. While CockroachDB is a general-purpose database system, its sweet spot is undoubtedly operational transactional processing. In many environments, the data that is processed within CockroachDB will be leveraged for business intelligence or data science purposes in combination with data from other operational systems. In these cases, we will want a mechanism for moving data into external systems. The CockroachDB change data capture (CDC) facility is invaluable for this purpose—we'll see how CDC can be used to move data into external systems such as Snowflake DB or Kafka. We'll also see how data can be dumped from CockroachDB directly to external files.

Loading Data

The first step in using CockroachDB is often to move data into the database from legacy systems or other sources. The most fundamental data load activity in CockroachDB is to load data from "flat files." CockroachDB can load data from delimited files—such as the ubiquitous CSV file—or from the Avro format. Data is loaded using the `IMPORT` command introduced in Chapter 4.

File Locations

In monolithic databases, loading data from flat files is typically done directly from files on filesystems—typically staged to the database server first to avoid network overhead. However, as a distributed cloud native database, CockroachDB takes a slightly different tack.

The `IMPORT` command requires that files are located on cloud storage (S3, GCP buckets, Azure containers), "userfiles" uploaded to the CockroachDB server, or HTTP file servers.

userfile storage

Let's start with uploading a file to cluster userfile storage. *Userfile* storage is a sort of virtual filestore maintained by the CockroachDB cluster, allowing access to files from the SQL layer across the entire cluster.

The `cockroach userfile upload` command allows you to copy a file to cluster storage. The file will be accessible only to the user who uploaded the file:

```
$ cockroach userfile upload employees.csv employees.csv --url $CRDB_CLUSTER

successfully uploaded to userfile://defaultdb.public.userfiles_guy/employees.csv
```

Nodelocal storage is similar to userfile storage but loads the file to just one of the nodes of the cluster. It is less secure than userfile storage—since it can be accessed from any CockroachDB database account—and less robust since an `IMPORT` from userfile storage can survive a node failure. On the other hand, a nodelocal upload is somewhat faster to execute.

The `cockroach nodelocal upload` command uploads a file to nodelocal storage:

```
$ cockroach nodelocal upload employees.csv employees.csv --url $CRDB_LOCAL

successfully uploaded to nodelocal://1/employees.csv
```

Both commands return the location for the file; you'll need that to load the file into tables later.

HTTP storage

CockroachDB can also access files held on local filesystems by running an HTTP file server such as Caddy (*https://cockroa.ch/3r2Dt9u*) or Nginx (*https://cockroa.ch/33SYmLC*).

Cloud storage

For large files, nodelocal and userlocal storage results in disk space and I/O being consumed on at least one of the cluster nodes, which may be less than ideal. Therefore, CockroachDB supports cloud storage locations, including Google Cloud Storage, Amazon S3 buckets, and Azure Storage containers.

In this example, we create a Google Cloud Storage bucket and upload a CSV file to that location. The example assumes that we are already logged in to Google Cloud.

```
$ ~ gsutil mb gs://cockroachdefinitiveguide
Creating gs://cockroachdefinitiveguide/...
$ gsutil cp employees.csv gs://cockroachdefinitiveguide
Copying file://employees.csv [Content-Type=text/csv]...
/ [1 files][  8.8 KiB/  8.8 KiB]
Operation completed over 1 objects/8.8 KiB.
$ gsutil ls gs://cockroachdefinitiveguide/
gs://cockroachdefinitiveguide/employees.csv
```

Here we upload the same file to an Azure container with the URL:

```
$ az storage container create --name cockroachdbdefinitiveguide
    --account-name crdbdg

{
  "created": true
}
$ az storage copy -s employees.csv -d
    https://crdbdg.blob.core.windows.net/cockroachdbdefinitiveguide

 <snip>
TotalBytesTransferred: 9011
Final Job Status: Completed
```

Finally, we upload this file to Amazon S3 storage. As with the other examples, we've already configured our AWS authentication:

```
$ aws s3 mb s3://cockroachdefinitiveguide
make_bucket: cockroachdefinitiveguide
$ aws s3 cp employees.csv s3://cockroachdefinitiveguide
upload: ./employees.csv to s3://cockroachdefinitiveguide/employees.csv
```

Importing Files

Once you have your file in cloud, userlocal, or other accessible storage, you'll typically use the IMPORT command to load the data.

Data can be loaded from an uploaded file by using the IMPORT INTO command.

Figure 7-1 shows the syntax of the IMPORT statement.

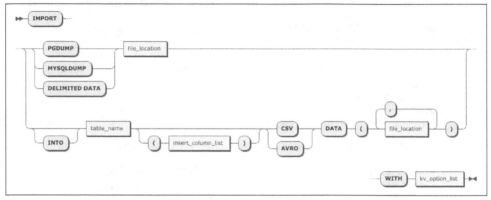

Figure 7-1. IMPORT statement syntax

You'll need appropriate privileges (*https://cockroa.ch/3x4SdIq*) on the target table.

Importing from userfile storage

Here's an example of IMPORT INTO, loading data into a new table and loading data from the userfile location that we created in the previous section.

First, we upload the CSV file:

```
$ cockroach userfile upload departments.csv departments.csv \
    --url $CRDB_CLUSTER
  uploaded to userfile://defaultdb.public.userfiles_guy/departments.csv
```

Now we create the table and import the data:

```
guy@cockroachlabs.cloud:26257/defaultdb>
CREATE TABLE departments
    (   department_id integer PRIMARY KEY,
        department_name varchar,
        manager_id integer,
        location_id integer

    ) ;
CREATE TABLE

Time: 40ms total (execution 24ms / network 16ms)
```

```
guy@cockroachlabs.cloud:26257/defaultdb>
IMPORT INTO departments
    ( department_id,department_name,manager_id,location_id  )
    ("userfile://defaultdb.public.userfiles_guy/departments.csv")
        WITH skip='1', nullif = '';

        job_id       | status   | fraction_c | rows | index_entries | bytes
--------------------+----------+------------+------+---------------+--------
  678724479937937414 | succeeded |          1 |   27 |             0 |   771
(1 row)


Time: 550ms total (execution 532ms / network 18ms)
```

In the previous examples, we specified WITH skip=1, nullif = ''; this signified that we should skip the first line of the CSV file (which consisted of a header line) and treat blanks as null values. These two options are commonly used. Other options are shown in in Table 7-1.

Table 7-1. Common options for IMPORT

Option	Usage	Default
delimiter	The Unicode character that delimits columns in your rows.	,
comment	The Unicode character that identifies rows to skip.	
strict_quotes	Use if CSV import files have quotes ("") within rows to prevent multiple rows from being treated as single rows.	Off
nullif	The string that should be converted to NULL.	
skip	The number of rows to be skipped while importing a file.	0.
decompress	The decompression codec to be used: gzip, bzip, auto, or none. Default: *auto*, which guesses based on file extension (.gz, .bz, .bz2). none disables decompression.	
rows_terminated_by	The Unicode character to indicate newlines in the input file.	\n
fields_terminated_by	The Unicode character is used to separate fields in each input line.	\t
fields_enclosed_by	The Unicode character that encloses fields.	"
fields_escaped_by	The Unicode character, when preceding one of the above DELIMITED DATA options, to be interpreted literally. Often the "\" symbol serves the purpose.	

Importing from Cloud Storage

Specifying userfile or nodelocal file locations is relatively simple, but in many cases, cloud storage is a more suitable option. When specifying a cloud location, we need to also specify credentials to allow the connection to succeed. For instance, if we uploaded the departments data to Amazon S3 as follows:

```
$ aws s3 cp departments.csv s3://cockroachdefinitiveguide
upload: ./departments.csv to s3://cockroachdefinitiveguide/departments.csv
```

we need to specify our AWS access keys when referencing the file from within an IMPORT statement:

```
defaultdb>
IMPORT INTO  departments
   ( department_id,department_name,manager_id,location_id  )
    CSV DATA (
"s3://cockroachdefinitiveguide/departments.csv?
AWS_ACCESS_KEY_ID=key
&AWS_SECRET_ACCESS_KEY=key")
       WITH skip='1', nullif = '';

        job_id      | status   | fraction | rows | index_entries | bytes
--------------------+----------+----------+------+---------------+--------
  678728775096893441 | succeeded |       1 |   27 |            0 |   771
(1 row)

Time: 1.379s total (execution 1.363s / network 0.016s)
```

To avoid including access keys in SQL commands, you can specify authentication in environment variables. Similar authentication mechanisms are provided for Google Cloud and Azure Storage systems. See the CockroachDB documentation (*https://cock roa.ch/3Jcq58C*) for more information.

Publicly Accessible Cloud Storage

Specifying cloud storage authentication parameters can be awkward. You might be tempted to use publicly accessible buckets or file settings to avoid the pain. This is usually a Very Bad Idea—it potentially exposes sensitive data to the world and may even be illegal if the confidential information protected by HIPAA (the US Health Insurance Portability and Accountability Act) or similar legislation is exposed.

Note that IMPORT INTO invalidates all foreign key constraints on the target table. These foreign keys need to be re-enabled using the VALIDATE CONSTRAINT command.

We'll see some examples of using IMPORT with PostgreSQL and MySQL dump files later in the chapter.

Import Performance

Import performance can vary markedly depending on the format of the data, and the sequencing of DDL commands. It's often best to defer index and constraint creation until after the data load and to use compact data formats. The effectiveness of these strategies can depend on network bandwidth, memory constraints, and other factors. For a discussion of import performance, consult the CockroachDB documentation (*https://cockroa.ch/3DBBlKE*).

Migrating from Another Database

There are a variety of ways to migrate from one database system to another. The most straightforward way is:

1. Extract DDL from the source system and convert that DDL to CockroachDB-compatible CREATE TABLE, INDEX, VIEW, and other statements.

2. Dump table data from the source system to CSV or another flat-file format.

3. Import the flat files using the IMPORT or IMPORT INTO statements.

This procedure copies static data only—for a live system, you may need to implement custom procedures to synchronize the state of the source and target system and perform a cutover with minimal downtime. Every software migration will be different, but we discuss a few common approaches next.

Extracting and Converting DDL

Most database systems provide mechanisms for generating DDL statements for schema objects. Coming up, we'll look at a few platform-specific techniques. However, some cross-platform IDEs can generate DDL for multiple types of database systems.

For example, we can generate DDL from the DBeaver object tree for most of the SQL database systems supported by DBeaver (which is practically all). In Figure 7-2, we generate a CREATE TABLE statement for the departments table in the AdventureWorks sample schema.

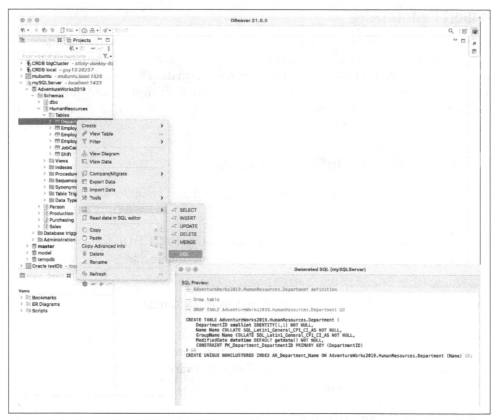

Figure 7-2. Generating DDL using DBeaver (large format version (https://cockroa.ch/cockroachDB-figs))

Extracting Oracle DDL

Oracle includes the dbms_metadata package, which can generate DDL for Oracle objects. The package includes settings that suppress or allow various storage clauses and other Oracle-specific information, resulting in an output that is closer to Cock-roachDB compatibility than would otherwise be the case. Example 7-1 shows a script that will emit DDL for all Oracle tables, indexes, and views in a specific Oracle account.

Example 7-1. Script to extract Oracle DDL

```
set long 100000
set head off
set echo off
set pagesize 0
set verify off
set feedback off
```

```
col DDL format a256

REM These statements limit Oracle-specific clauses generated
EXECUTE dbms_metadata.SET_TRANSFORM_PARAM(
dbms_metadata.SESSION_TRANSFORM,'SEGMENT_CREATION',false);
EXECUTE dbms_metadata.SET_TRANSFORM_PARAM(
dbms_metadata.SESSION_TRANSFORM,'CONSTRAINTS_AS_ALTER',true);
EXECUTE dbms_metadata.set_transform_param(
dbms_metadata.session_transform,'TABLESPACE',false);
EXECUTE dbms_metadata.set_transform_param(
dbms_metadata.session_transform,'STORAGE',false);
EXECUTE dbms_metadata.set_transform_param(
dbms_metadata.session_transform,'SEGMENT_ATTRIBUTES',false);
EXECUTE dbms_metadata.set_transform_param (
dbms_metadata.session_transform, 'SQLTERMINATOR', true);
EXECUTE dbms_metadata.set_transform_param (
dbms_metadata.session_transform, 'PRETTY', true);

SELECT dbms_metadata.get_ddl('TABLE', table_name,user) AS  ddl FROM user_tables;
SELECT dbms_metadata.get_ddl('INDEX', index_name,user) AS  ddl FROM user_indexes;
SELECT dbms_metadata.get_ddl('VIEW',view_name,user) AS ddl FROM user_views;

EXIT
```

Example 7-1 generates the DDL shown in Example 7-2.

Example 7-2. Example of Oracle DDL

```
CREATE TABLE "HR"."EMPLOYEES"
   (   "EMPLOYEE_ID" NUMBER(6,0),
       "FIRST_NAME" VARCHAR2(20),
       "LAST_NAME" VARCHAR2(25) CONSTRAINT "EMP_LAST_NAME_NN" NOT NULL ENABLE,
       "EMAIL" VARCHAR2(25) CONSTRAINT "EMP_EMAIL_NN" NOT NULL ENABLE,
       "PHONE_NUMBER" VARCHAR2(20),
       "HIRE_DATE" DATE CONSTRAINT "EMP_HIRE_DATE_NN" NOT NULL ENABLE,
       "JOB_ID" VARCHAR2(10) CONSTRAINT "EMP_JOB_NN" NOT NULL ENABLE,
       "SALARY" NUMBER(8,2),
       "COMMISSION_PCT" NUMBER(2,2),
       "MANAGER_ID" NUMBER(6,0),
       "DEPARTMENT_ID" NUMBER(4,0)
   ) ;
CREATE UNIQUE INDEX "HR"."EMP_EMP_ID_PK" ON "HR"."EMPLOYEES" ("EMPLOYEE_ID")
  ;
ALTER TABLE "HR"."EMPLOYEES" ADD CONSTRAINT "EMP_EMP_ID_PK"
  PRIMARY KEY("EMPLOYEE_ID")
  USING INDEX "HR"."EMP_EMP_ID_PK"  ENABLE;
ALTER TABLE "HR"."EMPLOYEES" ADD CONSTRAINT "EMP_DEPT_FK"
  FOREIGN KEY ("DEPARTMENT_ID")
    REFERENCES "HR"."DEPARTMENTS" ("DEPARTMENT_ID") ENABLE;
```

We still have some work to do to make this DDL CockroachDB-compatible:

- First, we need to convert data types to CockroachDB types. The Oracle NUMBER type encapsulates both INTEGER and FLOAT types, depending on the precision provided. VARCHAR2 maps to VARCHAR. There are many esoteric Oracle data types, but in the majority of cases, date and number conversions will dominate.

- The ENABLE clauses are unknown to CockroachDB and need to be removed, as do the USING INDEX clauses.

The following **sed** commands will perform a lot of the edits required:

```
s/VARCHAR2(.*)/VARCHAR/g
s/NUMBER(.*,0)/INT/g
s/NUMBER(.*,.*)/DECIMAL(\1)/g
s/NUMBER\((.*),\*\)/FLOAT(\1)/g
s/NUMBER/FLOAT/g
s/USING INDEX (.*) ENABLE//g
s/USING INDEX //g
s/ENABLE//g
s/\"(.*)\"\.//g
```

So, if we called the script in Example 7-1 getDDLOracle.sql, then we could generate the DDL for a schema and perform some initial edits as follows:

```
sql -S hr/hr@local @getDDLOracle.sql |sed -f oracle.sed

CREATE TABLE "HR"."JOBS"
 (    "JOB_ID" VARCHAR,
      "JOB_TITLE" VARCHAR CONSTRAINT "JOB_TITLE_NN" NOT NULL,
      "MIN_SALARY" INT,
      "MAX_SALARY" INT
 ) ;
CREATE UNIQUE INDEX "HR"."JOB_ID_PK" ON "HR"."JOBS" ("JOB_ID")
;
ALTER TABLE "HR"."JOBS" ADD CONSTRAINT "JOB_ID_PK" PRIMARY KEY ("JOB_ID")
  "HR"."JOB_ID_PK"  ;
```

More changes to the SQL will usually be required. For instance, in the example DDL, the JOB_ID is initially created without the NOT NULL constraint—Oracle allows nullable primary keys. The primary key is added after the CREATE TABLE by an ALTER TABLE statement. However, in CockroachDB, a primary key column must also be NOT NULL. Furthermore, it's best practice in CockroachDB to specify the PRIMARY KEY within the CREATE TABLE statement; otherwise, a hidden primary key field will be created.

Extracting DDL from SQL Server

There's no direct way to generate DDL from SQL Server T-SQL commands, but you can extract DDL from the Microsoft Management Studio (From Tasks → Generate

Scripts). Some users have created stored procedures to generate DDL (*https://cock roa.ch/3uRymtu*). You can also use DBeaver as described previously.

Extracting DDL from MySQL

MySQL supports a SHOW CREATE command, which can be used to extract DDL for a particular object. For instance, in the following code, we extract the DDL for the customer table in the Sakila schema:

```
$ mysql -uroot -D sakila -s -N
mysql> show create table customer;

customer        CREATE TABLE `customer` (\n
`customer_id` smallint unsigned NOT NULL AUTO_INCREMENT,\n
`store_id` tinyint unsigned NOT NULL,\n
`first_name` varchar(45) NOT NULL,\n
`last_name` varchar(45) NOT NULL,\n  `email` varchar(50) DEFAULT NULL,\n
`address_id` smallint unsigned NOT NULL,\n
`active` tinyint(1) NOT NULL DEFAULT '1',\n
`create_date` datetime NOT NULL,\n
`last_update` timestamp NULL DEFAULT CURRENT_TIMESTAMP
        ON UPDATE CURRENT_TIMESTAMP,\n
PRIMARY KEY (`customer_id`),\n
KEY `idx_fk_store_id` (`store_id`),\n
KEY `idx_fk_address_id` (`address_id`),\n
KEY `idx_last_name` (`last_name`),\n
CONSTRAINT `fk_customer_address` FOREIGN KEY (`address_id`)
REFERENCES `address` (`address_id`) ON DELETE RESTRICT ON UPDATE CASCADE,\n
CONSTRAINT `fk_customer_store` FOREIGN KEY (`store_id`)
REFERENCES `store` (`store_id`) ON DELETE RESTRICT ON UPDATE CASCADE\n)
ENGINE=InnoDB AUTO_INCREMENT=600 DEFAULT CHARSET=utf8mb4
COLLATE=utf8mb4_0900_ai_ci
```

You can also dump all the DDL for a schema using the mysqldump command with the -d option. -d suppresses data in the output.

```
$ sakila-db mysqldump -d -u root sakila
-- MySQL dump 10.13  Distrib 8.0.23, for osx10.16 (x86_64)
--

/*!40101 SET @OLD_CHARACTER_SET_CLIENT=@@CHARACTER_SET_CLIENT */;
<snip>
/*!40111 SET @OLD_SQL_NOTES=@@SQL_NOTES, SQL_NOTES=0 */;


--
-- Table structure for table `actor`
--

DROP TABLE IF EXISTS `actor`;
CREATE TABLE `actor` (
  `actor_id` smallint unsigned NOT NULL AUTO_INCREMENT,
  `first_name` varchar(45) NOT NULL,
```

```
    `last_name` varchar(45) NOT NULL,
    `last_update` timestamp NOT NULL DEFAULT CURRENT_TIMESTAMP
      ON UPDATE CURRENT_TIMESTAMP,
    PRIMARY KEY (`actor_id`),
    KEY `idx_actor_last_name` (`last_name`)
  ) ENGINE=InnoDB AUTO_INCREMENT=201 DEFAULT CHARSET=utf8mb4
    COLLATE=utf8mb4_0900_ai_ci;
```

MySQL SQL is largely compatible with CockroachDB, but you will want to remove the `ENGINE` and `CHARSET` directives. CockroachDB does support the `COLLATE` keyword, but the syntax is not identical. Also, MySQL surrounds literal names with backticks (`` ` ``)—these will need to be changed to double quotes for CockroachDB. In the example, you'll also need to remove the `ON UPDATE` and `AUTO_INCREMENT` flags.

Finally, secondary indexes in MySQL `CREATE TABLE` statements are shown as `KEY` elements in the `CREATE TABLE` statement. These will need to be removed and transformed to `CREATE INDEX` statements or to `INDEX` statements embedded within the `CREATE TABLE` statement.

In some cases, you might be able to directly import a MySQL dump file; we'll look at this option later in this chapter.

Extracting DDL from PostgreSQL

You can extract DDL from a PostgreSQL database by using the `pg_dump` command with the `-s` or `--schema-only` options. Here we dump the SQL from the DVDRental sample database.[1] You can also specify the `-t` option to extract DDL for a specific table in the DVDRental database:

```
$ pg_dump -s dvdrental -t customer
--
-- PostgreSQL database dump
--


-- Dumped from database version 13.3
-- Dumped by pg_dump version 13.3
<snip>


--
-- Name: customer; Type: TABLE; Schema: public; Owner: postgres
--

CREATE TABLE public.customer (
    customer_id integer DEFAULT
nextval('public.customer_customer_id_seq'::regclass) NOT NULL,
    store_id smallint NOT NULL,
```

---

1 A DVD is a sort of 3D-printed representation of a movie. In ancient times, primitive people used DVDs in areas where Netflix was not available.

```
    first_name character varying(45) NOT NULL,
    last_name character varying(45) NOT NULL,
    email character varying(50),
    address_id smallint NOT NULL,
    activebool boolean DEFAULT true NOT NULL,
    create_date date DEFAULT ('now'::text)::date NOT NULL,
    last_update timestamp without time zone DEFAULT now(),
    active integer
);
```

CockroachDB and PostgreSQL are highly compatible, but you'll still probably want to amend this SQL. In the preceding example, the primary key is based on a sequence generator, and as we discussed in Chapter 5, there are better options for CockroachDB. Columns based on PostgreSQL domains will need amendment as well; we'll discuss this later when we look at importing PostgreSQL data directly.

General Considerations When Converting DDL

A lot of the drudgery involved in converting DDL to CockroachDB involves repetitively changing data types and removing syntax clauses that have no effect in CockroachDB. However, there are some more nuanced decisions that you'll need to make that are reflective of more substantial differences between CockroachDB and other SQL databases:

- In a distributed SQL system, the selection of the *primary keys* data type and population mechanisms are particularly significant. Review the section on primary keys in Chapter 5 and make sure that you choose a primary key type that will work well for your application.

- *Triggers* may be implemented in other systems that implement business logic or refine referential integrity constraints. Carefully review the trigger code and determine if this logic needs to be implemented in application logic.

- Some databases allow the definition of user-defined data types or *domains*, which will be associated with their own constraints and data types. Most of these will need to be folded into your DDL (although CockroachDB does support ENUMs as user-defined types).

- The sequence of SQL statements is important. FOREIGN KEY references in CockroachDB can be created only if the referenced table exists. You may need to adjust the sequence of SQL statements to ensure that there are no broken dependencies. If you can defer all foreign key constraint generation until after every table is created, then that would be ideal. You may also find that your overall migration is faster if all index and constraint creations are deferred until after table data has been loaded.

- Review the indexing scheme carefully. In particular, in CockroachDB, covering indexes are a more important optimization than in some other databases. See Chapter 5 for more information on this topic.

Exporting Data

Having created the tables and other schema objects in the CockroachDB target, the next task is to dump the target data to CSV format. Each database system provides some mechanism to do this. You can sometimes use an IDE to perform this task. For instance, as shown in Figure 7-3, DBeaver can export table data to CSV format from any of its supported database types.

Figure 7-3. Exporting data from DBeaver (large format version (https://cockroa.ch/cockroachDB-figs))

In Oracle, we can simply use the `set sqlformat csv` setting to cause the SQLcl command-line tool to write data out in CSV format. The script shown in Example 7-3 can perform this task.

Example 7-3. Oracle script to dump table data as CSV

```
set head on
set echo off
set pagesize 0
set verify off
```

```
set feedback off
set sqlformat csv

select  * from &1;

exit
```

In SQL Server, you can export data to CSV from the SQL Server Management Studio, or you can use the `sqlcmd` command line as follows:

```
sqlcmd -U SA -P **** -d AdventureWorks2019 \
  -Q 'SELECT * FROM HumanResources.Employee' \
  -W -w 1024 -s","
```

MySQL allows data to be dumped to CSV from the `mysqldump` command:[2]

```
$ mysqldump -u root --no-create-info  --tab=/tmp Sakila customer  \
  --fields-terminated-by=,
```

In PostgreSQL, we can copy files to CSVs using the `COPY` command:

```
dvdrental=# COPY customer to '/tmp/customer.csv' DELIMITER ',' CSV HEADER;
COPY 599
```

Loading Data Into CockroachDB

Once data is exported to CSV, and we have valid CockroachDB DDL, we can import the data using the `IMPORT INTO` command. For instance, this statement will load the EMPLOYEES data from Oracle that we first looked at back in Example 7-2, assuming that we've loaded the data into `nodelocal` storage:

```
defaultdb>
IMPORT INTO  "EMPLOYEES"
   ( "EMPLOYEE_ID","FIRST_NAME","LAST_NAME","EMAIL",
     "PHONE_NUMBER","HIRE_DATE",
     "JOB_ID","SALARY","COMMISSION_PCT","MANAGER_ID",
     "DEPARTMENT_ID")
   CSV DATA ("nodelocal://1/employees.csv") WITH skip='1', nullif = '';

    job_id      |  status   | fraction_c | rows | index_entries | bytes
------------------+-----------+------------+------+---------------+--------
678984786365906945| succeeded |          1 | 107  |             0 | 10955
(1 row)
```

Note that during an `IMPORT INTO`, all foreign key constraints are invalidated on the target table, so you have to use `VALIDATE CONSTRAINT` (*https://cockroa.ch/3JcqKa6*) to revalidate the data.

---

2 This technique requires that `secure-file-priv` allows files to be written to the nominated directory and that the command is run from the MySQL host.

Directly Importing PostgreSQL or MySQL Dumps

In some circumstances, you can directly import PostgreSQL or MySQL dump files in a single operation. The `IMPORT PGDUMP` and `IMPORT MYSQLDUMP` commands can read an entire dump file and attempt to create the tables and load the data directly.

For PostgreSQL, use `pg_dump` to dump the required data. In this case, we dump the DVDRental databases:

```
$ pg_dump dvdrental >dvdrental.pgdump
```

From MySQL, use `mysqldump`. In this example, we dump the Sakila sample database:

```
$ mysqldump -u root Sakila >Sakila.dump
```

Now, we load the files concerned into userfile storage:

```
$ cockroach userfile upload Sakila.dump Sakila.dump  --url $CRDB_CLUSTER
  uploaded to userfile://defaultdb.public.userfiles_guy/Sakila.dump
$ cockroach userfile upload dvdrental.pgdump  --url $CRDB_CLUSTER
  uploaded to userfile://defaultdb.public.userfiles_guy/dvdrental.pgdump
```

Now let's try to import the MySQL dump file:

```
guy@sticky-donkey-8sd:26257/sakila>
IMPORT MYSQLDUMP
   'userfile://defaultdb.public.userfiles_guy/Sakila.dump' ;
ERROR: unimplemented: cannot import GEOMETRY columns at this time
SQLSTATE: 0A000
HINT: You have attempted to use a feature that is not yet implemented.
See: https://go.crdb.dev/issue-v/32559/v21.1
```

Whoops. Let's try the PostgreSQL dump:

```
guy@sticky-donkey-8sd:26257/dvdrental>
IMPORT PGDUMP
  'userfile://defaultdb.public.userfiles_guy/dvdrental.pgdump'
  WITH ignore_unsupported_statements;
ERROR: cannot add a SET NULL cascading action on column "payment.rental_id"
which has a NOT NULL constraint
SQLSTATE: 42830
guy@sticky-donkey-8sd:26257/dvdrental>
```

No, that didn't work either. Alas, this is the most common experience when importing dump files directly. Unless the source database uses only very vanilla schema objects, something in the dump file will trip up CockroachDB. You are, therefore, probably better off extracting the DDL first—as shown in the previous sections—and hand-converting it to CockroachDB-compatible syntax and features.

Synchronizing and Switching Over

The extract DDL, export CSV, and import procedure is a good way to move over data for development and testing purposes. It's possible that you will be able to use the same technique for a production system, but it definitely requires an outage.

Because data from multiple tables will be dumped to CSV at different times, or at least within distinct transactional scopes, there will be no guarantee of consistency between tables. If you dump CSVs from an active transactional system, it's possible you will encounter a foreign key violation on import. Even worse, you may receive no error but still have inconsistent data. Furthermore, transactions that hit the production system during or after the dump will not be included. So if you plan on using a dump and load strategy, you'll need to ensure that the dumps occur during a period of inactivity.

Consequently, most production system cutovers involve sophisticated synchronization mechanisms between the source and the target system. In some cases, both systems are run concurrently, and the application layer switches from one system to another with no downtime or inconsistency. There's no one single correct way to do this and no off-the-shelf solution that can perform this sort of synchronization and seamless switchover. Each conversion usually involves some bespoke synchronization mechanism.

We can't cover every conceivable scenario here, but let's look at a simplified example in which we keep data in a CockroachDB database in sync with data in a PostgreSQL database before a seamless switchover.

Let's say we are migrating from the DVDRental sample database in PostgreSQL. Our DVD business is booming (who'd have thought?), and we need to move to a more scalable database platform.

The most important table in our application is the `rental` table. We can prevent updates to other tables for short intervals, but without rentals, we have no revenue. So we need to make sure that we can continue to add new rental records continuously until we are ready to switch over.

We can extract the PostgreSQL `CREATE TABLE` statement using the following command:

```
pg_dump -s dvdrental -t rental
```

A few edits to the DDL results in a CockroachDB-compatible table:

```
CREATE TABLE rental (
    rental_id integer PRIMARY KEY,
    rental_date timestamp without time zone NOT NULL,
    inventory_id integer NOT NULL,
    customer_id smallint NOT NULL,
    return_date timestamp without time zone,
```

```
    staff_id smallint NOT NULL,
    last_update timestamp without time zone DEFAULT now() NOT NULL
);
```

To ensure that we can add new rows to the PostgreSQL version of that table during the transition, we are going to set up a CDC stream between PostgreSQL and CockroachDB.

The following statement creates a CDC "slot" in PostgreSQL:[3]

```
dvdrental=#
SELECT * FROM
    pg_create_logical_replication_slot('cockroach_migration', 'wal2json');
     slot_name      | xlog_position
--------------------+---------------
 cockroach_migration | 0/1CF4F60
```

We're using the wal2json plug-in (*https://cockroa.ch/3KaSKMy*) to format the change records in an easy-to-parse JSON structure. This package might need to be installed on a default PostgreSQL deployment.

The first parameter to pg_create_logical_replication_slot is a unique name we are going to use to access the CDC stream. The second parameter specifies a plug-in that can be used to control how the change data feed is formatted and accessed. The test_decoding plug-in is included in the base PostgreSQL distribution; it translates the changefeed to text format, which we will use in our synchronization program.

Once the changefeed is created, we can use the pg_logical_slow_peek_changes function to pull change records from the stream. For instance:

```
dvdrental=#
SELECT *
FROM pg_logical_slot_get_changes('cockroach_migration',
                 NULL, NULL);

location  | xid |    data
----------+-----+-------------------
 0/1CFECC0 | 742 | {"change":[{"kind":"insert","schema":"public",
 "table":"rental",
"columnnames":["rental_id","rental_date","inventory_id","customer_id",
"return_date","staff_id","last_update"],
"columntypes":["integer",
"timestamp without time zone","integer","smallint",
"timestamp without time zone","smallint",
"timestamp without time zone"],
"columnvalues":[16051,"2021-08-19 08:28:52.748047",
367,130,null,1,"2006-02-15 21:30:53"]}]}
```

---

3 The PostgreSQL configuration parameter wal_level must be set to "logical" for this command to succeed.

You can see in the output a JSON document containing details about a new row in the rental table.

Our top-level migrate and synchronize logic might look something like this (in JavaScript):

```
await pgConnection.connect();
await crdbConnection.connect();

await startReplication();
await copyTable();
while (true) {
    await syncChanges();
}
```

We create a connection to PostgreSQL and to CockroachDB. We commence the PostgreSQL CDC stream, copy the table data from PostgreSQL to CockroachDB, then continuously synchronize any changes from PostgreSQL to CockroachDB.

The startReplication function is simple—it simply creates the replication slot that we're going to use to capture the changefeed:

```
async function startReplication() {
    try {
        const replicationStatus = await pgConnection.query(
            `SELECT *
              FROM pg_create_logical_replication_slot(
                  'cockroach_migration', 'wal2json')`
        );
        console.log(replicationStatus.rows[0]);
    } catch (error) {
        console.warn(
            'Warning ', error.message
        );
    }
}
```

The copyTable() function copies data from PostgreSQL to CockroachDB using SELECT and INSERT statements. You could substitute a more performant extract and load procedure using the principles outlined earlier in the chapter.

```
async function copyTable() {
    const pgData = await pgConnection.query('SELECT * from rental');
    for (let rowNo = 0; rowNo < pgData.rows.length; rowNo += 1) {
        const row = pgData.rows[rowNo];
        await crdbConnection.query(
            `INSERT INTO rental (rental_id,rental_date,inventory_id,
                                  customer_id,return_date,staff_id,last_update)
              VALUES ($1,$2,$3,$4,$5,$6,$7)`,
            [row.rental_id, row.rental_date, row.inventory_id, row.customer_id,
             row.return_date, row.staff_id, row.last_update]
        );
```

```
    }
    console.log(pgData.rows.length, ' rows copied');
}
```

Once the bulk of the data is migrated, we can keep the CockroachDB database in sync with PostgreSQL by monitoring the changefeed and issuing INSERTs or UPSERTs as appropriate. Each time we call pg_logical_slot_get_changes, we can retrieve one or more rows in the output:

```
async function syncChanges() {
    const changeSQL = await pgConnection.query(
        `SELECT * FROM pg_logical_slot_get_changes(
            'cockroach_migration', NULL, NULL)`
    );
    for (rowNo = 0; rowNo < changeSQL.rows.length; rowNo++) {
        const changePayload = changeSQL.rows[rowNo];
        await processSingleChange(changePayload);
    }
}
```

We pull change records using the pg_logical_slot_get_changes function. Note that this function removes change records once they are retrieved, so we never process the same record twice. However, we need to be sure that we definitely apply the change. There's no transactional consistency available to us here!

In the following example we process a single change record. This simplified implementation handles only INSERTs into the rental table but could be modified to dynamically process any changes to any table:

```
async function processSingleChange(rawPayload) {
    const jsonPayload = JSON.parse(rawPayload.data);
    if ('change' in jsonPayload) {
        for (let cindx = 0; cindx < jsonPayload.change.length; cindx++) {
            const changeData = jsonPayload.change[cindx];
            const columnCount = changeData.columnnames.length;
            if (changeData.kind === 'insert' && changeData.table === 'rental') {
                const newValue = {}; // Object containing CDC row values
                for (let colno = 0; colno < columnCount; colno++) {
                    const columnName = changeData.columnnames[colno];
                    newValue[columnName] = changeData.columnvalues[colno];
                }
                const insertSQL = `
                    UPSERT into rental
                        (rental_id,rental_date,inventory_id,
                         customer_id,return_date,staff_id,last_update)
                        VALUES ($1,$2,$3,$4,$5,$6,$7)`;
                const result = await crdbConnection.query(insertSQL,
                    [newValue.rental_id, newValue.rental_date,
                     newValue.inventory_id, newValue.customer_id,
                     newValue.return_date, newValue.staff_id,
                     newValue.last_update ]);
                console.log(result.rowCount, 'rows', result.command + 'ed');
```

```
            }
        }
    }
}
```

This code is a little hard to read but essentially retrieves the JSON structure containing the new row from PostgreSQL, unpacks it, and inserts it into CockroachDB.

Now, both databases can run in parallel, and all new rentals will be automatically copied from PostgreSQL to CockroachDB. When we're ready to switch over, we can switch the application over from PostgreSQL to CockroachDB and shut down the PostgreSQL database.

This is a very simplified example of database synchronization. There's a lot more we would need to do in real life:

- We should implement code to synchronize other tables.

- We should handle UPDATEs and DELETEs as well as INSERTs.

- We may need to consider using bulk inserts and parallel threads of execution to ensure that the CockroachDB target does not fall behind the PostgreSQL source.

- If the application is distributed, there may be a need to prevent inserts from hitting the PostgreSQL database after inserts commence on the CockroachDB side. *All* inserts into PostgreSQL should cease before *any* inserts commence on CockroachDB.

When a CDC option is not available, then you might be able to implement a similar functionality using database triggers. For example, if you wanted to synchronize with an Oracle database, you could write database triggers that capture changes to source tables and send these to a STAGING table.

Updating Application Code

Migrating the database schema and data is obviously only one step in migrating to CockroachDB. Application code will almost certainly have to change as well. The following considerations are important:

- Convert the application to use a PostgreSQL-compatible driver. For instance, if you're using the Node.js oracledb driver, you will want to convert your application to the pg driver. We discussed the range of compatible drivers available for each language in Chapter 6. This won't be necessary if your application is currently using PostgreSQL.

- If your application uses an ORM, then it needs to move to an ORM that is PostgreSQL-compatible. Most ORMs support PostgreSQL already, so this might be only a minor concern. Chapter 6 discusses ORMs that are compatible with CockroachDB.

- Any logic held in stored procedures, functions, and triggers will need to be migrated into application code.

- You should modify any SQL calls that use non-PostgreSQL syntax. For example, Oracle uses `SYSDATE` to refer to the current time, so references to `SYSDATE` should be changed to use `NOW()` or `CURRENT_TIMESTAMP`. Similarly, Oracle has a unique syntax for hierarchical queries and requires a "`FROM dual`" for `SELECT`s that operate on no data.

- It should go without saying that you should test your application thoroughly after any migration. Your testing should ensure that the migrated application is working correctly and that performance requirements are met.

The migration from one SQL database to another is certainly less involved than migrating to or from a SQL database to a non-SQL system such as MongoDB or Cassandra. Nevertheless, migrating from one database system to another is far from trivial and should be approached seriously.

Exporting CockroachDB Data

So far, we've seen how to bring data into CockroachDB. However, if we have an application that wants to consume CockroachDB data, we have a number of options:

1. We can simply write a program that reads data using `SELECT` statements and outputs it to files or feeds it to APIs.

2. We can use the `EXPORT` command to dump data into flat files.

3. We can use CDC to automatically capture changes to nominated tables.

We spent a lot of time looking at the CockroachDB `SELECT` command and CockroachDB-compatible drivers in Chapters 4 and 6. Let's look now at how we can use the `EXPORT` command to unload data.

We introduced the `EXPORT` command in Chapter 5. The syntax of `EXPORT` is shown in Figure 7-4.

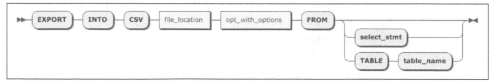

Figure 7-4. EXPORT statement syntax

EXPORT can write data to any of the file sources we discussed earlier in the context of IMPORT.

Here's an export of the `rides` table to `nodelocal` storage:

```
movr>
 EXPORT into csv 'nodelocal://self/rides'
   WITH nullas='' FROM TABLE rides;

                      filename                      | rows  | bytes
---------------------------------------------------+-------+----------
   export16976587190021a80000000000000000001-n1.0.csv | 13409 | 2374556
```

As discussed earlier, `nodelocal` storage is located in a deployment-specific location. On a single-node server, we might find it in the `extern` directory under the installation location:

```
$ ls -l /usr/local/var/cockroach/extern/rides
total 4640
-rw------- 1 guyharrison  admin  2374556  2 Aug 15:17
    export16976587190021a80000000000000000001-n1.0.csv
```

We can also export data to cloud storage locations, such as an Amazon S3 bucket:

```
movr> EXPORT INTO CSV
"s3://cockroachdefinitiveguide/?
AWS_ACCESS_KEY_ID=my-access-key&
AWS_SECRET_ACCESS_KEY=my-secret-key"
WITH nullas='' FROM TABLE rides;

                      filename                      | rows  | bytes
---------------------------------------------------+-------+----------
   export169765eed62b37b00000000000000000001-n1.0.csv | 13409 | 2374556
(1 row)
```

The EXPORT command can accept a SELECT statement that filters and projects the data to be exported:

```
movr> EXPORT INTO CSV
'userfile://defaultdb.public.userfiles_guy/'
WITH nullas='' FROM
SELECT rider_id,start_time,end_time
 FROM rides WHERE city='amsterdam';
                      filename                      | rows | bytes
---------------------------------------------------+------+--------
   export169766268b2faad80000000000000000001-n1.0.csv |  154 | 10972
(1 row)
```

EXPORT provides some switches to control the formatting, compression, and chunking of output. See the CockroachDB documentation (*https://cockroa.ch/3uQAyRX*) for information about these options.

There is also a quick-and-dirty way to export data from CockroachDB in CSV format. We can simply pass a SELECT statement to the CockroachDB shell and specify the --format=csv flag to request that the output be formatted as CSV:

```
$ cockroach sql -e "SELECT * from movr.rides;" \
--format=csv --url $CRDB_CLUSTER > rides.csv
```

Change Data Capture

CDC is an interface that tracks changes to nominated tables and allows you to respond to these changes or to forward them to an external system.

CockroachDB CDC comes in two forms:

- Core CDC is available in the CockroachDB Community License and allows you to respond to changes in your own code.
- Enterprise CDC allows you to feed changes to downstream systems automatically. These downstream sources can be cloud storage such as S3, messaging systems such as Kafka, or a generic "webhook."

Core Change Data Capture

Core CDC feeds changes to a client program that can then respond to these changes as it sees fit. Let's look at Core CDC in the CockroachDB shell.

The shell must be started with the --format=csv flag. Otherwise, the client keeps waiting for the data from the changefeed to end so it can construct a nice ANSI table display. Unfortunately, changefeeds stream indefinitely, so this backfires.

We also have to set the cluster setting kv.rangefeed.enabled to true.

CDC implies some performance overhead, estimated as between 5% and 10%. The actual overhead will depend heavily on the transaction rate of the system. Systems that are read-heavy might see less overhead:

```
$ cockroach sql --format csv --url $CRDB_CLUSTER
#
# Welcome to the CockroachDB SQL shell.

defaultdb>
use movr;
SET

Time: 29ms total (execution 11ms / network 17ms)

guy@sticky-donkey-8sd:26257/movr>
SET CLUSTER SETTING kv.rangefeed.enabled = true;
SET CLUSTER SETTING
```

```
Time: 35ms total (execution 18ms / network 17ms)

guy@sticky-donkey-8sd:26257/movr>
EXPERIMENTAL CHANGEFEED FOR rides;

table,key,value
rides,"[""washington dc"", ""547ae147-ae14-4c00-8000-0000000000a5""]",
"{""after"": {""city"": ""washington dc"",
""end_address"": ""59500 Eddie Union Apt. 0"",
""end_time"": ""2018-12-25T10:04:05"",
""id"": ""547ae147-ae14-4c00-8000-0000000000a5"",
""revenue"": 14.00,
 ""rider_id"": ""428f5c28-f5c2-4000-8000-00000000000d"",
""start_address"": ""81047 Perez Views"",
""start_time"": ""2018-12-25T03:04:05"",
""vehicle_city"": ""washington dc"",
""vehicle_id"": ""44444444-4444-4400-8000-000000000004""}}"
rides,"[""washington dc"", ""54fdf3b6-45a1-4c00-8000-0000000000a6""]",
"{""after"": {""city"": ""washington dc"",
""end_address"": ""78010 Woodard Plaza Apt. 9"", ""e
```

Initially, the changefeed displays all the current data in the table. It then will stop and wait for any changes to be made to the table concerned. For example, if we perform this transaction in a separate session:

```
guy@sticky-donkey-8sd:26257/movr>
update rides set revenue=revenue*1.1
  where id='c50d42a9-62ae-4501-97e0-38b9626502a1';
UPDATE 1
```

this new row of data will be emitted by the changefeed session:

```
rides,"[""amsterdam"", ""c50d42a9-62ae-4501-97e0-38b9626502a1""]",
"{""after"": {""city"": ""amsterdam"", ""end_address"": null,
""end_time"": null, ""id"": ""c50d42a9-62ae-4501-97e0-38b9626502a1"",
""revenue"": 10.00, ""rider_id"": ""ae147ae1-47ae-4800-8000-000000000022"",
""start_address"": ""54948 Direct St Via Apt. 28"",
""start_time"": ""2021-07-02T08:09:51.062777"",
""vehicle_city"": null,
""vehicle_id"": ""bbbbbbbb-bbbb-4800-8000-00000000000b""}}"
```

The changefeed will continue indefinitely. To terminate the changefeed, you would hit Control-C from a SQL prompt or, in a programming language, simply stop fetching new rows from the cursor.

The output of the CDC stream contains three columns. The first is the table name; the second is the primary key of the row concerned; and the third is a JSON-formatted representation of the row's new value. We can add the timestamp—and push out timestamps periodically during idle periods with the following syntax:

```
guy@sticky-donkey-8sd:26257/movr>
  EXPERIMENTAL CHANGEFEED FOR rides with updated, resolved='10s';
```

```
<snip>
rides,"[""amsterdam"", ""c5180421-4421-495f-ae7d-fa0ae08a7258""]",
"{""after"": {""city"": ""amsterdam"", ""end_address"": null,
""end_time"": null, ""id"": ""c5180421-4421-495f-ae7d-fa0ae08a7258"",
""revenue"": null, ""rider_id"": ""ae147ae1-47ae-4800-8000-000000000022"",
""start_address"": ""2 Pool St Via Apt. 28"",
""start_time"": ""2021-07-02T08:10:52.678899"",
""vehicle_city"": null,
""vehicle_id"": ""bbbbbbbb-bbbb-4800-8000-00000000000b""},
""updated"": ""1627285876946192391.0000000000""}"
NULL,NULL,"{""resolved"":""1627285883727456610.0000000000""}"
NULL,NULL,"{""resolved"":""1627285893772664924.0000000000""}"
```

The `resolved` attribute tracks the timestamp that the changefeed has "caught up to." So if you get a resolved message with timestamp t, you know that you have seen every message committed before timestamp t. This can be used for duplicate tracking or to downstream reorder messages. The `resolved=` flag specifies the minimum time between resolved messages.

Resuming a changefeed

If we've been tracking the timestamps emitted by the changefeed, you can use that timestamp to resume a changefeed at a later date. In the previous example, the most recent timestamp is `1627285893772664924.0000000000`, and we use that to resume the feed:

```
guy@sticky-donkey-8sd:26257/movr>
EXPERIMENTAL CHANGEFEED FOR rides with updated, resolved='10s',
cursor='1627285913863014169.0000000000';
```

Using the Changefeed Programmatically

There's not much you can really do with a changefeed from the CockroachDB shell. More typically, we would consume the changefeed programmatically.

Example 7-4 shows an example of consuming the changefeed in Java.

Example 7-4. Consuming a changefeed in Java

```
Statement stmt = connection.createStatement();
stmt.setFetchSize(1);
stmt.execute("use movr");
ResultSet rs = stmt.executeQuery("EXPERIMENTAL CHANGEFEED
FOR rides WITH updated, resolved;");
while (rs.next()) {
    String tableName = rs.getString("table");
    String keyString="";
    byte[] keyBytes = rs.getBytes("key");
    if (!rs.wasNull()) { // Key is null for resolved messages
        keyString=new String(keyBytes, "UTF-8");;
```

```
    }
    JsonObject valueJson = JsonParser.parseString(
        new String(rs.getBytes("value"),
"UTF-8")).getAsJsonObject();
    if (valueJson.has("resolved")) {
        System.out.println("Resolved timestamp: "+valueJson.get("resolved"));
    } else if (valueJson.has("updated")) {
        System.out.printf("Table %s new value for key %s at %s is\n\t%s\n",
            tableName,keyString,valueJson.get("updated"),
        valueJson.get("after"));
    }
}
```

The `setFetchSize` assignment is important. By default, `executeQuery` will pull all the rows from the result set before returning control to the program. Because change-feeds *never* return a last result, you need to set `fetchSize` to a value of 1 to prevent the program from hanging and to ensure that rows are emitted as they are received.

This program simply prints the contents of the changefeed in a human-readable format. However, in practice, we could use this code as the basis for something more ambitious. For example:

- The changefeed could be written to flat files that will be loaded into a down-stream system such as Hadoop or Snowflake DB.
- The changefeed could be examined to perform application-specific operations. For instance, every time a ride is commenced, we might send an alert to drivers in the area or update a real-time map of rides in progress.
- The changefeed could be used to trigger a refresh or a materialized view or to manually update a summary table.

Changefeeds can be consumed by some—but not all—database drivers. Of the four drivers we've focused on in this book, only Java and Go `pgx` work seamlessly with changefeeds.

The default query interface in the Node.js `pg` package attempts to retrieve all query results before allowing the program to navigate through the results. To navigate a changefeed, you'll need to stream data using an undocumented query streaming method. Example 7-5 illustrates this approach.

Example 7-5. Streaming changefeed data in JavaScript

```
async function main() {
    try {
        await connection.connect();
        const sql = 'EXPERIMENTAL CHANGEFEED FOR movr.rides WITH updated, resolved';
        const query = new pg.Query(sql);
```

```
        query.on('row', (row) => {
            console.log(row.value.toString());
        });
        query.on('error', (error) => console.eror(error));
        query.on('end', () => {
            console.log('Changefeed terminated');
            process.exit(0);
        });
        await connection.query(query);
    } catch (error) {
        console.error(error.stack);
    }
}
```

In the Python `psycopg2` driver, all cursor calls—`fetchmany()`, `fetchone()`, `fetch all()`—can be applied only to a cursor that has retrieved all the rows from the query. As we've noted earlier, changefeeds *never* provide a "last" row. Consequently, changefeeds cannot currently be used with `psycopg2`. Psycopg3 includes a `stream` interface (*https://cockroa.ch/3x3tt3m*) that was experimental at the time of writing but suitable for change streams.

Enterprise Change Data Capture

Enterprise CDC is a feature of the CockroachDB Enterprise edition. It has the following advantages over Core CDC:

- Once created, an Enterprise CDC is continuously running within the CockroachDB cluster—you are not responsible for running the job or tracking the last resolved timestamp.

- Enterprise CDC output can be directed to cloud storage destinations ("sinks") (S3, Google Cloud Storage, Azure Blob storage) or to Kafka.

- Enterprise change streams operate in a distributed manner, doling out the workload across the cluster.

CockroachDB Enterprise Trial

If you want to try out any of the CockroachDB Enterprise features, sign up for a 30-day trial (*https://www.cockroachlabs.com/get-cockroachdb/enterprise*).

Using cloud sinks

Cloud sinks are storage destinations for public cloud systems. These are defined using the same mechanisms that we discussed when using the IMPORT command. See the CockroachDB documentation (*https://cockroa.ch/3j4U9se*) for details on specifying authentication and configuring these sinks.

Cloud sinks are a perfect mechanism for connecting two disparate systems that share only the ability to connect to the internet and, in particular, are the perfect medium for cloud-based applications. However, do bear in mind that there is a certain latency involved in writing to cloud sinks—changes are batched to ensure that the destination does not fill up with many tiny files, so some delay will be expected.

In this section, we'll configure an enterprise changefeed for tables in the movr sample database, which we will feed to an Amazon S3 bucket.

The syntax for creating a changefeed is relatively simple. You specify the Amazon S3 bucket name, optionally adding the AWS access key and secret access key. Access keys may also be loaded from environment variables (*https://cockroa.ch/3Jcq58C*):

```
defaultdb>
CREATE CHANGEFEED FOR TABLE movr.rides,movr.users,movr.vehicles INTO
    's3://cockroachdefinitiveguide/movrFeed?
AWS_ACCESS_KEY_ID=my_access_key&
AWS_SECRET_ACCESS_KEY=my_secret_access_key
    WITH updated, resolved='10s';


        job_id
---------------------
  680908602728218625
(1 row)
```

CREATE CHANGEFEED creates a background job that will continuously process the changefeed. We can examine the job with the SHOW JOB or SHOW CHANGEFEED JOBS command:

```
defaultdb> \set display_format=records;
defaultdb> show job 680908602728218625;

-[ RECORD 1 ]
job_id          | 680908602728218625
job_type        | CHANGEFEED
description     | CREATE CHANGEFEED FOR TABLE movr.rides, movr.users,
movr.vehicles INTO 's3://cockroachdefinitiveguide/movrFeed?
AWS_ACCESS_KEY_ID=my_access_key&
AWS_SECRET_ACCESS_KEY=redacted' WITH resolved = '10s', updated
statement       |
user_name       | root
status          | running
running_status  | running: resolved=1627867221.708330000,0
created         | 2021-08-02 01:20:14.797451+00:00:00
```

```
started           | 2021-08-02 01:20:15.014177+00:00:00
finished          | NULL
modified          | 2021-08-02 01:21:09.273081+00:00:00
fraction_completed | NULL
error             |
coordinator_id    | NULL

Time: 40ms total (execution 40ms / network 0ms)
```

We can also monitor jobs from the Jobs section of the admin console, as shown in Figure 7-5.

Figure 7-5. Showing job status in the Jobs console

We are able to examine the changefeed output from the Amazon S3 console, as shown in Figure 7-6.

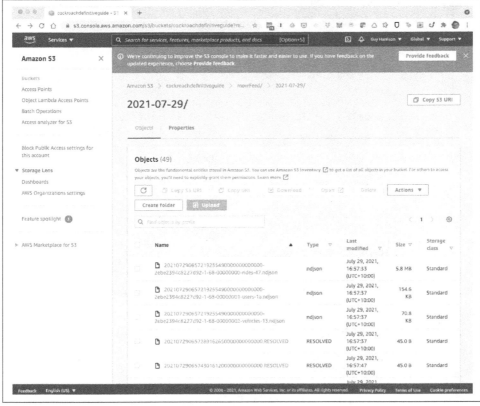

Figure 7-6. Changefeed files in the Amazon S3 console

Webhook sinks

CockroachDB version 21.2 introduced a beta version of webhook sinks, which allow changefeed messages to an arbitrary HTTP endpoint. A webhook sink URL has the following format:

```
'webhook-https://{your-webhook-endpoint}?insecure_tls_skip_verify=true'
```

See the CockroachDB documentation (*https://cockroa.ch/3j6haLe*) for more information.

Managing jobs

Once commenced, Enterprise changefeeds continue indefinitely. You can examine the status and configuration of these jobs in the admin console, as shown in Figure 7-5 or from using the SHOW JOBS command. Changefeeds can be paused or canceled using PAUSE JOB or CANCEL JOB:

```
movr>
SELECT job_id,description,running_status
  FROM [show jobs]
 WHERE job_type='CHANGEFEED';

        job_id        |     description
----------------------+----------------------------
  680908602728218625  | CREATE CHANGEFEED FOR TABLE movr.rides, movr.users, mo
  680913149274030081  | CREATE CHANGEFEED FOR TABLE movr.rides, movr.users, mo
(2 rows)

Time: 29ms total (execution 28ms / network 0ms)

movr> pause job 680913149274030081;
PAUSE JOBS 1

Time: 57ms total (execution 56ms / network 0ms)

movr> cancel job 680913149274030081;
CANCEL JOBS 1
```

Paused changefeeds can be resumed with the RESUME JOB command.

Errors in the changefeed will normally be revealed by the SHOW JOBS command. For instance, here we see a changefeed created with an invalid access key:

```
movr> \set display_format=records;
movr> SHOW JOB 680937397724741633;
-[ RECORD 1 ]
job_id             | 680937397724741633
job_type           | CHANGEFEED
description        | CREATE CHANGEFEED FOR TABLE movr.rides, movr.users,
movr.vehicles INTO
's3://cockroachdefinitiveguide/movrFeed?AWS_ACCESS_KEY_ID=notAValidKey
&AWS_SECRET_ACCESS_KEY=redacted' WITH resolved = '10s',
 updated
statement          |
user_name          | root
status             | running
running_status     | retryable error: retryable changefeed error: failed
to put s3 object: InvalidAccessKeyId: The AWS Access Key Id
you provided does not exist in our records.+
                   |     status code: 403, request id: D1QT6FJS60SNX461,
host id: k7e18TvfvGn5OdZJ3JJlywcApEjU+a3++ =
created            | 2021-08-02 03:46:42.332999+00:00:00
started            | 2021-08-02 03:46:42.587753+00:00:00
finished           | NULL
modified           | 2021-08-02 03:48:02.009441+00:00:00
fraction_completed | 0
error              |
coordinator_id     | NULL
```

Change Data Capture to Kafka

Enterprise changefeeds can be sent directly to Kafka topics, to which any interested downstream system can subscribe.

The first step is to create a topic in Kafka matching the table names for which feeds will be created.[4] This can be done using the `kafka-topics` command:

```
$ kafka-topics --create --topic users --bootstrap-server localhost:9092
Created topic users.
```

You can also create topics using the Confluent Kafka console, as shown in Figure 7-7.

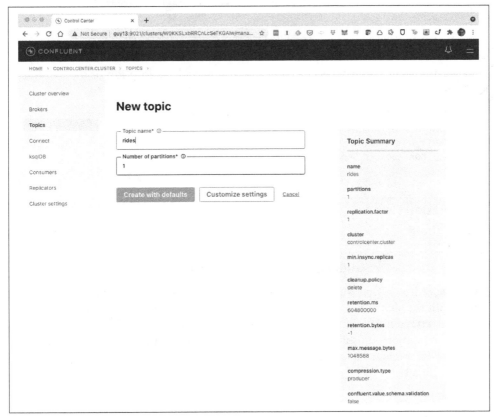

Figure 7-7. Creating a topic in the Kafka console

---

4 See the CockroachDB documentation (*https://cockroa.ch/3LIR3Gr*) for guidance on how to fine-tune topic names.

Once the Kafka topics are created, you can create a changefeed with a Kafka URL as the destination:

```
defaultdb> CREATE CHANGEFEED FOR TABLE movr.rides,movr.users  INTO
      'kafka://localhost:9092'
   WITH updated, resolved='120s';
```

In this example, we have an unsecured Kafka server running on localhost. For enterprise deployments of Kafka, you would normally configure a connection to a broker and supply authentication credentials, as in this example:

```
'kafka://broker.address.com:9092?topic_prefix=bar_&tls_enabled=true&
ca_cert=LS0tLS1CRUdJTiBDRVJUSUZ&sasl_enabled=true&sasl_user=petee&
sasl_password=bones&sasl_mechanism=SASL-SCRAM-SHA-256'
```

Avro is an alternative data format for changefeeds with Kafka. Like JSON, Avro documents are self-describing, but Avro data is more efficient and strongly typed. When using an Avro feed, specify the avro format and the location of the Confluent Kafka registry:

```
CREATE CHANGEFEED FOR TABLE movr.rides,movr.users
   INTO 'kafka://localhost:9092'
   WITH format = experimental_avro,
        confluent_schema_registry = 'http://localhost:8081';


        job_id
---------------------
   679859316344848385
(1 row)
```

Duplicate Change Stream Messages

Changefeeds can feed duplicate messages in some circumstances—the communication with the sink is not transactional, so in the event of a network error, a message may be retransmitted. Furthermore, unless you have an append-only workload, there could be many modification messages for a single row. You may have to implement some programmatic logic to ensure that the changefeed data is accurately represented in your target.

Change Data Capture to Snowflake

Once data from a changefeed is sent to Kafka or cloud storage, it can be consumed by a huge variety of downstream systems. Let's consider one of those possible integrations.

Like CockroachDB, Snowflake DB is a modern, cloud native SQL database. But where CockroachDB is optimized for transactional workloads, Snowflake is optimized for analytics. The two platforms are, therefore, very complementary.

We can use Enterprise CDC to automate the feeding of CockroachDB data changes into a Snowflake data warehouse.

To start, we create a changefeed into an Amazon S3 bucket:

```
defaultdb>
CREATE CHANGEFEED FOR TABLE movr.rides,movr.users,movr.vehicles INTO
    's3://cockroachdefinitiveguide/movrFeed?
AWS_ACCESS_KEY_ID=my_access_key&
AWS_SECRET_ACCESS_KEY=my_secret_access_key'
    WITH updated, resolved='10s';
        job_id
---------------------
  680913149274030081
(1 row)

Time: 373ms total (execution 373ms / network 0ms)
```

On the Snowflake side, we create a table to receive the changes. We use the VARIANT data type, which can store the JSON-structured documents from the changefeed:

```
GHARRISO#COMPUTE_WH@(no database).(no schema)>
 CREATE DATABASE movrfeed;

+-----------------------------------------+
| status                                  |
|-----------------------------------------|
| Database MOVRFEED successfully created. |
+-----------------------------------------+
1 Row(s) produced. Time Elapsed: 0.309s

GHARRISO#COMPUTE_WH@MOVRFEED.PUBLIC>
CREATE TABLE movr (changefeed_record VARIANT);

+--------------------------------+
| status                         |
|--------------------------------|
| Table MOVR successfully created. |
+--------------------------------+
1 Row(s) produced. Time Elapsed: 0.327s
```

We associate our Amazon S3 bucket with a Snowflake *external stage*. A stage is an Amazon S3 bucket, Google Cloud Storage, or Azure container that contains data that will be loaded into Snowflake.

```
GHARRISO#COMPUTE_WH@MOVRFEED.PUBLIC>
CREATE STAGE cdc_stage url='s3://cockroachdefinitiveguide/movrFeed/'
  credentials=(aws_key_id='my_access_key'
               aws_secret_key='kLKkZjS/my_secret_access_key')
  file_format = (type = json);


+--------------------------------------------+
| status                                     |
|--------------------------------------------|
| Stage area CDC_STAGE successfully created. |
+--------------------------------------------+
1 Row(s) produced. Time Elapsed: 1.020s
```

The next step is to connect the stage with the table that will receive the changefeed. This is done by creating a Snowflake *pipe*. The pipe links the external stage with a Snowflake table:

```
GHARRISO#COMPUTE_WH@MOVRFEED.PUBLIC>
CREATE PIPE cdc_pipe auto_ingest = true
    as
  COPY INTO movr FROM @cdc_stage;


+-------------------------------------+
| status                              |
|-------------------------------------|
| Pipe CDC_PIPE successfully created. |
+-------------------------------------+
1 Row(s) produced. Time Elapsed: 1.204s
```

We need to obtain the notification_channel associated with the pipe for the next section. Use the SHOW PIPES command to extract pipe information:

```
GHARRISO#COMPUTE_WH@(no database).(no schema)>
!set output_format=expanded;
GHARRISO#COMPUTE_WH@(no database).(no schema)>
show pipes;
***************************[ 1 ]***************************
created_on           | 2021-08-01 18:42:05.898 -0700
name                 | CDC_PIPE
database_name        | MOVRFEED
schema_name          | PUBLIC
definition           | COPY INTO movr FROM @cdc_stage
owner                | SYSADMIN
notification_channel | arn:aws:sqs:ap-southeast-2:757948394836:
sf-snowpipe-AIDA3A6J6VVKNSPOHQ7NX-EswnTwnSGDYt8ve10d5hnA
comment              |
integration          | NULL
pattern              | NULL

1 Row(s) produced. Time Elapsed: 0.276s
```

The notification channel is used to trigger data loads from the Amazon S3 bucket into CockroachDB. We want to configure the Amazon S3 bucket so that every time a change is made to the bucket, it notifies the pipe.

From the Amazon S3 bucket properties, find the "Event notifications" section and click "Create event notification" (Figure 7-8).

Figure 7-8. Creating a topic in the Kafka console

Under "Events types," specify all the object create events (Figure 7-9).

Event types
Specify at least one type of event for which you want to receive notifications. Learn more

☑ **All object create events**
s3:ObjectCreated:*

  ☑ Put
  s3:ObjectCreated:Put

  ☑ Post
  s3:ObjectCreated:Post

  ☑ Copy
  s3:ObjectCreated:Copy

  ☑ Multipart upload completed
  s3:ObjectCreated:CompleteMultipartUpload

☐ **All object delete events**
s3:ObjectRemoved:*

  ☐ Permanently deleted
  s3:ObjectRemoved:Delete

  ☐ Delete marker created

Figure 7-9. Amazon S3 event types for event notification

Finally, in the Destination section, specify "SQS queue" as the destination and paste in the `notification_channel` value from the Snowflake `SHOW PIPES` command (Figure 7-10).

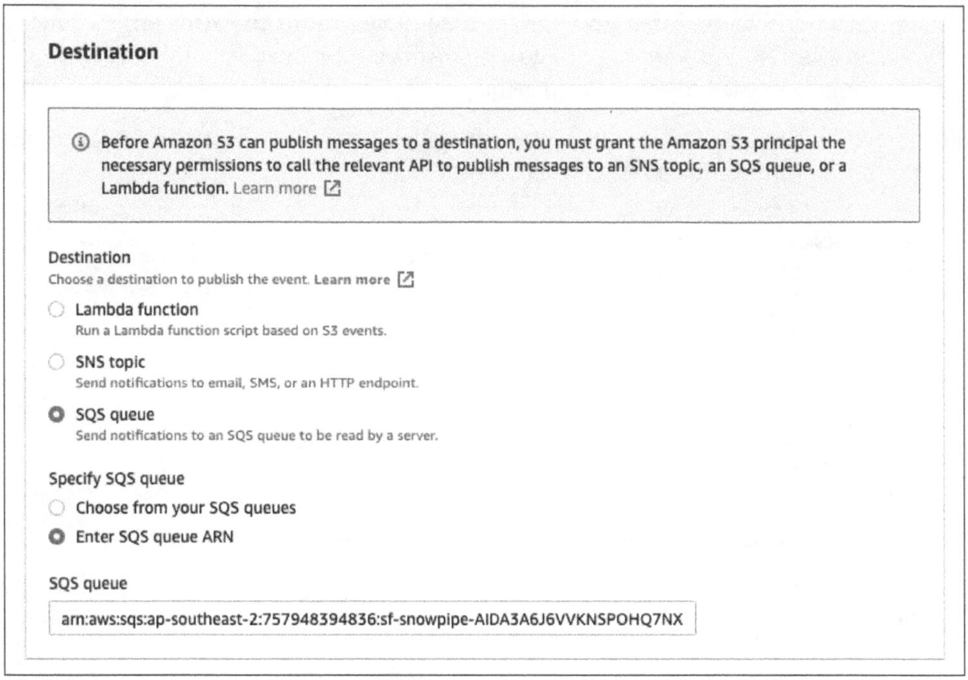

Figure 7-10. Amazon S3 event destination

We've now hooked up a changefeed to an Amazon S3 bucket and the Amazon S3 bucket to a Snowflake pipe. If we query the Snowflake `movr` table, we can see it now contains the changefeed records that have been created as changes to the `movr` tables are processed:

```
GHARRISO#COMPUTE_WH@MOVRFEED.PUBLIC>
select * from movr limit 10;
+-----------------------------------------------------------+
| CHANGEFEED_RECORD                                         |
|-----------------------------------------------------------|
| {                                                         |
|   "after": {                                              |
|     "city": "rome",                                       |
|     "end_address": null,                                  |
|     "end_time": null,                                     |
|     "id": "000288ee-56e9-42f3-9991-9831a668c76a",         |
|     "revenue": null,                                      |
|     "rider_id": "cfeb35ff-a826-439e-83da-c633a158315d",   |
|     "start_address": "54948 Pool St Via Apt. 28",         |
|     "start_time": "2021-07-02T07:47:58.526734",           |
|     "vehicle_city": null,                                 |
|     "vehicle_id": "e9f53976-9fc0-4a7a-b049-34b6ee286be7"  |
|   },                                                      |
|   "key": [                                                |
```

```
|    "rome",                                         |
|    "000288ee-56e9-42f3-9991-9831a668c76a"          |
|  ],                                                |
|  "updated": "1627871552959954000.0000000000"       |
| }
```

Summary

In this chapter, we looked at how to migrate to CockroachDB and how to integrate CockroachDB with other systems.

CockroachDB provides import facilities that allow data to be loaded from flat files. These files can be loaded to storage locations within the cluster—userfile and nodelocal storage, or from cloud storage locations such as S3, Google Cloud Storage, or Azure containers.

Migrating from another SQL database to CockroachDB is generally a three-stage project. First, we extract DDL from the source systems and modify it to support CockroachDB syntax and best practices. Second, we dump data from the source system into a flat-file format. Finally, we import the data into a CockroachDB database. For a production system, there are usually additional configurations around synchronization and switchover.

We can export data from CockroachDB to flat files using the EXPORT command. Alternatively, we can capture changes to nominated tables with CDC. Core CDC allows these changes to be managed programmatically, while Enterprise CDC allows changefeeds to be automatically forwarded to cloud storage or to Kafka.

SQL Tuning

CockroachDB was designed to be a scalable, distributed, transactional database system. It is capable of delivering the demands of high-performance, highly available, globally distributed applications. However, it's not a magic box that can eliminate all inefficiencies in application code or schema design. From time to time, developers and applications will send SQL statements to a database that do not run as fast as they should. Consequently, since the dawn of time—or at least the emergence of relational databases—SQL tuning has been a major concern for database developers and administrators.

In this chapter, we'll explain how CockroachDB optimizes SQL statements and how you can help CockroachDB make these queries run faster. We'll also show you how to find queries that might need tuning, how to determine if those SQL statements are optimized, and discuss ways of making them faster.

Finding Slow SQL

Assuming that we have up-to-date and comprehensive query statistics in place, we should monitor our cluster to identify any problematic SQL statements.

Many applications will log SQL statements or logical transaction times and provide insight into the SQL statements that are performing poorly. However, if we don't have application-level tracing, CockroachDB itself can provide information about overall SQL execution times.

The best place to start is probably the Statements page on the CockroachDB Console —as shown in Figure 8-1.

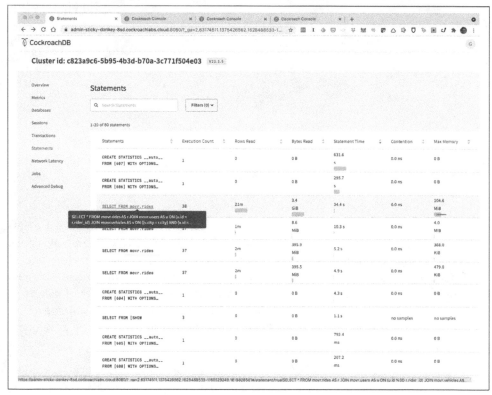

Figure 8-1. CockroachDB Console Statements page (large format version (https://cock roa.ch/cockroachDB-figs))

The Statements page lists SQL statements that have run on the server together with basic execution statistics. We can sort by average statement time or cumulative execution time to identify SQL statements that may require attention. Clicking on a specific SQL statement takes us to the Statement Details, as shown in Figure 8-2.

There are a few other ways we can identify SQL statements that might need tuning. The SHOW STATEMENTS command shows SQL statements currently running and may show long-running queries that are currently consuming resources.

CockroachDB can log "slow" queries to the log (*https://cockroa.ch/3LEKEfv*) by setting the cluster variable sql.log.slow_query.latency_threshold to a nonzero value. This will cause queries exceeding the threshold to emit records to a slow query log. The log records will look like this:

```
I210809 07:47:09.663658 12467601 10@util/log/event_log.go:32 ⋮
  [n1,client=‹192.168.0.245:57136›,hostnossl,user=root] 17
```

```
={"Timestamp":1628495229538628000,"EventType":"slow_query","Statement":
"‹SELECT city, id FROM \"\".\"\".vehicles WHERE city = $1›",
"User":"‹root›","ApplicationName":"‹movr›","PlaceholderValues":
["‹'amsterdam'›"],"ExecMode":"exec","NumRows":25,
"Age":125.039,"TxnCounter":11310}
```

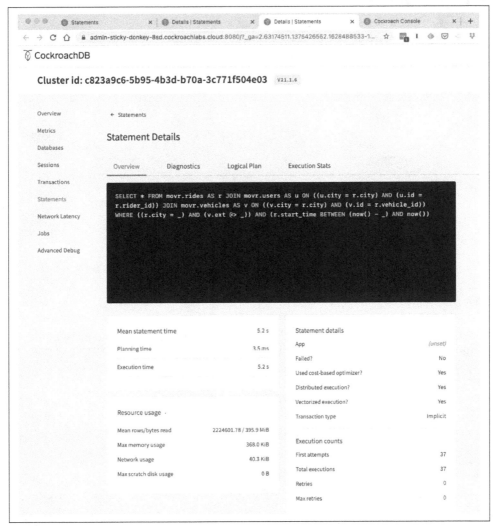

Figure 8-2. CockroachDB Console Statement Details page (large format version (https://cockroa.ch/cockroachDB-figs))

Identifying slow-running SQL statements in the log is not straightforward. You will need to somehow aggregate the entries to identify repetitive SQL statements, and it can be difficult to access these logs if you don't have access to the server (which you won't in CockroachDB Cloud).

Regardless of how you do it, finding SQL that is failing to deliver acceptable performance is a critical task. Now that we've found them, let's see how we tune them.

Explaining and Tracing SQL

When we find a SQL statement that is underperforming, the first thing to do is to determine exactly how the SQL is being executed. This is where the EXPLAIN command comes in.

The EXPLAIN command syntax is shown in Figure 8-3.

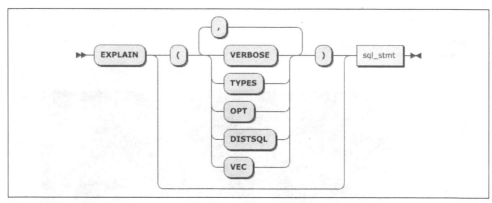

Figure 8-3. EXPLAIN statement syntax

EXPLAIN reveals exactly how the optimizer decided that the SQL statement could be resolved.

Let's look at a simple example. Example 8-1 shows an EXPLAIN for a simple SELECT statement with a single table and a single WHERE clause condition.

Example 8-1. Simple EXPLAIN statement

```
movr> EXPLAIN SELECT *
FROM rides
WHERE end_address = '66037 Belinda Plaza Apt.93';

                        info
-----------------------------------------------------------
  distribution: full
  vectorized: true

  • filter
  | estimated row count: 1
  | filter: end_address = '66037 Belinda Plaza Apt. 93'
  |
  └── • scan
```

```
estimated row count: 20,000,063 (100% of the table;
 stats collected 4 days ago)
table: rides@primary
spans: FULL SCAN
```

The output of EXPLAIN is generally read "bottom-up" and "inside-out." The most heavily indented statements, which are almost invariably those at the bottom of the plan, are read first. So, in the case of Example 8-1, the first operation is scan followed by filter.

The scan step involves a read of one or more rows in a table. In this case, the table is denoted as rides@primary—that is the base table for rides. spans: FULL SCAN tells us that every row in that table must be read.

The output from the scan step is passed to a filter clause that removes any row not matching the filter condition (in this case, the end_address).

Each step includes estimated row counts—these are based on the optimizer statistics that we discussed in the previous section.

We'll discuss the details of SQL tuning later in the chapter, but for now, it's worth noting that full table scans on a table of nontrivial size are generally undesirable. So, if we are concerned about the execution time of the statement, we would probably want to avoid the full table scan by creating an index.

Let's look now at a query plan for a statement that uses an index. Example 8-2 shows an execution plan that involves an index scan.

Example 8-2. Example of an EXPLAIN on an indexed query

```
movr> EXPLAIN SELECT rider_id
FROM rides
WHERE vehicle_id = 'aaaaaaaa-aaaa-4800-8000-00000000000a'
AND vehicle_city = 'amsterdam'
AND end_address = '63002 Sheila Fall';

                                  info
-----------------------------------------------------------------------------
  distribution: local
  vectorized: true

  • filter
  │ estimated row count: 1
  │ filter: end_address = '63002 Sheila Fall'
  │
  └── • index join
        │ estimated row count: 888
        │ table: rides@primary
        │
```

```
└── • scan
        estimated row count: 888 (<0.01% of the table;
        stats collected 2 hours ago)
        table: rides@rides_auto_index_fk_vehicle_city_ref_vehicles
        spans: [/'amsterdam'/'aaaaaaaa-aaaa-4800-8000-00000000000a'-
                /'amsterdam'/'aaaaaaaa-aaaa-4800-8000-00000000000a']
```

Looking at Example 8-2 from the inside out, we see three steps:

1. A scan step, but this time the "table" is the `rides_auto_index_fk_vehi cle_city_ref_vehicles` index. The `span` shows us that this index was used to find all rows with a specific `vehicle_city` and `vehicle_id` combination.

2. The next step is an `index join`. An `index join` connects index entries with the corresponding entry in the base table. In this case, we are retrieving the rows for the matching `vehicle_city` and `vehicle_id` combination to obtain the corresponding `rider_id`.

3. The `filter` condition eliminates rows that don't match the specific `end_address` value.

Figure 8-4 diagrammatically represents these steps.

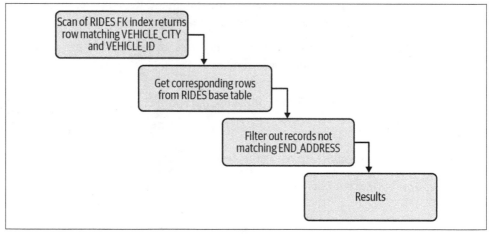

Figure 8-4. Diagrammatic representation of execution plan from Example 8-2

Although this plan uses an index, it's far from optimal. The index brings us only part of the way to the answer since we still have to retrieve rows from the base table and filter out the addresses that don't match those shown in the `WHERE` clause. This query would be better optimized by a *covering* index on `vehicle_city`, `vehicle_id`, `end_address`, and `rider_id`.

For instance, if we create an index as follows:

```
movr> CREATE INDEX rides_vehicle_address_rider_ix1
    ON rides(vehicle_city,vehicle_id,end_address)
    STORING (rider_id);
```

the execution plan will show just a single scan operation:

```
• scan
  estimated row count: 1 (<0.01% of the table; stats collected 6 minutes ago)
  table: rides@rides_vehicle_address_rider_ix1
  spans: [/'amsterdam'/'aaaaaaaa-aaaa-...-00000000000a'/'63002 Sheila Fall'
- /'amsterdam'/'aaaaaaaa-aaaa-4800-8000-00000000000a'/'63002 Sheila Fall']
```

The new index can satisfy the query without the index_join or filter operations.
Now let's look at a more complex example. Example 8-3 shows a SQL statement that
includes a JOIN and ORDER BY.

Example 8-3. An EXPLAIN for a JOIN operation

```
movr> EXPLAIN SELECT *
FROM rides r
JOIN vehicles v ON
    (r.vehicle_city = v.city
      AND r.vehicle_id = v.id)
WHERE vehicle_id = 'aaaaaaaa-aaaa-4800-8000-00000000000a'
AND vehicle_city = 'amsterdam'
AND end_address = '63002 Sheila Fall'
ORDER BY start_address;
                                    info
-------------------------------------------------------------------------------
  distribution: full
  vectorized: true

  • sort
  | estimated row count: 1
  | order: +start_address
  |
  └── • lookup join
      | estimated row count: 1
      | table: rides@primary
      | equality: (city, id) = (city,id)
      | equality cols are key
      | pred: end_address = '63002 Sheila Fall'
      |
      └── • lookup join
          | estimated row count: 823
          | table: rides@rides_auto_index_fk_vehicle_city_ref_vehicles
          | equality: (city, id) = (vehicle_city,vehicle_id)
          | pred: (vehicle_id = 'aaaaaaaa-aaaa-4800-8000-00000000000a')
          |     AND (vehicle_city = 'amsterdam')
          |
          └── • scan
              estimated row count: 1 (<0.01% of the table;
```

```
        stats collected 4 days ago)
      table: vehicles@primary
      spans: [/'amsterdam'/'aaaaaaaa-aaaa-4800-8000-00000000000a'-
            /'amsterdam'/'aaaaaaaa-aaaa-4800-8000-00000000000a']
```

The four steps in this query are:

1. The primary key of the `vehicles` table index is used to retrieve a specific city/vehicle location.

2. That `vehicles` row is joined to the `rides` foreign key index to obtain the primary key for rides that used that vehicle.

3. We then `JOIN` to the `rides` table itself to retrieve the rest of the RIDE columns. During that step, we also apply the filter condition on the `end_address`.

4. Finally, we sort the results on `start_address`.

Figure 8-5 illustrates the execution plan.

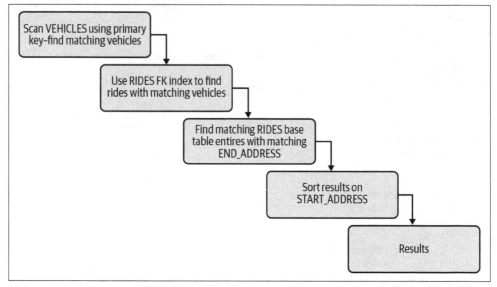

Figure 8-5. Diagrammatic representation of execution plan from Example 8-3

We'll elaborate further on `EXPLAIN` plan interpretation and optimization later in the chapter.

EXPLAIN ANALYZE

`EXPLAIN ANALYZE` is a more powerful variant of the `EXPLAIN` command. `EXPLAIN` tells you what the optimizer *thinks* will happen if it runs the command, while `EXPLAIN ANALYZE` actually runs the command and tells you what *actually* happened.

The syntax for EXPLAIN ANALYZE is shown in Figure 8-6.

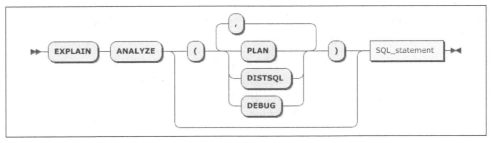

Figure 8-6. EXPLAIN ANALYZE statement syntax

Let's look at the output of EXPLAIN ANALYZE for a relatively simple SQL statement:

```
movr> EXPLAIN ANALYZE
SELECT *
FROM vehicles v
WHERE v.ext@> '{"brand":"Fuji"}'
AND v.city = 'paris'
AND v.status = 'in_use';
                                        info
--------------------------------------------------------------------------
  planning time: 568µs
  execution time: 9ms
  distribution: local
  vectorized: true
  rows read from KV: 2,240 (348 KiB)
  cumulative time spent in KV: 6ms
  maximum memory usage: 380 KiB
  network usage: 0 B (0 messages)
  regions: gcp-australia-southeast1

  • filter
  | nodes: n7
  | regions: gcp-australia-southeast1
  | actual row count: 63
  | estimated row count: 136
  | filter: (ext @> '{"brand": "Fuji"}') AND (status = 'in_use')
  |
  └── • scan
        nodes: n7
        regions: gcp-australia-southeast1
        actual row count: 2,240
        KV rows read: 2,240
        KV bytes read: 348 KiB
        estimated row count: 2,220 (11% of the table; stats collected 5 days ago)
        table: vehicles@primary
        spans: [/'paris'–/'paris']
```

As with EXPLAIN, EXPLAIN ANALYZE shows us the execution plan, and for each step, the estimated row counts. It also shows the actual row counts together with the number of operations performed at the storage layer. In addition, it shows the actual execution time and memory usage for the query.

Actual row counts are better than estimated row counts and real elapsed times are also very useful. However, the downside of EXPLAIN ANALYZE is that because it actually executes the operations on the cluster, it takes time and generates real load. For a time-consuming SQL statement, this might be undesirable.

EXPLAIN Options

EXPLAIN takes a number of modifiers that can enhance or change the EXPLAIN output. You will rarely use these, but they are still important tools in your tuning toolbox.

The VERBOSE flag can be added to EXPLAIN with or without any additional options and, as you might expect, increases the amount of output:

```
movr> EXPLAIN (VERBOSE) SELECT *
FROM rides
WHERE end_address = '66037 Belinda Plaza Apt. 93';
                              info
-----------------------------------------------------------------------
  distribution: full
  vectorized: true

  • filter
  | columns: (id, city, vehicle_city, rider_id, vehicle_id,
  |   start_address, end_address, start_time, end_time, revenue)
  | estimated row count: 0
  | filter: end_address = '66037 Belinda Plaza Apt. 93'
  |
  └── • scan
        columns: (id, city, vehicle_city, rider_id, vehicle_id,
          start_address, end_address, start_time, end_time, revenue)
        estimated row count: 13,409 (100% of the table;
          stats collected 9 days ago)
        table: rides@primary
        spans: FULL SCAN
```

The OPT option displays the query plan tree generated by the cost-based optimizer. On its own, this is a simplified version of a normal EXPLAIN, but by specifying both OPT and VERBOSE, EXPLAIN will expose some of the cost calculations used in the plan. To include all details used by the optimizer, including statistics, use OPT and ENV. This option will generate a URL that you can use to print a detailed optimizer report.

Here's an example of an OPT,VERBOSE EXPLAIN. The bulky histogram information has been removed:

```
movr> EXPLAIN (OPT,VERBOSE)
SELECT start_address
FROM rides
WHERE end_address = '63002 Sheila Fall';
                        info
---------------------------------------------
  project
   ├── columns: start_address:6
   ├── stats: [rows=0.0468389869]
   ├── cost: 15167.4105
   ├── prune: (6)
   └── select
        ├── columns: start_address:6 end_address:7
        ├── stats: [rows=0.0468389869, distinct(7)=0.0468389869, null(7)=0]
        │    histogram(7)=  0        0.046839
        │                    <--- '63002 Sheila Fall'
        ├── cost: 15167.4
        ├── fd: ()-->(7)
        ├── scan rides
        │    ├── columns: start_address:6 end_address:7
        │    ├── stats: [rows=13409, distinct(7)=627, null(7)=12781]
        │    │    histogram(7)=  0 12781
        │              <--- NULL --- '10093 Julie Prairie' -----
        │                          '99954 Sarah Rapids'
        │    ├── cost: 15033.29
        │    └── prune: (6,7)
        └── filters
             └── end_address:7 = '63002 Sheila Fall' [outer=(7),
                   constraints=(/7: [/'63002 Sheila Fall
                     '-/'63002 Sheila Fall']; tight), fd=()-->(7)]
```

The DISTSQL option generates a URL that can be used to generate a Distributed SQL execution map. For example:

```
movr> EXPLAIN (DISTSQL) SELECT *
FROM rides
WHERE end_address = '63002 Sheila Fall';
                   info
---------------------------------------------
  distribution: full
  vectorized: true

  • filter
  │ estimated row count: 1
  │ filter: end_address = '63002 Sheila Fall'
  │
  └── • scan
        estimated row count: 20,000,063 (100% of the table;
          stats collected 4 days ago)
        table: rides@primary
        spans: FULL SCAN

  Diagram: https://cockroachdb.github.io/distsqlplan/decode.html#eJzE..._8GK5vg=
```

Following the link generates a diagram such as that shown in Figure 8-7.

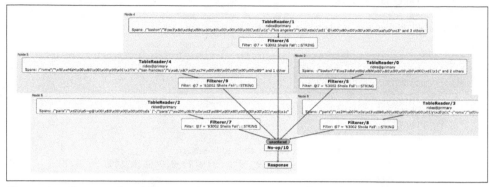

Figure 8-7. Digram from the `DISTSQL EXPLAIN` option (large format version (https://cockroa.ch/cockroachDB-figs))

Distributed SQL diagrams can be a little difficult to interpret, but the very complexity of the diagram in Figure 8-7 should give us pause. We can see that there are five "TableReader" nodes involved in resolving this query. Because the movr schema is geographically distributed (e.g., rides for specific cities are located on specific nodes), why did we need to involve five nodes to retrieve rides to a single address? The answer is that we specified the end_address column but not the city column. If we generate a Distributed SQL diagram for a query that includes the city column:

```
movr> EXPLAIN (DISTSQL) SELECT *
FROM rides
WHERE city='new york'
  AND end_address = '63002 Sheila Fall';
```

we see a much less complicated—and much less time-consuming—single-node operation as shown in Figure 8-8.

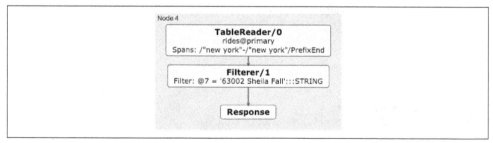

Figure 8-8. `DISTSQL` diagram for a single-node query

Note that the structure of these diagrams are specific to the distributed system upon which they are run. A `DISTSQL` diagram on a single-node cluster will usually be simpler than one run on a widely distributed cluster.

EXPLAIN DEBUG

The DEBUG option of EXPLAIN ANALYZE creates a package of information that contains just about everything you could possibly want when tuning a SQL statement:

```
movr>  EXPLAIN ANALYZE (DEBUG)
SELECT *
  FROM rides r
JOIN vehicles v ON
 (r.vehicle_city=v.city and r.vehicle_id=v.id)
 WHERE vehicle_id='aaaaaaaa-aaaa-4800-8000-00000000000a'
AND vehicle_city='amsterdam'
AND end_address='63002 Sheila Fall'
ORDER BY start_address;


                             info
----------------------------------------------------------------
   Statement diagnostics bundle generated. Download from the Admin UI (Advanced
   Debug -> Statement Diagnostics History), via the direct link below, or using
   the command line.
   Admin UI: https://guyharrison1-506-0:8080
   link: https://guyharrison1-506-0:8080/_admin/v1/stmtbundle/682491029549164305
   Command line: cockroach statement-diag list / download
```

The debug packet can be retrieved from the URL shown in the output of EXPLAIN ANALYZE (DEBUG) or accessed using the cockroach statement-diag command:

```
$ cockroach statement-diag list --url $CRDB_CLUSTER

Statement diagnostics bundles:
   ID                   Collection time          Statement
   682648827880505350   2021-08-08 04:51   EXPLAIN ANALYZE (DEBUG) SELECT v.id…
   667946704191422465   2021-06-17 06:32   INSERT INTO seq_cached(id, rnumber, …
 .
$ cockroach statement-diag download 682648827880505350 myExplainDebug.zip \
  --url $CRDB_CLUSTER

$ unzip myExplainDebug.zip
Archive:  myExplainDebug.zip
  inflating: statement.txt
  inflating: opt.txt
  inflating: opt-v.txt
  inflating: opt-vv.txt
  inflating: plan.txt
  inflating: distsql.html
  inflating: trace.json
  inflating: trace.txt
  inflating: trace-jaeger.json
  inflating: env.sql
  inflating: schema.sql
  inflating: stats-movr.public.vehicles.sql
  inflating: stats-movr.public.rides.sql
```

The ZIP file contains text representations of the plan, definitions for the schema object, and a URL for the Distributed SQL chart that we looked at earlier. It also includes a Jaeger-compatible trace file. Jaeger is a popular framework for visualizing and analyzing distributed trace information.

The Jaeger trace file shows exactly how much time was consumed on each node within various parts of the CockroachDB code. Although this sounds great, in practice, you're usually better off just looking at the EXPLAIN plan—sometimes less information leads you more directly to a solution. However, in complex cases, the Jaeger trace might be just the thing.

Figure 8-9 shows an example of a Jaeger trace.

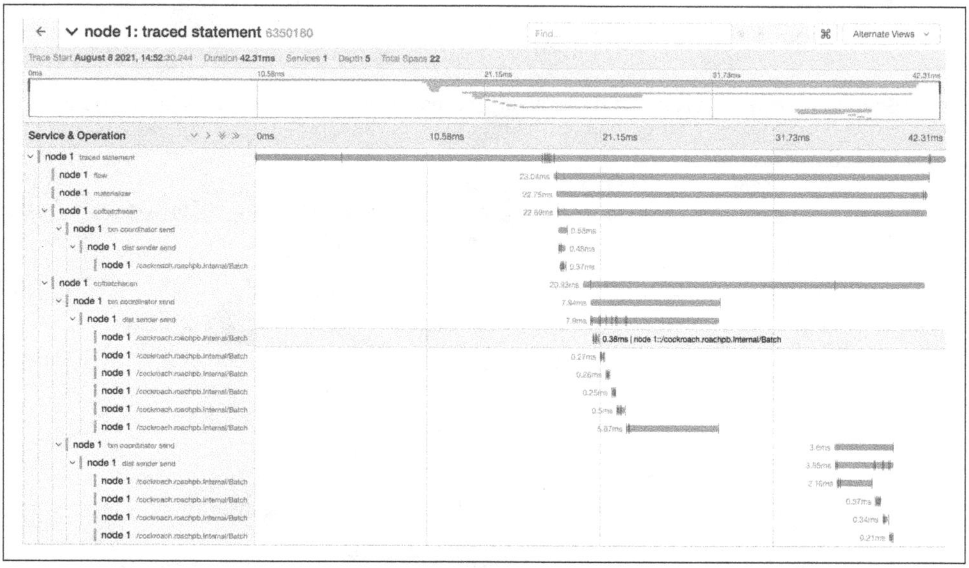

Figure 8-9. Jaeger trace from EXPLAIN ANALYZE DEBUG (large format version (https:// cockroa.ch/cockroachDB-figs))

Changing SQL Execution

You've determined that SQL statement needs to go faster, and you've collected EXPLAIN information to help understand the current execution profile. So, what now?

Improvements in SQL performance usually come down to one of the following options:

Changing or adding indexes
> Indexes exist mainly to improve performance, so not surprisingly, you can often use an index to improve performance. Beware, however, of creating redundant or excessive indexes.

SQL rewrites

It may be that you have expressed your SQL in such a way as to suppress a desirable plan. Additionally, you can use *hints* to force specific execution paths. We'll discuss hints in the context of specific optimization scenarios soon.

Optimizing Table Lookups

Before we can join, sort, or otherwise manipulate table data, we have to first read from at least one table. Optimizing table lookups is, therefore, a key task.

In some SQL databases, indexes and tables are structured differently, and there's a decision to be made as to whether a table access should be index-based or table scan–based. However, in CockroachDB, the structure of tables and indexes is identical, so the question is not so much "index or table?" as "which index?"

Index lookups

In CockroachDB, the best resolution for a table access is through an index that has all of the WHERE clause predicates as part of the key and any additional SELECT list columns within the STORING clause.

For instance, consider this query:

```
movr> EXPLAIN
SELECT start_time, end_time
FROM rides
WHERE city = 'amsterdam'
AND start_address = '67104 Farrell Inlet'
AND end_address = '57998 Harvey Burg Suite 87'
  ;
                                 info
-------------------------------------------------------------------
  distribution: local
  vectorized: true

  • filter
  | estimated row count: 0
  | filter: (start_address = '67104 Farrell Inlet')
      AND (end_address = '57998 Harvey Burg Suite 87')
  |
  └── • scan
        estimated row count: 2,257,435 (11% of the table;
          stats collected 2 days ago)
        table: rides@primary
        spans: [/'amsterdam'-/'amsterdam']
```

This query starts with `rides@primary`, which represents the base table and primary key index for `rides`. In some other databases, the primary key index is a separate structure from the table itself; however, in CockroachDB, the primary key index *is* the base table.

If we create an index on all the columns in the `WHERE` clause:

```
movr> CREATE INDEX rides_address_ix ON rides(city,start_address,end_address);
```

our execution plan now looks like this:

```
• index join
│ estimated row count: 0
│ table: rides@primary
│
└── • scan
        estimated row count: 0 (<0.01% of the table; stats collected 2 days ago)
        table: rides@rides_address_ix
        spans: [/'amsterdam'/'67104 Farrell Inlet'/'57998 Harvey Burg Suite 87'
           -/'amsterdam'/'67104 Farrell Inlet'/'57998 Harvey Burg Suite 87']
```

We are using a new index, but now we have this strange `index join` step. We have no `JOIN` condition in the query, so why do we have to do a `JOIN`?

Effectively, this `index join` step indicates that we are joining the results from the index back into the base table to retrieve the columns that we want to display in the `SELECT` list. In other words, it represents the navigation from the index entry to the base table row.

An even better index would have been one that stored those columns so that we did not have to perform this join:

```
movr> CREATE INDEX rides_address_times_ix
     ON rides(city,start_address,end_address)
STORING (start_time,end_time);
```

Now that our table access is optimized, we have just a single scan of the index:

```
• scan
    estimated row count: 0 (<0.01% of the table; stats collected 9 minutes ago)
    table: rides@rides_address_times_ix
    spans: [/'amsterdam'/'67104 Farrell Inlet'/'57998 Harvey Burg Suite 87'-
           /'amsterdam'/'67104 Farrell Inlet'/'57998 Harvey Burg Suite 87']
```

You may remember from Chapter 5 that we can use a concatenated index to resolve a query provided any of the *leading columns* are specified. For example, the index we just created could be used to efficiently resolve queries like this one—where the leading `start_address` column is included in the `WHERE` clause:

```
movr> EXPLAIN
SELECT start_time, end_time
FROM rides
```

```
WHERE city = 'amsterdam'
AND start_address = '67104 Farrell Inlet';
                                 info
--------------------------------------------------------------------
  distribution: local
  vectorized: true

  • scan
    estimated row count: 0 (<0.01% of the table; stats collected 10 minutes ago)
    table: rides@rides_address_times_ix
    spans: [/'amsterdam'/'67104 Farrell Inlet'-
      /'amsterdam'/'67104 Farrell Inlet']
```

However, the index cannot be used to optimize queries like the following one, which has the trailing end_address in the WHERE clause:

```
movr> EXPLAIN
SELECT start_time, end_time
FROM rides
WHERE city = 'amsterdam'
AND end_address = '57998 Harvey Burg Suite 87';
                                 info
--------------------------------------------------------------------
  distribution: local
  vectorized: true

  • index join
  | estimated row count: 1
  | table: rides@primary
  |
  └── • filter
      | estimated row count: 1
      | filter: end_address = '57998 Harvey Burg Suite 87'
      |
      └── • scan
            estimated row count: 2,277,448
(11% of the table;
stats collected 10 minutes ago)
            table: rides@rides_address_ix
            spans: [/'amsterdam'-/'amsterdam']
```

Note that this query exhibits two clues that an indexing optimization might be possible: the index join and filter steps.

> The presence of index join or filter steps in an execution plan may be an indication that a better indexing solution is possible.

Index merges

When a query filters on multiple columns, each of which is indexed separately, CockroachDB may perform an index merge—identified in the EXPLAIN output as a zigzag join.

For instance, imagine there are two indexes on a table named iotData:

```
CREATE INDEX iotState_ix ON iotData(state_code);
CREATE INDEX iotType_ix ON iotData(obs_type);
```

If we issue a query using both of these columns, we'll see the zigzag join step:

```
EXPLAIN SELECT avg(measurement)
  FROM iotData
 WHERE obs_type=10
   AND state_code=10;
                                info
------------------------------------------------------------
  distribution: full
  vectorized: true

  • group (scalar)
  | estimated row count: 1
  |
  └── • lookup join
      | table: iotdata@primary
      | equality: (rowid) = (rowid)
      | equality cols are key
      |
      └── • zigzag join
            estimated row count: 197
            pred: (obs_type = 10) AND (state_code = 10)
            left table: iotdata@iotstate_ix
            left columns: (state_code, rowid)
            left fixed values: 1 column
            right table: iotdata@iottype_ix
            right columns: (obs_type)
            right fixed values: 1 column
```

The zigzag join starts reading from one of the two indexes, then for each row matching the condition does a quick lookup on the second index for rows with a matching primary key and filter condition. Depending on the distribution of data, the zigzag merge of two indexes can be more efficient than using just one of the indexes and almost certainly more efficient than a scan of the base table.

Figure 8-10 shows the performance of various approaches to the query shown. The zigzag merge outperformed either of the individual indexes and was far better than a full scan. However, as always, a composite index—(state_code,obs_type) STORING(measurement)—provided the ultimate in performance.

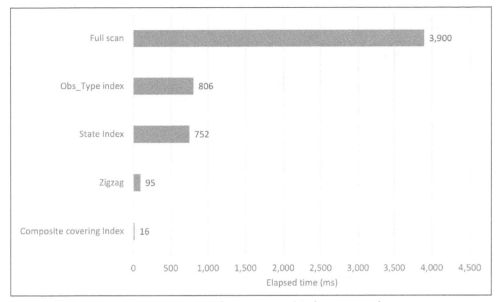

Figure 8-10. Comparison on zigzag index merge with other approaches

Query distribution

EXPLAIN ANALYZE output includes a `nodes` attribute for each step, which identifies the nodes that needed to be involved in the execution step, and a `distribution` attribute, which identifies queries that could be resolved by a single node (the gateway node) as compared to those that needed to be forwarded to other nodes in the cluster.

Bear in mind that even if the distribution is "local," the node concerned can fetch data from other nodes. However, all the SQL processing of that data (sorting, joining, filtering) will occur on the gateway node.

There's no right or wrong number of nodes that need to be involved in a query. When aggregating larger amounts of data, the use of multiple nodes helps to parallelize the processing and avoid network transmission of data—because each node can partially aggregate the data. On the other hand, for single-row lookups, we might expect and hope that a single node can resolve the query, and we would be concerned if we see multiple nodes participating.

For instance, consider this query:

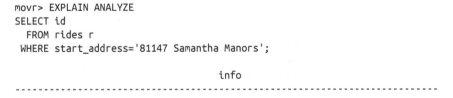

```
movr> EXPLAIN ANALYZE
SELECT id
  FROM rides r
 WHERE start_address='81147 Samantha Manors';

                              info
------------------------------------------------------------------------
```

```
planning time: 263µs
execution time: 13.1s
distribution: full
vectorized: true
rows read from KV: 20,012,724 (3.3 GiB)
cumulative time spent in KV: 25.4s
maximum memory usage: 450 KiB
network usage: 184 B (13 messages)
regions: gcp-australia-southeast1

• filter
│ nodes: n2, n3, n4, n5, n6, n8, n9
│ regions: gcp-australia-southeast1
│ actual row count: 1
│ estimated row count: 0
│ filter: start_address = '81147 Samantha Manors'
│
└── • scan
        nodes: n2, n3, n4, n5, n6, n8, n9
        regions: gcp-australia-southeast1
        actual row count: 20,012,724
        KV rows read: 20,012,724
        KV bytes read: 3.3 GiB
        estimated row count: 20,012,724 (100% of the table;
         stats collected 2 days ago)
        table: rides@primary
        spans: FULL SCAN
```

The full scan required the query to be distributed to seven nodes. Not surprising, since we are, of course, scanning the entire table, and its data is distributed across those nodes. An index on the `filter` column results in a "local" query distribution involving just a single node:

```
movr> CREATE INDEX rides_start_add_ix ON rides(start_address);
CREATE INDEX

Time: 84.540s

movr> EXPLAIN ANALYZE
SELECT id
  FROM rides r
 WHERE start_address='81147 Samantha Manors';
                                            info
-------------------------------------------------------------------------
  planning time: 703µs
  execution time: 10ms
  distribution: local
  vectorized: true
  cumulative time spent in KV: 9ms
  maximum memory usage: 10 KiB
  network usage: 0 B (0 messages)
  regions: gcp-australia-southeast1
```

```
 • scan
    nodes: n2
    regions: gcp-australia-southeast1
    actual row count: 0
    KV rows read: 0
    KV bytes read: 0 B
    estimated row count: 0 (<0.01% of the table; stats collected 18 minutes ago)
    table: rides@rides_start_add_ix
    spans: [/'81147 Samantha Manors'-/'81147 Samantha Manors']
 (18 rows)
```

In general, when you're looking for single rows, you would hope to see a single node involved in the lookup.

Index hints

If we want to force a particular index access path for a table access, we can do so by specifying the index name in the FROM clause. For instance, if we specify rides@primary, then we'll use the base table (or primary key index, if you like). An EXPLAIN with the OPT option will show that we have a "force-index" operation:

```
movr> EXPLAIN (OPT)
SELECT start_time, end_time
FROM rides@primary
WHERE city = 'amsterdam'
AND end_address = '57998 Harvey Burg Suite 87';
                                  info
  project
   └─ select
       ├─ scan rides
       │   ├─ constraint: /2/1: [/'amsterdam'-/'amsterdam']
       │   └─ flags: force-index=primary
       └─ filters
           └─ end_address = '57998 Harvey Burg Suite 87'
```

Likewise, we can force the use of a specific index:

```
movr> EXPLAIN (OPT)
SELECT start_time, end_time
FROM rides@rides_address_ix
WHERE city = 'amsterdam'
AND end_address = '57998 Harvey Burg Suite 87';
                                  info
  project
   └─ index-join rides
       └─ select
           ├─ scan rides@rides_address_ix
           │   ├─ constraint: /2/6/7/1: [/'amsterdam'-/'amsterdam']
           │   └─ flags: force-index=rides_address_ix
           └─ filters
               └─ end_address = '57998 Harvey Burg Suite 87'
```

Be Careful with Index Hints

Specifying a specific index in the `FROM` clause can improve performance if the optimizer is not choosing the best index. However, this practice has a host of pitfalls and should be used sparingly:

- If the index specified is dropped, your SQL may fail.
- If a better index is created in the future, the optimizer will be prevented from taking advantage of the new index.
- Changes in table data distributions might suggest a better plan in the future, which the index hint will prevent.

Use index hints as a last resort or to evaluate the performance of various indexes in test environments.

Full scans

The most notorious undesirable query step is the full scan of a large table. When performing analytic workloads, these full scans are commonplace. However, in transactional contexts, they usually indicate a missing index or badly formed query.

Here's an example:

```
movr> EXPLAIN
SELECT start_time, end_time
FROM rides
WHERE end_address = '57998 Harvey Burg Suite 87';
                                     info
-----------------------------------------------------------------------------
  distribution: full
  vectorized: true

  • filter
  | estimated row count: 0
  | filter: end_address = '57998 Harvey Burg Suite 87'
  |
  └── • scan
        estimated row count: 20,012,724 (100% of the table;
stats collected 58 minutes ago)
        table: rides@primary
        spans: FULL SCAN
```

The `spans: FULL SCAN` entry against the `scan` step tells us that every row in the table or index was read. This is often a Bad Thing—it may indicate that you need a new index to support the query or that you have failed to include a leading column of an existing index in your `WHERE` clause. In the previous case, it's the latter error: The `city` column should have been included together with the `end_address` column.

Full Scans

A FULL SCAN span in a scan step may indicate a missing index or a failure to include the leading columns of an existing index.

Full scans can also occur on indexes and are sometimes hard to spot. For instance, suppose we have an index to support username lookups by address:

```
CREATE INDEX user_address_ix ON users(address) STORING (name);
```

This works well when we supply the entire address:

```
EXPLAIN SELECT name FROM users WHERE address='20069 Tara Cove';
                              info
----------------------------------------------------------------
  distribution: local
  vectorized: true

  • scan
    estimated row count: 0 (<0.01% of the table; stats collected 43 seconds ago)
    table: users@user_address_ix
    spans: [/'20069 Tara Cove'-/'20069 Tara Cove']
```

However, if we don't know the street number and provide a wildcard, we see that we access a lot more rows. Indeed, while the infamous FULL SCAN span is not shown, the span of NULL— is effectively the same thing; we had to scan the entire index to find matching rows:

```
EXPLAIN SELECT name FROM users WHERE address LIKE '% Tara Cove';
                              info
----------------------------------------------------------------
  distribution: local
  vectorized: true

  • filter
  | estimated row count: 269,875
  | filter: address LIKE '% Tara Cove'
  |
  └── • scan
        estimated row count: 809,626 (100% of the table;
stats collected 43 seconds ago)
        table: users@user_address_ix
        spans: (/NULL—]
```

We can also inadvertently cause a full scan by applying operations to query predicates. For instance, if we're not sure how addresses are capitalized in the database, we might be tempted to do something like this:

```
movr>   EXPLAIN SELECT name FROM users
        WHERE LOWER(address)=LOWER('20069 Tara Cove');
                              info
```

```
---------------------------------------------------------------
  distribution: full
  vectorized: true

  • filter
  | estimated row count: 33,333
  | filter: lower(address) = '20069 tara cove'
  |
  └── • scan
        estimated row count: 100,000 (100% of the table;
        table: users@primary
        spans: FULL SCAN
```

As you can see, by changing the case of the column in the WHERE clause, we have prevented CockroachDB from matching those values with index entries, and a FULL SCAN has resulted.[1] An expression index (see Chapter 5) can be created to support WHERE clauses like this.

Computed columns to the rescue

The solution to a lot of these problems is to create indexed computed columns on the expressions concerned. In the following example, we create a computed column for the address with the street number removed and then create an index on that column:

```
movr>
movr> ALTER TABLE users ADD address_no_number STRING
          AS (SUBSTR(address,POSITION(' ' IN address)+1) )
          VIRTUAL;
ALTER TABLE

movr>
CREATE INDEX users_add_no_num_ix ON users(address_no_number)
 STORING (name);
CREATE INDEX
```

We can now use that index to effectively search for addresses without the street number:

```
movr>
EXPLAIN SELECT name FROM users
WHERE address_no_number = 'Tara Cove';
                                        info
---------------------------------------------------------------
  distribution: local
  vectorized: true
```

---

1 CockroachDB does support a case-insensitive comparison operator—ILIKE. However, the use of ILIKE still results in a full index scan.

```
• scan
    estimated row count: 2 (0.18% of the table; stats collected 13 seconds ago)
    table: users@users_add_no_num_ix
    spans: [/'Tara Cove'-/'Tara Cove']
```

A similar technique can be used to perform case-insensitive searches. We'd create a computed column on the uppercased address column and index that computed column.

Computed Columns

Indexed computed columns can often be used to provide indexed access methods when operations on SQL columns (substrings or case-insensitive searches, for instance) would otherwise suppress an index.

Optimizing Joins

Joins can multiply the overhead of SQL queries. Every join involves additional storage engine operations, and in the case of badly executed joins, the overhead can be extreme.

Furthermore, the complexity of join optimization grows exponentially as more joins are added to the SQL. In extreme cases, the number of possible plans will exceed the factorial of the number of tables involved. For instance, for a 5-table join with no filter conditions, the number of possible orders may be as high as 5! (120). Since CockroachDB supports multiple join methods for each of these orders, the number of possible plans may be in the hundreds.

The session parameter `reorder_joins_limit` limits the number of join recordings that the optimizer will consider. By default, the optimizer will reorder only subtrees containing four or fewer joins by default. For a join with a high elapsed time, increasing this value might allow the optimizer to find a better option.

Join Methods

Most CockroachDB SQL joins will use one of the following algorithms:

Lookup join
   CockroachDB performs a search of the second (or "inner") table for each row found in the first (or "outer") table. This type of join is most effective when the inner table is fully indexed on the join condition because otherwise, each search would require a full or partial range scan. The *index join*, which we've seen earlier in this chapter, is a special case of the lookup join.

Hash join

> CockroachDB creates a hash table (in memory, if possible; on disk, if necessary) from the smaller of the two tables, then uses that hash table as a sort of on-the-fly index to look up rows matching the join conditions from the larger table. Hash joins provide scalable performance when joining all or most of the table's rows or where there is no supporting index for the join.

Merge join

> Both tables must have equivalent indexes on the join conditions. Merge joins are used in similar circumstances to hash joins but will normally outperform the hash join because there's no need to create an in-memory hash table.

inverted join

> This algorithm is less commonly used. It occurs when there is a join condition that leverages values in JSONB or ARRAYs and which can be joined only by the use of an inverted index on those values (see Chapter 5 for a discussion of inverted indexes).

Let's look at some examples.

Lookup joins

For most transactional workloads, you'll be hoping for lookup joins that can leverage indexes and which do not need to scan large numbers of rows.

In this example, we get ride identifiers for a specific rider by name:[2]

```
movr> EXPLAIN
 SELECT r.id FROM rides r
   JOIN users u ON (u.city=r.city AND u.id=rider_id)
  WHERE u.city='amsterdam'
    AND u.name='Thomas Smith';

                               info
-----------------------------------------------------------------
  distribution: full
  vectorized: true

  • lookup join
  | estimated row count: 1
  | table: rides@rides_auto_index_fk_city_ref_users
  | equality: (city, id) = (city,rider_id)
  | pred: city = 'amsterdam'
  |
  └── • scan
        estimated row count: 0 (<0.01% of the table; )
```

---

2 For this example, we created an index on users(name), which is not in the standard movr schema.

```
        table: users@user_names_idx
        spans: [/'Thomas Smith'/'amsterdam'-/'Thomas Smith'/'amsterdam']
```

For each row retrieved from the users@user_names_idx index we perform a lookup on the rides@rides_auto_index_fk_city_ref_users index (this is the foreign key constraint index linking users and RIDERS).

As we saw in the section on table accesses, you'll often see "joins" between an index and its base table. So, for example, if we projected the user's address and the ride date in the WHERE clause, we'd see joins from the indexes to the base table to retrieve those columns:

```
movr> EXPLAIN
 SELECT r.start_time ,u.address FROM rides r
   JOIN users u ON (u.city=r.city AND u.id=rider_id)
 WHERE u.city='amsterdam'
   AND u.name='Thomas Smith';
                                    info
-----------------------------------------------------------------------
  distribution: full
  vectorized: true

  • lookup join
  | table: rides@primary
  | equality: (city, id) = (city,id)
  | equality cols are key
  |
  └── • lookup join
      | estimated row count: 0
      | table: rides@rides_auto_index_fk_city_ref_users
      | equality: (city, id) = (city,rider_id)
      | pred: city = 'amsterdam'
      |
      └── • index join
          | estimated row count: 0
          | table: users@primary
          |
          └── • scan
                estimated row count: 0 (<0.01% of the table;
                 stats collected 6 minutes ago)
                table: users@user_names_idx
                spans: [/'Thomas Smith'/'amsterdam'-/'Thomas Smith'/'amsterdam']
```

This two-table, three-joins plan might seem a little confusing to those more familiar with other databases. Remember: in CockroachDB, an index and a table are more or less equivalent structures. What we see here is a join from the users@user_names_idx to the users@primary table, then a join from there to the rides@rides_auto_index_fk_city_ref_users foreign key index and then to the rides@primary table. In databases such as Oracle, the index to table "joins" would be described as index lookups.

We might think of this execution plan in pseudocode as follows:

```
FOR each row found in users@user_names_idx with matching value:
        FIND matching row in users@primary
        FOR each row found in rides@fk index with matching rider_id
                FIND matching row in rides@primary
                ADD joined row to result set.
```

There's nothing to be alarmed about when seeing the index joins and additional lookup joins. However, consider this join situation:

```
movr>
EXPLAIN
 SELECT r.start_time ,u.address FROM rides r
   JOIN users u ON (u.city=r.city AND u.address=r.end_address)
   WHERE u.city='amsterdam'
     AND u.name='Thomas Smith';
                                           info
-------------------------------------------------------------------------------
  distribution: full
  vectorized: true

  • lookup join
  | estimated row count: 1
  | table: rides@primary
  | equality: (city) = (city)
  | pred: (address = end_address) AND (city = 'amsterdam')
  |
  └── • index join
      | estimated row count: 0
      | table: users@primary
      |
      └── • scan
            estimated row count: 0 (<0.01% of the table;
              stats collected 13 minutes ago)
            table: users@user_names_idx
            spans: [/'Thomas Smith'/'amsterdam'-/'Thomas Smith'/'amsterdam']
```

This join has a similar "shape" to the previous example but is less efficient. Note that in the top-most lookup join, the equality condition includes *only* the city and that the address comparison is shown in the pred: (predicate) section. What this means is that not all of the join could be satisfied using the index.

Sure enough, if we do an EXPLAIN ANALYZE, we see that more than two million rows (all rides in *amsterdam*) needed to be processed in that final step:

```
EXPLAIN ANALYZE
 SELECT r.start_time ,u.address FROM rides r
   JOIN users u ON (u.city=r.city AND u.address=r.end_address)
   WHERE u.city='amsterdam'
     AND u.name='Thomas Smith';
                                    info
-------------------------------------------------------------------------------
```

```
planning time: 3ms
execution time: 12.8s
distribution: full
vectorized: true
rows read from KV: 2,223,731 (379 MiB)
cumulative time spent in KV: 5.3s
maximum memory usage: 1.8 MiB
network usage: 0 B (2 messages)
regions: gcp-australia-southeast1

• lookup join
│ nodes: n8
│ regions: gcp-australia-southeast1
│ actual row count: 0
│ KV rows read: 2,223,715
│ KV bytes read: 379 MiB
│ estimated row count: 1
│ table: rides@primary
│ equality: (city) = (city)
│ pred: (address = end_address) AND (city = 'amsterdam')
│
└── • index join
    │ nodes: n8
    │ regions: gcp-australia-southeast1
    │ actual row count: 8
    │ KV rows read: 8
    │ KV bytes read: 911 B
    │ estimated row count: 0
    │ table: users@primary
    │
    └── • scan
        nodes: n8
        regions: gcp-australia-southeast1
        actual row count: 8
        KV rows read: 8
        KV bytes read: 628 B
        estimated row count: 0 (<0.01% of the table;
            stats collected 18 minutes ago)
        table: users@user_names_idx
        spans: [/'Thomas Smith'/'amsterdam'-/'Thomas Smith'/'amsterdam']
```

If the equality condition in a join plan does not include all the
columns in the join condition, then it may indicate that the join is
only partially supported by an index.

Hash and merge joins

When no index exists to support a join, then a hash join will be performed, as in the following example:

```
movr> EXPLAIN
SELECT COUNT(*)
  FROM rides r
  INNER  JOIN vehicles v ON ( v.id=r.vehicle_id)
;
                                        info
-------------------------------------------------------------------------
  distribution: full
  vectorized: true

  • group (scalar)
  │ estimated row count: 1
  │
  └── • hash join
      │ estimated row count: 18,576,034
      │ equality: (vehicle_id) = (id)
      │
      ├── • scan
      │     estimated row count: 20,012,724 (100% of the table;
      │      stats collected 6 hours ago)
      │     table: rides@rides_auto_index_fk_vehicle_city_ref_vehicles
      │     spans: FULL SCAN
      │
      └── • scan
            estimated row count: 20,429 (100% of the table;
              stats collected 3 days ago)
            table: vehicles@vehicles_auto_index_fk_city_ref_users
            spans: FULL SCAN
```

A hash join is often the best solution for a join in which all or most of two tables must be joined. However, if an index is available, we might also see a merge join:[3]

```
movr> EXPLAIN
SELECT COUNT(*)
  FROM rides r
  INNER MERGE JOIN vehicles v ON ( v.id=r.vehicle_id);
                                  info
-------------------------------------------------------------------------
distribution: full
vectorized: true

• group (scalar)
│ estimated row count: 1
│
└── • merge join
```

---

3 Note that we've forced the merge join algorithm here using the MERGE JOIN directive.

```
| estimated row count: 2,064,004
| equality: (vehicle_city, vehicle_id) = (city, id)
| right cols are key
|
├── • scan
|     estimated row count: 20,012,724 (100% of the table;
|      stats collected 6 hours ago)
|     table: rides@rides_auto_index_fk_vehicle_city_ref_vehicles
|     spans: FULL SCAN
|
└── • scan
      estimated row count: 20,429 (100% of the table;
       stats collected 3 days ago)
      table: vehicles@primary
      spans: FULL SCAN
```

If there is an appropriate index, we also have the option of forcing a lookup join. In this case (because there is a supporting index), the optimizer prefers the lookup join:

```
• group (scalar)
| estimated row count: 1
|
└── • lookup join
    | estimated row count: 2,064,004
    | table: vehicles@primary
    | equality: (vehicle_city, vehicle_id) = (city,id)
    | equality cols are key
    |
    └── • scan
          estimated row count: 20,012,724 (100% of the table;
           stats collected 6 hours ago)
          table: rides@rides_auto_index_fk_vehicle_city_ref_vehicles
          spans: FULL SCAN
```

Join performance is notoriously sensitive to data distributions. However, for what it's worth, Figure 8-11 compares the performance of hash, merge, and lookup joins when joining the vehicles and rides tables. You'll note that the optimizer's decision to use a lookup join was arguably not the best decision in this case—a hash join may have been faster. The optimizer's decisions are based on heuristics, algorithms, and estimates of cardinalities and should not be regarded as infallible.

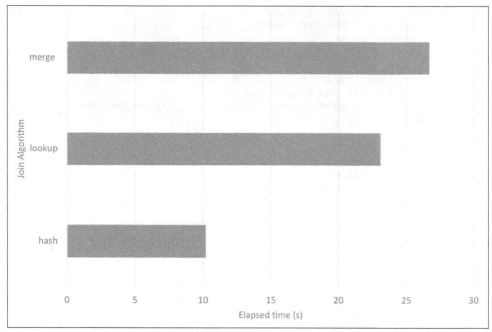

Figure 8-11. Comparison of hash, merge, and lookup joins when joining rides and vehicles

Join hints

We can specify the join algorithm we prefer in the SQL statement itself. These "join hints" are useful when we believe the optimizer has chosen a suboptimal plan. However, they have the same drawbacks we discussed earlier in the context of index hints. By forcing the optimizer's hand, we prevent it from adapting to changes in indexing or data distribution in the future. Here are examples of a join forcing each of the three methods:

```
SELECT COUNT(*)
  FROM rides r
  INNER MERGE JOIN vehicles v
    ON ( r.vehicle_city=v.city AND v.id=r.vehicle_id);

SELECT COUNT(*)
  FROM rides r
  INNER LOOKUP JOIN vehicles v
    ON ( r.vehicle_city=v.city AND v.id=r.vehicle_id);

SELECT COUNT(*)
  FROM rides r
  INNER HASH JOIN vehicles v
    ON ( r.vehicle_city=v.city AND v.id=r.vehicle_id);
```

When you specify a join method, you are also forcing a particular join *order*. In the previous examples, we are forcing CockroachDB to start with the `rides` table and join that to `vehicles`. So, when using join hints, be sure that the sequence of join operations is the one you want.

Outer joins and anti-joins

So far, we've looked at the inner join types. Let's briefly look at outer joins and anti-joins.

Outer joins are executed using the same algorithms as inner joins. However, outer joins limit the possible join orders because inner tables have to be accessed before the outer tables. The lookup join algorithm cannot, therefore, be used with right outer joins (because you can't start a lookup from a value that doesn't exist on the "right" table).

An anti-join is one that returns rows that do not match rows in another table. There are a few ways to express this in SQL. One way is to perform a `NOT IN` subquery:

```
movr>  EXPLAIN
 SELECT r.id  FROM rides r
 WHERE (city,rider_id) NOT IN
  (SELECT city,user_id FROM user_promo_codes upc );
                                    info
------------------------------------------------------------------------
   distribution: full
   vectorized: true

   • cross join (anti)
   | estimated row count: 13,341,816
   | pred: (column20 = (city, rider_id)) IS NOT false
   |
   ├── • scan
   |     estimated row count: 20,012,724 (100% of the table;
   |       stats collected 6 hours ago)
   |     table: rides@rides_auto_index_fk_city_ref_users
   |     spans: FULL SCAN
   |
   └── • render
       | estimated row count: 3,179
       |
       └── • scan
             estimated row count: 3,179 (100% of the table;
              stats collected 6 hours ago)
             table: user_promo_codes@primary
             spans: FULL SCAN
```

Another option is NOT EXISTS:

```
movr>  EXPLAIN
 SELECT r.id FROM rides r
  WHERE NOT EXISTS (
        SELECT city,user_id
          FROM user_promo_codes upc
         WHERE upc.city=r.city
           AND upc.user_id=r.rider_id)
   -> ;
                                  info
----------------------------------------------------------------------
  distribution: full
  vectorized: true

  • merge join (anti)
  | estimated row count: 19,957,371
  | equality: (city, rider_id) = (city, user_id)
  |
  ├── • scan
  |     estimated row count: 20,012,724 (100% of the table;
  |       stats collected 6 hours ago)
  |     table: rides@rides_auto_index_fk_city_ref_users
  |     spans: FULL SCAN
  |
  └── • scan
        estimated row count: 3,179 (100% of the table;
          stats collected 6 hours ago)
        table: user_promo_codes@primary
        spans: FULL SCAN
```

Finally, we can perform an OUTER JOIN and filter on the NULL values returned on rows that don't have a match:

```
movr> EXPLAIN
SELECT r.id
  FROM rides r
  LEFT OUTER JOIN user_promo_codes upc
       ON (upc.city=r.city
           AND upc.user_id=r.rider_id)
 WHERE upc.user_id IS NULL;
                                 info
----------------------------------------------------------------------
  distribution: full
  vectorized: true

  • filter
  | estimated row count: 20,003,984
  | filter: user_id IS NULL
  |
  └── • merge join (left outer)
     | estimated row count: 20,012,724
     | equality: (city, rider_id) = (city, user_id)
```

```
|
├─ • scan
|     estimated row count: 20,012,724 (100% of the table;
|       stats collected 6 hours ago)
|     table: rides@rides_auto_index_fk_city_ref_users
|     spans: FULL SCAN
|
└─ • scan
      estimated row count: 3,179 (100% of the table;
        stats collected 6 hours ago)
      table: user_promo_codes@primary
      spans: FULL SCAN
```

Each of these three formulations returns the same data but with significantly different execution plans. The "best" execution plan will often depend on the nature of the data and, in particular, the size of the two tables. In our example, user_promo_codes is a small fraction of the size of rides. However, the cross join (anti) plan used to implement the NOT IN syntax can lead to particularly poor results. Figure 8-12 illustrates the results for the preceding test queries.

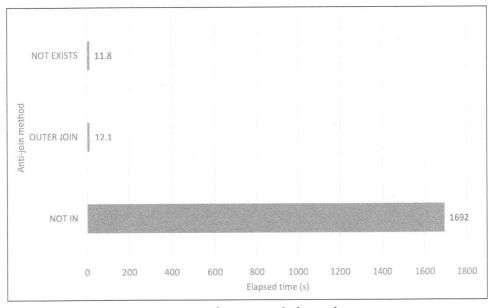

Figure 8-12. NOT IN anti-joins can perform particularly poorly

Optimizing Sorting and Aggregation

Transactional workloads typical in CockroachDB do not generally involve the large-scale aggregations that are typical of a data warehousing database. Nevertheless, there's almost always some reporting or analytic requests that will aggregate nontrivial data sets, and it's important that these SQL statements don't swamp the database unnecessarily.

It's also commonplace for a transactional query to retrieve "latest" or "next" rows in some ordered data set, which can require sorting of data.

For instance, we might want to select the most recent rides commenced in a particular city:

```
movr> EXPLAIN
SELECT start_address
FROM rides
WHERE city = 'paris'
ORDER BY start_time DESC
LIMIT 10;
                                    info
-------------------------------------------------------------------------
  distribution: full
  vectorized: true

  • limit
  │ estimated row count: 10
  │ count: 10
  │
  └── • sort
      │ estimated row count: 2,279,450
```

```
| order: -start_time
|
└── • scan
        estimated row count: 2,279,450 (11% of the table;
         stats collected 7 hours ago)
        table: rides@primary
        spans: [/'paris'-/'paris']
```

Here you can see we scan `rides` for Paris entries, then sort that result—about two million rows must be sorted.

As usual, the best solution is to create an index. Indexes can be used not just to filter rows but also to return rows in a specific order. If we create an index:

```
movr> CREATE INDEX rides_start_time_address ON
rides(city, start_time) STORING (start_address);
```

we can retrieve rows in the specified order with far lower overhead:

```
movr> EXPLAIN
SELECT start_address
FROM rides
WHERE city = 'paris'
ORDER BY start_time DESC
LIMIT 10;
                              info
-----------------------------------------------------------------------
  distribution: local
  vectorized: true

  • revscan
    estimated row count: 10 (<0.01% of the table;
        stats collected 2 minutes ago)
    table: rides@rides_start_time_address
    spans: [/'paris'-/'paris']
    limit: 10
```

GROUP BY and aggregation queries tend to deal with larger sets of rows, but the use of an index to reduce overhead is still significant. Consider this query, which sums up revenue by city and vehicle:

```
movr> EXPLAIN analyze
SELECT vehicle_city, vehicle_id, sum(revenue)
FROM rides
GROUP BY vehicle_city, vehicle_id
ORDER BY 3 DESC
LIMIT 10
   -> ;
                              info
-----------------------------------------------------------------
  planning time: 850µs
  execution time: 29.7s
  distribution: full
```

```
vectorized: true
rows read from KV: 20,012,724 (3.3 GiB)
cumulative time spent in KV: 43s
maximum memory usage: 30 MiB
network usage: 1.4 MiB (212 messages)
regions: gcp-australia-southeast1

• limit
| nodes: n9
| regions: gcp-australia-southeast1
| actual row count: 10
| estimated row count: 10
| count: 10
|
└── • sort
    | nodes: n2, n5, n6, n8, n9
    | regions: gcp-australia-southeast1
    | actual row count: 50
    | estimated row count: 21,937
    | order: -sum
    |
    └── • group
        | nodes: n2, n5, n6, n8, n9
        | regions: gcp-australia-southeast1
        | actual row count: 21,972
        | estimated row count: 21,937
        | group by: vehicle_city, vehicle_id
        |
        └── • scan
            nodes: n2, n5, n6, n8, n9
            regions: gcp-australia-southeast1
            actual row count: 20,012,724
            KV rows read: 20,012,724
            KV bytes read: 3.3 GiB
            estimated row count: 20,012,724 (100% of the table;
              stats collected 1 day ago)
            table: rides@primary
            spans: FULL SCAN
```

The full scan of the base table is followed by a GROUP and SORT operation. If an index exists on all of the columns involved, then the overhead of grouping is reduced because rows can be consumed in sorted order—Figure 8-13 illustrates the performance improvement.

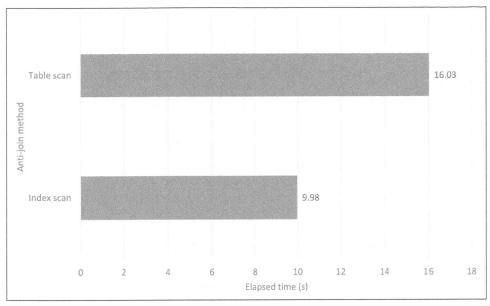

Figure 8-13. Creating a dedicated index can reduce GROUP BY overhead

Disk sorts

When a sort operation exceeds the threshold defined by `sql.distsql.temp_stor age.workmem`, CockroachDB will write to temporary disk files during the sort operation. By default, the limit is 64 MB:

```
show cluster setting sql.distsql.temp_storage.workmem;

  sql.distsql.temp_storage.workmem
------------------------------------
    64 MiB
```

64 MB is not a huge amount of memory and while you might not want every session concurrently consuming 64 MB (although we've heard worse ideas), you definitely should consider increasing the value if large sorts appear to be executing slowly.

For example, consider this horrible query that sorts all the rows in the `rides` table after joining to several other tables:

```
movr> EXPLAIN ANALYZE
SELECT *
  FROM rides r
    INNER HASH JOIN users u
       ON (r.city=u.city AND r.rider_id=u.id)
    INNER HASH JOIN vehicles v
       ON (v.city=r.vehicle_city AND v.id=r.vehicle_id)
    LEFT OUTER HASH JOIN user_promo_codes upc
       ON (upc.city=u.city AND upc.user_id=u.id)
```

```
          LEFT OUTER  HASH JOIN promo_codes pc
              ON (upc.code=pc.code)
     ORDER BY r.city,v.TYPE,u.address,pc.description LIMIT 10;
                                          info
-----------------------------------------------------------------------------
     planning time: 49ms
     execution time: 7m29s
     distribution: full
     vectorized: true
     rows read from KV: 20,854,691 (3.4 GiB)
     cumulative time spent in KV: 1m23s
     maximum memory usage: 204 MiB
     network usage: 38 GiB (8,715,885 messages)
     regions: gcp-australia-southeast1

  <snip>
```

If we increase the value of sql.distsql.temp_storage.workmem, we can reduce its execution time by about 40% (Figure 8-14):

```
movr> SET  cluster setting sql.distsql.temp_storage.workmem='500 MiB';
SET CLUSTER SETTING

Time: 49ms

movr> EXPLAIN ANALYZE
SELECT *
  FROM rides r
    INNER HASH JOIN users u
      ON (r.city=u.city AND r.rider_id=u.id)
    INNER HASH JOIN vehicles v
      ON (v.city=r.vehicle_city AND v.id=r.vehicle_id)
    LEFT OUTER HASH JOIN user_promo_codes upc
      ON (upc.city=u.city AND upc.user_id=u.id)
    LEFT OUTER  HASH JOIN promo_codes pc
      ON (upc.code=pc.code)
 ORDER BY r.city,v.TYPE,u.address,pc.description LIMIT 10;
                                  info
----------------------------------------------------------------------
     planning time: 2ms
     execution time: 4m38s
     distribution: full
     vectorized: true
     rows read from KV: 20,854,691 (3.4 GiB)
     cumulative time spent in KV: 1m24s
     maximum memory usage: 822 MiB
     network usage: 33 GiB (5,982,233 messages)
     regions: gcp-australia-southeast1
```

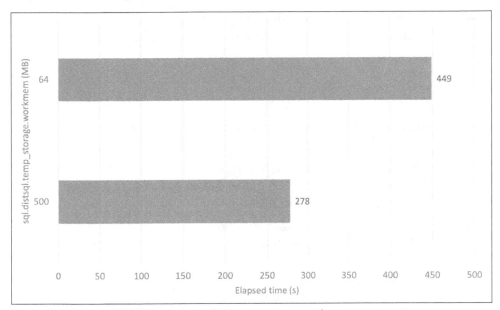

Figure 8-14. Increasing memory available to sorts can reduce execution time

Disk sorts can result from a variety of SQL operations, including ORDER BY, GROUP BY, window functions, hash joins, and merge joins. There are also per-node limits to the amount of memory available for sorting; these will be discussed in Chapter 14.

Optimizing DML

Data manipulation language (DML) statements—INSERT, UPDATE, UPSERT, and DELETE—are the bread and butter of a transactional system. However, we generally concentrate on tuning queries because even in an intensive online transaction processing (OLTP) system, queries outnumber DML and because many of the principles involved in DML optimization involve WHERE clause optimization.

Most DML statements include a query component—to identify the rows to be processed or to gather the new rows to be inserted. Optimizing this query aspect—tuning the WHERE clause in an UPDATE or DELETE statement, for instance—is usually the first step in DML tuning.

Indexes exist mainly to optimize query performance, but this benefit comes at a high cost for DML statements. Index maintenance is often the single biggest component of DML performance. Therefore, make sure that all indexes are needed. The crdb_internal.index_usage_statistics (*https://cockroa.ch/3DGCMat*) table contains statistics about the utilization of indexes and can be consulted to find "unused" indexes. Referential integrity constraints create an overhead on DML as well.

When optimizing a WHERE clause with an index, try to avoid creating an index that itself must be changed during the update. For instance, consider this UPDATE:

```
movr> EXPLAIN ANALYZE
UPDATE users u
   SET credit_card='9999804075'
 WHERE city='rome'
   AND name='Anna Massey'
   AND address='75977 Donna Gateway Suite 52';
```

Without a new index, this UPDATE is going to have to perform a fairly expensive SCAN of all Rome users and filter on name and address. Based on our repeated recommendations of adding all the columns referenced in a query within the INDEX, you might create a covering index like this:

```
movr> CREATE  INDEX users_city_name_add_cc_idx
         ON users(city,name,address)
      STORING(credit_card);
```

Alas, the STORING clause in this index actually hurts performance. Because the credit_card number is changing, the index will have to be updated as well as the base table. The correct index to optimize the update would be:

```
movr> CREATE  INDEX users_city_name_add_idx
         ON users(city,name,address);
```

So while STORING columns that appear in the SELECT list is often a good practice, STORING columns in the SET list can be counterproductive.

As with a lot of indexing decisions, you need to balance the cost/benefit of various indexes. While the STORING clause shown is detrimental to the performance of the UPDATE, it might be beneficial to a SELECT statement. The important thing to remember is that the STORING clause should not necessarily be added to an index without a clear idea of its positive effect on SELECT statements versus its possible detrimental effect on UPDATEs.

Denormalizations that have been introduced to reduce SELECT overhead—to avoid joins, in particular—will often exact a cost during update operations. Make sure you are not maintaining pointless or ineffective denormalizations. We discussed denormalization in Chapter 5.

Inserts can be optimized by using bulk inserts—inserting multiple rows in a single operation. Methods of doing this were covered in Chapter 6.

The total elapsed time for a multistatement DML can be strongly affected by the transaction design. Check out Chapter 6 for a discussion on optimizing transactions.

Optimizing the Optimizer

SQL is a declarative language—it specifies a logical operation on data without defining exactly how that operation should be executed. The declarative nature of SQL makes it relatively easy to understand and is one of the major reasons that SQL has become so ubiquitous. Like all SQL database systems, CockroachDB includes a *query optimizer* that will determine how to transform the SQL logical request into physical database operations. We introduced the SQL optimizer in Chapter 2. The decisions that the optimizer makes can be influenced favorably by cluster configuration and table statistics.

In practice, you don't need to think too much about optimizer internals when tuning CockroachDB SQL. In the vast majority of cases, the optimizer will make a decision that is as good as can be achieved given the available indexes and constraints of the SQL.

However, the optimizer is dependent on statistics that give it an idea of the distribution of data within various tables and indexes. You do have some control over these statistics, and in some cases, you might want to tweak these.

Optimizer Statistics

The optimizer is only as good as its input statistics, so it's important to ensure that those statistics are up-to-date and comprehensive. CockroachDB collects statistics automatically, and most of the time, these automatic statistics will be sufficient. However, you do have the option to tweak statistics collections or to collect them manually.

Viewing Statistics

The SHOW STATISTICS command allows us to look at the statistics collected for a specific table:

```
movr> SHOW STATISTICS FOR table rides;
```

statistics_name	column_names	created	row_count	distinct_co	null_c
__auto__	{city}	2021-08-03	20000000	9	0
__auto__	{id}	2021-08-03	20000000	31265268	0
__auto__	{city,id}	2021-08-03	20000000	47560228	0
__auto__	{rider_id}	2021-08-03	20000000	834396	0
__auto__	{city,rider_id}	2021-08-03	20000000	825716	0
__auto__	{vehicle_city}	2021-08-03	20000000	9	0
__auto__	{vehicle_id}	2021-08-03	20000000	20074	0
__auto__	{vehicle_city,v	2021-08-03	20000000	20033	0
__auto__	{start_address}	2021-08-03	20000000	48346139	0

By default, all collected statistics are displayed, including those from previous collection jobs. To see just the most recent statistics, you could issue a query like this:

```
movr> WITH rides_statistics AS (
  SELECT *
    FROM [SHOW STATISTICS FOR TABLE rides])
SELECT column_names,row_count,distinct_count,null_count
  FROM rides_statistics r
 WHERE created =(
        SELECT max(created)
      FROM rides_statistics
     WHERE column_names=r.column_names
);
        column_names        | row_count | distinct_count | null_count
----------------------------+-----------+----------------+------------
  {city}                    | 20000566  |              9 |          0
  {id}                      | 20000566  |       20121839 |          0
  {city,id}                 | 20000566  |       19805157 |          0
  {rider_id}                | 20000566  |         805159 |          0
  {city,rider_id}           | 20000566  |         797137 |          0
  {revenue}                 | 20000566  |            100 |          0
  {vehicle_id}              | 20000566  |          20136 |          0
  {vehicle_city,vehicle_id} | 20000566  |          20108 |          0
  {start_address}           | 20000566  |       20001958 |          0
  {end_address}             | 20000566  |       19982168 |        461
  {start_time}              | 20000566  |            596 |          0
  {end_time}                | 20000566  |            862 |        461
  {vehicle_city}            | 20000566  |              9 |          0
  {start_address,end_address} | 20000566 |      20385247 |          0
(14 rows)

Time: 36ms
```

Automatic Statistics

Statistics are collected when:

- Tables are created
- Schema changes occur
- Time passes
- Changes to the table exceed a threshold

SQL statistics are controlled by the cluster settings shown in Table 8-1. You can modify these using the SET CLUSTER SETTING command.

Table 8-1. Cluster configuration settings for automatic statistics collection

Cluster setting	Description
`sql.stats.automatic_collection.enabled`	Automatic statistics collection mode
`sql.stats.automatic_collection.fraction_stale_rows`	Target fraction of stale rows per table that will trigger a statistics refresh
`sql.stats.automatic_collection.min_stale_rows`	Target minimum number of stale rows per table that will trigger a statistics refresh
`sql.stats.histogram_collection.enabled`	Histogram collection mode
`sql.stats.multi_column_collection.enabled`	Multicolumn statistics collection mode

Normally, we would not recommend changing these parameters, though if automatic statistics correction was causing an unacceptable overhead, you might increase the `fraction_stale_rows` parameter if you're comfortable that the general shape of your data was not changing.

Manually Collecting Statistics

You can create or refresh statistics for an entire table by issuing a `CREATE STATISTICS` command:

```
movr> create statistics manualStats from rides
   -> ;
CREATE STATISTICS

Time: 51.450s
```

You can also create statistics for a nominated set of columns. For instance, here we create statistics for `start_address` and `end_address`:

```
movr> CREATE STATISTICS city_addresses ON city, end_address
         FROM movr.public.rides
;
CREATE STATISTICS

Time: 10.235s
```

This gives the optimizer an idea of the cardinality for that *combination* of columns. We might do this when two columns are related in some way that the optimizer doesn't know about. In this case, we know intuitively that each address resides within a single city. Unless we collect the statistics, the optimizer will assume that they are independent and consequently overestimate the number of distinct values.

Background jobs are created to collect statistics. You can view the status of these jobs through the `SHOW JOBS` command.

There are a relatively limited number of situations in which changing statistics would be warranted. The automatic statistics collection triggers (on average) when 20% of a table has changed. In some cases, this is insufficient when a specific column is subject to frequent changes. For example, if you have a timestamp column where the values are increasing over time, the histogram will show no recent values most of the time, which can make the optimizer choose an index on that column even when it's a bad idea. Another example would be a "status" column that showed whether some task was complete or in progress. Depending on when the statistics were collected, the histogram might show no in-progress tasks.

Summary

SQL tuning is a big topic—whole books have been written on it, so in this chapter, we've necessarily only been able to provide an introduction.

The CockroachDB query optimizer will attempt to determine the best possible plan for a SQL statement given the table statistics that it has at hand and the available access paths. You can help the optimizer by making sure that statistics are up-to-date and relevant, but more importantly, by ensuring that the best set of indexes exist to support the queries that will be executed.

Finding queries that may need tuning can be done through the database console Statements page or through the SHOW STATEMENTS statement. The EXPLAIN command can be used to reveal how a SQL statement will be executed. No serious SQL tuning effort will omit the use of the EXPLAIN command, particularly EXPLAIN ANALYZE, which shows actual statement tuning times.

Single table accesses are the building block of more complex SQL statements, so make sure these are optimized by using appropriate indexes and avoiding accidental full scans. You can force the use of indexes with index "hints," though the use of hints should be the exception, not the rule; hints may prevent the optimizer from evolving superior plans in the future.

Joins are generally also optimized by making sure that indexes exist on join conditions, though for joins on complete tables, hash or merge joins that do not use indexes might be appropriate. Join hints can be used to control the types and order of joins, though again, these should not be used frequently.

When data is needed in a specific order, an index retrieval is usually preferred to a sort operation. If a sort operation is required, consider changing the amount of memory available to the sort to avoid disk sorts.

DML optimization uses the principles of query optimization—particularly where the DML has a WHERE clause. Avoiding excessive indexing and effective transactions design is also important.

Deploying and Administering CockroachDB

Planning a Deployment

In the preceding chapters, we've described how to get started with CockroachDB and how to develop highly available and performant applications with the CockroachDB platform.

Now it's time to consider how to set up a production CockroachDB cluster to support your application.

The distributed nature of CockroachDB allows for a large range of deployment topologies. Choosing the right topology requires an understanding of your application's requirements and the cost and performance implications of various CockroachDB options. In this chapter, we review the steps in planning a deployment and provide an overview of the most common deployment patterns.

There are two main categories of CockroachDB deployments:

- A fully managed CockroachDB Cloud deployment, in which all aspects of Cockroach-DB cluster management are handled by the CockroachDB dedicated cloud platform. Within CockroachDB Cloud, you can choose from serverless or dedicated hardware options.

- A self-hosted or "do it yourself" deployment in which you install CockroachDB on your own hardware platform or on cloud-based virtual machines (VMs) that you have available.

In any of these scenarios, you may deploy *single-region* or *multiregion* topologies.

Within a self-hosted deployment, you have two additional dimensions of choice. Whether using on-premise hardware or cloud resources, you can install CockroachDB directly onto the OS, or you can install CockroachDB into a Kubernetes cluster.

Know Your Requirements

Choosing the best deployment pattern for your circumstances is hard unless you have a clear handle on your business requirements. Here are some of the considerations you should clarify before finalizing your deployment plan:

Total cost of ownership
> The total cost of ownership for a CockroachDB deployment includes the capital costs of hardware (for on-premise deployments) or hardware rental (for cloud deployments) together with the software licensing costs and staffing costs for administrators. A fully managed cloud deployment, such as CockroachDB Cloud, minimizes the staffing costs and encapsulates all other costs into a single subscription. An on-premise deployment might have higher staffing costs and higher initial hardware costs but lower software subscription costs, especially if the CockroachDB community distribution is used.

High availability
> CockroachDB is a high-availability system, but failures can occur, and outages can result. In a three-node cluster, a failure of two nodes may render the cluster unavailable. If this scenario is unacceptable, then a more sophisticated topology might be required. A topology can be designed that can tolerate a data center failure or even the failure of a cloud vendor. However, these topologies have cost and performance implications.

Latency
> The time taken to respond to a single request is often a key service-level agreement (SLA) for a business application. Some topologies are more resilient in the case of regional disruptions but at the cost of write latency.

Geographical considerations
> Applications that require global availability can take advantage of CockroachDB's rich multiregion capabilities. Within these capabilities, there are trade-offs involving survivability, latency, and total costs that need to be understood.

Comparison of Deployment Options

Table 9-1 provides a quick summary of deployment options together with some advantages and disadvantages.

Table 9-1. Comparison of deployment options

Deployment type	Advantages	Disadvantages
CockroachDB Serverless	Minimal operational costs. Pay only for the resources that you use (after free allowance). No need for predeployment capacity planning. Automatic and seamless scaling with demand.	Your deployment is cotenanted with other Serverless users. This may result in less predictable performance when compared to a dedicated deployment. May conflict with some security policies regarding colocation of data with other tenants. Billing may be unpredictable if monthly budgets are set too high, or performance may be throttled if monthly budgets are set too low.
CockroachDB Dedicated	Reduced operational costs. Rapid deployment. Rapid scaling and reconfiguration.	Reduced control over hardware and software configuration. Unlike Serverless, you still have to determine the number and sizes of nodes.
Self-hosted on bare metal	Maximum control over hardware and OS configuration. Lower ongoing hardware "rental" costs, compared to a cloud deployment. Reduced latency for applications running on-premise.	The highest cost in terms of skilled human resources. High initial cost in terms of hardware acquisition. Paying for computing resources that are unused during idle periods.
Self-hosted on cloud VMs	Ability to reconfigure computing resources dynamically. Reduced capital hardware expenditure. Availability of additional services such as Amazon S3 for backup storage.	Increased operational expenditure (hardware "rental").
Self-hosted with Kubernetes (bare metal or cloud VMs)	Reduced complexity of deployment and management. Ability to share hardware resources with other applications. Ability to migrate to cloud-based Kubernetes platforms.	Reduced control over fine-grained configuration. Requires high-level Kubernetes expertise and infrastructure. Multiregion deployments are currently difficult to configure.

As emphasized earlier, the deployment that is best for you depends strongly on your requirements, and there is not (yet) a "one size fits all" deployment option that will suit every enterprise. However, it's worth noting that there's a strong and increasing pull in the database industry toward fully managed deployments (such as CockroachDB Dedicated cloud) and toward containerized development platforms such as Kubernetes.

About Kubernetes

Kubernetes is one of the fastest-growing and most significant technologies in the distributed systems realm. However, it's still relatively young, and there's still a large cohort of software professionals who have not yet used Kubernetes.[1]

Kubernetes controls—orchestrates—the components of a distributed application. These components are independently distributed as pods, which are themselves typically composed of one or more Docker containers. The CockroachDB Kubernetes Operator is a Kubernetes pod that understands how to create and maintain a CockroachDB deployment of arbitrary size. Once you've created a CockroachDB cluster on Kubernetes, you can move it to any environment where Kubernetes is supported, which includes all the major cloud platforms as well as on-premise Kubernetes clusters.

Kubernetes is incredibly powerful and has been described by some as the "Linux of the cloud." However, it does involve a learning curve. O'Reilly has books (such as *Production Kubernetes*) and learning paths (such as this CKAD Prep Course) that can help.

Kubernetes excels at running stateless application servers. A stateful service like a CockroachDB cluster is much more complicated. If this is the first time you're using Kubernetes, consider starting with a stateless service to gain an understanding of the basics before moving on to run CockroachDB on Kubernetes.

Fully managed database as a service (DBaaS) solutions such as CockroachDB Cloud offer significant compelling advantages when compared to self-managed deployments. In particular:

- Fully managed deployments reduce the human costs involved in managing a database cluster. A globally distributed database cluster might require a team of highly skilled administrators, possibly located across multiple time zones. In a DBaaS solution, most of these staff are not required.

- Operational risks are reduced. The team managing the DBaaS has a greater depth of experience with the technology and is generally less likely to misconfigure the cluster. The DBaaS can incorporate more redundancy in human and computing resources than might be practical in a self-hosted deployment. Therefore, the risk of failure for most organizations is reduced.

---

1 In the 2021 StackOverflow survey, only 19.5% of professional developers reported that they were using Kubernetes.

- The time to implement is radically reduced. A DBaaS cluster can be configured in minutes—an equivalent self-hosted cluster might take months of planning and implementation.

- A fully managed DBaaS can be scaled in either direction with ease. In a self-hosted configuration, adding or removing nodes can be a laborious process. Although adding nodes to a CockroachDB cluster is relatively straightforward, the provisioning of hardware in an on-premise environment is not something that can be done quickly. Even on a cloud platform, you still have many manual tasks to perform before a new node can be instantiated.

For organizations where a fully managed DBaaS is, for some reason, not acceptable, a containerized deployment using Kubernetes is often the next most attractive option. A Kubernetes deployment has the following advantages:

- If using a Kubernetes Operator provided by the database vendor, then best practices are baked into the configuration.

- Assuming a Kubernetes environment already exists, the time to deploy is significantly reduced.

- A Kubernetes-based deployment can be scaled in either direction with less effort than on a bare-metal configuration.

The advantages of Kubernetes are widely accepted. Indeed, CockroachDB Cloud itself is deployed on Kubernetes infrastructure. However, Kubernetes is a sophisticated platform and requires experienced administrators to establish and maintain it. If no Kubernetes resources exist in your organization, and CockroachDB Cloud is for some reason not suitable, then you may decide that a self-hosted implementation is required.

However, given the complexity involved in a large CockroachDB cluster deployment, you might still give some thought to a Kubernetes deployment. Perhaps now is the time to invest in Kubernetes training and expertise and to deploy your CockroachDB on your first Kubernetes cluster. The advantages in terms of portability and scalability in the future may well justify the investment at this time.

Serverless Deployments

The most fundamental question for a fully managed solution is between a Dedicated deployment and a Serverless deployment.

In a Dedicated deployment, you choose the number and size of the CockroachDB nodes. These nodes are dedicated to your cluster and are under your control.

In a Serverless deployment, you don't have to worry about any of that. You simply sign up to CockroachDB Serverless in a specific region and provide a limit on the amount of monthly spending you're willing to commit to. Resources will be applied to your service as your workload requires, and you'll only ever be charged for the resources that you use.

There's a lot to like in a Serverless deployment:

- You are paying only for the resources that you use, so if your application has peaks and troughs of activity, you will probably save money.

- Resources applied to your workload will scale dynamically—as the workload demands increase or decrease, CPU and memory will be adjusted to suit. As a result, you may not need to perform benchmarks or otherwise determine ahead of time the hardware resources needed to support the application workload.

- You have a monthly "free" allowance of Request Units,[2] so you can develop for free and then seamlessly transition to a paid service when your application moves into production.

These advantages are compelling across a wide range of use cases. However, there are some limitations:

- In a Serverless deployment, your application shares some physical resources with other Serverless users. In particular, an individual storage node will contain data from multiple CockroachDB Serverless users. Of course, you can't see data from other users, but some organizations with hyper-sensitive security requirements might find this co-tenanting unacceptable.

- This co-tenanting also allows for the possibility that a "noisy neighbor" might disrupt your performance. Because some hardware resources are shared, it's possible that very high load on another tenant causes a noticeable drop in throughput on your service. Furthermore, during periods of low activity, your data in cache memory may be replaced by data from other tenants. When your application starts to ramp back up, it will experience a "cold cache" scenario in which physical I/O rates are higher than normal, and consequently, query latencies are increased.

- In dedicated mode, both your cost and resource utilization are relatively fixed, so there'll be no surprises in billing or in performance. In Serverless mode, you "cap" your bill at a certain amount; if your resource utilization exceeds that cap, then you'll be throttled back to the performance limitations provided by the free tier. There are, of course, ways to monitor and manage your resource utilization. Nevertheless, if you're not paying attention to your application's workload, you might be surprised by an unusually large bill or by the throttling of resources.

---

2 All resource usage in CockroachDB Serverless (beta) is measured in Request Units. RUs represent the compute and I/O resources used by a simple query.

When the throttling occurs, the resources available to the serverless cluster will be abruptly reduced, leading to increases in latency and reduced throughput.

To plan a serverless deployment, you need to establish an upper limit on your monthly spending, a cloud provider, and the region that your serverless deployment will work within. Figure 9-1 shows the configuration panel for a serverless deployment.

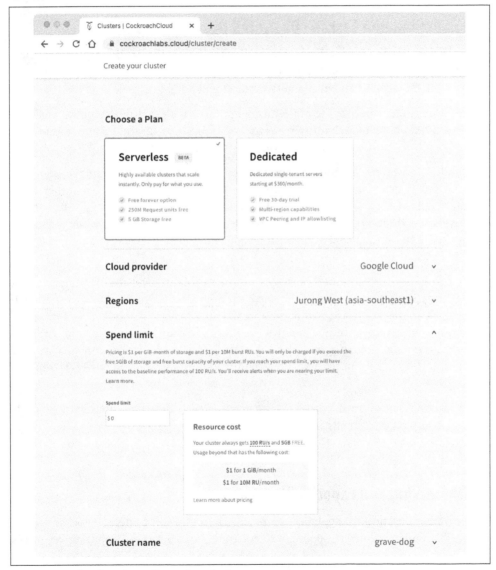

Figure 9-1. Configuring a Serverless deployment page

Single-Region Dedicated Deployments

If your deployment is not serverless, then you will be looking at a dedicated deployment. We'll start with planning a dedicated single-region deployment, which in many respects represents the building blocks for a more complex multiregion deployment. We'll discuss more complex deployments later in this chapter and in subsequent chapters.

Common Planning Tasks—Dedicated Deployments

Regardless of whether you are planning a CockroachDB Dedicated deployment or a self-hosted deployment, you should determine how many nodes will be required to satisfy your throughput and availability requirements.

While more nodes can provide more throughput, from a price-performance perspective, it's often more effective to "scale up"—purchase or configure more powerful servers or VMs—rather than to "scale out"—by adding more nodes to the cluster.

Availability, however, cannot be increased by "scaling up." The number of nodes that can fail is determined by the number of nodes in the cluster. Remember from Chapter 2 that each replica range must maintain a majority of its ranges to survive a failure. So a three-node cluster can survive just one node failure, while a suitably configured five-node cluster (one with a replication factor of five) can survive two node failures.

Configuring an even number of nodes is unhelpful for availability because, in a network partition, neither side of the partition might have a majority. For instance, if a four-node cluster is split in half by a network issue, neither side will have a majority, so processing cannot continue because neither side can be sure that the other is not processing conflicting operations. Likewise, a four-node cluster can survive only a single node failure since a two-node failure fails to leave a majority of replicas running.

When adding nodes to a cluster to improve availability due to individual node failures, you would normally increase the default replica factor to match the number of nodes by issuing an ALTER RANGE default command.[3] We'll discuss the detailed implications of replication factors in Chapter 11.

Benchmarking and Capacity Planning

Before an application is deployed to production, it's somewhere between almost impossible and absolutely impossible to accurately predict the computing resources

---

3 For instance, if the cluster has five nodes, ALTER RANGE default CONFIGURE ZONE USING num_replicas = 5.

required to sustain a given business workload. So how can we successfully configure the correct number and sizes of nodes to support our database?

Broadly speaking, there are three approaches:

- We can perform a benchmark in which we simulate the expected workload as accurately as possible.

- We can extrapolate from another running production application that has a similar workload.

- We can try to model the workload and mathematically predict resource requirements.

None of these approaches is particularly easy or practical. Benchmarking requires some means of simulating a realistic workload. For a geographically distributed, high-throughput application, the complexity of the simulation can approach the complexity of the production deployment itself. Nevertheless, there are many benchmarking tools that we can use to capture test workloads and scale the workload to simulate a larger workload. Regardless, if you intend to run a pre-production benchmark, then be sure to budget for the time, staff, and equipment (virtual or real) required to perform the benchmarks.

Extrapolating from another application is a superficially attractive proposition. "So and so has a similar application, and they use eight m2.extra.fabulous EC2 instances." However, it's a risky proposition—a similar workload in terms of users and queries per second may translate to very different I/O, CPU, and memory requirements depending on the data volumes, data model, and technologies employed. However, you might be able to get close to a reasonable first-order approximation of hardware requirements, especially if you're comparing with another application using CockroachDB. Cockroach Labs' professional services may be able to share their experiences.

Modeling the workload and mathematically predicting the resource requirements is a viable means of creating a low-precision estimation of at least certain aspects of resource requirements. For instance, if you have EXPLAIN ANALYZE output for the SQL statements that make up key transactions and those have been performed on representative data volumes, then you will have a sense of the I/O operations required to support those operations. Given those individual I/O rates, you can extrapolate to aggregate "logical" I/O requirements. The number of physical I/Os will be reduced somewhat by caching at the storage layer—typically by 80% to 90%. This sort of "back of an envelope" I/O estimation may give you a first-cut sense of how many nodes might be required given the aggregate I/O rate. Similar rough estimates might provide some idea of CPU requirements—working out how many simple queries per second a single CPU can sustain and extrapolating that to a higher workload.

Each of these approaches has as much art as science; typically, the guesses of experienced practitioners are at least as accurate. You should always be prepared for your estimates to be inaccurate and either overconfigure your hardware to avoid any chance of a performance bottleneck or be prepared to quickly increase your deployment by adding nodes or increasing the size of your virtual nodes.

The difficulty in predicting exactly what hardware resources will be required to support CockroachDB (or, indeed, any database) provides a strong advantage for cloud-based, orchestrated, or serverless deployments. So, the less able you are to accurately predict your current or future workload, the more motivation you have to deploy on an elastically scalable cloud platform or, indeed, a serverless deployment.

Regardless of the approach you use, you're going to have to make a call on sizing the four main attributes of the deployment:

CPU
> CPU is required for virtually all operations, and is often the limiting factor for a CockroachDB deployment. Every connection, SQL execution, and internal operation consumes CPU resources and CockroachDB.

Memory
> Memory is consumed by every connection and for SQL internal workspaces. Furthermore, memory is used to cache frequently held data to reduce disk I/O.

I/O bandwidth
> Physical disk operations are slower than most other operations and can become a limiting factor. You should ensure that your disks support enough I/O operations per second (IOPS) so that they do not become a limiting factor.

Disk storage
> Obviously, your disks need to support enough storage to store your data. Data storage can be higher than a back of an envelope calculation might suggest: the replication factor will multiply your storage needs, and indexes may consume as much storage as the base tables.

CockroachDB Cloud Deployments

A CockroachDB Dedicated deployment takes away a lot of the effort for a CockroachDB deployment, but there are still some pre-deployment decisions to make.

First, you will want to choose a cloud provider and region. CockroachDB Cloud is available within Google Cloud and AWS across a variety of regions. Generally, you will want to choose a cloud provider and region that is "close" to your application workload. Specifically:

- If your application is already running on a public cloud, then it makes sense to locate your cluster within that cloud and region. For instance, if you have a Node.js-based application running in AWS region us-east-1 (North Virginia), then it makes sense to locate your CockroachDB Cloud cluster in that region because the network delay between application and database will be minimized. Furthermore, you can use virtual private cloud (VPC) peering (*https://cockroa.ch/ 36OzMgz*)—such as Google Cloud VPC Network Peering—to create more secure internal IP addresses and reduce latency.

- If your application is running off-cloud or in some other cloud provider, then locate your CockroachDB Cloud cluster as geographically close to your workload as possible. Geographical closeness does not always result in low network latencies, but large geographical distances are certain to create latency.

The considerations for choosing the number of nodes are the same as for any dedicated deployment. Scaling up can be somewhat more cost-effective from a performance point of view, but a larger number of nodes can provide more redundancy and availability.

At the time of writing, the standard node configurations available in CockroachDB Cloud are shown in Table 9-2.

Table 9-2. Default node configurations in CockroachDB Cloud

Virtual CPUs	Disk size	Memory[a]	I/O per second[b]
2	60 GB	8	600
4	150 GB	16	900
8	500 GB	32	1800
16	900 GB	64	2000

[a] The amount of memory per node is not advertised or guaranteed by CockroachDB, but these numbers were accurate at the time of writing.
[b] Based on AWS disk types, similar I/O rates are provided by other cloud types.

You can approach CockroachDB support if you would like to deploy a nonstandard node size. You might want to do this if you have determined that your CPU/I/O ratios are particularly unique; for instance, if you need a higher amount of storage but don't want to buy more CPU to go with it.

Self-Hosted on a Cloud Platform

In this scenario, we are deploying CockroachDB ourselves to VM images running in a cloud platform such as Amazon EC2 or GCP. Our decision-making process is rather similar to a CockroachDB Dedicated deployment. The unique consideration is the configuration of the VM to be deployed.

Each cloud platform offers a bewildering variety of instance types. You will typically want to choose instance types with at least two virtual CPUs and with 4 GB of RAM per virtual CPU.

On the GCP, these would be the n2-standard, e2_standard, or n2-highcpu family of VMs. On AWS, the m5 or c5 family of EC2 instances are suitable, and on Microsoft Azure, the standard_F family of instances. Keep in mind that these are general guidelines, not concrete recommendations. Each application will have different CPU and memory requirements, so in some cases, you might want to have a different ratio of memory to CPU. It's also true that we all have to live within our budgets, so sometimes you have to make do with what you can afford.

The disk devices attached to these VMs will be an important factor on performance. The guiding principle for optimizing I/O is to provision disks based on I/O rates, not storage capacities. You should ensure that you have provisioned sufficient I/O capacity for your nodes. In AWS use provisioned IOPS solid-state drive (SSD), in Google Cloud Platform the SSD persistent disk (pd-ssd) type, and in Azure premium SSD disks.

We recommend against using "ephemeral" disk devices, which do not survive beyond the life of the VM. These disks are directly attached to the physical machine hosting the VM, and while they can provide low-latency I/Os, they are not guaranteed to survive VM reboots. These disks are referred to as *ephemeral OS disks* or *Lsv2-series disks* on Azure, *ephemeral* or *instance storage* on AWS, and *local SSD* on Google Cloud.

Table 9-3 compares the VM configurations for a "large" node (16 vCPU and 64 GB of memory).

Table 9-3. Comparison of "large" (16 vCPU, 64 GB) VM instances in each of the clouds

Cloud	VM type	Disk type
AWS EC2	m4.4xlarge	Provisioined IOPS SSD (io2)
Azure	D16s_v4	Premium SSD (P30 or better)
Google Cloud Platform	n2-standard-16	SSD persistent disk (pd-ssd)

CockroachDB runs comfortably on most recent versions of Linux. The "standard" Linux distributions provided by the cloud vendor are often preconfigured for optimized time synchronization, which can save configuration time later.

When deploying on cloud platforms, take advantage of the native load balancing and time synchronization mechanisms provided by the cloud. Although it's possible to use external Network Time Protocol (NTP) and load balancers in the cloud, the native cloud offerings are usually superior in terms of manageability, performance, and reliability.

On AWS (*https://cockroa.ch/3r1059W*), you will want to use AWS load balancing and the Amazon Time Sync Service.

On GCP (*https://cockroa.ch/36XvKCl*), use Google TCP proxy load balancing and the Google internal NTP service.

On Azure (*https://cockroa.ch/3j4g02V*), we recommend that you *disable* the Hyper-V Time Synchronization Service in favor of standard NTP and use Azure load balancing.

Chapter 10 contains detailed instructions for configuring time synchronization.

Self-Hosted "Bare-Metal" On-Premise

The considerations for a self-hosted, on-premise deployment are the same as for other dedicated self-hosted options (see "Common Planning Tasks—Dedicated Deployments" on page 288), but there are some specific considerations that you need to take into account.

Primarily, in every other scenario, you have the option of changing the CPU or memory on demand, but with physical hardware, it's much harder to change the configuration on the fly, and consequently, it's more important to correctly configure the nodes initially.

You will also have fewer options for automatic scaling compared with a CockroachDB Cloud deployment, and you will be responsible for your own backup and disaster recovery scenarios.

In a "bare-metal" configuration, you are installing CockroachDB software directly onto the OS of a physical host. That physical host should be configured with sufficient CPU, memory, and I/O resources to sustain the projected workload.

Remember, in a self-hosted, bare-metal configuration, you are limited in your ability to "scale up": while it's possible to reconfigure the memory or CPU of a node, it's not something that can be done with minimal risk or downtime. However, you are still able to "scale out" by adding more nodes. Consequently, it's a good idea to pick a node configuration that provides a good balance between price and performance.

As we will see in later chapters, memory is an important resource for the storage engine, avoiding unnecessary I/O and improving sort performance. For a production implementation, 16 to 64 GB per node is typical. Up to 4 GB per CPU core is typical.

CPU typically constrains the amount of concurrent activity that can occur on each node. At the time of writing, 8-core CPU processors offer the best price-performance ratio, and at least two processors are typical. Systems that have very high concurrency—a higher number of inbound connections, for instance—may benefit from more CPU. Some SQL execution steps—hash joins and sorts, for example—may also be CPU-hungry.

Each CockroachDB node has dedicated disk devices. These devices must satisfy both the storage requirements (e.g., total terabytes [TB]) and the I/O requirements (e.g., IOPS at acceptable latencies). An easy mistake is to buy drives with a certain TB of storage without considering the I/O capacity of the devices. While magnetic disk devices (hard disk drive [HDD]) provide the best GB/dollar ratio, they provide the worst IOPS/dollar ratio. To avoid a CockroachDB node becoming I/O-bound, you will want to use SSDs.

Not all SSDs are created equally, however. SSDs may be connected over the traditional Serial Advanced Technology Attachment (SATA) interface or through the Peripheral Component Interconnect (PCI) (nonvolatile memory express [NVMe]) interface. The NVMe interface provides lower latency and higher performance, though typically at a premium price point. The SSD drive itself may be a single-level cell (SLC), multilevel cell (MLC), triple-level cell (TLC), or quad-level cell (QLC). SLCs are the fastest and QLCs are relatively slower, so if money is no object, then a PCI-based SLC drive would be preferred. However, there are price-performance trade-offs involved in each configuration, and TLCs are quite common in production scenarios.

The absolute I/O throughput of a node is dependent not just on the type of disk but also on the number of disks. Multiple disks can either be striped (RAID0) to provide greater throughput, or the CockroachDB node can be launched with multiple `--store` flags, allowing each disk to, in effect, act as a distinct replication group. Configuring the node with stores—through multiple `--store` flags—provides more parallelism since each node becomes a separately managed Raft store. However, due to the internals of replication, multiple `--store` flags are ineffective unless there are more than three nodes in the cluster. For three-node clusters, you may want to use RAID0 to create a logical volume. Do not configure disks for a CockroachDB node as RAID5 or similar—the write penalty is unacceptably high (*https://cockroa.ch/ 3r1a5Ah*) for anything other than a read-only workload.

It's almost always a good idea to keep each node in the cluster equivalent in terms of configuration and capacity. An unbalanced cluster tends to scale poorly, with the slowest node in the cluster becoming a bottleneck.

Other Self-Hosted Considerations

In any self-hosted scenario, you will need to establish the following:

- Firewalls will need to be established to allow applications to connect to the CockroachDB cluster without allowing access to unwanted parties. We'll discuss firewall and network configuration in detail within Chapters 10 and 12.

- Clock synchronization in CockroachDB affects the stability and performance of the cluster. We'll discuss this in Chapter 10.

- You will almost always want to configure a load balancer in front of your cluster to distribute load and handle node failures. This will also be discussed in Chapter 10.

Self-Hosted Kubernetes

An orchestrated deployment removes a lot of the overhead involved in the deployment and management of distributed containerized applications and frameworks. Kubernetes has emerged as the most influential Orchestration framework, and in this section, we'll discuss planning a Kubernetes deployment, whether on-premise or on a cloud platform.

Kubernetes concepts and administration are beyond the scope of this book, so for the purposes of this section, we'll assume you are familiar with Kubernetes and have a Kubernetes environment available. If you're looking for a guide to deploying Kubernetes in production, we'd suggest *Production Kubernetes* by Ross, Lander, Brand, and Harris.

We talked earlier about the advantages of deploying CockroachDB on Kubernetes. In particular, a Kubernetes deployment is inherently portable—the steps to install the software are identical regardless of where the Kubernetes framework resides. Consequently, we don't have to distinguish here between installing Kubernetes on-premise and installation on one of the major cloud platforms. The core activities are identical.

Your Kubernetes cluster must be running a reasonably up-to-date version of Kubernetes. For CockroachDB version 21.2, the Kubernetes version must be at least 1.18. Newer versions of CockroachDB are likely to require newer versions of Kubernetes—consult the CockroachDB documentation (*https://cockroa.ch/3J7oReM*) for guidance.

Each CockroachDB node will run within a Kubernetes pod, and these pods should be sized similarly to those for on-premise or cloud deployments. As a rule of thumb, each pod should have between 2 and 16 vCPUs and 4 GB of RAM per vCPU.

A Kubernetes node failure will at least temporarily result in the failure of a CockroachDB node. To prevent that node failure from disabling the cluster, you should align the Kubernetes nodes with CockroachDB nodes. For instance, if you deploy a three-node CockroachDB cluster on a three-node Kubernetes cluster, then it's important that each CockroachDB node be located on a separate Kubernetes node. Otherwise, a single Kubernetes node failure might disable the CockroachDB cluster.

In many serious production deployments, CockroachDB will run on dedicated Kubernetes cluster nodes. However, in some cases, a Kubernetes cluster will share CockroachDB workloads with other applications. In these cases, it's important to ensure that each CockroachDB node has sufficient access to CPU and memory resources to avoid conflicts. Typically, this is done by using `Resource requests` for each CockroachDB node that guarantee that a Kubernetes node does not over-commit resources to competing applications. We'll come back to this in the next chapter, but from a planning point of view, you want to be sure that each Cock-roachDB node can actually have exclusive access to the vCPU and memory resources required. This requires some awareness of the resource requirements of the other pods running within the cluster.

Historically, Kubernetes has been used for applications more than databases—CPU and memory have been more influential than I/O. Consequently, many Kubernetes clusters—particularly those on Cloud platforms—are configured with economical "storage by the GB" disks. For instance, when creating a Kubernetes cluster on GCP, the default disk type for the node pool is `standard persistent disk`, whereas an `SSD persistent disk` is a much better option for a database deployment.

When configuring Kubernetes nodes for CockroachDB, follow the guidelines for on-premise hardware; in particular, you should use high-performance SSDs.

In many cases, the Kubernetes cluster will have multiple disk types available and exposed as `storageclasses`. During CockroachDB initialization, you can select the storage type most applicable to your workload. We'll come back to this in Chap-ter 10. From a planning point of view, you need to be sure that high-performance disk devices are available to the Kubernetes cluster to which you intend to deploy CockroachDB.

Configuring for Self-Hosted High Availability

One of the reasons for using a distributed database system is that the database can survive the sorts of failures that would cause a monolithic database to fail. The original SQL databases might fail catastrophically if even a single disk device failed—and the disks of those eras were far less resilient than those of today.

In a distributed database like CockroachDB, single points of failure like these are completely survivable. We've outlined in previous chapters—particularly Chapter 2 —how CockroachDB topologies can be made fault-tolerant. In a production deploy-ment, it's time to put these principles into practice.

Survivable failures fall into one of the following categories:

- A hardware failure that does not cause a node to fail. In particular, the failure of a disk device.
- The failure of one or more nodes.
- A network failure.

- The failure of an availability zone (perhaps a data center failure).
- Failure of a larger region.

Disk Failure

In a default configuration, the failure of a disk device will cause the CockroachDB node to fail. However, it's long been possible to configure disk devices in redundant arrays that allow for individual disk failures. It's possible in self-hosted configuration to configure RAID10 (mirrored and striped) directly attached disks for availability purposes. If this is done, then a disk failure will not necessarily cause a node failure. However, it's completely acceptable to use standalone disks and rely on CockroachDB replication to handle disk failures. Note that the disks recommended on cloud platforms are often replicated transparently.

Node Failures

The default configuration of CockroachDB provides for three replicas of each range. This allows for only a single node failure. To tolerate more than one node failure, we need to increase the replication factor.

The replication factor is controlled by CockroachDB replication zones. The `crdb_internal.zones` table contains the definitions for these zones. The zone with target RANGE `default` defines the default zone:

```
/movr>  SELECT raw_config_sql FROM crdb_internal.zones
   WHERE target='RANGE default';
               raw_config_sql
---------------------------------------------
   ALTER RANGE default CONFIGURE ZONE USING
       range_min_bytes = 134217728,
       range_max_bytes = 536870912,
       gc.ttlseconds = 90000,
       num_replicas = 3,
       constraints = '[]',
       lease_preferences = '[]'
```

To survive two node failures, we need a replication factor of at least five. We can configure this as follows:

```
/movr> ALTER RANGE default CONFIGURE ZONE USING
     num_replicas=5;
CONFIGURE ZONE 1
```

Remember, only by increasing the number of replicas to an odd number do we increase the number of node failures that can be tolerated. There must always be a majority of replicas available to survive a node failure—so to survive two failures, we need five replicas.[4] In general, we don't recommend setting the replication factor above five—if you're concerned about survivability beyond individual node failures, you should consider availability zone configurations as discussed in Chapter 11.

Also, bear in mind that when we increase the replication factor, we increase the write overhead for transactions. As always, in distributed systems, there is a trade-off between write throughput and availability. The higher the replication factor, the more failures we can endure, but at the cost of slower transactional consensus.

In many CockroachDB deployments, multiregion configurations are used to protect against larger-scale node failures. For this reason, if you're considering a replication factor above five, we think you might want to consider if a multiregion topology is better for your specific circumstances.

Network Failure

A distributed database is highly vulnerable to network failures because all nodes need to communicate with each other to continue. If the network as a whole fails, the cluster cannot continue.

Luckily, complete network failures are unlikely. Simple network failures may cause a node to become isolated and fail—in which case we rely upon the standard CockroachDB replication to continue operations.

More severe network failures create more interesting scenarios. When a network becomes partitioned such that the CockroachDB cluster is split in two, the side of the partition with the smaller number of nodes is effectively unavailable. For a three-node cluster, this will be the same as a single node failure. However, for larger clusters, the network partition may result in a larger number of nodes becoming disconnected. This is why we normally want to increase the replication factor as we increase the size of the cluster.

In the case of a zone survival goal, data unavailability will occur if the number of nodes that become partitioned is more than half of the zone replication factor.

Many of these concepts will be elaborated on in Chapter 12.

Zone and Region Topologies

Multiregion deployments allow a CockroachDB database to span multiple geographic regions.

---

4 CockroachDB includes some system ranges whose default replication is set to five. If you are increasing the general replication factor above five, you should increase the replication factor for these as well (*https://cockroa.ch/36S8CVW*).

In a multiregion deployment, each node is allocated to one *region*. A region can consist of multiple *zones*. These concepts are roughly analogous to the regions and zones that exist in cloud systems such as AWS or GCP.

Generally, a *region* is a collection of computing resources that are close enough together that you can mostly ignore network latency between them. Regions are often aligned with cities.

An *availability zone* is ideally a collection of resources that do not have any points of failure in common with other availability zones. For the major cloud providers, each availability zone consists of a separate building with separate connections to the power grid and network with independent backup generators and so on.

Each database within the cluster can be assigned to one or more regions, with one of the regions being the primary.

When planning for a multiregion deployment, it's important to understand your objectives. Broadly speaking, multiregional deployments can deliver one of two desirable objectives:

- By distributing data close to its users, a multiregional deployment can reduce latency and improve performance for a widely distributed application. For instance, you can ensure that Australian users can update their shopping basket without having to send updates to a US data center and vice versa.
- By replicating data widely across multiple geographical regions, a multiregion deployment can allow a cluster to survive severe outages that would otherwise be close to catastrophic. For instance, you could ensure that the database cluster continues to function even if every data center in the eastern US region fails.

Of course, these two objectives are somewhat in conflict—in one case, we localize data, and in the other case, we broadly distribute it. It's usually possible to provide good read performance to all regions, but writes are either going to be distributed broadly (for high availability) or restricted to local regions (for low latency). Be clear on which objective is more important to you before planning your deployment. It's also possible to pick different objectives for specific parts of the database—see Chapter 11 for more details on configuring tables and databases for specific survival goals.

The failure considerations for regional survival are an extension of zone survival logic. Replicas are distributed across regions in such a way that the loss of any single region still leaves a majority of voting replicas in place.

Although a cluster may be configured to survive the failure of a single region, it may not be resilient to the failure of the same number of nodes in a single region arbitrarily spread across regions in the cluster. For example, in a nine-node cluster with three nodes in three regions each, the loss of a single region would result in the loss of three nodes from the cluster. If we configure the replication factor of the data in the cluster to maintain five copies, CockroachDB will spread the replicas across the three regions with at most two copies in any single region. This way, the failure of a single region will only remove two out of five replicas of data, which ensures that all data would still be available. However, that doesn't mean that any three nodes can fail. If one node from each region failed, then some ranges at least would lose three of five replicas and become unavailable.

The lesson here is that if you want to survive the failure of *any* three nodes in a nine-node cluster, you would need a replication factor of at least seven.

We'll elaborate on these considerations in Chapter 12.

Summary

CockroachDB supports a very wide range of deployment scenarios, and in this chapter, we've attempted to give you an overview of the decision points for the various deployment options and outlined the pre-deployment planning tasks.

A CockroachDB Serverless deployment is probably the simplest option for deploying CockroachDB. In a Serverless deployment, you need only decide upon an execution region and monthly budget. CockroachDB Cloud will scale automatically to suit workload, and you need only pay for what you use.

If serverless is not suitable, you can deploy a dedicated CockroachDB cluster. The dedicated cluster can be deployed in CockroachDB Cloud or in a self-hosted manner either on a public cloud or your own hardware. Cloud deployments provide more flexibility in terms of scaling, but a Kubernetes "local cloud" can provide most of the same advantages.

Managed cloud deployments and Kubernetes managed deployments are definitely increasing in popularity; both options reduce operational complexity and allow for more reactive scaling. However, an on-premise "bare metal" deployment is still a common and fully supported configuration.

In the next chapter, we'll go through the steps required to turn our planning into reality by deploying CockroachDB.

Single-Region Deployment

In this chapter, we will describe the steps required to set up a self-hosted CockroachDB cluster.

If you've decided to use—or are already using—a CockroachDB Dedicated or Serverless deployment, then congratulations! You can safely skip over this chapter. However, if you're deploying on your own hardware or on a cloud platform, you have some work to do, and this chapter describes that work.

CockroachDB is not difficult to install, but distributed systems have more moving parts than other software products, so it may seem more difficult than—for example—installing MySQL or PostgreSQL.

CockroachDB installation instructions can change with each release, and there are some edge cases that we don't have space for in this chapter, so make sure that you check out the "Production Checklist" (*https://cockroa.ch/3J3Xylz*) and "Manual Deployment" (*https://cockroa.ch/3NM1oU5*) pages in the CockroachDB docs.

In this chapter, we will focus on the tasks involved in deploying to a single region. In Chapter 12, we'll extend to the additional considerations involved in a multiregion deployment.

Deploying On-Premise or On-Cloud

For the on-premise parts of this section, we are deploying a three-node CockroachDB cluster on Ubuntu servers, with a fourth Ubuntu node running a load balancer. The CockroachDB nodes are called gubuntu1, gubuntu2, and gubuntu3. The load balancer is mubuntu. Each node has a cockroachdb user installed, and the CockroachDB binaries already installed in */usr/local/bin*. We'll be using a fifth machine—a Mac laptop—to perform the installation; we have called that the "home system."

Firewall Configuration

CockroachDB nodes expect to be able to communicate with each other over the SQL port (by default 26257, configurable through the `--sql-addr` flag)—this port should be accessible to all nodes in the cluster from all nodes in the cluster.

Applications also require access to the SQL port; any program that wishes to connect to CockroachDB and anyone who wants to issue `cockroach sql` or other CLI commands will need access to the port. It's generally wise, however, to limit as much as possible the IP addresses that have access to the port since this is potentially a cyber-attack vector. Use allowlists to restrict access to this port as much as possible.

Access to port 8080 is required to access the DB Console.

Operating System Configuration

CockroachDB can run successfully on most default configurations of Linux. However, there are a couple of things to check.

Your Linux should have the standard C library *glibc* installed as well as the `libcurses` library.

CockroachDB can require more than the default number of open file descriptors. The absolute minimum number is about 2,000, but setting the file descriptors to unlimited or at least 15,000 is recommended. The exact configuration procedures can be OS, and version-specific; see the CockroachDB documentation (*https://cockroa.ch/3u6BBy3*) for full instructions.

To increase the file descriptor limit on Ubuntu, we add `nofile` entries to the */etc/security/limits.conf* file. First, we see if any entries already exist:

```
guyharrison@gubuntu2:~$ sudo -i

root@gubuntu2:~# grep nofile  /etc/security/limits.conf
#          - nofile - max number of open file descriptors
```

Because there are no entries, we append new entries. If there were existing entries, we would, of course, need to edit them:

```
root@gubuntu2:~# echo '*  soft  nofile  unlimited' \
    >>/etc/security/limits.conf
root@gubuntu2:~# echo '*  hard  nofile  unlimited' \
    >>/etc/security/limits.conf
```

We need to make sure the line `session required pam_limits.so` appears both in */etc/pam.d/common-session* and */etc/pam.d/common-session-noninteractive*:

```
root@gubuntu2:~# grep pam_limits /etc/pam.d/common-session
root@gubuntu2:~# grep pam_limits /etc/pam.d/common-session-noninteractive
root@gubuntu2:~# echo 'session required pam_limits.so' \
```

```
  >>/etc/pam.d/common-session
root@gubuntu2:~# echo 'session required pam_limits.so' \
  >>/etc/pam.d/common-session-noninteractive
```

Also, check that the system-wide value in */proc/sys/fs/file-max* is sufficient:

```
root@gubuntu2:~# cat /proc/sys/fs/file-max
9223372036854775807
```

You will need to reboot the system to ensure these settings are applied to all processes.

Clock Synchronization On-Premise

We emphasized in Chapter 2 that CockroachDB requires robust time synchronization between nodes. By default, any clock skew higher than 500 ms may cause a node to become unavailable. Clock skews below 500 ms affect performance because Cockroach DB will sometimes need to retry reads whose transactional sequence cannot be determined. In short, we want time synchronization to be as tight as possible.

Linux operating systems will almost always be configured with an NTP service active. You can check the current configuration with timedatectl:

```
$ timedatectl
              Local time: Thu 2021-09-16 22:08:51 PDT
          Universal time: Fri 2021-09-17 05:08:51 UTC
                RTC time: Fri 2021-09-17 05:08:51
               Time zone: America/Los_Angeles (PDT, -0700)
System clock synchronized: yes
             NTP service: active
           RTC in local TZ: no
```

If timedatectl reports that the NTP service is inactive (unlikely), then enable it:[1]

```
$ timedatectl set-ntp true
```

The show-timesync argument can be used to show the existing NTP server configuration:

```
$ timedatectl show-timesync
FallbackNTPServers=ntp.ubuntu.com
ServerName=ntp.ubuntu.com
ServerAddress=91.189.94.4
RootDistanceMaxUSec=5s
PollIntervalMinUSec=32s
PollIntervalMaxUSec=34min 8s
PollIntervalUSec=8min 32s
NTPMessage={ Leap=0, Version=4, Mode=4, Stratum=2, … }
Frequency=-1224761
```

---

1 On some Linux systems you may have to install system-timesyncd: sudo apt install systemd-timesyncd.

For an on-premise deployment, the CockroachDB team recommends the use of Google NTP servers because their "time smearing" (*https://cockroa.ch/3J1Rava*) implementation avoids issues relating to leap seconds.

To implement the Google NTP servers, edit */etc/systemd/timesyncd.conf* so that the Google time servers are listed in the NTP entry within the [Time] section:

```
[Time]
NTP=time1.google.com time2.google.com time3.google.com time4.google.com
```

Now restart the timesyncd service and check that the service is pointing to Google NTP servers:

```
$ systemctl restart systemd-timesyncd.service
$ timedatectl show-timesync
SystemNTPServers=time1.google.com time2.google.com time3.google.com time4.goo
FallbackNTPServers=ntp.ubuntu.com
ServerName=time1.google.com
ServerAddress=216.239.35.0
RootDistanceMaxUSec=5s
PollIntervalMinUSec=32s
PollIntervalMaxUSec=34min 8s
PollIntervalUSec=1min 4s
NTPMessage={ Leap=0, Version=4, Mode=4, Stratum=1, Precision=-20, … }
Frequency=2568984
```

All looks good! Of course, we need to do this on every node in the cluster.

If your hosts are using chrony or ntpd to synchronize time, then the procedure is similar. Add the Google time servers to */etc/chrony.conf* or */etc/ntp.conf* as appropriate and restart the service. It's very important that all nodes use the same time synchronization mechanism—although time is time everywhere, small inconsistencies between time sync can have large implications for a distributed CockroachDB cluster.

Clock Synchronization on Cloud Platforms

While it is possible to use the on-premise time synchronization configuration on a cloud platform, there are strong advantages to using the vendor's own time synchronization services when deploying on a public cloud such as Amazon or Google. The vendor's cloud synchronization generally involves specialized hardware installed in each data center and region and is, therefore, capable of delivering tighter time synchronization than would be possible using a generic configuration.

On Amazon AWS, the Amazon Time Sync Service is enabled by default if the EC2 instance is based on the latest version of Amazon Linux. If you're using a non-Amazon image or an older Amazon Machine Image (AMI), then follow the instructions provided by Amazon (*https://cockroa.ch/3J6aKGM*) to install and configure the chrony time service to use the Amazon time service using the 169.254.169.123 IPV4 address or fd00:ec2::123 IPV6 address.

If all is well, you should see 169.254.169.123 IPV4 address or fd00:ec2::123 from the output of a `chronyc sources` command:

```
[ec2-user@ip-172-30-0-188 ~]$ chronyc sources
MS Name/IP address         Stratum Poll Reach LastRx Last sample
===============================================================================
^* 169.254.169.123               3    4   377     2  -8333ns[  -13us] +/-  477us
^- 165.227.219.198               2    6    77    41   +45us[  +35us] +/-   43ms
^- clock.sjc.he.net              1    6   137    38 +2869us[+2859us] +/-   34ms
^- hc-007-ntp1.weber.edu         1    6    77    40 +8155us[+8145us] +/-   33ms
^- ntp.wdc1.us.leaseweb.net      2    6    77    40  +194us[ +184us] +/-  125ms
```

On Google Cloud, follow the Google instructions (*https://cockroa.ch/3JcVYOd*) to configure your time service to use `metadata.google` or `metadata.google.internal`. You should then see `metadata.google` or `metadata.google.internal` as a source from the `chronyc sources` command:

```
gharriso@ubuntu-us:~$ chronyc sources
210 Number of sources = 1
MS Name/IP address         Stratum Poll Reach LastRx Last sample
===============================================================================
^* metadata.google.internal      2    6    77    24   -27us[ +302us] +/-  499us
```

On Microsoft Azure, CockroachDB recommends that you *disable* the default Hyper-V Time Synchronization Service and configure the NTP service as shown for an on-premise deployment.[2]

To disable the service, obtain the address of the Time Synchronization device:

```
$ sudo -i
$ cd /tmp
$ curl -O \
  https://raw.githubusercontent.com/torvalds/linux/master/tools/hv/lsvmbus

  % Total    % Received % Xferd  Average Speed   Time    Time     Time  Current
                                 Dload  Upload   Total   Spent    Left  Speed
100  3555  100  3555    0     0  79000      0 --:--:-- --:--:-- --:--:-- 79000

$ python lsvmbus -vv | grep -w "Time Synchronization" -A 3
VMBUS ID 11: Class_ID = {9527e630-...ab0175caf} - [Time Synchronization]
        Device_ID = {2dd1ce17-079e-403c-b352-a1921ee207ee}
        Sysfs path: /sys/bus/vmbus/devices/2dd1ce17-079e-403c-b352-a1921ee207ee
        Rel_ID=11, target_cpu=0
```

Now, push that Device ID into the unbind file at */sys/bus/vmbus/drivers/hv_utils* (or */sys/bus/vmbus/drivers/hv_util* on some Linuxes):

---

2 This recommendation is based on clock drift issues observed on Azure by the CockroachDB team. Check the documentation (*https://cockroa.ch/3LC5Ena*) for updates for this issue.

```
$ echo 2dd1ce17-079e-403c-b352-a1921ee207ee \
  >/sys/bus/vmbus/drivers/hv_utils/unbind
```

You can now install the NTP service using the instructions for on-premise that we presented earlier in this chapter.

Creating Certificates

Each CockroachDB node will require a certificate to prove its identity to other members of the cluster and to clients that are requesting to connect. Of course, it's possible to run CockroachDB in insecure mode (*https://cockroa.ch/3NMliOz*), but this is not a recommended production configuration, so we don't describe it here.

We generally create certificates on a separate host from the production system for security reasons. We can create certificates on any secure system that has the Cockroach binary installed—the home system.

On the home system, we start by creating a certificate authority (CA) certificate:

```
mkdir -p $HOME/cockroach/certs
mkdir -p $HOME/cockroach/ca-cert

cockroach cert create-ca \
    --certs-dir=$HOME/cockroach/certs \
    --ca-key=$HOME/cockroach/ca-cert/ca.key
```

Using a Public Certificate Authority

For an internal cluster, our self-generated CA certificate is sufficient for most purposes. However, it does result in some warnings when accessing the DB Console.

The alternative is to use a certificate generated by a public CA that is trusted by browsers such as Google Chrome. See the CockroachDB documentation (*https://cockroa.ch/33ULHrA*) for more information.

Next, we generate certificates for each node in the cluster. Each certificate should list the endpoints that the node can respond from, including those of any load balancers. Our load balancer is going to be installed on the mubuntu host (IP address 192.168.0.197). The certificate lists gubuntu1, gubuntu1's IP address, localhost addresses, and addresses for the mubuntu load balancer:

```
$ cockroach cert create-node \
    gubuntu1 \
    localhost \
    127.0.0.1 \
    mubuntu \
    mubuntu.local \
    192.168.0.197 \
```

```
--certs-dir=$HOME/cockroach/certs \
--ca-key=$HOME/cockroach/ca-cert/ca.key \
--overwrite
```

We copy that certificate to the `gubuntu1` node:

```
$ cd $HOME/cockroach/certs
$ scp ca.crt node.crt node.key cockroachdb@gubuntu1:cockroach/certs
cockroachdb@gubuntu1's password:
ca.crt    100% 1151    300.6KB/s    00:00
node.crt  100% 1281    302.1KB/s    00:00
node.key  100% 1675    395.6KB/s    00:00
```

We then repeat this process for each of the other nodes. For example, here, we perform the same certificate generation and copy for `gubuntu2`:

```
cockroach cert create-node \
    192.168.0.50      \
    gubuntu2 \
    gubuntu2.local    \
    localhost \
    127.0.0.1 \
    mubuntu \
    mubuntu.local \
    192.168.0.197 \
--certs-dir=$HOME/cockroach/certs \
--ca-key=$HOME/cockroach/ca-cert/ca.key

ssh cockroachdb@gubuntu2 "mkdir -p cockroach/certs"

cd $HOME/cockroach/certs
scp ca.crt node.crt node.key cockroachdb@gubuntu2:cockroach/certs
```

To connect remotely to our cluster without a password (for initial setup), we'll need a root client certificate. For now, we'll just create this on the home system:

```
$ cockroach cert create-client \
    root \
    --certs-dir=$HOME/cockroach/certs \
    --ca-key=$HOME/cockroach/ca-cert/ca.key
```

Configuring the Nodes

To start each Cockroach server node, we need to copy the certificates into the appropriate directory and configure a service to run the cockroach program. In the previous step, we copied the certificates into the directory *~cockroachdb/cockroach/certs*. Now we move those certificates into the */var/lib/cockroachdb/certs* directory:

```
cockroachdb@gubuntu1:~$ sudo mkdir /var/lib/cockroachdb
[sudo] password for cockroachdb:
cockroachdb@gubuntu1:~$ sudo chown cockroachdb:cockroachdb /var/lib/cockroachdb
cockroachdb@gubuntu1:~$ mv ~/cockroach/certs /var/lib/cockroachdb
```

To configure CockroachDB as a service, we create a `systemd` service definition in */etc/system/system*. This file defines the command line (`ExecStart`), working directory (`WorkingDirectory`), and the account that runs the CockroachDB binary (`User`). Note in particular that the `--advertise-addr` argument within the `ExecStart` entry should match the current node:

```
$ cat /etc/systemd/system/cockroachdb.service
[Unit]
Description=Cockroach Database cluster node
Requires=network.target
[Service]
Type=notify
WorkingDirectory=/var/lib/cockroachdb
ExecStart=/usr/local/bin/cockroach start --certs-dir=certs
      --advertise-addr=gubuntu1 --join=gubuntu1,gubuntu2,gubuntu3
TimeoutStopSec=60
Restart=always
RestartSec=10
StandardOutput=syslog
StandardError=syslog
SyslogIdentifier=cockroachdb
User=cockroachdb
[Install]
```

The settings for the `ExecStart` are the simplest that could possibly work. However, on a production system, you'll want to additionally specify the following:

- `--cache` specifies the amount of memory to cache data in the KV store. It defaults to 128 MB, which is usually too small. You may specify an exact amount or a proportion of physical memory (0.5 for 50% of physical memory, for instance). We'll come back to this setting in Chapter 14.

- `--max-sql-memory` specifies the amount of memory for the SQL engine. This includes sort and hash areas and intermediate data sets. This defaults to .25 (25% of physical memory).

- `--locality` includes information about the node's physical location. These values can be used later when configuring multiregion deployment. So, for instance, to start a server in the `us-west-1` region, `us-west-1a` zone with 35% of memory allocated to SQL memory and 35% allocated to KV store cache, our `ExecStart` might look like this:

```
ExecStart=/usr/local/bin/cockroach start --certs-dir=certs
--advertise-addr=gubuntu2 --join=gubuntu1,gubuntu2,gubuntu3
--locality=region=us-west-1,zone=us-west-1a
--max-sql-memory=.35 --cache=.35
```

Once the file is created, we can start the service using `systemctl`:

```
cockroachdb@gubuntu1:~$ sudo systemctl start cockroachdb
cockroachdb@gubuntu1:~$ sudo systemctl status cockroachdb
```

- cockroachdb.service - Cockroach Database cluster node
      Loaded: loaded (/etc/systemd/system/cockroachdb.service;)
      Active: active (running) since Sun 2021-09-05 11:49:43 AEST; 1min 31s ago
    Main PID: 8650 (cockroach)
       Tasks: 10 (limit: 9485)
      Memory: 119.3M
      CGroup: /system.slice/cockroachdb.service
              └─8650 /usr/local/bin/cockroach start --certs-dir=certs
--advertise-addr=gubuntu1 --join=gubuntu1,gubuntu2,gubuntu3

    Sep 05 11:49:43 gubuntu1 systemd[1]: Started Cockroach Database cluster node.

We now repeat these steps for the other nodes—gubuntu2 and gubuntu3. We make sure that the --advertise-addr listed in the *cockroachdb.service* file is different for each node in the cluster.

Creating a Ballast File

In the event that the filesystem containing CockroachDB data files fills up, the CockroachDB system might be unable to start up. To mitigate this possibility, CockroachDB automatically creates a *ballast file* at node startup. Should disk space be exhausted, the ballast file can be removed, and the node can continue to function.

The ballast file defaults to 1% of total disk capacity or 1 GiB, whichever is smaller. The size of the ballast file may be configured using the --store flag to cockroach start with a ballast-size field; this field accepts the same value formats as the size field.

During node startup, if available disk space on at least one store is less than or equal to half the ballast file size, the process will exit immediately with the exit code 10, signifying *Disk Full*.

To allow the node to start, you can manually remove the *EMERGENCY_BALLAST* file, which is located in the store's *cockroach-data/auxiliary* directory.

In versions of CockroachDB earlier than 21.2, ballast files could be created manually with the cockroach debug ballast command.

Initializing the Cluster

Once the CockroachDB service is running on each node, we can initialize the cluster. From the home machine, we issue a cockroach init command:

```
$ cockroach init --certs-dir=$HOME/cockroach/certs --host=gubuntu1
Cluster successfully initialized
```

We should now be able to connect to nodes in the cluster using the `cockroach sql` command:

```
$ cockroach sql --certs-dir=$HOME/cockroach/certs --host=gubuntu1
#
# Welcome to the CockroachDB SQL shell.
# All statements must be terminated by a semicolon.
# To exit, type: \q.
#
# Enter \? for a brief introduction.
#
root@gubuntu1:26257/defaultdb>
```

We can also issue a `cockroach node status` command to make sure that all the nodes are working:

```
$ cockroach node status --certs-dir=$HOME/cockroach/certs --host=gubuntu2
```

id	address	started_at	is_av	is_live
1	gubuntu1:26257	2021-09-05 22:57:56.58651+00:00:00	true	true
2	gubuntu2:26257	2021-09-05 22:58:11.223174+00:00:00	true	true
3	gubuntu3:26257	2021-09-05 23:02:37.353788+00:00:00	true	true

If there's trouble, try looking at the logs for each node in the */var/lib/cockroachdb/cockroach-data/logs* directory. This command will tail the most recent log:[3]

```
cd /var/lib/cockroachdb/cockroach-data/logs;tail -f `ls -t |head -1`
```

Typical problems that can occur during cluster setup include:

- Incorrect certificates—for instance, you might accidentally copy the certificate for node1 to node2.

- DNS errors—each node needs to be able to correctly resolve the address of each node listed in the `-join` argument.

- Firewall errors—the ports for 26257 and 8080 need to be open to other nodes in the cluster and to the client node.

CockroachDB documentation (*https://cockroa.ch/3LXmAoz*) lists other troubleshooting steps that you can undertake in the event your cluster does not initialize.

Creating the First User

To connect to the DB Console and to connect from SQL clients without the client root certificate, we'll need to create a user in the database:

---

3 Log location and configuration can be fine-tuned (*https://cockroa.ch/3r21JIy*). We'll come back to that in a later chapter.

```
$ cockroach sql --host=gubuntu1 --certs-dir=$HOME/cockroach/certs
#
# Welcome to the CockroachDB SQL shell.
# All statements must be terminated by a semicolon.
# To exit, type: \q.
#
# Enter \? for a brief introduction.
#
root@gubuntu1:26257/defaultdb>
  CREATE USER consoleAdmin WITH PASSWORD
    'EfV2ZwV1oHlsQdW9XW9ovKDx0vm6GB';
CREATE ROLE

Time: 126ms total (execution 121ms / network 5ms)
```

You might want to assign other roles to this user depending on your needs. We'll discuss user configuration further in Chapter 12.

We can then navigate to *https://${nodeName}:8080* to visit the DB Console. If you use a self-generated CA certificate, you'll get a warning because your browser won't recognize the CA certificate. Figure 10-1 shows the warning.

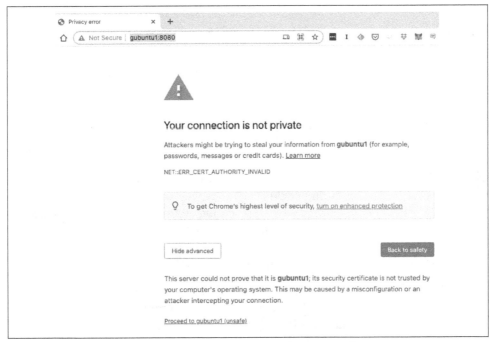

Figure 10-1. Insecure warning when connecting to cluster console

It's safe to proceed past this warning, but if it concerns you, you should consider signing your certificates with a public certificate authority generated certificate (*https://cockroa.ch/33ULHrA*).

Figure 10-2 shows the database console for our freshly created three-node cluster.

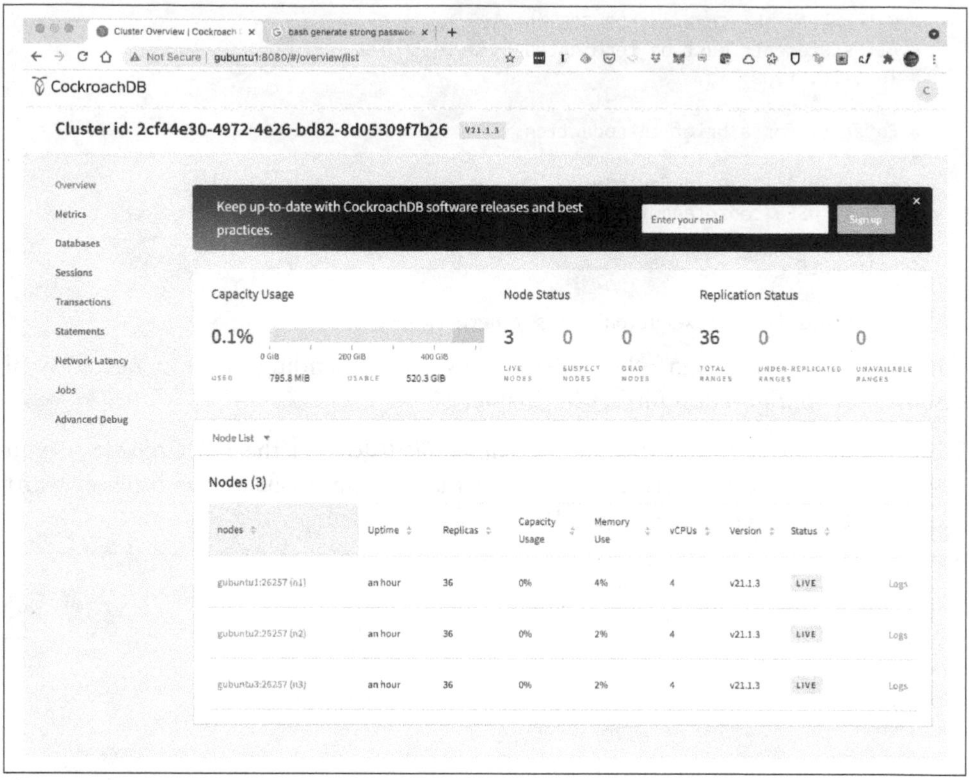

Figure 10-2. DB Console for a three-node cluster (large format version (https://cock roa.ch/cockroachDB-figs))

The DB Console shown in Figure 10-2 shows the cluster UUID. If the user specifies the `--cluster-name` flag during `cockroach init`, the console will show that name instead. This has the added benefit of preventing nodes from being added to the wrong cluster—the cluster name must match across all nodes.

Installing a Load Balancer (On-Premise)

As we discussed way back in Chapter 2, a load balancer distributes the load across the members of a CockroachDB cluster and thereby improves performance as well as improving maintainability by allowing seamless connection shifting when a node goes down.

With a single load balancer, client connections are resilient to node failure, but the load balancer itself is a point of failure. Therefore, it's best to make load balancing resilient as well by using multiple load-balancing instances, with a mechanism such as floating IPs or DNS to select load balancers for clients.

For an on-premise implementation, the HAProxy load balancer is a popular choice and directly supported by CockroachDB, so we'll use that here.

On our home machine, we can generate a *haproxy.cfg* configuration file as follows:

```
$ cockroach gen haproxy \
--certs-dir=$HOME/cockroach/certs \
--host=gubuntu1
```

The default settings for HAProxy are usually adequate, but you may modify settings as appropriate:

```
$ cat haproxy.cfg

global
  maxconn 4096

defaults
    mode                tcp
    # Timeout values should be configured for your specific use.
    timeout connect     10s
    timeout client      1m
    timeout server      1m
    # TCP keep-alive on client side. Server already enables them.
    option              clitcpka

listen psql
    bind :26257
    mode tcp
    balance roundrobin
    option httpchk GET /health?ready=1
    server cockroach1 gubuntu1:26257 check port 8080
    server cockroach2 gubuntu2:26257 check port 8080
    server cockroach3 gubuntu3:26257 check port 8080
```

We copy *haproxy.cfg* to the load balancer node:

```
$ scp haproxy.cfg cockroachdb@mubuntu:~
haproxy.cfg
```

On the load balancer node (mubuntu in this case), we install the HAProxy software:

```
$ sudo apt install haproxy
Reading package lists... Done
Building dependency tree
<snip>
Created symlink /etc/systemd/system/multi-user.target.wants/haproxy.service
```

```
      → /lib/systemd/system/haproxy.service.
<snip>
Processing triggers for ureadahead (0.100.0-21) ...
ureadahead will be reprofiled on next reboot
```

Now we copy the config file that we copied over earlier into the standard location for the HAProxy service (in this case */etc/haproxy*):

```
root@mubuntu:~# cd /etc/haproxy
root@mubuntu:/etc/haproxy# cp haproxy.cfg haproxy.cfg.old
root@mubuntu:/etc/haproxy# cp ~cockroachdb/haproxy.cfg .
```

With the new configuration file in place, we can now restart the HAProxy service:

```
cockroachdb@mubuntu:~$ sudo systemctl restart haproxy
cockroachdb@mubuntu:~$ sudo systemctl status haproxy
● haproxy.service - HAProxy Load Balancer

    Active: active (running) since Mon 2021-09-06 10:29:16 AEST; 4s ago
      Docs: man:haproxy(1)
    CGroup: /system.slice/haproxy.service
            ├─3319233 /usr/sbin/haproxy -Ws -f /etc/haproxy/haproxy.cfg
              -p /run/haproxy.pid
            └─3319235 /usr/sbin/haproxy -Ws -f /etc/haproxy/haproxy.cfg
              -p /run/haproxy.pid
```

Back on the home system, confirm that you can connect to the cluster through the node balancer node:

```
$ cockroach sql --host=mubuntu --certs-dir=$HOME/cockroach/certs
#
# Welcome to the CockroachDB SQL shell.
# All statements must be terminated by a semicolon.
# To exit, type: \q.
#
# Enter \? for a brief introduction.
#
root@mubuntu:26257/defaultdb> show databases;
  database_name | owner | primary_region | regions | survival_goal
----------------+-------+----------------+---------+----------------
  defaultdb     | root  | NULL           | {}      | NULL
  postgres      | root  | NULL           | {}      | NULL
  system        | node  | NULL           | {}      | NULL
(3 rows)
```

Cloud Load Balancers

HAProxy is a good choice for an on-premise deployment, but if you're deploying to a public cloud, then the cloud vendor's load-balancing solutions are preferable.

Load-balancing configuration for the cloud platforms is straightforward. The load balancer should listen to TCP port 26257 and distribute requests in a round-robin

---

fashion to the CockroachDB nodes. The health check should be configured to use port 8080 with the /health?ready=1 path.

On AWS, use the *AWS Load Balancing* service. Create a target group that contains all of the instances in your cluster and listens on port 26257. You should then be able to connect to your cluster using the provisioned IP address for the load balancer. See the CockroachDB documentation (*https://cockroa.ch/3u6Uj8R*) for more details.

On Google Cloud, you can use the *TCP Proxy Load Balancing* service, which creates a single IP address that is routed to the instances closest to the user. Note that the TCP Proxy load balancer does not support fine-grained firewall access rules, so in some cases, HAProxy might be a better alternative. See the CockroachDB documentation (*https://cockroa.ch/3J9MgfH*) for more details.

On Azure, you can use *Azure load balancing*, listening on port 26257. See the CockroachDB documentation (*https://cockroa.ch/3u4GVlB*) for more details.

Configuring Regions and Zones

We'll go into some depth on the deployment of a multiregion distribution in the next chapter. However, if your deployment is going to be multiregion, then you should be setting regions and zones with the -locality flag during node startup. For instance, if gubuntu2 was in the us-west-1 region, us-west-1a zone, then we'd specify the following in the *cockroachdb.service* file:

```
ExecStart=/usr/local/bin/cockroach start --certs-dir=certs
--advertise-addr=gubuntu2 --join=gubuntu1,gubuntu2,gubuntu3
--locality=region=us-west-1,zone=us-west-1a
```

Deploying on Kubernetes

We've waxed lyrical about Kubernetes in previous chapters, but now we'll let the rubber meet the road in an actual production Kubernetes installation. In this section, we'll configure a three-node cluster with a similar configuration to the self-hosted example from the previous section.

In this example, we'll install CockroachDB on Google Kubernetes Engine (GKE), though the instructions are mostly generic and should work on other Kubernetes implementations. We created our Kubernetes cluster using a command like this:

```
$ gcloud container clusters create crdb --zone=us-central1-c \
--machine-type n2-standard-4 \
--disk-type=pd-ssd --disk-size-200GB

Creating cluster crdb in us-central1-c...done.

Created [https://container.googleapis.com/v1/projects/
        /zones/us-central1-c/clusters/crdb].
```

```
kubeconfig entry generated for crdb.
NAME LOCATION      MASTER_VERSION MASTER_IP     MACHINE_TYPE N_NODES STATUS
crdb us-central1-c 1.20.9-gke.701 35.239.71.140 n2-standard-4 3      RUNNING
```

```
$ gcloud container clusters get-credentials crdb --zone us-central1-c
```

Note that we chose a machine type (n2-standard-4) that has 4 vCPUs and 16 GB of memory. This matters when we configure our CockroachDB nodes later. We also chose pd-ssd as the disk type, ensuring that we have high-performance SSD drives.

Initializing the Operator

Our first step is to apply the CockroachDB Kubernetes Operator CustomResource-Definition (CRD) to the cluster:

```
$ kubectl apply -f https://cockroa.ch/crds_yaml
```

```
customresourcedefinition.apiextensions.k8s.io/crdbclusters.crdb.cockroachlabs.com
created
```

We then apply the operator manifest. First, let's download the default manifest:

```
$ wget https://cockroa.ch/operator-yaml -O operator.yaml
```

```
2021-12-30 15:00:31 (28.2 MB/s) - 'operator.yaml' saved [7123/7123]
```

You probably won't need to edit this file unless you want to change the namespace in which CockroachDB is to run. The *operator.yaml* file installs everything into the cockroach-operator-system namespace. If you want to install into a different namespace, then change all instances of namespace: cockroach-operator-system accordingly.

Once you've edited the *operator.yaml* file if necessary, apply it to your cluster:

```
$ kubectl apply -f operator.yaml
namespace/cockroach-operator-system created
serviceaccount/cockroach-operator-sa created
clusterrole.rbac.authorization.k8s.io/cockroach-operator-role created
clusterrolebinding.rbac.authorization.k8s.io/cockroach-operator-rolebinding
  created
service/cockroach-operator-webhook-service created
deployment.apps/cockroach-operator-manager created
mutatingwebhookconfiguration.admissionregistration.k8s.io/
  cockroach-operator-mutating-webhook-configuration created
validatingwebhookconfiguration.admissionregistration.k8s.io/
  cockroach-operator-validating-webhook-configuration created
```

We should now see the CockroachDB operator running in a pod within the cluster:

```
$ kubectl get pods --namespace cockroach-operator-system
NAME                                         READY  STATUS   RESTARTS  AGE
cockroach-operator-manager-74f6c548b8-2sxgr  1/1    Running  0         3m57s
```

Initializing the Cluster

Now we can initialize the cluster. Let's grab the example configuration from the operator's GitHub repository:

```
$ wget https://cockroa.ch/example_yaml -O example.yaml

Saving to: 'example.yaml'
```

The file *example.yaml* contains the specification for a default three-node cluster. You should get familiar with this file because it includes parameters that you may well want to change. For instance, you can see in the upcoming example that the minimum and maximum resource allocations are specified in the `requests` and `limits` sections.

You might *increase* the `limit` setting to ensure that the CockroachDB nodes have access to a reasonable amount of the memory for each node and make sure that the `request` value is not so high that they might not be able to obtain those resources. Remember, if the `limits` are too high, then you might waste cluster resources, but if the `requests` are too high, Kubernetes might be unable to find enough resources to run the CockroachDB pod.

```
apiVersion: crdb.cockroachlabs.com/v1alpha1
kind: CrdbCluster
metadata:
  # this translates to the name of the statefulset that is created
  name: cockroachdb
spec:
  dataStore:
    pvc:
      spec:
        accessModes:
          - ReadWriteOnce
        resources:
          requests:
            storage: "60Gi"
        volumeMode: Filesystem
  resources:
    requests:
      cpu: "2"
      memory: "8Gi"
    limits:
      cpu: "2"
      memory: "8Gi"
  tlsEnabled: true
# You can set either a version of the db or a specific image name
# cockroachDBVersion: v21.1.7
  image:
    name: cockroachdb/cockroach:v21.1.7
    # nodes refers to the number of crdb pods that are created
```

```
# via the statefulset
nodes: 3
```

Remember from earlier that our Kubernetes nodes have four vCPUs and 16 GB of memory each, in the *example.yaml* we've specified a limit of 2 CPUs and 8 GB of memory per CockroachDB node. So, in this case, we should consider raising the limit to allow CockroachDB to use more of the cluster's resources. However, don't assume that the CockroachDB pod can use the entire resources of a Kubernetes node. Kubernetes clusters will have some internal pods deployed, and the operator itself requires resources. Therefore, you should never try to acquire *all* of a pod's resources. For our 4 CPU, 16 GB Kubernetes configuration, we should request no more than 3 CPUs and perhaps 12 GB of memory.

You can also change the number of nodes in the CockroachDB cluster by simply modifying the nodes value.

The operator will install self-signed certificates for the cluster by default. If you want to use a public CA, consult the CockroachDB documentation (*https://cockroa.ch/3DI6cFw*).

When you are happy with the YAML file, you can issue a create command to create the cluster:

```
$ kubectl create -f example.yaml
crdbcluster.crdb.cockroachlabs.com/cockroachdb created
```

When all is well, you should see three database pods and the cockroach operator running in the cluster:

```
$ kubectl get pods --namespace cockroach-operator-system
NAME                                        READY   STATUS    RESTARTS   AGE
cockroach-operator-manager-74f6c548b8-2sxgr 1/1     Running   0          10m
cockroachdb-0                         .      1/1     Running   0          86s
cockroachdb-1                               1/1     Running   0          86s
cockroachdb-2                               1/1     Running   0          86s
```

It's handy to default the Kubernetes namespace to the CockroachDB namespace, so we don't have to include --namespace cockroach-operator-system in every command:

```
$ kubectl config set-context --current --namespace=cockroach-operator-system
Context "crdb" modified.
```

The most likely failure scenario at this point would be a resource limitation. For instance, if a pod stays in Pending status indefinitely, it may be that Kubernetes is unable to find enough memory to launch it. You can use the describe pod command to look for warnings or errors:

```
$ kubectl describe pod cockroachdb-2 |grep Warning
  Warning  FailedScheduling        4m43s (x2 over 4m43s)  default-scheduler
    0/3 nodes are available: 3 pod has unbound immediate PersistentVolumeClaims.
```

```
  Warning  FailedScheduling         4m41s                      default-scheduler
    0/3 nodes are available: 3 Insufficient cpu, 3 Insufficient memory.
```

You can use the kubectl logs command to examine the logs for individual pods:

```
$ kubectl logs cockroachdb-0 |tail
```

```
‹compact       1     0 B            (size == estimated-debt)›
‹ memtbl       2    64 M›
‹zmemtbl       0     0 B›
‹   ztbl       0     0 B›
‹ bcache     704    66 M   87.2%  (score == hit-rate)›
‹ tcache      98    59 K   96.8%  (score == hit-rate)›
‹ titers       3›
‹ filter       -     -     72.2%  (score == utility)›
I210920 01:39:10.955848 266 server/status/runtime.go:525 ⦂ [n1] runtime stats:
I210920 01:39:20.954284 266 server/status/runtime.go:525 ⦂ [n1] runtime stats:
```

Creating a Client Pod

It's handy to have a "client" pod in the cluster that is able to issue cockroach sql commands. The following command creates such a pod:

```
$ kubectl create -f https://cockroa.ch/client-secure-operator_yaml
pod/cockroachdb-client-secure created
```

We can attach to that pod and issue cockroach sql commands. Here we create our first user in the cluster (we'll need it later):

```
kubectl exec -it cockroachdb-client-secure \
-- ./cockroach sql \
--certs-dir=/cockroach/cockroach-certs \
--host=cockroachdb-public
#
# Welcome to the CockroachDB SQL shell.
# All statements must be terminated by a semicolon.
# To exit, type: \q.
#
# Enter \? for a brief introduction.
#
root@cockroachdb-public:26257/defaultdb>
CREATE USER guy WITH PASSWORD
    'N2U0OWEyMDE2OGMyNjkwNDI1MzVhYmU5';

CREATE ROLE
```

Load Balancing

The CockroachDB Kubernetes Operator creates a cockroachdb-public service that can be used as the target for connections. We used that service earlier to connect from the CockroachDB client. However, despite its name, the cockroachdb-public service is not really public—the IP address it creates is available only within the cluster.

You could use this service to connect an application running inside the Kubernetes cluster, but not for external connections.

To connect to the DB from outside the cluster, we're going to need a load balancer service. The following definition creates a load-balancing service:

```
apiVersion: v1
kind: Service
metadata:
  name: cockroach-lb-service
spec:
  selector:
    app.kubernetes.io/component: database
    app.kubernetes.io/instance: cockroachdb
    app.kubernetes.io/name: cockroachdb
    crdb: is-cool
  type: LoadBalancer
  ports:
  - name: sql
    protocol: TCP
    port: 26257
    targetPort: 26257
  - name: http
    protocol: TCP
    port: 8080
    targetPort: 8080
```

We can then create the load-balancing service as follows:

```
$ kubectl apply -f loadBalancer.yaml
```

After a while, we'll see the load balancer operational and serving external ports:

```
$ kubectl get service cockroach-lb-service
NAME                     TYPE          CLUSTER-IP      EXTERNAL-IP
PORT(S)
cockroach-lb-service    LoadBalancer   10.27.252.140   104.197.158.47
26257:31430/TCP,8080:30088/TCP
```

We can use the EXTERNAL-IP address to connect to the database console. While it's possible to connect to https://104.197.158.47:8080 to view the database console, your browser will protest that it doesn't recognize the CA.[4]

---

4 This is one reason for using a CA certificate (*https://cockroa.ch/3NM34Nn*) from a known public authority.

For a database connection, we are going to need at least the CA certificate. We can copy that from one of the CockroachDB pods:

```
$ mkdir certs
```

```
$ kubectl exec cockroachdb-client-secure -it -- cat cockroach-certs/ca.crt \
  >certs/ca.crt
```

```
$ chmod 600 certs/*
```

Now we can connect to the CockroachDB cluster using the username and password that we created earlier, the IP address of the load balancer, and the CA certificate we just copied:

```
$ cockroach sql --url
'postgres://guy:N2U0OWEyMDE2OGMyNjkwNDI1MzVhYmU5@104.197.158.47:26257
?sslmode=verify-ca&sslrootcert=certs/ca.crt'
#
# Welcome to the CockroachDB SQL shell.
# All statements must be terminated by a semicolon.
# To exit, type: \q.
#
#
# Enter \? for a brief introduction.
#
guy@104.197.158.47:26257/defaultdb>
```

Exposing the CockroachDB cluster to a wide area network or the internet may be desirable in some cases but does raise security concerns. We'll discuss mitigations in Chapter 13, but the following are possible configurations to mitigate the risk:

- Instead of creating an external load balancer, colocate the application that needs access to the CockroachDB cluster in the same Kubernetes cluster.
- If the application runs outside of the Kubernetes environment, consider VPC Network Peering (*https://cockroa.ch/3DDMkmC*) to enable connectivity between the application and the internal cockroach-public service.
- If VPC peering is not an option, then you should set up firewall rules (*https://cockroa.ch/36Ms32B*) to limit connections to known IP addresses.

Other Kubernetes Tasks

We've really just scratched the surface of the management of a Kubernetes console. The CockroachDB documentation (*https://cockroa.ch/3j5z7tn*) has further details on configuring, scaling, and monitoring a Kubernetes deployment. However, it's worth recognizing just how powerful Kubernetes is. The entire process of deploying a production CockroachDB cluster in the cloud can be completed in under one hour, and it's not much more difficult to create an 80-node cluster than a three-node cluster.

Summary

If you've made your way through this chapter, then you're probably particularly well placed to appreciate the benefits of a CockroachDB Serverless or Dedicated cloud deployment. None of the activities outlined in this chapter are required for cloud deployments!

However, while a self-hosted deployment does involve some complexity, it's by no means overwhelming. The tasks outlined in this chapter should allow you to set up a production cluster without too much trouble. As we've seen, creating a self-hosted cluster on Kubernetes is even easier since Kubernetes automates most of the tasks required in the self-hosted procedure.

Nonetheless, we're still arguably at the starting point for some production implementations. We have not yet addressed many operational tasks such as security, monitoring, and backup, and we have yet to fully explore the configuration of a multiregion cluster. In the next chapter, we'll deep dive into multiregion deployment, and in the following chapters, we'll go farther into the world of production CockroachDB administration.

Multiregion Deployment

Multiregion deployments allow a CockroachDB database to span multiple geographic regions, The configuration of a multiregion deployment has implications for the cluster's fault-tolerance and for regional performance. Generally speaking, we configure a CockroachDB cluster into regions to achieve one or both of two objectives:

- To allow the cluster to continue servicing requests when the computing resources in one of the cluster's regions becomes unavailable.
- To ensure that users of a geographically distributed database can enjoy low-latency database operations.

These two objectives are not completely incompatible, but there are some trade-offs involved between the two. It's important to understand how to balance latency and high availability in a manner that suits your circumstances.

Multiregion Concepts

The multiregion capabilities of CockroachDB exercise some of CockroachDB's most unique architectural features. Some of the underlying algorithms can be challenging. However, the core concepts of a multiregion CockroachDB helpfully abstract much of that around simple concepts such as regions, zones, and survival goals.

Regions and Zones

A region is a broad geographical region that has a set of CockroachDB nodes deployed within it. Regions can be anything you want them to be, but it only really makes sense to define a region across an area that either has some sort of network adjacencies, distinct workload or user characteristics, or legal requirements.

One of the regions in a database is the *primary region*. The primary region is the default region for all the tables in a database.

Within a region, you define one or more zones. Zones are again defined arbitrarily but will typically be aligned with data centers within a region (though they might just as easily be defined as racks within a highly redundant data center).

In other contexts, zones are sometimes called *availability zones*. The idea is that a zone represents some sort of single point of failure. When a zone is defined as a data center, then we can assume that in the event of a data center failure, all the nodes within that zone will fail. It makes a lot less sense to define a zone spanning data centers unless the data centers had some common point of failure (both dependent on the same power station, for instance).

Figure 11-1 provides an example of a three-region global deployment with three zones in each region.

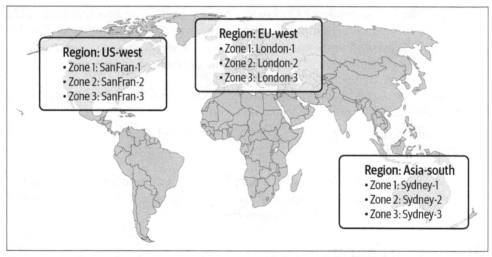

Figure 11-1. Example of regions and zones in a global CockroachDB deployment

Each region represents a broad geographical region that we assume has some importance to the CockroachDB application. Each zone in the region is represented by a city in which one or more CockroachDB nodes are running.

In practice, regions are often more narrowly defined and often align with the region and zone maps for a public cloud platform. For instance, if you are running on Amazon AWS, then your zones will almost certainly align with AWS zones that represent specific data centers. Amazon supports over 20 regions, with 4 in the US. Each of these regions has three availability zones, representing three distinct data centers in the region.

Survival Goals

Each database in the cluster has a survival goal that determines the trade-off between latency and survivability. Be aware that sometimes we might say database to refer to an entire CockroachDB deployment, but in this case, we are talking about databases as defined by CREATE DATABASE statements. Each of these databases can have different survival goals:

- *Zone failure* is the default survival goal. The database will remain available for reads and writes even if a node in a zone fails. Multiple zone failures might still be survivable provided you have configured enough nodes in the region and an appropriate replication factor.

- When a database is configured for *region failure* then the database will be fully available even in the event of a full region failure. To achieve this, data must be replicated to another region, which in most circumstances will reduce write performance.

Figure 11-2 illustrates a zone failure within a database with a zone survival goal. The data ranges in question are maintained in three replicas within the US region (the default region), and a failure of any single zone (in this case, the New York zone) in that region allows the database to continue to function with two replicas. Two failures in any region would have the same effect, albeit based on different ranges of data becoming unavailable.

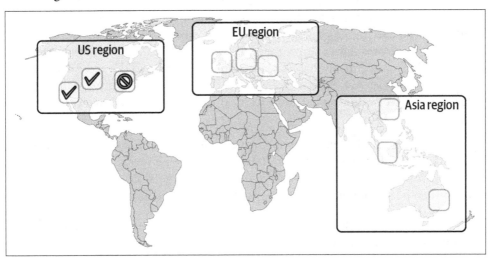

Figure 11-2. Example of a zone failure in zone survival goal

Figure 11-3 shows a region failure for a database with a regional survival goal. As a consequence of setting regional survival goal for a database, the replication factor is automatically increased to five instead of the default three and the replicas are distributed across regions. When the US region fails, there are still three copies of the data in other regions and database operations can continue.

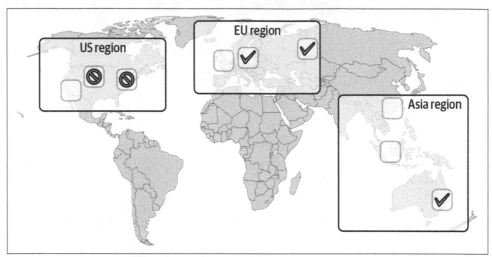

Figure 11-3. Example of a region failure in regional survival goal

It's true that three replicas in different regions would be enough to survive region-level failures. However, CockroachDB increases the replication factor to improve the handling of smaller (node or zone level) failures within the primary region. If the replication factor was left at three, then the failure of one node or zone within the primary region would mean that all reads would have to go to the secondary region, greatly increasing latency. Because node failures are much more common than region failures, we increase the replication factor so that they have a smaller impact on performance.

The region/zone survival goal is your biggest single "switch" to configure a multi-region deployment. Zone survival results in the best performance, while regional survival promotes greater survivability in case of large-scale outages or network partitions. When deciding between the two, the following considerations are relevant:

- In the big public cloud platforms, failures of entire regions are rare but not unheard of. For instance, as we write this, the Google Cloud Australian southeast region had recently suffered a 90-minute outage. The configuration shown in Figure 11-2 could not have remained completely available during that period. You shouldn't assume on any platform that a regional outage is vanishingly rare.

- Regional survival implies zone survival. By default, a regional survival goal protects against the loss of any single region or the failure of any two zones.

- Just as we need at least three nodes to allow for survivability in a single-region cluster, we need three regions to allow for regional survival. With only two regions, the failure of any one region would make the majority of replicas for some ranges unavailable.

Locality Rules

Regardless of the survival goal, we can fine-tune the distribution within a table to optimize access from specific regions.

Tables in the database may have *locality rules* that determine how their data will be distributed across zones:

- A *global table* will be optimized for low-latency reads from any region.
- A *regional table* will be optimized for low-latency reads and writes from a single region.
- A *regional by row table* will have specific rows optimized for low-latency reads and writes for a region. Different rows in the table can be assigned to specific regions.

With a global table, replicas for all ranges within the table will exist in each region. This ensures that read time is optimized but creates the highest overhead for writes because all regions must coordinate on a write request. Global tables are suitable for relatively static lookup tables that are relevant across all regions. A product table might be a relevant example—product information is often shared across regions, and not subject to frequent updates; therefore, performance is optimized if each region has a complete copy of the product table. The downside is that writes to the product table will require participation for all regions and therefore be relatively slow.

With a regional table, as much replica information as possible (subject to failure configuration) for all ranges in the table is located in a single region. This makes sense either if that region is way more important to the business than other regions or if the data is particularly relevant to that region. For instance, if in an internationalized application error codes for each language were located in separate tables, then it might make sense to locate these in particular regions (though this, of course, would rekindle the age-old debate on where *English* should reside). Note that REGIONAL BY TABLE IN PRIMARY REGION is the default configuration.

A regional by row table locates the replicas for specific rows in specific regions. A hidden column (crdb_region) in each row determines where the row will reside. This column can be populated directly by the application or can be derived from other information. For example, in a users table, we could assign rows to the US region if their country code was "USA", "Canada," or any country in North or South

America. Regional by row is a very powerful way of moving data close to the regions in which it is required.

Now, if you're very alert, you might be wondering about how regional survivability interacts with these table region settings. If I'm in regional survival mode, I have to have replicas in other regions, so then how does this regional setting work? The answer is that CockroachDB compromises between the two settings. For a regional table in region survival mode, two voting replicas and the leaseholder for the entire table or the ranges in question will be located in the region, while the other voting replicas will be located in other regions. The end result is a slight advantage in performance for the "home" region.

In essence, there are three types of tables in a CockroachDB cluster, listed in decreasing order of survivability and increasing order of performance:

- GLOBAL
- REGIONAL SURVIVE REGION
- REGIONAL SURVIVE ZONE

The reason it's presented as two separate settings has to do with which combinations are sensible and how database and table-level settings interact. If there are *any* SURVIVE ZONE tables in your database, your application is probably going to break in a regional failure (unless you're *very* careful about which tables you use and when), so mixing REGIONAL SURVIVE ZONE and REGIONAL SURVIVE REGION tables in one DB doesn't make a lot of sense (why pay the performance cost of SURVIVE REGION for some tables if you're still going to have downtime in a region failure?). That's why the survival goals are a database-level setting. On the other hand, it does make sense to have mixtures of global and regional tables, so that's a table-level setting.

Reads from regional or regional by row tables will be slower by default from outside the region concerned. However, low-latency "stale" reads can be performed by using AS OF SYSTEM TIME. AS OF SYSTEM TIME can take advantage of nonvoting replicas that are located in each nonprimary region. These nonvoting replicas aren't involved in transaction commit processing and so, therefore, may be slightly out-of-date.

Planning Your Mutliregion Deployment

Hopefully, we have enough background on multiregion deployments to talk sensibly about how they can be used in practice.

The default configuration—in which all tables are regional tables housed in the default region and in which only zone failures are survivable—might be a useful starting point, but it's unlikely to be the optimal configuration.

If your primary goal is high performance in all geographies, then you are probably going to be motivated toward zone survival. In this scenario, carefully determining your table locality settings will make a big difference. Tables that have "global" relevance and that are read-intensive should probably be set to global. Tables that contain regional-specific data should probably become regional by row. Only if a table is specific to a region—such as a language-specific table—should it be left as regional.

If your primary goal is high availability, then you're probably going to need regional survival. Table localities are less important in this scenario for write performance because writes are distributed across multiple regions by default. However, you will still see advantages in configuring global, regional, and regional by row settings for selected tables for read performance and can also distribute the workload more evenly across your cluster.

Deploying in Multiregion

Let's put theory into practice by configuring a highly available multiregion database. We'll use CockroachDB's own movr sample database, which is designed to illustrate multiregional principles.

You can replicate these commands using a free-trial CockroachDB nine-node cluster.[1] The cluster configuration for this example is shown in Figure 11-4:

---

1 You can get a one-month free trial (*https://cockroa.ch/3nXObwe*) of a nine-node CockroachDB cluster across three regions.

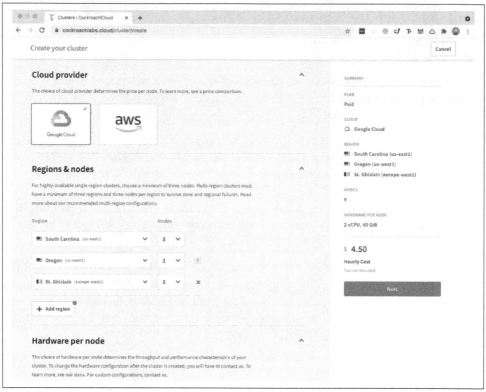

Figure 11-4. CockroachDB nine-node regional cluster setup (large format version (https://cockroa.ch/cockroachDB-figs))

Once the cluster is created, you'll want to initialize the movr schema with the following command:

```
cockroach workload init movr <url>
```

Alternatively, you can run a local demo system that simulates a nine-node cluster with this command:

```
cockroach demo movr init \
--nodes=9 \
--demo-locality=region=gcp-us-east1,az=gcp-us-east1a:\
region=gcp-us-east1,az=gcp-us-east1b:\
region=gcp-us-east1,az=gcp-us-east1c:\
region=gcp-us-west1,az=us-west-1a:\
region=gcp-us-west1,az=us-west-1b:\
region=gcp-us-west1,az=gcp-us-west1c:\
region=gcp-europe-west1,az=gcp-europe-west1a:\
region=gcp-europe-west1,az=gcp-europe-west1b:\
region=gcp-europe-west1,az=gcp-europe-west1c
```

There's no need to initialize the movr database with the demo cluster.

If all is well, then SHOW REGIONS should reveal the three regions and nine availability zones:

```
movr> show regions;
        region      |                              zones
--------------------+----------------------------------------------------------------
  gcp-europe-west1  | {gcp-europe-west1a,gcp-europe-west1b,gcp-europe-west1c}
  gcp-us-east1      | {gcp-us-east1a,gcp-us-east1b,gcp-us-east1c}
  gcp-us-west1      | {gcp-us-west1c,us-west-1a,us-west-1b}
```

By default, the tables in movr will be in the default replication zone, which is defined with three replicas:

```
/movr> \set display_format=records;
/movr>  SELECT raw_config_sql FROM crdb_internal.zones
  WHERE target='RANGE default';
-[ RECORD 1 ]
raw_config_sql | ALTER RANGE default CONFIGURE ZONE USING+
               |         range_min_bytes = 134217728,+
               |         range_max_bytes = 536870912,+
               |         gc.ttlseconds = 90000,+
               |         num_replicas = 3,+
               |         constraints = '[]',+
               |         lease_preferences = '[]'
```

If we examine a range from a table in movr, we'll see that it is indeed replicated over three nodes with one replica in each region:

```
/movr> \set display_format=records;
/movr> SHOW RANGE FROM INDEX users@primary
FOR ROW ('amsterdam','ae147ae1-47ae-4800-8000-000000000022')
;

-[ RECORD 1 ]
start_key              | NULL
end_key                | /"amsterdam"/"\xb333333@\x00\x80\x00\x00\x00\x00\x00\x00#"
range_id               | 37
lease_holder           | 5
lease_holder_locality  | region=gcp-us-west1,az=us-west-1b
replicas               | {1,5,9}
replica_localities     | {"region=gcp-us-east1,az=gcp-us-east1a",
                           "region=gcp-us-west1,az=us-west-1b",
                           "region=gcp-europe-west1,az=gcp-europe-west1c"}
```

Note that you have to provide a valid primary key-value for a user in the preceding command. The UUID in the example may not exist in your database.

Converting to a Multiregion Database

To get started in converting movr to a multiregion database, we assign a primary region and associate the nonprimary regions with the database:

```
/movr> ALTER DATABASE movr SET PRIMARY REGION="gcp-us-east1";
ALTER DATABASE PRIMARY REGION

/movr> ALTER DATABASE movr ADD REGION  "gcp-europe-west1";
ALTER DATABASE ADD REGION

/movr> ALTER DATABASE movr ADD REGION "gcp-us-west1";
ALTER DATABASE ADD REGION
```

SHOW REGIONS now reveals that movr is associated with each region and with a primary region of gcp-us-east1:

```
/movr> \set display_format=records;
/movr> show regions;
-[ RECORD 1 ]
region           | gcp-europe-west1
zones            | {gcp-europe-west1a,gcp-europe-west1b,gcp-europe-west1c}
database_names   | {movr}
primary_region_of | {}
-[ RECORD 2 ]
region           | gcp-us-east1
zones            | {gcp-us-east1a,gcp-us-east1b,gcp-us-east1c}
database_names   | {movr}
primary_region_of | {movr}
-[ RECORD 3 ]
region           | gcp-us-west1
zones            | {gcp-us-west1c,us-west-1a,us-west-1b}
database_names   | {movr}
primary_region_of | {}
```

We can see that each table in the movr database now is a REGIONAL BY TABLE IN PRIMARY REGION table:

```
/movr> SELECT name,locality
  FROM crdb_internal."tables"
 WHERE schema_name='public'
   AND database_name='movr';
```

```
             name            |                locality
-----------------------------+----------------------------------------
   users                     | REGIONAL BY TABLE IN PRIMARY REGION
   vehicles                  | REGIONAL BY TABLE IN PRIMARY REGION
   rides                     | REGIONAL BY TABLE IN PRIMARY REGION
   vehicle_location_histories | REGIONAL BY TABLE IN PRIMARY REGION
   promo_codes               | REGIONAL BY TABLE IN PRIMARY REGION
   user_promo_codes          | REGIONAL BY TABLE IN PRIMARY REGION
```

As a consequence of distributing movr over three regions, CockroachDB creates a new replication zone for the movr database, with a replication factor of five:

```
/movr> \set display_format=records;
/movr>  SELECT raw_config_sql FROM crdb_internal.zones
   WHERE target='DATABASE movr';
-[ RECORD 1 ]
raw_config_sql | ALTER DATABASE movr CONFIGURE ZONE USING+
               |         num_replicas = 5,+
               |         num_voters = 3,+
               |         constraints = '{+region=gcp-europe-west1: 1,
 +region=gcp-us-east1: 1, +region=gcp-us-west1: 1}',+
               |         voter_constraints = '[+region=gcp-us-east1]',+
               |         lease_preferences = '[[+region=gcp-us-east1]]'
```

Note the constraints on replication—while there should be five replicas in total, just three of these nodes should be voting nodes, and those nodes should be restricted to the primary region (region=gcp-us-east1). This is the configuration for a REGIONAL BY TABLE IN PRIMARY REGION table—by default, the voting nodes should be located in the primary region so that consensus can be reached without having to consult other regions synchronously.

Configuring Regional by Row

The nature of MovR is that most transactions are restricted to a single region. We don't normally take ride shares from the East of the US to the West and hardly ever take a MovR car from Europe to the US! Therefore, we probably want the transaction tables to be REGIONAL BY ROW rather than REGIONAL BY TABLE IN PRIMARY REGION.

Let's set it up. For a REGIONAL BY ROW table, CockroachDB expects to find a hidden CRDB_REGION column that maps to one of the regions assigned to the database. We can alter the application so that it inserts an appropriate value into the row when it is created, or we could to use a *computed* column. Here we define such a computed crdb_internal_region column for the users table:

```
/movr> ALTER TABLE users ADD COLUMN crdb_region crdb_internal_region AS (
   CASE
     WHEN city IN ('new york', 'boston', 'washington dc') THEN 'gcp-us-east1'
     WHEN city IN ('san francisco', 'seattle', 'los angeles') THEN 'gcp-us-west1'
     WHEN city IN ('amsterdam', 'paris', 'rome') THEN 'gcp-europe-west1'
     ELSE 'gcp-us-east1'
   END
) STORED;
ALTER TABLE
```

We can see that the column is mapping correctly:

```
/movr> SELECT DISTINCT city,crdb_region FROM users;
     city     |   crdb_region
--------------+------------------
  boston      | gcp-us-east1
  new york    | gcp-us-east1
  rome        | gcp-europe-west1
  amsterdam   | gcp-europe-west1
  los angeles | gcp-us-west1
  paris       | gcp-europe-west1
  san francisco | gcp-us-west1
  seattle     | gcp-us-west1
  washington dc | gcp-us-east1
```

Now that the CRDB_REGION column is defined, we can set the table LOCALITY to REGIONAL BY ROW, after first making the column NOT NULL:

```
/movr> ALTER TABLE users ALTER COLUMN crdb_region SET NOT NULL;
ALTER TABLE

/movr> ALTER TABLE users SET LOCALITY REGIONAL BY ROW;
NOTICE: LOCALITY changes will be finalized asynchronously;
further schema changes on this table may be restricted until the job completes
ALTER TABLE SET LOCALITY
```

The shift to REGIONAL BY ROW is implemented by a set of background jobs. Here we can see that the core jobs have been completed, and a garbage collection is still in progress:

```
/movr> \set display_format=records;
/movr> SELECT  job_type,description,status
  FROM [show jobs]
 WHERE description LIKE '%REGIONAL%';

-[ RECORD 1 ]
job_type    | SCHEMA CHANGE
description | ALTER TABLE movr.public.users SET LOCALITY REGIONAL BY ROW
status      | succeeded
-[ RECORD 2 ]
job_type    | SCHEMA CHANGE
description | CLEANUP JOB for 'ALTER TABLE movr.public.users
                               SET LOCALITY REGIONAL BY ROW'
status      | succeeded
-[ RECORD 3 ]
job_type    | SCHEMA CHANGE GC
description | GC for CLEANUP JOB for 'ALTER TABLE movr.public.users
                                SET LOCALITY REGIONAL BY ROW'
status      | running
```

Under the hood, the primary index for the users table now includes the CRDB_REGION column:

```
/movr> \set display_format=table;
SELECT DISTINCT index_name,column_Name
  FROM crdb_internal.index_columns
 WHERE descriptor_name='users';

  index_name | column_name
-------------+--------------
   primary   | crdb_region
   primary   | city
   primary   | id
```

Let's look at the distribution of ranges for a row in Amsterdam:

```
/movr> set display_format=records;

/movr> SHOW RANGE FROM INDEX users@primary FOR ROW
('gcp-europe-west1','amsterdam','ae147ae1-47ae-4800-8000-000000000022');

-[ RECORD 1 ]
start_key              | /"@"
end_key                | /"@"/PrefixEnd
range_id               | 98
lease_holder           | 8
lease_holder_locality  | region=gcp-europe-west1,az=gcp-europe-west1b
replicas               | {3,6,7,8,9}
replica_localities     | {"region=gcp-us-east1,az=gcp-us-east1c",
"region=gcp-us-west1,az=gcp-us-west1c","region=gcp-europe-west1,
az=gcp-europe-west1a","region=gcp-europe-west1,az=gcp-europe-west1b",
"region=gcp-europe-west1,az=gcp-europe-west1c"}
```

We can see that there are three replicas in Europe and one replica each in the other two zones. This maps to the zone survival goal—we can sustain a failure of any one node in any region, but should the entire gcp-Europe-west1 region fail, then the table would be unavailable. Compare that to a row for a New York user:

```
/movr> \set display_format=records;

/movr> SHOW RANGE FROM INDEX users@primary
FOR ROW ('gcp-us-east1','new york','00000000-0000-4000-8000-000000000000');
-[ RECORD 1 ]
start_key              | /"\x80"
end_key                | /"\x80"/PrefixEnd
range_id               | 100
lease_holder           | 1
lease_holder_locality  | region=gcp-us-east1,az=gcp-us-east1a
replicas               | {1,2,3,4,8}
replica_localities     | {"region=gcp-us-east1,az=gcp-us-east1a",
"region=gcp us east1,az=gcp-us-east1b","region=gcp-us-east1,
az=gcp-us-east1c","region=gcp-us-west1,az=us-west-1a",
"region=gcp-europe-west1,az=gcp-europe-west1b"}
```

The New York row has three copies in the gcp-us-east1 region and one copy in each of the other regions.

We should repeat the process of assigning CRDB_REGION and setting REGIONAL BY ROW locality for the other transactional tables that are region-specific: RIDES, VEHICLES, VEHICLE_LOCATION_HISTORIES, and USER_PROMO_CODES.

The PROMO_CODES table is not region-specific—promo codes are equally applicable in every location. We should probably make this a GLOBAL table since it is read from every region and not subject to high transaction rates:

```
/movr> ALTER TABLE promo_codes SET LOCALITY GLOBAL;
ALTER TABLE SET LOCALITY
```

Our final table locality configuration would look like this:

```
/movr> SELECT name,locality
  FROM crdb_internal."tables"
 WHERE schema_name='public'
   AND database_name='movr';
                name            |     locality
--------------------------------+------------------
  users                         | REGIONAL BY ROW
  vehicles                      | REGIONAL BY ROW
  rides                         | REGIONAL BY ROW
  vehicle_location_histories    | REGIONAL BY ROW
  promo_codes                   | GLOBAL
  user_promo_codes              | REGIONAL BY ROW
```

Setting Regional Survival Goal

What we've done so far enhances regional performance by moving rows close to the regions in which they are accessed and modified. However, our high-availability configuration may actually have decreased. Prior to the REGIONAL BY ROW configuration, we could have survived a nonprimary region failure. We are now vulnerable to failure of any region because each region has the majority of replicas for at least some ranges,

To achieve global high availability, we need to move to a regional survival goal. We can do that with a single command:

```
/movr> ALTER DATABASE movr SURVIVE REGION FAILURE;

ALTER DATABASE SURVIVE
```

As with other reconfigurations, this kicks off a background job that oversees the necessary redistribution of ranges:

```
/movr> \set display_format=records;
/movr>
SELECT description,status
  FROM [show jobs]
 WHERE description like '%SURVIVE%';

-[ RECORD 1 ]
```

```
description | ALTER DATABASE movr SURVIVE REGION FAILURE
status      | succeeded
```

To see what exactly has changed, let's look at the distribution of ranges for an Amsterdam row. You might recall that previously this row had three replicas in the EU region and one replica in each of the US regions. Let's see what it looks like now:

```
movr> \set display_format=records;
/movr>
SHOW RANGE FROM INDEX users@primary FOR ROW
('gcp-europe-west1','amsterdam','ae147ae1-47ae-4800-8000-000000000022');

-[ RECORD 1 ]
start_key             | /"@"
end_key               | /"@"/PrefixEnd
range id              | 98
lease_holder          | 8
lease_holder_locality | region=gcp-europe-west1,az=gcp-europe-west1b
replicas              | {2,4,7,8,9}
replica_localities    | {"region=gcp-us-east1,az=gcp-us-east1b",
  "region=gcp-us-west1,az=us-west-1a","region=gcp-europe-west1,
  az=gcp-europe-west1a","region=gcp-europe-west1,az=gcp-europe-west1b",
  "region=gcp-europe-west1,az=gcp-europe-west1c"}
```

Now we have two replicas in gcp-Europe-west1, two replicas in us-west1, and one replica in us-east1. If any region fails, there will still be a majority of replicas available—hence we can survive a region failure. The trade-off is write performance; since only a minority of replicas exist in the primary region, we cannot achieve Raft consensus without another region receiving the write.

Placement Restricted Databases

The ALTER DATABASE...PLACEMENT RESTRICTED statement constrains replica placement for a multiregion database's regional tables to the home regions assoiated with those tables.

In practice, this prevents nonvoting replicas of a table or row being located outside the table or rows region.

Since the consequence of this may be slower reads, why would we do this? There are at least three reasons:

- We are attempting to comply with data domiciling requirements that restrict the storage of data outside of a geographical or political zone. For instance, EU General Data Protection Regulation (GDPR) compliance might require that certain data be hosted only within the EU.

- We reduce the number of replicas, and therefore reduce the total disk storage requirements for the cluster.

- We reduce the write overhead that might be involved in replicating data across a large number of regions. For more information, consult the CockroachDB documentation (*https://cockroa.ch/3j4F1ek*).

Summary

In this chapter, we've outlined the theory and practice of CockroachDB multiregion deployments.

Multiregion deployments allow a CockroachDB cluster to span multiple geographies and to potentially survive failures of entire regions. Multiregion configurations also allow you to fine-tune the distribution of data such that data resides where it is most likely to be used, thus reducing latency both for reads and writes.

There are some trade-offs between latency and availability. Most critically, where regional survival is required, some increase in write latency at least will occur, because multiple regions will have to participate in transaction consensus.

Highly available CockroachDB configurations, including the multiregion options, protect against a large subset of possible failure scenarios. However, there are situations in which even the most robust distributed database may need to be recovered from backups—in the next chapter, we'll provide an overview of the CockroachDB backup and recovery facilities.

Backup and Disaster Recovery

High availability is the only option for most modern applications. In previous chapters, we've seen how to configure a distributed CockroachDB cluster that can survive all but the most extreme circumstances.

Nevertheless, even a cluster with the most resilient replication scheme may encounter a circumstance from which it cannot recover. There might be a coordinated failure of multiple data centers—as a result of a cyber attack, for instance—that renders all the data within the cluster irrecoverable.

There are also circumstances in which the cluster infrastructure remains intact, but the data within it becomes corrupted. For instance, a database administrator (DBA) might inadvertently modify data thinking that they are working on the development system, a ransomware attack might attempt to wipe all the data, or an application bug might subtly corrupt data over time.

While CockroachDB has a number of features that can assist you when recovering from data corruption (primarily based on the AS OF SYSTEM TIME clause), backups provide the ultimate insurance policy against loss of or corruption of data in your databases.

Backups also provide some ability to recover the stage of data in the relatively distant past. This might be required for regulatory purposes or in the event that data becomes so logically corrupted that a "do-over" from some point in time is required.

> ### Backup Versus High Availability
>
> In distributed databases such as CockroachDB, backup and high-availability patterns differ significantly from those of a monolithic database such as Oracle or SQL Server. In a monolithic database such as Oracle, replication and backup are both based on a write-ahead transaction log (called the *redo log* in Oracle). This log is the first recipient of durable commit records and is used both as the source of replication to standby databases (for high-availability purposes) and to "roll forward" the database from a static backup in case of a total failure.
>
> In CockroachDB, the Raft logs serve the same logical function as the transaction logs of the monolithic database, but there is no single log to base recovery on, and consequently, the procedures are a little different. In short, the dominant pattern for HA and disaster recovery in CockroachDB involves:
>
> - Using redundant distributed copies of data to maintain availability in the event of predictable infrastructure failure.
> - Taking periodic backups of the database to protect against disasters that overwhelm the replication.
>
> These two techniques are used in combination to provide high availability for foreseeable infrastructure failure together with a fallback solution should the entire infrastructure fail or the database becomes logically corrupt.

Backups

CockroachDB backups are the primary means of creating offline copies of CockroachDB data that can be rapidly restored in the event of a disaster or data corruption issue.

Backups can be made of the entire cluster or of individual databases or tables. An Enterprise edition backup can include not only the current state of the data but also all history known to the database at the time of the backup (by default, a 25-hour window of data).

In the Enterprise edition, backups may be automatically executed on a schedule and may include both incremental and full backups.

Backups may be taken using the AS OF SYSTEM TIME clause, which uses historical data to create the backups. This reduces performance overhead and transactional conflicts but does mean that the backup will not include all committed transactions at its execution time.

The BACKUP Command

The BACKUP statement creates full or incremental backups of the data in the entire cluster, one or more databases, or one or more tables. Incremental backups require an Enterprise license.

The user performing a backup needs read access on all objects being backed up and write access to the target destination. You'll also need the USAGE privilege to back up user-defined schemas or types. For a full backup, you'll need to be a member of the admin role.

Figure 12-1 shows the syntax of the BACKUP statement.

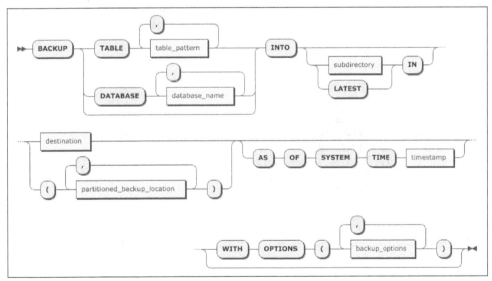

Figure 12-1. Syntax of the BACKUP command

Backup Destinations

Backup destinations follow the same format as for file imports, which we introduced in Chapter 7. In short, the backup can be written to cloud storage destinations such as S3, Google Cloud Storage, or Azure containers to CockroachDB cluster storage—userfile and nodelocal destinations—or to custom HTTP storage locations.

For instance, the following command generates a full backup to a nodelocal destination:

```
/defaultdb> backup database bank into 'nodelocal://1/bank.backup/';
         job_id       | status  | f_completed | rows | index_entries | bytes
--------------------+-----------+-------------+------+---------------+---------
   694816704807895041 | succeeded |           1 | 1031 |            16 | 239079
(1 row)

Time: 764ms total (execution 727ms / network 36ms)
```

Nodelocal destinations are still based within cluster storage and are not always suitable for disaster recovery purposes. If you do back up to a nodelocal location, then you might want to mount the destination on a Network File System (NFS) or other remote durable filesystem. Also, note that nodelocal locations are not available in CockroachDB Cloud.

In the next example, a backup for the Bank database is written to a Google Cloud destination. The authentication is stored in the `cloudstorage.gs.default.key` cluster parameter:

```
root@guy13:26257/defaultdb>
SET CLUSTER SETTING cloudstorage.gs.default.key = '{
  "type": "service_account",
  "project_id": "ghreqs",
  "private_key_id": "048d8c08c90032758aba99d77676a84c1ceef9fa",
  "private_key": "-----BEGIN PRIVATE KEY----- \ 7udawwrrGI\n6/...
  … ==\n-----END PRIVATE KEY-----\n",
  "client_email": "592053976296-compute@developer.gserviceaccount.com",
  "client_id": "112395942388993483786",
  "auth_uri": "https://accounts.google.com/o/oauth2/auth",
  "token_uri": "https://oauth2.googleapis.com/token",
  "auth_provider_x509_cert_url": "https://www.googleapis.com/oauth2/v1/certs",
  "client_x509_cert_url":
"https://www.googleapis.com/robot/v1/metadata/x509/592053976296-
compute%40developer.gserviceaccount.com"
}';

Time: 122ms total (execution 121ms / network 0ms)

/defaultdb>
BACKUP DATABASE bank INTO 'gs://ghcrdb/bank.backup' ;
```

```
        job_id       | status   | fraction_c| rows | index_entries | bytes
---------------------+----------+-----------+------+---------------+---------
  694812435375915009 | succeeded |         1 | 1000 |             0 | 114634
(1 row)


Time: 4.550s total (execution 4.549s / network 0.000s)
```

For more information about configuring cloud storage destinations, see the Cock-roachDB documentation (*https://cockroa.ch/3J7LQXf*).

Full Backup

A full backup copies all data and all metadata (such as permissions and users) to the destination. It is sufficient to simply specify the destination of the backup:

```
/defaultdb> BACKUP INTO 'gs://ghcrdb/full.backup' ;

        job_id       | status   |  rows  | index_entries |  bytes
---------------------+----------+--------+---------------+-----------
  694818421848604673 | succeeded | 214148 |        401210 | 63225717
(1 row)


Time: 14.772s total (execution 14.758s / network 0.014s)
```

Note that full-cluster backups can be restored only into a brand-new cluster in a pristine state—you can't simply apply it over the top of a damaged server. So you will want to make sure that your recovery procedure includes the initialization of the cluster.

Table- and Database-Level Backups

Table- and database-level backups use an intuitive syntax. Here we back up select tables and then the whole database:

```
/defaultdb>
BACKUP TABLE movr.rides, movr.users
INTO 'nodelocal://1/movr.rides.backup/';
        job_id       | status   |  rows  | index_entries |  bytes
---------------------+----------+--------+---------------+-----------
  694832106547740673 | succeeded | 210128 |        400130 | 62401452
(1 row)


Time: 875ms total (execution 868ms / network 7ms)

/defaultdb>
BACKUP DATABASE movr INTO 'nodelocal://1/movr.full.backup/';
        job_id       | status   |  rows  | index_entries |  bytes
---------------------+----------+--------+---------------+-----------
  694832216177213441 | succeeded | 214887 |        401149 | 63027704
(1 row)
```

```
Time: 943ms total (execution 938ms / network 5ms)
```

Unlike a full backup, table- or database-level backups do not include metadata. In particular, users and permissions will not be included within the backup. Therefore, if you're restoring a table or database backup, you will need to maintain scripts to restore the appropriate user and permission structures. You will also need to separately restore system settings, schedules, and any other aspects of the system configuration that you want to be preserved.

For a table-level backup, it's possible that there will be dependent objects—foreign key references, for example—that will be required to completely restore the table. Some of these dependencies can be ignored during a restore by setting the appropriate options.

Incremental Backups

Incremental backups are an Enterprise-only feature. An incremental backup includes only the changes since the full backup. They are denoted by the use of the LATEST IN clause. For instance, if we have a full backup created as follows:

```
/defaultdb> BACKUP INTO 'nodelocal://1/fullClusterBackup/';

        job_id        |  status   |  rows  | index_entries |   bytes
----------------------+-----------+--------+---------------+----------
  694822827753701377  | succeeded | 215369 |        401314 | 63320592
(1 row)
```

Then by specifying the LATEST IN clause and the same location, we create an incremental backup:

```
/defaultdb>
BACKUP INTO LATEST IN 'nodelocal://1/fullClusterBackup/';

        job_id        |  status   | rows | index_entries | bytes
----------------------+-----------+------+---------------+-------
  694823197287415809  | succeeded |  681 |            63 | 57054
(1 row)

Time: 382ms total (execution 377ms / network 5ms)
```

AS OF SYSTEM TIME Backup

By default, the backup will be consistent as of the time the backup command was executed. However, you can use the AS OF SYSTEM TIME clause to take a backup using "time travel." The backup copies data current as of the specified time using the MVCC records, which are (by default) kept for one day or for the value of the replication zone parameter gc.ttlseconds.

Here we take a backup as of one hour ago:

```
/defaultdb>
BACKUP INTO 'nodelocal://1/onehourago.backup/'
AS OF SYSTEM TIME '-1h';

         job_id        |  status   |  rows  | index_entries |  bytes
-----------------------+-----------+--------+---------------+----------
  694821661481992193   | succeeded | 58057  |         95076 | 15687164
(1 row)


Time: 641ms total (execution 638ms / network 3ms)
```

These time-travel backups represent the fulfillment of an age-old DBA dream—to be able to take a backup of the database *after* screwing it up by doing something stupid! So if we were to drop an important table by mistake in production (thinking it was development), we could quickly take a backup of the database as it was before our mistake.

It is also best practice to use the AS OF SYSTEM TIME clause with a small offset (−10 s is recommended) to reduce overhead and conflicts during the backup process. Without AS OF SYSTEM TIME, the backup will attempt to read the current state of all ranges, which may involve blocking on uncommitted transactions or retrying reads when necessary. By using AS OF SYSTEM TIME, these conflicts are eliminated, resulting in a faster backup with less impact on the production database.

WITH REVISION HISTORY

WITH REVISION HISTORY is another Enterprise edition feature. The WITH REVISION HISTORY clause adds all known data history into the backup.

As we've seen numerous times in this book, CockroachDB keeps changes to data for the duration of the replication zone gc.ttlseconds configuration variable. WITH REVISION HISTORY causes this information to be included in the backup. The backup will, of course, be much larger, but you'll have the option of performing a point-in-time RESTORE option that might be useful if you need to recover the database to a point in time.

SHOW BACKUP

The SHOW BACKUP command lists backups and their attributes. Its syntax is shown in Figure 12-2.

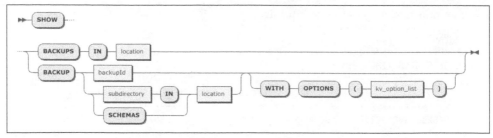

Figure 12-2. Syntax of the SHOW BACKUP command

In its simplest form, `SHOW BACKUPS IN location` lists the backups that have been written to a particular destination. For instance, for the full and incremental backup that we took earlier, we could issue this command to find the backup ID:

```
/defaultdb> SHOW BACKUPS IN
'nodelocal://1/fullClusterBackup/';
          path
------------------------
  2021/09/20-045139.32
```

We can now list properties of that backup:

```
/defaultdb> \set display_format=records
/defaultdb> SHOW BACKUP '2021/09/20-045139.32'
IN 'nodelocal://1/fullClusterBackup/';

-[ RECORD 1 ]
database_name      | NULL
parent_schema_name | NULL
object_name        | system
object_type        | database
start_time         | NULL
end_time           | 2021-09-20 04:51:39.325918+00:00:00
size_bytes         | NULL
rows               | NULL
is_full_cluster    | true
...
-[ RECORD 72 ]
database_name      | bank
parent_schema_name | public
object_name        | backup_upload_payload
object_type        | table
start_time         | 2021-09-20 04:53:32.054603+00:00:00
end_time           | 2021-09-20 04:59:38.075636+00:00:00
size_bytes         | 0
rows               | 0
is_full_cluster    | true

Time: 59ms total (execution 45ms / network 13ms)
```

Although the output is verbose, we can manipulate it using SQL. So, for instance, to see the start and end times of each full and incremental backup, we could do this:

```
/defaultdb>
SELECT distinct start_time,end_time
 FROM [SHOW BACKUP '2021/09/20-045139.32'
   IN 'nodelocal://1/fullClusterBackup/']
;
              start_time              |              end_time
--------------------------------------+--------------------------------------
  NULL                                | 2021-09-20 04:51:39.325918+00:00:00
  2021-09-20 04:51:39.325918+00:00:00 | 2021-09-20 04:53:32.054603+00:00:00
  2021-09-20 04:53:32.054603+00:00:00 | 2021-09-20 04:59:38.075636+00:00:00
(3 rows)
```

We see one full backup and two incremental backups in the backup container.

Managing Backup Jobs

By default, BACKUP commands block until the backup is complete. If the WITH DETACHED clause is added, then the backup proceeds in the background. For instance:

```
/defaultdb>
BACKUP INTO 'gs://ghcrdb/myFullBackup/'
WITH DETACHED;
        job_id
---------------------
  694835817555918849
(1 row)

Time: 2.148s total (execution 2.088s / network 0.060s)
```

The SHOW JOB, CANCEL JOB, and PAUSE JOB commands can help manage the backup:

```
/defaultdb> \set display_format=records;
/defaultdb> SHOW JOB 694835817555918849
;
-[ RECORD 1 ]
job_id              | 694835817555918849
job_type            | BACKUP
description         | BACKUP INTO '/2021/09/20-055741.77'
 IN 'gs://ghcrdb/myFullBackup/' WITH detached
statement           |
user_name           | root
status              | succeeded
running_status      | NULL
created             | 2021-09-20 05:57:41.779563+00:00:00
started             | 2021-09-20 05:57:50.462355+00:00:00
finished            | 2021-09-20 05:58:04.257721+00:00:00
modified            | 2021-09-20 05:58:04.177931+00:00:00
fraction_completed  | 1
error               |
coordinator_id      | 0
```

Scheduling Backups

The Enterprise command CREATE SCHEDULE FOR BACKUP allows you to create a schedule for periodic backups. Figure 12-3 shows the syntax of the CREATE SCHEDULE FOR BACKUP command.

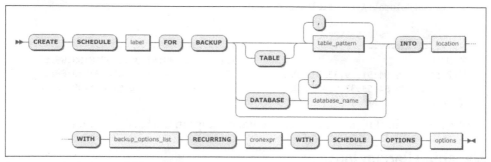

Figure 12-3. Syntax of the CREATE SCHEDULE FOR BACKUP command

Most of these options are the same as for the BACKUP command itself as well as advanced options that you can read about in the CockroachDB documentation (*https://cockroa.ch/3NLrqqs*).

The RECURRING arguments control the scheduling of the backup. RECURRING uses the familiar crontab format that has been in use since the 1970s. A crontab expression consists of five fields separated by white space. These fields correspond to:

- Minute in the hour
- Hour in the day (1 to 24)
- Day of month
- Month of year (1 to 12 or JAN to DEC)
- Day of the week (0 to 6 or SUN to SAT)

Asterisks can be used to indicate all ranges for the field, dashes (-) can be used to indicate ranges, and comma-separated lists might specify multiple entries. A crontab of:

```
5,35 0-6 1 * *
```

would fire at 5 minutes and 35 minutes past the hour, from midnight to 6 A.M. on the first day of every month. CockroachDB also accepts the nonstandard cron shortcuts @yearly, @annually, @monthly, @weekly, @daily, and @hourly. For more options, see the crontab manual page (*https://cockroa.ch/3j1BOMC*).

The following example takes a full backup, stored to a Google Cloud Storage bucket, every morning at 1:05 A.M.:

```
/movr> \set display_format=records;

/movr>
 CREATE SCHEDULE mydailyfullbackup
  FOR BACKUP INTO 'gs://ghcrdb/dailybackup'
    WITH revision_history
    RECURRING '5 1 * * *' FULL BACKUP ALWAYS;
-[ RECORD 1 ]
schedule_id | 695961487290531841
label       | mydailyfullbackup
status      | ACTIVE
first_run   | 2021-09-25 01:05:00+00:00:00
schedule    | 5 1 * * *
backup_stmt | BACKUP INTO 'gs://ghcrdb/dailybackup'
WITH revision_history, detached
```

This example takes an incremental backup every hour at 15 minutes past the hour and a daily full backup:

```
/movr> \set display_format=records;

/movr>  CREATE SCHEDULE myhourlybackup
    FOR BACKUP INTO 'gs://ghcrdb/hourly'
    WITH revision_history
    RECURRING '15 * * * *' FULL BACKUP '@daily';
-[ RECORD 1 ]
schedule_id | 695961540785733633
label       | myhourlybackup
status      | PAUSED: Waiting for initial backup to complete
first_run   | NULL
schedule    | 15 * * * *
backup_stmt | BACKUP INTO 'gs://ghcrdb/hourly'
WITH revision_history, detached
-[ RECORD 2 ]
schedule_id | 695961540796055553
label       | myhourlybackup
status      | ACTIVE
first_run   | 2021-09-25 00:00:00+00:00:00
schedule    | @daily
backup_stmt | BACKUP INTO 'gs://ghcrdb/hourly'
WITH revision_history, detached
```

Note that this command created two schedules—one for the hourly incremental backups and one for the daily full backup.

We can view schedules using the SHOW SCHEDULES command:

```
/movr> \set display_format=records;

/movr> SELECT * FROM [SHOW SCHEDULES] WHERE label='myhourlybackup';
```

```
-[ RECORD 1 ]
id              | 695961540785733633
label           | myhourlybackup
schedule_status | PAUSED
next_run        | NULL
state           | Waiting for initial backup to complete
recurrence      | 15 * * * *
jobsrunning     | 0
owner           | demo
created         | 2021-09-24 05:23:24.936047+00:00:00
command         | {"backup_statement": "BACKUP INTO LATEST
    IN 'gs://ghcrdb/hourly' WITH revision_history, detached",
    "backup_type": 1}
-[ RECORD 2 ]
id              | 695961540796055553
label           | myhourlybackup
schedule_status | ACTIVE
next_run        | 2021-09-25 00:00:00+00:00:00
state           | NULL
recurrence      | @daily
jobsrunning     | 0
owner           | demo
created         | 2021-09-24 05:23:24.936047+00:00:00
command         | {"backup_statement": "BACKUP INTO 'gs://ghcrdb/hourly'
WITH revision_history, detached", "unpause_on_success": 695961540785733633}
```

We can manage schedules using the SHOW SCHEDULES, PAUSE SCHEDULE, RESUME SCHEDULE, and DROP SCHEDULE commands.

Locality-Aware Backups

Locality-aware backups are an Enterprise-only feature in which each node writes its backup files to a specific backup destination. The idea is that a node in one region will write its backup to a cloud store in the same region. This will consequently optimize the network traffic and data transfer costs for the backup.

The following backup command specifies three Google Cloud Storage buckets assigned to corresponding CockroachDB locality regions. Note that a default bucket is also assigned to ensure that any ranges not assigned to one of these regions will still have a destination:

```
/movr> BACKUP INTO
    ('gs://crddg-us-east?COCKROACH_LOCALITY=default',
     'gs://crddg-us-east?COCKROACH_LOCALITY=region%3Dgcp-us-east1',
     'gs://crddg-us-west?COCKROACH_LOCALITY=region%3Dgcp-us-west1',
     'gs://crddg-eu-west?COCKROACH_LOCALITY=region%3Dgcp-europe-west1'
    );
      job_id       |  status   | rows | index_entries | bytes
--------------------+-----------+------+---------------+---------
  695965008766107649 | succeeded | 2613 |          1063 | 475741
(1 row)
```

Restoring Data

There's only one thing more important than taking backups—being able to restore them! The syntax for the restore command is straightforward, and a simple example is, well, simple. This might make you feel relaxed about the restore procedure. If so, un-chill out! There is nothing more nerve-wracking than trying to recover a mission-critical production system in the middle of the night with everyone—absolutely everyone—breathing down your neck.

You do not want to be doing your first restore procedure in these circumstances. What you need is to be following an extremely well-documented, foolproof, and *practiced* procedure for the recovery. Make sure that you perform disaster recovery drills at regular intervals and that the procedures are well understood.

Having said all that, it's true that the CockroachDB restore procedure is relatively straightforward. Figure 12-4 shows the syntax of the RESTORE command.

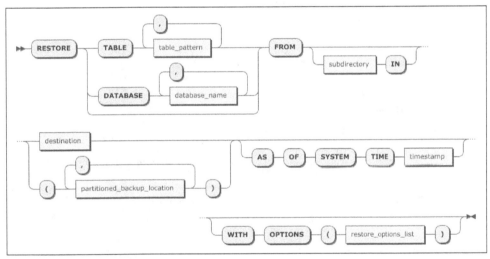

Figure 12-4. Syntax of the RESTORE command

Full cluster restores can be run only by members of the admin role. By default, the root user belongs to the this role.

For all other restores, the user must have write access (CREATE or INSERT) on all affected objects.

Let's step through a simplistic example. We create a backup of the entire cluster and then drop the movr database:

```
/defaultdb> BACKUP INTO 'gs://ghcrdb/gubuntu1.backup' ;
        job_id       | status   | rows   | index_entries | bytes
---------------------+----------+--------+---------------+----------
  694844860424978433 | succeeded | 216047 |        401379 | 63374661
(1 row)

Time: 13.930s total (execution 13.911s / network 0.018s)

/defaultdb> DROP DATABASE movr CASCADE;
DROP DATABASE
```

Now, to restore, we look at the backups in the cloud store:

```
/defaultdb> show backups in 'gs://ghcrdb/gubuntu1.backup';
          path
----------------------
  2021/09/20-064056.37
  2021/09/20-064341.66
(2 rows)
```

We pick the most recent backup and restore the database:

```
/defaultdb>
RESTORE DATABASE movr FROM '2021/09/20-064056.37'
IN 'gs://ghcrdb/gubuntu1.backup' ;

        job_id       | status   | rows   | index_entries | bytes
---------------------+----------+--------+---------------+----------
  694845589288714242 | succeeded | 214887 |        401149 | 63027704
(1 row)
```

Alternatively, we can specify a fully qualified backup location:

```
/defaultdb>
RESTORE DATABASE movr
  FROM 'gs://ghcrdb/gubuntu1.backup/2021/09/20-064056.37' ;
        job_id       | status   | rows   | index_entries | bytes
---------------------+----------+--------+---------------+----------
  694848192927858689 | succeeded | 214887 |        401149 | 63027704
(1 row)
```

Simple! The RESTORE command allows restoration of the entire cluster or selected databases and tables. A few things to note about a RESTORE:

- If a backup was taken WITH REVISION HISTORY, then a restore may use the AS OF SYSTEM TIME clause to restore data at a point in time. This might be useful if the database became corrupted before the backup was initiated, and you need to restore it to a point in time before the corruption.

- After a restore operation, your data will be restored to a point in time without history: AS OF SYSTEM TIME queries cannot access data prior to the restore point.

- RESTORE accepts the WITH DETACHED clause and creates a restore job that can be managed with SHOW JOB, CANCEL JOB, and PAUSE JOB commands.

- If an incremental backup is stored in the same location as the full backup, then a restore will leverage the incremental backups transparently.

- You may restore tables from one database into another using the INTO_DB option. This works only when restoring individual tables, not entire databases.

- RESTORE accepts a variety of options that can be used to fine-tune the restoration. For instance, you can ignore various dependencies such as foreign keys or sequences, or you can change the target database when restoring a table. See the CockroachDB documentation (*https://cockroa.ch/36OE6MP*) for more details.

Backups are a lot like home fire insurance—you hope that you never need it—and, given the high-availability features of CockroachDB, the chances are you never will. However, when you need it, you really need it. The principles of backup and restore are relatively straightforward, but there are many things that can go wrong in the real world. Crusty old DBAs are full of horror stories about backup and recovery. One thing these stories have in common is that the recovery procedure was not thoroughly tested.

Remember that it's very likely that a restore operation on a production system will occur in a high-stress environment and without any chance for preparation. You should be certain that your backups are safe and sound and that your procedures are documented and practiced.

Exporting Data

EXPORT is used to write table data or SQL result sets into CSV files. Although you could theoretically create a backup regimen around EXPORT and IMPORT (see Chapter 7), in practice, BACKUP and RESTORE, which allow for scheduled and incremental backups as well as all the other features we've outlined in this chapter, are a far superior solution for disaster recovery purposes.

EXPORT, however, has the advantage of storing data in a platform-independent format that can be used to load data into other systems (data warehouses, for instance) or for long-term archival purposes.

We looked at EXPORT in detail back in Chapter 7. Please refer to that chapter for more details.

Disaster Recovery Best Practices

Now that we're familiar with the various backup and restore commands, let's review how best to use the commands in real-world scenarios.

Backup Scheduling and Configuration

There are several considerations that bear on the scheduling and configuration of backups:

- Backups should be scheduled to minimize the possibility of any data loss.
- Backups should be scheduled and configured to minimize the time taken to restore from the backup: sometimes called mean time to recovery (MTTR).
- Backups should be scheduled and configured to avoid placing undue overhead on the live database.

Not all of these motivations are in perfect alignment. Very frequent backups will reduce the MTTR and the possibility of data loss but will increase the overhead on the system. Furthermore, different approaches are required for CockroachDB Community and CockroachDB Enterprise because the Community edition lacks some of the Enterprise backup facilities.

However, the following guidelines are suggested as general-purpose best practices.

For any edition (Community or Enterprise):

- Perform a full backup at least once within each garbage collection window (by default, 25 hours). The parameter `gc.ttlseconds` determines how long data will be retained before being discarded. In the event of a data corruption issue, you will always be able to retrieve data up to `gc.ttlseconds` in the past. You want to make sure that there is no gap between the last backup and the current garbage collection window.
- Use the `AS OF SYSTEM TIME` clause to base the backup of a snapshot of historical data rather than on the current state of the database. Without `AS OF SYSTEM TIME`, the backup will attempt to read the current state of data ranges and may need to restart reads if there are unresolved write intents or block if the read encounters an uncommitted write. By specifying a `SYSTEM TIME` in the very recent past (10 seconds is recommended), you avoid these conflicts, which results in a faster backup with less impact on other sessions.
- Use cloud storage for backup destinations when possible. Directing backups to destinations in the same region as your cluster can optimize backup performance by reducing network latency but raises the risk that an outage might affect both the cluster and the cloud store. Most cloud stores offer geo-redundant options

in which data is replicated to multiple regions: these would be preferred destinations for important backups.

For an Enterprise edition cluster:

- Use a combination of full and incremental backups to achieve a balance between overhead, frequency, and time to recover. The more frequently an incremental backup is executed, the lower its overhead (because it is backing up fewer changes). Therefore, you can issue incremental backups reasonably frequently—once per hour is a typical choice.

- Use the `WITH REVISION HISTORY` if you want to be able to recover a backup to a point in time.

- Use CockroachDB scheduling instead of an external scheduler such as `cron`. The CockroachDB scheduler understands some of the nuances of the CockroachDB backup system, such as using the `AS OF SYSTEM TIME` clause to reduce overhead.

Recovering from Human Errors

Most of the backup and high-availability scenarios we've discussed involve hardware or software failures that render the CockroachDB cluster partially or completely unavailable. While it's true that hardware failures occur, all too often a database is compromised because of a human error or a fault in application code. For instance, a DBA might accidentally drop a table or delete some data or an application developer might roll out a patch that incorrectly updates important information.

The most important mitigation that CockroachDB offers for these categories of errors is the ability to access data `AS OF SYSTEM TIME`. By default, "old" versions of data are maintained within the system for at least the time period specified by the replication zone setting `gc.ttlseconds`. By default, this parameter is set to 90,000 seconds (25 hours). This allows us to retrieve data after it has been modified for over a day.

`AS OF SYSTEM TIME` can be used to recover from a variety of data-corruption scenarios:

- Fine-grained changes to a table can be reversed by replacing the table's contents with that of a simple `SELECT` query with a specific `AS OF SYSTEM TIME`. Individual row changes can similarly be reversed.

- A backup can be taken with the `AS OF SYSTEM TIME` clause. This backup can effectively represent the state of the database or selected tables at the time prior to corruption. It sounds kind of amazing to be restoring from a backup taken *after* a logical corruption, but it's a powerful way of undoing any undesirable changes.

- If a backup is created with the `WITH REVISION HISTORY` option, then the backup can be restored to a point in time. So even if the backup was taken after the logical corruption, it could still be restored to a point before that corruption.

Summary

CockroachDB backups are typically used as a mechanism for recovering a CockroachDB cluster in the event of a truly catastrophic failure. They also play a role in allowing us to recover from a variety of data corruption issues that can be the result of human failures or application errors. CockroachDB supports a rich range of backup and restore options, though some of these require an Enterprise license.

Backups are needed less frequently in distributed databases because replication allows the database to continue functioning in the presence of failures that would break a monolithic database such as Oracle or MySQL. However, this doesn't reduce the need to implement a robust and tested backup and restore facility. You don't cancel your fire insurance just because you've installed some fire suppression equipment. Likewise, you should not neglect backups just because you have a fault-tolerant database cluster.

Security

In the Information Age, data is one of the world's most valuable commodities. It can confer competitive advantage through enhanced operational intelligence, and it is often subject to the most stringent privacy regulations. Databases are frequently the target of data theft, ransomware attacks, and data tampering.

CockroachDB supports industrial-strength security features that protect your database from malicious attacks and also to some degree from human error and application bugs.

A well-secured CockroachDB deployment uses defense-in-depth to protect the database: multiple levels of security that protect against intrusion or unauthorized activities. These include:

- Firewall rules that restrict cluster connections to known and trusted network addresses.
- Transport Layer Security (TLS) encryption in flight to prevent access of data in transit. TLS authentication can also be used to defeat man-in-the-middle attacks and to provide a level of client authentication.
- Encryption at rest: an enterprise feature that allows data files on disk to be encrypted.
- A variety of authentication mechanisms to determine a user's identity, including username/password, key file, Kerberos, and OAuth.
- A role-based authorization system that controls access to data and to system commands.

- Logging options that allow for tracking of user access. Standard logging allows tracking of authentication events and SQL executions, while *audit* logging allows for fine-grained tracking of access to sensitive data.

We'll discuss each of these in detail within this chapter.

Firewall Configuration

Most attempts to gain access to a CockroachDB database will occur through the SQL port—which by default is listening on port 26257. Restricting access to this port to authorized IP addresses is an obvious first step in securing a cluster.

IP Allowlist with CockroachDB Dedicated

CockroachDB Dedicated provides an IP allowlist function that serves as a global firewall for the cluster. Using the allowlist, we can allow individual IP addresses or IP address ranges in Classless Inter-Domain Routing (CIDR) format to connect to the cluster. Figure 13-1 shows us adding a new CIDR range to a CockroachDB Dedicated cluster.

Figure 13-1. Setting up an allowlist in CockroachDB Dedicated

VPC Peering and PrivateLink with CockroachDB Dedicated

Virtual private cloud (VPC) peering allows a CockroachDB Dedicated cloud cluster to be exposed on the private cloud IP addresses that you are using for your application. VPC peering is available for only the CockroachDB Dedicated clusters on the Google Cloud Platform. On AWS, you can achieve the same result with AWS PrivateLink. AWS PrivateLink and GCP VPC peering reduce operational overhead because you don't have to manually maintain a list of IP addresses in an allowlist. They may also reduce your cloud networking billing costs.

Figure 13-2 shows us setting up VPC peering during cluster creation. You can also configure VPC peering after the fact on the networking/VCP peering page of the CockroachDB Console.

On AWS, you can achieve a similar result with AWS PrivateLink, which links an AWS VPC to an AWS endpoint associated with your CockroachDB cluster.

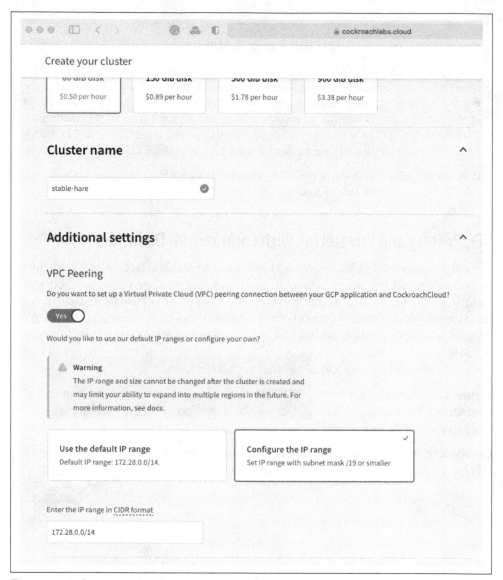

Figure 13-2. Setting up VPC peering in Google Compute Cloud

To create a PrivateLink, navigate to the Networking section on your CockroachDB Dedicated cluster and select the PrivateLink option. The console will display the CockroachDB endpoint (Figure 13-3).

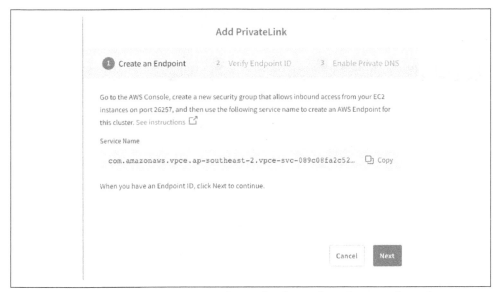

Add PrivateLink

1 **Create an Endpoint**　　　2　Verify Endpoint ID　　　3　Enable Private DNS

Go to the AWS Console, create a new security group that allows inbound access from your EC2
instances on port 26257, and then use the following service name to create an AWS Endpoint for
this cluster. See instructions

Service Name

`com.amazonaws.vpce.ap-southeast-2.vpce-svc-089c08fa2c52…`　　☐ Copy

When you have an Endpoint ID, click Next to continue.

Cancel　　**Next**

Figure 13-3. Creating an AWS VPC endpoint for the CockroachDB Dedicated instance

The dialog shown in Figure 13-3 has a link to detailed instructions for setting up the
link on the AWS side (*https://cockroa.ch/3j1U5JV*). The core activity is to associate the
service name shown in Figure 13-3 with an AWS endpoint associated with a security
group and private DNS that allows your AWS application within a VPC to connect to
CockroachDB Dedicated.

Figure 13-4 shows the service name from Figure 13-3 with a new AWS endpoint.

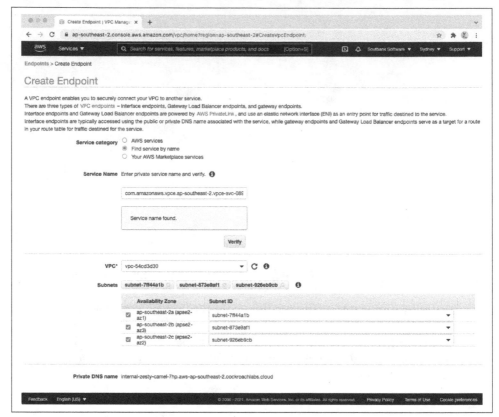

Figure 13-4. Associating an AWS endpoint with a CockroachDB Dedicated service (large format version (https://cockroa.ch/cockroachDB-figs))

Native Linux Firewall

Linux kernels incorporate firewall functionality that can be used to restrict inbound access to nominated IP ranges.

On modern Ubuntu-based systems, the ufw (Uncomplicated Firewall) is the default firewall configuration tool. If ufw is disabled, it should first be enabled:

```
$ sudo ufw status
Status: inactive
$ sudo ufw enable
Command may disrupt existing ssh connections. Proceed with operation (y|n)? y
Firewall is active and enabled on system startup
```

By default, only `ssh` will be enabled:

```
$ sudo ufw status
Status: active

To                         Action      From
--                         ------      ----
22/tcp                     ALLOW       Anywhere
22/tcp (v6)                ALLOW       Anywhere (v6)
```

For a CockroachDB node to communicate to other nodes of the cluster and for client connections to succeed, we need to enable access from those addresses:

```
$ sudo ufw allow proto tcp from 192.168.0.50 to any port 26257
Rule added
$ sudo ufw allow proto tcp from 192.168.0.53 to any port 26257
Rule added
$ sudo ufw status
Status: active

To                         Action      From
--                         ------      ----
22/tcp                     ALLOW       Anywhere
26257/tcp                  ALLOW       192.168.0.50
26257/tcp                  ALLOW       192.168.0.53
22/tcp (v6)                ALLOW       Anywhere (v6)
```

To allow clients to connect to the cluster, their IP addresses also need to be added. You can add each client individually, but it's often easier to specify an IP address range in CIDR format:

```
$ sudo ufw allow proto tcp from 192.168.0.0/24 to any port 26257
Rule added
$ sudo ufw status
Status: active

To                         Action      From
--                         ------      ----
22/tcp                     ALLOW       Anywhere
26257/tcp                  ALLOW       192.168.0.50
26257/tcp                  ALLOW       192.168.0.53
26257/tcp                  ALLOW       192.168.0.0/24
22/tcp (v6)                ALLOW       Anywhere (v6)
```

You will want to configure similar firewall rules for the DB Console (port 8080) and for the load balancer machine. The load balancer allows access from behind the firewall to the CockroachDB nodes, so it's essential that it not be open to the wide network. The DB Console is a lesser risk, but a hacker could still potentially retrieve sensitive information or discover cluster vulnerabilities if they got access to the console.

Configuring a Firewall in GCP

If you have a CockroachDB self-hosted cluster on a public cloud, you will generally control access to the CockroachDB ports using the cloud vendor's security rules.

In the GCP, these rules can be found under Networking → VPC network → Firewall, as shown in Figure 13-5.

Figure 13-5. Setting firewall rules in Google Cloud Platform (large format version (https://cockroa.ch/cockroachDB-figs))

The firewall rules in Figure 13-5 can also be created using the following gcloud command:

```
gcloud compute --project=just-rhythm-211204 firewall-rules \
  create cdb-firewall-rule --description="CockroachDB server SQL port" \
  --direction=INGRESS --priority=1000 --network=default \
  --action=ALLOW --rules=tcp:26257 --source-ranges=192.168.4.0/24 \
  --target-tags=cdb-server
```

Once the rule is created, you can add the associated target tag to a VM (*https://cock roa.ch/3j1Zwbs*). This can be done from the VM Instances page, using the following gcloud syntax:

```
$ ~ gcloud compute --project=just-rhythm-211204 instances add-tags instance-1 \
    --tags cdb-server --zone us-central1-a
```

Configuring a Firewall in AWS

AWS security groups control port access to EC2 instances. They can be created and associated with EC2 machines as they are created. Figure 13-6 shows us making a new rule during the creation of a new EC2 VM.

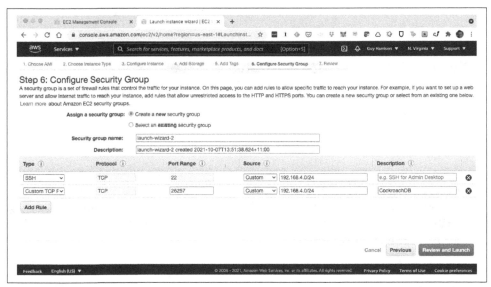

Figure 13-6. Configuring an AWS security group during EC2 initialization (large format version (https://cockroa.ch/cockroachDB-figs))

Alternatively, you can create a named firewall rule and add it to existing EC2 instances, as shown in Figure 13-7.

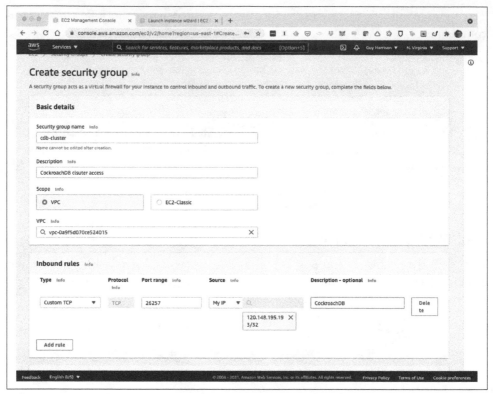

Figure 13-7. Configuring an ASWS security group (large format version (https://cock roa.ch/cockroachDB-figs))

Configuring Ports for Microsoft Azure

We can specify security rules for Azure VMs during VM creation or with Azure network security groups. Once created, this security group can be reused by other VMs by referring to the name given during its creation. Figure 13-8 shows us creating a security rule for the `Centos8` VM called `crdb-server`. Once created, we can add that security group to other servers supporting the cluster.

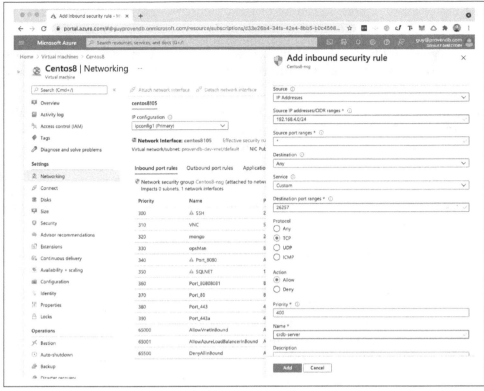

Figure 13-8. Creating a security rule during Microsoft Azure VM creation (large format version (https://cockroa.ch/cockroachDB-figs))

Encryption and Server Certificates

Transmissions between clients and servers will be encrypted unless the server is running in `insecure` mode. Running in `insecure` mode is definitely not an option for a production system.

CockroachDB Dedicated and CockroachDB Serverless cloud connections will always be encrypted. The certificates necessary to establish the connection are provided by Cockroach Labs and can be downloaded from the Cloud console.

For a self-hosted deployment, you are responsible for creating a server certificate that is used to encrypt wire protocol transmissions between client and server. This certificate is used to encrypt both the SQL protocol messages (usually over port 26257) and the DB Console (usually port 8080).

We showed how to create self-signed certificates in Chapter 10. The Cockroach binary can create both a self-signed CA certificate (`cockroach cert create-ca`) and certificates for each node signed by that CA certificate (cockroach cert create-node).

A self-signed certificate is sufficient to ensure that communication across the wire is encrypted. However, such a certificate cannot be used to definitively prove that a server is what it claims to be.

Because a self-signed certificate cannot be used to definitively establish the identity of a server, web browsers will object when an HTTPS connection is established to a CockroachDB server that uses a self-signed certificate. Consequently, when you connect to the database console for a self-signed CockroachDB server, your browser will require that you click through a series of alarming-sounding warnings.

The CockroachDB documentation (*https://cockroa.ch/3qWPw7Z*) has more information about using custom CA certificates.

Encryption at Rest

Encryption at rest is an Enterprise feature that allows for the encryption of a CockroachDB node's data on disk. Without encryption at rest, an attacker who gets access to the machine hosting a node's data files might be able to extract data from those files, even if they do not have the necessary CockroachDB credentials to read that data. An attacker might also be able to extract meaningful data from OS snapshots of the store files taken for backup purposes.

CockroachDB uses two layers of encryption keys. The *store key* is provided by the user at node startup. It is used to encrypt *data keys* that are used to encrypt files on disk.

We can create a store key using the cockroach gen encryption-key command:

```
$ cockroach gen encryption-key -s 128 $HOME/.cockroachKeys/crdb-aes-128.key
  created AES-128 key: /home/cockroachdb/.cockroachKeys/crdb-aes-128.key
```

Here we use that key to start a new single-node cluster:

```
$ cockroach start-single-node \
  --store=/var/lib/cockroachdb/encrypted-cockroach-data \
  --enterprise-encryption=path=\
  /var/lib/cockroachdb/encrypted-cockroach-data\
  ,key=/home/cockroachdb/.cockroachKeys/crdb-aes-128.key\
  ,old-key=plain \
  --certs-dir=/var/lib/cockroachdb/certs
*
*
*
CockroachDB node starting at 2021-10-10 23:40:39.232036716 +0000 UTC (took 0.5s)
nodeID:                1
```

The old-key argument allows us to rotate from one key to another. It's best practice to rotate keys to reduce the risk of a key becoming compromised. The special key plain indicates that the files are not encrypted; when we first encrypt, we use plain as the old key, indicating that the files are not currently encrypted.

Here we create a new key and restart our cluster to use that new key:

```
$ cockroach gen encryption-key -s 128 \
 $HOME/.cockroachKeys/new-crdb-aes-128.key
 created AES-128 key: /home/cockroachdb/.cockroachKeys/new-crdb-aes-128.key
$ cockroach start-single-node \
 --store=/var/lib/cockroachdb/encrypted-cockroach-data \
 --enterprise-encryption=path=\
 /var/lib/cockroachdb/encrypted-cockroach-data,\
  key=/home/cockroachdb/.cockroachKeys/new-crdb-aes-128.key,\
 old-key=/home/cockroachdb/.cockroachKeys/crdb-aes-128.key \
 --certs-dir=/var/lib/cockroachdb/certs
*
*
CockroachDB node starting at 2021-10-10 23:46:03.452508125 +0000 UTC (took 0.3s)
clusterID:          dd842f97-4833-4ff6-ae9f-03bb23a4b953
```

In Chapter 10, we created a three-node self-hosted cluster that was managed by a systemctl service. To implement encryption on that server, we would modify the *cockroachdb.service* file as follows:

```
$ cat  /etc/systemd/system/cockroachdb.service
[Unit]
Description=Cockroach Database cluster node
Requires=network.target
[Service]
Type=notify
WorkingDirectory=/var/lib/cockroachdb
ExecStart=/usr/local/bin/cockroach start --certs-dir=certs
--advertise-addr=gubuntu2 --join=gubuntu1,gubuntu2,gubuntu3
--locality=region=us-west-1,zone=us-west-1a --max-sql-memory=.35
--cache=.35
--enterprise-encryption=path=/var/lib/cockroachdb/cockroach-data,
key=/home/cockroachdb/.cockroachKeys/crdb-aes-128.key,
old-key=plain
TimeoutStopSec=60
Restart=always
RestartSec=10
StandardOutput=syslog
StandardError=syslog
SyslogIdentifier=cockroachdb
User=cockroachdb
[Install]
```

And then restart:

```
$ sudo systemctl daemon-reload
$ sudo systemctl restart cockroachdb
```

You can see the status of encryption on the console "stores" report within the DBConsole at *https://nodeaddress:8080/#/reports/stores/local*. Figure 13-9 provides an example of a cluster that has just been restarted with encryption on.

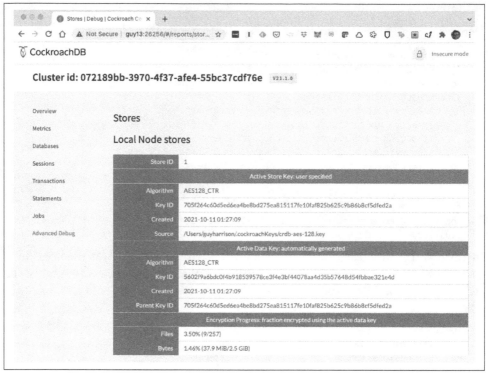

Figure 13-9. Viewing encryption progress on the CockroachDB Console

Best Practices for Key Management

Although the *store key* is not directly used to encrypt data files, a talented hacker would be able to use this key to decrypt CockroachDB data files. Furthermore, loss of the key could render your CockroachDB database unusable.

To prevent loss of the encryption key, your encryption keys should always be securely stored outside of the CockroachDB host, ideally in a Key Management Service (KMS) specifically designed to secure and protect keys.

Because the store key is needed only when the CockroachDB server is started, it may be advisable to make the store key available only during system startup. That way, an attacker who gains root access to the server will not automatically gain access to the store key.

Authentication Mechanisms

Authentication allows CockroachDB to determine the identity of the entity attempting to establish a connection. Members of the cluster authenticate themselves using node certificates and keys—as outlined in Chapter 10.

Standard Authentication

Clients—programs that wish to interact with the CockroachDB server—use a combination of username/password authentication together with client certificate and key authentication.

CockroachDB Dedicated and CockroachDB Serverless cloud clusters use a server certificate together with username and passwords. The server certificate guarantees the identity of the server and allows for encrypted communication, while the username and password are used to authenticate the specific user.

In the initial set up of our self-hosted cluster in Chapter 10, we created a CA certificate (`ca.crt`) as well as certificates and keys for the root user. Our certificates directory looked like this:

```
$ tmp ls certs
ca.crt          client.root.crt client.root.key
```

Because we had both the certificate and the key for the root user, we were able to connect to that user without a password:

```
$ tmp cockroach sql --host gubuntu1 --user=root --certs-dir=certs
#
# Welcome to the CockroachDB SQL shell.
# All statements must be terminated by a semicolon.
# To exit, type: \q.
#
# Enter \? for a brief introduction.
#
root@gubuntu1:26257/defaultdb>
```

Without the client certificates, we can still connect to the cluster, but we must provide a password for the username concerned:

```
$ tmp cockroach sql --host gubuntu1 --user=root --certs-dir=certs
#
# Welcome to the CockroachDB SQL shell.
# All statements must be terminated by a semicolon.
# To exit, type: \q.
#
Enter password:
```

Without the CA certificate, we're unable to connect to the server in secure mode:

```
$ tmp cockroach sql --host gubuntu1 --user=root --certs-dir=certs
#
# Welcome to the CockroachDB SQL shell.
# All statements must be terminated by a semicolon.
# To exit, type: \q.
#
ERROR: cannot load certificates.
Check your certificate settings, set --certs-dir,
 or use --insecure for insecure clusters.
```

If we want to allow unencrypted communications, we can specify `--accept-sql-without-tls` when starting the server. This should be done only if transport-level encryption is implemented by the underlying infrastructure.

Advanced Authentication

CockroachDB supports additional authentication mechanisms that can be used to integrate with enterprise and third-party systems:

Single sign-on
> An enterprise feature that allows a DB Console user to authenticate using an OAuth credential, such as a Google or GitHub account. This is an experimental feature only available in CockroachDB Enterprise. See the CockroachDB documentation (*https://cockroa.ch/3LFLpoJ*) for more details.

GSSAPI
> This authentication uses the Generic Security Services API to authenticate SQL connections against Kerberos-compatible systems such as Active Directory. To use GSSAPI authentication, you need to use a GSSAPI-compatible Postgres client such as the `psql` client distributed with PostgreSQL. For more information, check out the CockroachDB documentation (*https://cockroa.ch/3u3GcRE*).

Authorization

Authorization determines the privileges granted to authenticated users. CockroachDB uses the familiar role, privilege, and objects model for determining the operations that an authenticated user can perform:

- Users and roles in CockroachDB are technically interchangeable, though, by default, roles will be configured with the `NOLOGIN` option, preventing a client from directly authenticating as a role.

- Privileges can be granted to users or roles, though it's generally easier administratively if privileges are granted only to roles, and then users are assigned privileges via roles.

- Privileges may have specific objects to which they apply. For instance, the UPDATE privilege must be associated with a table.

There is just one default user in CockroachDB—the root user is created automatically upon cluster creation.

Two roles are created by default: admin and public. The public role is assigned by default to all new users and is used to control global privileges. The admin role has access to all privileges on all objects.

Managing Users

As mentioned previously, USERs and ROLEs are mostly interchangeable. Figure 13-10 shows the syntax for creating a user or a role.

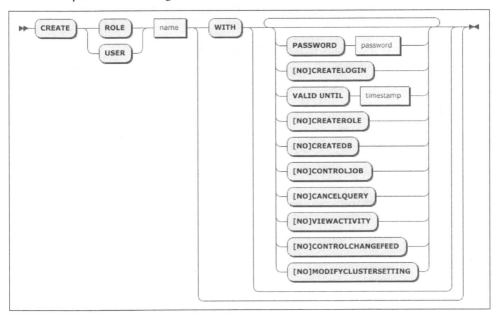

Figure 13-10. CREATE USER statement syntax

The options associated with the CREATE USER and ROLE statement represent high-level options that cannot be assigned using GRANT statements—see Table 13-1.

Table 13-1. Create USER and ROLE options

Option	Description
[NO]CREATEROLE	Determines whether the user or role can create other users or roles
[NO]CREATEDB	Determines whether the user or role can create databases
[NO]CONTROLJOB	Determines if the user can pause, resume, or cancel jobs

Option	Description
[NO]CANCELQUERY	Determines if the user can cancel queries of other users
[NO]VIEWACTIVITY	Determines if the user can use SHOW STATEMENTS or SHOW SESSIONS to examine other users' activity
[NO]CONTROLCHANGE FEED	Determines if the user can control changefeeds
[NO]MODIFYCLUSTER SETTING	Determines if the user can modify cluster settings with the sql.defaults prefix

Managing Privileges

The GRANT command allows privileges to be assigned to roles or users. Although roles and users are broadly interchangeable, the best practice is to assign privileges to roles and then roles to users. This way, privileges are grouped around workload requirements, not against individual accounts.

Figure 13-11 shows the syntax of the GRANT statement.

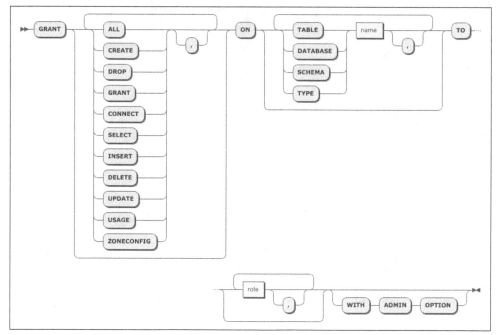

Figure 13-11. GRANT statement syntax

The GRANT statement can assign one, some, or all privileges on one or more database objects to one or more roles or users. Table 13-2 lists the privileges that may be used.

The WITH ADMIN OPTION clause allows for the target user to grant these privileges to other roles or users.

Table 13-2. Privileges that may be assigned with the GRANT statement

Privilege	Description
CREATE	Allows the user or role to create a database, schema, or table
DROP	Allows the user or role to drop a database or table
GRANT	Allows the user or role to grant privileges on a database, schema, table, or type
CONNECT	Allows the user or role to connect to a database
SELECT	Allows the user or role to select from a table or all tables in a database
INSERT	Allows the user or role to insert into a table
DELETE	Allows the user or role to delete rows in a table
UPDATE	Allows the user or role to update rows in a table
USAGE	Allows the user or role to use a user-defined type
ZONECONFIG	Allows the user or role to change the zone configuration for a database

Fine-Grained Access Control with Views

The GRANT system allows us to grant SELECT, INSERT, UPDATE, and DELETE access to individual tables, but they don't provide a mechanism for granting access to individual rows or columns. For instance, let's say we had a table with a security level column, like this:

```
defaultdb > SELECT description, security_restriction FROM documents;

            description                | security_restriction
---------------------------------------+----------------------
  Why CockroachDB is better than Oracle | OPEN
  Ben Darnell - the inside story        | TOP SECRET
  MongoDB - plans for their destruction | SECRET
```

We want everybody to be able to read the "Why CockroachDB is better than Oracle" document, and insiders can read the MongoDB destruction document, but if the inside story of Ben Darnell got out, there would be a scandal!

We can restrict a user's access to specific rows by creating a table containing usernames and security access levels:

```
defaultdb> SELECT * FROM document_access;
  username | security_access
-----------+------------------
  ben      | TOP SECRET
  ben      | SECRET
  jesse    | SECRET
  root     | SECRET
```

Then we can create a view that joins the documents table to the document_access table and returns rows only for which the current_user has access:

```
defaultdb> CREATE VIEW restricted_documents_view AS
SELECT id,description,document FROM documents
 WHERE security_restriction='OPEN'
 UNION
 SELECT d.id, d.description,d.document
   FROM documents d JOIN document_access da
     ON(d.security_restriction=da.security_access)
   WHERE da.username=current_user;
CREATE VIEW

Time: 482ms total (execution 174ms / network 308ms)

defaultdb> GRANT SELECT ON document_access TO PUBLIC;
GRANT

Time: 306ms total (execution 103ms / network 203ms)
```

Now, unless we have TOP SECRET clearance, we can't see those documents:

```
defaultdb> SELECT description FROM restricted_documents_view;
                description
----------------------------------------
   Why CockroachDB is better than Oracle
   MongoDB - plans for their destruction
```

Ben's secrets are safe! Of course, you need to ensure that access to the base documents table is restricted.

As well as restricting access to rows, a view can also restrict access to columns, either by simply not including a column in a definition or by using a CASE statement to mask the contents of the column if the user lacks the appropriate authorization.

Logging and Auditing

Not all cyber attacks can be prevented. Furthermore, most organizations have a responsibility not just to stop attacks but also to be able to demonstrate that to regulators.

CockroachDB supports logging and auditing features that allow access to data within the database to be recorded.

CockroachDB logging is a general-purpose facility used for troubleshooting, administration, and performance management, as well as for access security. We'll dig into logging in depth in the next chapter.

Logging in CockroachDB is organized around channels. In Chapter 14, we'll see how to configure the verbosity, format, and destination for those channels. For now, we will use the default logging configuration.

The SESSIONS, PRIVILEGE, USER_ADMIN, and SQL_EXEC channels can be used to get a high-level view of user and SQL activity across all tables.

The server.auth_log.sql_connections.enabled cluster setting can be used to log connections over the SQL channel to the server:

```
/defaultdb> SET CLUSTER SETTING
            server.auth_log.sql_connections.enabled = true;
SET CLUSTER SETTING
```

This will result in client_connection_start and client_connection_end messages being logged to the *cockroach-sql-auth.log* file:

```
I211012 22:01:56.625060 6885 4@util/log/event_log.go:32 :
 [n1,client=‹192.168.0.242:55773›]
2 ={"Timestamp":1634076116625055000,
"EventType":"client_connection_start","InstanceID":1,
"Network":"tcp","RemoteAddress":"‹192.168.0.242:55773›"}

I211012 22:02:16.542770 6885 4@util/log/event_log.go:32 :
[n1,client=‹192.168.0.242:55773›,hostnossl] 3
={"Timestamp":1634076136542761000,
"EventType":"client_connection_end","InstanceID":1
"Network":"tcp","RemoteAddress":"‹192.168.0.242:55773›",
"Duration":19917706000}
```

This is primarily useful to track the IP addresses that are connecting to the server. Accesses from unexpected IP addresses might indicate attacks or the need to refine your firewall or network access rules.

The PRIVILEGE channel shows privilege changes. Cyber attacks might involve unauthorized attempts to elevate privilege for nonadmin users. Here we can see that the user guy has been given all privileges on the movr database:

```
I211012 22:34:29.137386 12700 7@util/log/event_log.go:32 :
 [n1,client=‹192.168.0.242:59281›,hostssl,user=root] 286
={"Timestamp":1634078069088688947,"EventType":"change_database_privilege",
"Statement":"‹GRANT ALL ON DATABASE movr TO guy›","Tag":"GRANT","User":"root",
"DescriptorID":98,"ApplicationName":
"$ cockroach sql","Grantee":"‹guy›","GrantedPrivileges":["ALL"],
"DatabaseName":"‹movr›"}
```

The USER_ADMIN channel logs the creation and modifications of roles. Here we see the creation of the blackhat role has been logged:

```
I211012 22:40:15.472921 12700 6@util/log/event_log.go:32 :
[n1,client=‹192.168.0.242:59281›,hostssl,user=root]
337 ={"Timestamp":1634078415319346771,"EventType":"create_role",
```

```
"Statement":"‹CREATE USER 'blackhat' WITH PASSWORD '*****'›",
"Tag":"CREATE ROLE","User":"root","ApplicationName":"$ cockroach sql",
"RoleName":"‹blackhat›"}
```

Finally, the SQL_EXEC channel logs SQL executions into the cockroach-sql-exec.log if the cluster setting sql.trace.log_statement_execute is true:

```
root@:26257/defaultdb> SET CLUSTER SETTING sql.trace.log_statement_execute = true;
SET CLUSTER SETTING
```

This setting creates verbose log output. However, it does provide the ability to identify any suspicious activity. For instance, what follows is a SQL statement that appears to be the result of SQL injection (we first looked at this SQL injection use case in Chapter 6):

```
211012 22:48:34.565430 89972 9@util/log/event_log.go:32 ⋮
[n1,client=‹192.168.0.242:61454›,hostssl,user=root] 341 =
{"Timestamp":1634078914296526204,"EventType":"query_execute","Statement":
"‹SELECT u.name FROM \"\".movr.rides AS r JOIN \"\".movr.users AS u
ON (r.rider_id = u.id)
WHERE r.id = 'aaaae297-396d-4800-8000-00000001046b'
UNION SELECT credit_card FROM \"\".movr.users ORDER BY 1, name›",
"Tag":"SELECT","User":"root",
"ApplicationName":"‹DBeaver 21.1.3 - SQLEditor <Console>›",
"ExecMode":"exec","NumRows":1001,
"Age":458.3223,"FullTableScan":true,"FullIndexScan":true,
"TxnCounter":12}
```

All of these logging options are system-wide; in particular, the SQL_EXEC channel will log all SQL statements, regardless of the target object or the type of operation.

The EXPERIEMENTAL_AUDIT clause allows you to track SQL operations against selected tables for either read or write operations—you can think of it as a more targeted variant of the SQL_EXEC channel.

For instance, we track read and write operations against the movr.users table in the following way:

```
root@:26257/defaultdb> ALTER TABLE movr.users EXPERIMENTAL_AUDIT SET READ WRITE;
ALTER TABLE

Time: 758ms total (execution 140ms / network 618ms)
```

Any operations that read from or write to movr.users will be logged to the *cockroach-sql-audit.log* file (or wherever the SENSITIVE_ACCESS channel is directed):

```
I211012 23:05:06.816793 89972 8@util/log/event_log.go:32 ⋮
[n1,client=‹192.168.0.242:61454›,hostssl,user=root]
3 ={"Timestamp":1634079906720036907,
"EventType":"sensitive_table_access",
"Statement":"‹SELECT u.name FROM \"\".movr.rides AS r
JOIN \"\".movr.users AS u ON (r.rider_id = u.id)
```

```
WHERE r.id = 'aaaae297-396d-4800-8000-00000001046b'
UNION
SELECT credit_card FROM \"\".movr.users ORDER BY 1, name›",
"Tag":"SELECT","User":"root",
"DescriptorID":99,
"ApplicationName":"‹DBeaver 21.1.3 - SQLEditor <Console>›",
"ExecMode":"exec","NumRows":1001,
"Age":96.941925,"FullTableScan":true,"FullIndexScan":true,
"TxnCounter":18,"TableName":"‹movr.public.users›","AccessMode":"r"}
```

Note that the format for the SENSITIVE_ACCESS channel is the same as for the SQL_EXEC channel.

Security Best Practices

We've seen that CockroachDB supports a variety of industrial-strength security measures that are intended to protect your data from unauthorized access. Let's sum up how we would normally use these features in practice:

- Production CockroachDB clusters will normally be protected from public access by firewall and network security rules. We will normally restrict the IP addresses that are authorized to connect to those associated with the application and with authorized administrators. The methods for doing this vary depending on your deployment pattern, but all deployment options allow for the restriction of IP addresses.

- Traffic between clients and the CockroachDB server should be encrypted using TLS certificates. These certificates may be self-signed when CockroachDB is running in a trusted environment, but ideally, we would expect a CA-signed certificate to be used that can definitively identify the CockroachDB server to prevent man-in-the-middle attacks.

- Optionally, we can encrypt the CockroachDB data files to prevent an attacker who gains access to a CockroachDB server from accessing data directly in the data files.

- Clients should authenticate themselves to the server using client certificates. Password-based authentication is also available, but since passwords may be brute-forced, certificate authentication is preferred.

- Access to table data should be configured using users, ROLES, and GRANTS. Roles should be constructed that represent various job descriptions and application roles. Login accounts (users) can be associated with the roles, and the roles may be granted appropriate access to appropriate tables.

- Alternatively, we can use views to implement columnar or row-based access to table data.

- Logging and auditing can be used to ensure that a record of access is preserved, and these logs can be used for forensic purposes should unauthorized access be suspected.

Summary

In this chapter, we've examined the mechanisms provided by CockroachDB for protecting your database from unauthorized access. Cybersecurity is a major focus for all large organizations, and protecting your database from attack should be a primary consideration for CockroachDB administrators.

CockroachDB supports the following security features:

- Firewalls and network security groups can be used to prevent access to the cluster from unauthorized IP addresses.
- Communications between clients and servers can be encrypted using TLS.
- Data at rest can be encrypted (in CockroachDB Enterprise edition).
- Clients can be authenticated using client certificates and/or passwords.
- Access to specific operations on specific database objects can be restricted using roles and grants.
- CockroachDB can log a variety of activities providing an audit trail to ensure that no unauthorized activity has occurred or for forensic purposes in the event of a breach.

Administration and Troubleshooting

In previous chapters, we've shown you how to design and implement applications for the CockroachDB platform and how to create a CockroachDB deployment either in a fully managed cloud platform—CockroachDB Dedicated and Serverless—or in a self-hosted implementation on your own hardware or in a public cloud.

Now that you have your CockroachDB application implemented and your CockroachDB cluster in place, it's time to consider the day-to-day administration and configuration tasks that are required to keep a CockroachDB deployment healthy and happy.

We'll leave one of the most significant tasks—cluster optimization—to the final chapter because that topic is deep enough to require its own chapter.

Note that while a lot of these tasks are required only for self-hosted deployments, even a CockroachDB Dedicated or Serverless cloud cluster does require some care and attention. Choosing a CockroachDB Cloud option reduces your administration overhead dramatically; however, there still are some troubleshooting and configuration tasks, which we'll cover in this chapter.

Monitoring

Production systems require some form of monitoring software that makes sure that the system is healthy and responsive and which collects performance and utilization metrics for longer-term planning. Without a monitoring system, you may not know if your database has stopped responding to requests. Furthermore, you might be unable to detect slow-moving performance or capacity problems. With a good monitoring system, you would be immediately notified if the database fails or has a problem that requires attention. You'll have in your possession metrics allowing you to predict resource requirements for the future.

A good monitoring solution will support both detection and diagnostic capabilities:

- The monitoring system will detect problems and will notify the appropriate person of that problem.
- The monitoring system will collect enough information to allow the administrator to determine the root cause of the problem.

The monitoring system might also offer resolution tools to help with the correction of problems and predictive capabilities that can predict an incipient problem before it occurs.

CockroachDB Dedicated Alerts

CockroachDB Dedicated clusters can send email alerts when certain utilization thresholds are exceeded. These can be enabled on the Alerts page of the cluster dashboard (Figure 14-1).

These alerts generally suggest that your cluster is approaching its capacity. You may respond by reducing demand through workload tuning (as discussed in Chapter 8 and elsewhere) or by scaling your cluster.

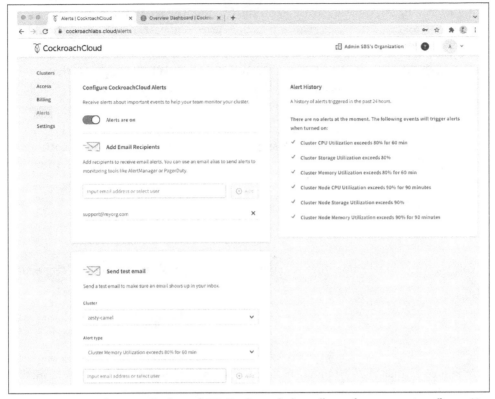

Figure 14-1. Configuring CockroachDB Dedicated alerts (large format version (https://cockroa.ch/cockroachDB-figs))

CockroachDB Serverless Alerts

The Alerts page is accessible on CockroachDB Dedicated clusters. For CockroachDB Serverless (beta) clusters, all Console Admins will automatically receive email alerts when your cluster reaches 50%, 75%, and 100% of its spend limit, burst capacity, or storage limit.

You can react to these alerts by either increasing your spend limit to avoid a performance degradation when resource throttling kicks in, or by tuning your workload to reduce demand—for instance, by tuning SQL as outlined in Chapter 8.

Availability Monitoring

As we noted earlier, the most important measure of availability is application-specific. The database is not truly available unless the application can connect using the authentication mechanisms specific to the application and can issue the sort of requests that implement application logic. Therefore, a well-architected application will implement its own database monitoring and report if there are any issues connecting to the database. That application-level database monitoring should be the primary indicator of database health.

However, the CockroachDB system also contains a set of HTTP endpoints that can be used to determine if the cluster "thinks" it is healthy. These endpoints are available in all contexts other than for serverless clusters.

The health endpoint implements a simple database ping. This performs a very basic health check of the server process. A server that is repeatedly unhealthy according to this endpoint should be terminated and restarted. If it succeeds, it returns an empty payload:

```
$ curl https://admin-zesty-camel-7hp.cockroachlabs.cloud:8080/health
{

}
```

If you want to check a host that is using self-signed certificates, add the `--insecure` flag:

```
$ curl --insecure https://gubuntu1.local:8080/health
{

}%
```

Any failure in that HTTP request indicates that the database HTTP server is unable to respond to even the simplest request.

An HTTP readiness check verifies that nodes are ready to receive SQL requests. As before, an empty return indicates success:

```
$ curl https://admin-zesty-camel-7hp.cockroachlabs.cloud:8080/health\?ready\=1
{

}%
```

Here's an example of a failure response:

```
$ curl --insecure https://gubuntu1.local:8080/health\?ready\=1
{
  "error": "node is not healthy",
  "code": 14,
  "message": "node is not healthy",
  "details": [
  ]
}%
```

The Cluster API

The cluster API is a secure REST API that allows monitoring tools—either third-party or homegrown—to interrogate a CockroachDB cluster. The API requires that you first retrieve a token for authentication purposes. Here we connect to a cluster, providing the username and password (same as we would provide when logging on to the console) and supplying the location of the CA certificate for that cluster:

```
$ curl -d "username=guy&password=xxxxxxx" \
    -H 'Content-Type: application/x-www-form-urlencoded' \
    --cacert $HOME/cockroach/certs/ca.crt \
    https://gubuntu1.local:8080/api/v2/login/

{"session":"CIGAhIHnq53gCRIQVNCsD2E1HFc4cAYbhbuYjQ=="}%
```

Now that we have the token, we can use it to retrieve a variety of information. Let's get the status of each node:

```
$ curl --request GET \
  --url 'https:/gubuntu1.local:8080/api/v2/nodes/' \
  --cacert $HOME/cockroach/certs/ca.crt \
  --header 'X-Cockroach-API-Session:CIGAhJ7p153gCRIQvCerkilIMUfjcS1M/uJHmA==' | jq

{
  "nodes": [
    {
      "node_id": 1,
      "address": {
        "network_field": "tcp",
        "address_field": "gubuntu1.local:26257"
      },
      "attrs": {},
      "locality": {
        "tiers": [
          {
            "key": "region",
            "value": "us-east-1"
          },
          {
            "key": "zone",
            "value": "us-east-1a"
          }
        ]
      },
      "ServerVersion": {
        "major_val": 21,
        "minor_val": 1,
```

The cluster API supports a wide variety of endpoints. Table 14-1 lists a few of the most useful.

Table 14-1. CockroachDB cluster API endpoints

Endpoint	Name	Description
/health	Check node health	Determine if the node is running and ready to accept SQL connections.
/nodes	List nodes	Get details on all nodes in the cluster, including node IDs, software versions, and hardware.
/nodes/{node_id}/ranges	List node ranges	For a specified node, get details on the ranges that it hosts.
/ranges/hot	List hot ranges	Get information on ranges receiving a high number of reads or writes.
/ranges/{range_id}	Get range details	Get detailed technical information on a range. Typically used by Cockroach Labs engineers.
/sessions	List sessions	Get SQL session details of all current users or a specified user.
/login	Log in	Authenticate as a SQL role that is a member of the admin role to retrieve a session token to use with further API calls.
/logout	Log out	Invalidate the session token.

Complete Cluster API documentation can be found in the CockroachDB documentation (*https://cockroa.ch/3DFEGIL*).

Monitoring and Alerting with Prometheus

Some sites will use the Cluster API to integrate CockroachDB monitoring into a customized alerting and monitoring framework. However, even more, we will use CockroachDB with an existing monitoring and alerting tool. Let's look quickly at how to integrate with a few of the most popular options.

Prometheus is probably the most widely used open source tool for monitoring time-series data. It's often used together with Grafana for data visualization.

CockroachDB provides Prometheus configuration files. We first download the files:

```
$ wget https://cockroa.ch/prometheus_yml -O prometheus.yml

2021-10-18 11:20:34 (12.7 MB/s)–'prometheus.yml' saved [746/746]

$ mkdir rules
$ wget https://cockroa.ch/aggregation_rules_yml -O rules/aggregation.rules.yml

2021-10-18 11:25:25 (20.3 MB/s)–'rules/aggregation.rules.yml' saved [5653/5653]

$ wget https://cockroa.ch/alerts_rules_yml -O rules/alerts.rules.yml

2021-10-18 11:25:33 (29.0 MB/s)–'rules/alerts.rules.yml' saved [7234/7234]
```

Edit the `targets` section of the *Prometheus.yml* file to list the nodes in your cluster:

```
static_configs:
-targets: ['gubuntu1.local:8080,gubuntu2.local:8080,gubuntu3.local:8080']
  labels:
    cluster: 'my-cockroachdb-cluster'
```

You might also need to modify the `rule_files` section if you have placed the rules file in a different directory and change the `scheme` and `tls_config` if you have a secure cluster.

Once everything is running, you can start Prometheus:

```
$ prometheus --config.file=prometheus.yml

...
level=info ts=2021-10-18T00:29:18.516Z caller=main.go:794
msg="Server is ready to receive web requests."
```

Go to the Prometheus dashboard at `localhost:9090`, and check out the Status/Targets page. You should see the status of each of your nodes, as shown in Figure 14-2.

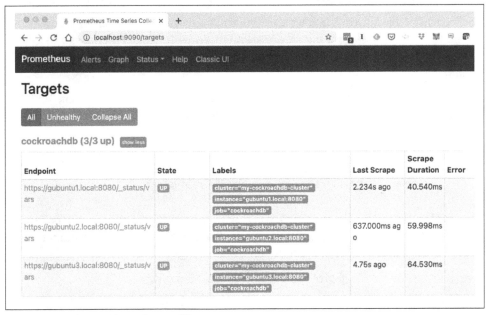

Figure 14-2. Prometheus Status/Targets page

The Prometheus AlertManager tool (*https://cockroa.ch/3u7uXYw*) can be used to forward alerts to email addresses, Slack, WeChat, and even—if you're still living in the 1990s—pagers. AlertManager also handles deduplication, acknowledgments, and other aspects of a production alerting system.

Grafana (*https://grafana.com*) is an open source visualization tool that is well integrated with Prometheus. Using Grafana, you can create custom dashboards that help visualize the data collected by Prometheus from the CockroachDB server. The CockroachDB team maintains a starter Grafana dashboard (*https://cockroa.ch/3DF6Gfh*) though the monitoring screens provided by the DB Console are generally preferred for diagnostic purposes.

The Cockroach documentation (*https://cockroa.ch/3x3Bq8D*) contains more information about integrating CockroachDB with Prometheus and Grafana.

By default, the CockroachDB rules will generate alerts when instability in the cluster is detected, when resource utilization is approaching capacity, and when certificate expiration is imminent.

Monitoring and Alerting with Datadog

While Prometheus is the most widely used open source monitoring solution, commercial products such as Datadog are widely deployed in the Enterprise.

CockroachDB monitoring is integrated within the base Datadog distribution. After installing the datadog agent on a CockroachDB node, find the *cockroach.d* directory with your *datadog-agent/conf.d* directory (typically located in */etc/datadog-agent* or *~/.datadog-agent* directories).

Rename the *conf.yaml.example* file in that directory to *conf.yaml*. Then, edit the *conf.yaml* file so that your Prometheus endpoint is pointing to the members of your cluster:

```
instances:

 –prometheus_url: http://gubuntu1.local:8080/_status/vars
    tls_ca_cert: /Users/guyharrison/cockroach/certs/ca.crt
```

The configuration file also supports some advanced options, such as the collection of logs and advanced authentication options. See the CockroachDB documentation (*https://cockroa.ch/3qXEXBu*) for more information.

Figure 14-3 shows the default Datadog CockroachDB dashboard.

The Datadog system can integrate with an alerting system, custom dashboard creation, and the ability to integrate data from many other data sources such as OS and cloud platforms. See the Datadog documentation (*https://docs.datadoghq.com*) for more details.

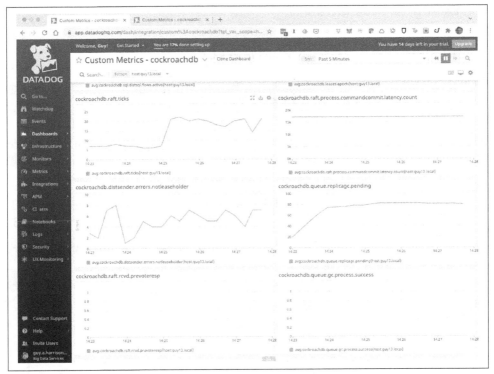

Figure 14-3. Datadog CockroachDB integration (large format version (https://cock roa.ch/cockroachDB-figs))

Log Configuration

Logging is one of the most important diagnostic resources provided by Cock-roachDB. CockroachDB logs are organized by *channel*. Each channel can have its own verbosity setting and can be directed to separate logfiles or other "sinks." In particular, logs can be directed to Fluentd-compatible log servers rather than, or in addition to, file destinations.

Logging configuration is controlled by a YAML file that can be provided on startup to the CockroachDB server by the `-log-config-file` flag. We might include a reference to our log configuration file in the startup command in our CockrochDB service:

```
ExecStart=/usr/local/bin/cockroach start --certs-dir=certs
  --advertise-addr=gubuntu1.local
  --join=gubuntu1.local,gubuntu2.local,gubuntu3.local
  --locality=region=us-east-1,zone=us-east-1a
  --log-config-file=log-config.yaml
```

The YAML file has four sections:

file-defaults
> Defines the defaults inherited by all file sinks.

fluent-defaults
> Defines the defaults inherited by all Fluentd sinks.

sinks
> Defines the specific sinks that are configured, the channels to which they are associated, and any overrides on those sinks.

capture-stray-errors
> Defines what happens to outputs that are not specifically assigned to a channel. This would include stack traces and other "panicky" outputs from CockroachDB.

The cockroach debug check-log-config command returns a summary of the current configuration and a URL to a graphical visualization of the current config:

```
cockroachdb@gubuntu1:~$ cockroach debug check-log-config
# configuration after validation:
file-defaults:
  dir: /home/cockroachdb/cockroach-data/logs
  max-file-size: 10MiB
  max-group-size: 100MiB
  buffered-writes: true
  filter: INFO
  format: crdb-v2
  redact: false
  redactable: true
  exit-on-error: true
  auditable: false

...
# graphical diagram URL:
http://www.plantuml.com/plantuml/uml/X9H1Zzem48NlyokidDf3oX88xFPG
```

Figure 14-4 shows the visualization that is provided for a default log configuration.

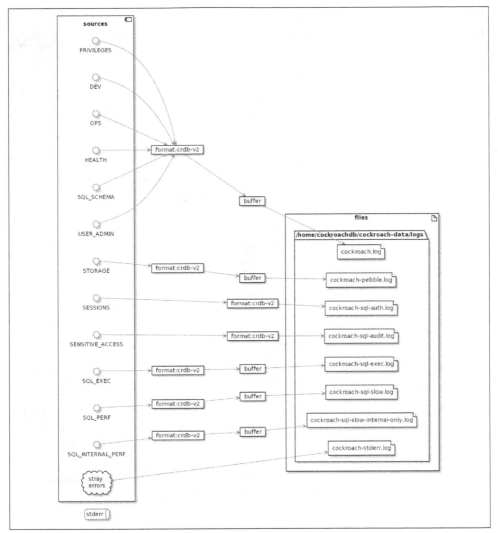

Figure 14-4. Summary of log configuration provided by the cockroach debug check-log-config *command (large format version (https://cockroa.ch/cockroachDB-figs))*

Log Channels

CockroachDB log messages are directed to several channels (Table 14-2). These channels can have independent settings for verbosity, format, destination, and so on.

Table 14-2. CockroachDB logging channels

Channel	Description
DEV	The DEV channel is used during development to collect log details useful for troubleshooting that fall outside the scope of other channels. It is also the default logging channel for events not associated with a channel.
OPS	The OPS channel is used to report "point" operational events initiated by user operators or automation. This includes startup and shutdown events, node additions, removals, decommissions, etc.
HEALTH	The HEALTH channel is used to report "background" operational events initiated by CockroachDB or reporting on automatic processes.
STORAGE	The STORAGE channel is used to report low-level storage layer events.
SESSIONS	The SESSIONS channel is used to report connection and authentication events and is enabled by the cluster settings `server.auth_log.sql_connections.enabled` and/or `server.auth_log.sql_sessions.enabled`.
SQL_SCHEMA	The SQL_SCHEMA channel is used to report changes to the SQL schema objects, other than privilege and ownership changes (which are reported separately on the PRIVILEGES channel) and zone configuration changes (which go to the OPS channel).
USER_ADMIN	The USER_ADMIN channel is used to report changes in users and roles.
PRIVILEGES	The PRIVILEGES channel is used to report data authorization changes.
SENSI TIVE_ACCESS	The SENSITIVE_ACCESS channel is used to report SQL data access to tables for which the EXPERIMENTAL_AUDIT option has been provided and SQL statements are executed by users with the admin role. We discussed this in detail in Chapter 13.
SQL_EXEC	The SQL_EXEC channel is used to report SQL statement executions when enabled via the `sql.trace.log_statement_execute` cluster setting.
SQL_PERF	The SQL_PERF channel is used to log SQL executions that are "slow" as defined by the cluster variable `sql.log.slow_query.latency_threshold`. We introduced this facility in Chapter 8.
SQL_INTER NAL_PERF	The SQL_INTERNAL_PERF channel is like the SQL_PERF channel but is aimed at helping developers of CockroachDB itself.
TELEMETRY	The TELEMETRY channel reports telemetry events. Telemetry events describe feature usage within CockroachDB and anonymizes any application-specific data.

Log Format

The format for all logs or for individual sinks can be controlled by the `format` property. Logs can be formatted in `json` format or `crdb-v2` format (the default). The `crdb-v2` format is a traditional format that is sometimes laughably referred to as "human-readable." Parsing the `crdb-v2` format programmatically is problematic. The `json` format, on the other hand, can easily be handled by programming languages that support JSON (which might exclude COBOL but not much else).

The `crdb-v2` format lines look like this:

```
I211018 04:52:13.141036 195 2@server/status/runtime.go:569 ⋮ [n1] 277
runtime stats: 294 MiB RSS, 254 goroutines (stacks: 4.2 MiB), 42 MiB/81 MiB
Go alloc/total (heap fragmentation: 8.1 MiB, heap reserved: 12 MiB,
heap released: 126 MiB), 73 MiB/102 MiB CGO alloc/total (0.1 CGO/sec),
7.5/8.2 %(u/s)time, 0.0 %gc (0x), 645 KiB/879 KiB (r/w)net
```

We could use regular expressions or Linux file munging tools (awk, Perl, etc.) to process this sort of output.

If the format were `json`, then the relevant lines would look like this:

```
{"channel_numeric":2,"channel":"HEALTH","timestamp":"1634532949.122393871",
"cluster_id":"2cf44e30-4972-4e26bd828d05309f7b26","node_id":1,
"severity_numeric":1,"severity":"INFO","goroutine":138,
"file":"server/status/runtime.go","line":569,"entry_counter":58,
"redactable":1,"tags":{"n":"1"},"message":"runtime stats: 170 MiB RSS,
240 goroutines (stacks: 4.1 MiB), 41 MiB/60 MiB Go alloc/total
(heap fragmentation: 3.5 MiB, heap reserved:
2.3 MiB, heap released: 13 MiB), 75 MiB/94 MiB CGO alloc/total
(0.0 CGO/sec), 0.0/0.0 %(u/s)time, 0.0 %gc (0x),
 472 KiB/283 KiB (r/w)net"}
```

The JSON format is far easier for programs to process; there's no need for complex regular expressions to parse the output format. The `jq` command can be used to format these messages in a way that can be easier for humans as well:

```
$ jq 'select (.severity=="ERROR")' <cockroach.log
{
  "channel_numeric": 0,
  "channel": "DEV",
  "timestamp": "1635309437.656563146",
  "severity_numeric": 3,
  "severity": "ERROR",
  "goroutine": 94,
  "file": "kv/kvserver/replica_write.go",
  "line": 292,
  "entry_counter": 91,
  "redactable": 0,
  "tags": {
    "n": "1",
    "s": "1",
    "r": "2/1:/System/NodeLiveness{-Max}"
  },
  "message": "range unavailable: have been waiting 60.00s for
proposing command RequestLease …\n"
}
```

Filter Levels

The `filter` setting controls the verbosity of the channels. By default, the filter is set to INFO, which is the most verbose setting. Other settings, in order of decreasing verbosity, are shown in Table 14-3.

Table 14-3. CockroachDB log filters

Filter	Description
INFO	The INFO severity is used for informational messages that do not require action.
WARNING	The WARNING severity is used for situations that may require special handling, where normal operation is expected to resume automatically.
ERROR	The ERROR severity is used for situations that require special handling, where the normal operation could not proceed as expected. Other operations can continue mostly unaffected.
FATAL	The FATAL severity is used for situations that require an immediate, hard server shutdown. A report is also sent to telemetry if telemetry is enabled.

Note that each filter encompasses all the higher-level filters. So if you specify INFO, you will also receive WARNING, ERROR, and FATAL. If you specify ERROR, you will also receive FATAL.

In this fragment of YAML, we set the default filter to WARNING, effectively eliminating INFO messages from the log stream:

```
file-defaults:
  max-file-size: 10MiB
  max-group-size: 100MiB
  buffered-writes: true
  filter: WARNING
  format: json
```

In this fragment, we set the filter for the `sql-audit-channel` to INFO, overriding the WARNING filter applied to other logs:

```
sql-audit:
  channels: [SENSITIVE_ACCESS]
  filter: INFO
  auditable: true
```

Log Destinations

File-based destinations can be changed by modifying the default `dir` value or the `dir` value for a specific sink. For instance, here we direct the `SENSITIVE_ACCESS` channel to the */tmp* directory:

```
sql-audit:
  channels: [SENSITIVE_ACCESS]
  filter: INFO
  auditable: true
  redact: true
  dir: /tmp
```

The files are named after the name of the filegroup. For instance, in the example shown, the filegroup name is `sql-audit`, and the full logfile name is *cockroach-sql-audit.gubuntu1.cockroachdb.2021-10-23T03_54_47Z.016225.log*.

The full log name embeds the process ID, start time, host, and file owner in the following format: *{process}-{file group}.{host}.{user}.{start timestamp in UTC}.{process ID}.log*.

There is always a shorter symbolic link to the file that simply lists the filegroup name. So, for instance, in the preceding example, we would find the latest SENSTIVE_ACCESS channel log in */tmp/sql-audit.log*.

Logging to Fluentd

CockroachDB can log to Fluentd-compatible network logging systems. *Fluentd* is an open source, general-purpose data collection engine used for real-time ingestion of semi-structured data such as logfiles.

To configure a Fluentd sink, we simply add a `fluent-servers` entry to our `sinks` section and specify the channels to be forwarded and the address of the Fluentd server (`xps13.local` in this example):

```
sinks:
  fluent-servers:
    health:
      channels: [HEALTH,SENSITIVE_ACCESS]
      address: xps13.local:8888
```

Using a network logging destination is good practice, especially for audit logging. Attackers frequently remove edit logs to hide evidence of their attacks. Sending the logs to a network destination makes it harder for them to do this.

Redaction

The redaction flag removes any log entries that might contain sensitive information. This pertains most significantly to SQL tracing, where personally identifiable information (PII) might be embedded within WHERE clauses:

```
sql-audit:
    channels: [SENSITIVE_ACCESS]
    filter: INFO
    auditable: true
    redact: true
    dir: /tmp
```

While redaction does limit the possibility of data leaking through logs, it places a fairly significant restriction on log usefulness. For instance, as a result of the change shown, an attempt to read from a table identified for audit logging has the entire SQL statement removed:

```
"event": {
  "Timestamp": 1634970161209797400,
  "EventType": "sensitive_table_access",
  "Statement": "×",
  "Tag": "SELECT",
  "User": "root",
  "DescriptorID": 99,
  "ApplicationName": "$ cockroach sql",
  "ExecMode": "exec",
  "NumRows": 10,
  "Age": 85.1666,
  "TxnCounter": 4,
  "TableName": "×",
  "AccessMode": "r"
}
```

With the SQL statement removed from the log, we are now unable to determine if the SQL statement was valid or the result of a cyber attack. Indeed, we can no longer even identify the table involved.

Logs in Cloud Deployments

In a cloud deployment, you don't have direct access to the log destinations. Instead, you can retrieve the logs from the DB Console at the /_status/logs endpoints. To access the logs, you'll need to have the cluster configuration variable server.remote_debugging.mode set to any. Figure 14-5 shows the DB Console logs page.

Figure 14-5. Accessing logs for a Dedicated or Serverless cloud deployment (large format version (https://cockroa.ch/cockroachDB-figs))

Cluster Management

We spent a few chapters outlining the procedure for installing a fresh cluster. Let's examine some of the considerations around modifying that cluster configuration.

Upgrading the Cluster Version

It's generally advisable to upgrade your software version to ensure that you have the latest performance, security, and availability features.

Before upgrading, carefully review the upgrade checklist on the CockroachDB website (*https://cockroa.ch/3J7NJ64*). While most new features in CockroachDB are Good Things, there may be deprecated features or backward-incompatible changes that will adversely affect your application or require some coding changes. These will typically be listed on the CockroachDB website (*https://cockroa.ch/37kuadS*).

CockroachDB supports upgrades only from one major version to the next. So if you are on version 20.1 and wish to upgrade to version 22.0, you must first upgrade to version 21.x.

Preserving a Downgrade Option

By default, an upgrade will perform certain changes that cannot be undone. This might be the result of changes to internal data structures or because some new features might cause changes to schema objects that have no analog in previous versions.

To make sure that a downgrade is possible, use the cluster setting `cluster.pre serve_downgrade_option`. This option will disable new features following the upgrade but will allow a downgrade if needed.

Prior to upgrade, set the `cluster.preserve_downgrade_option`:

```
defaultdb>
SET CLUSTER SETTING cluster.preserve_downgrade_option = '21.1';
SET CLUSTER SETTING
```

When you are content that the new version is stable and wish to enable new features that cannot be downgraded, reset the cluster setting:

```
defaultdb>
RESET CLUSTER SETTING cluster.preserve_downgrade_option;
SET CLUSTER SETTING
```

For CockroachDB Dedicated cloud deployments, minor upgrades (for instance, v21.1.0 → v21.2.1) will be performed automatically, but major upgrades (v21 → v22, for example) can be performed from the CockroachDB Cloud console.

In CockroachDB Serverless cloud deployments, upgrades will occur automatically and transparently.

In a Kubernetes deployment, it's simply a matter of changing the Docker image in the YAML definition file. So, for instance, if our YAML file contained this line:

```
image:
  name: cockroachdb/cockroach:v21.1.7
```

we might change it as follows:

```
image:
  name: cockroachdb/cockroach:v21.2.7
```

then apply the changes:

```
kubectl apply -f example.yaml
```

In a self-hosted deployment, you have a more complex task, though it's generally pretty straightforward. We would normally perform a rolling upgrade in which we upgrade each node serially. For each node in the cluster:

- Shut down the node.
- Install the new version binaries.
- Restart the node.

After each node restart, perform appropriate checks (run some SQL statements, check logs, visit DB Console Status page, etc.) to make sure that the upgrade is successful before proceeding to the next node.

When all the nodes are upgraded, and if you had preserved the ability to downgrade, you can finalize the upgrade by resetting the `cluster.preserve_downgrade_option` variable. See "Preserving a Downgrade Option" on page 398 for details.

Adding Nodes to a Cluster

The procedure for adding nodes to an existing cluster is the same as the steps involved in adding the first nodes.

In a CockroachDB Dedicated cloud deployment, this is done simply by requesting more nodes and specifying their locations. Navigate to the cluster's Overview page, Click the Actions button in the top-right corner, then select "Add/remove nodes."

In a Kubernetes deployment, we simply edit the `nodes` entry in the operator YAML file and then apply the file. The operator will do the rest.

In a self-hosted cluster, we need to follow the steps outlined in Chapter 10. That is:

- Set up the host with appropriate kernel configuration and clock synchronization.
- Create and distribute certificates to the new nodes.
- Issue a `cockroach start` command with a `--join` flag pointing to three of the existing nodes of the cluster.
- Configure the load balancer to balance connection requests to the new node.

Once the new nodes join the cluster, data ranges will automatically be rebalanced across the new nodes. You can observe the rebalancing in real time using the Replication dashboard. Figure 14-6 shows an example of ranges being redistributed from a three-node to a four-node cluster.

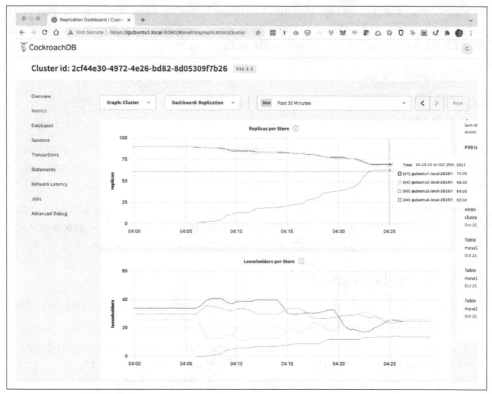

Figure 14-6. Ranges being rebalanced after a new node is added to a cluster (large format version (https://cockroa.ch/cockroachDB-figs))

Check out Chapter 10 for more details on each of these activities.

Decommissioning Nodes

Removing a node from a cluster—decommissioning a node—requires that we first migrate all range replicas to other nodes. Once that has happened, the node can be shut down and will be removed from the cluster after it has been idle for `server.time_until_store_dead`, which defaults to five minutes.

You can decommission a node only if there are other nodes available to meet replication requirements. For instance, if your replication factor is three, then you cannot decommission a node in a three-node cluster without first adding the fourth node.

Before decommissioning, make sure that there are no under-replicated or unavailable ranges (this is something you should be keeping an eye on at all times!). This can be seen from the front page of the DB Console in Figure 14-7.

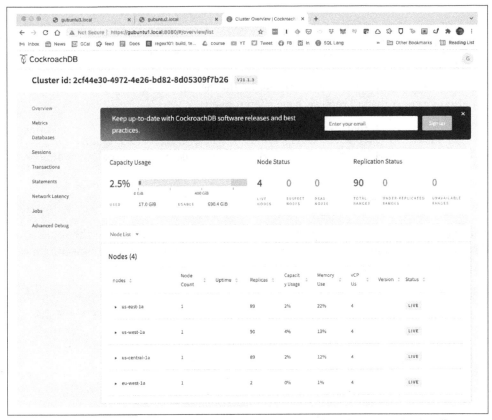

Figure 14-7. Check that no ranges are under-replicated before decommissioning (large format version (https://cockroa.ch/cockroachDB-figs))

Make sure that you will have enough capacity after removing the node(s). For example, if you have a six-node cluster, you would not want to decommission if your peak CPU load is above 66%. (Because 66% of a six-node cluster is 80% of a five-node cluster, and above that point, you cannot afford to lose a single node without disruption.)

Decommission the node by running the `cockroach node decommission` command from the node to be decommissioned:

```
$ cockroach node decommission --self --certs-dir=/var/lib/cockroachdb/certs
  --host=gubuntu4.local

 id | is_live | replicas | is_decommissioning |   membership   | is_draining
----+---------+----------+--------------------+----------------+-------------
  4 |  true   |    83    |        true        | decommissioning |   false
(1 row)

........
```

```
id | is_live | replicas | is_decommissioning |   membership    | is_draining
----+---------+----------+--------------------+-----------------+-------------
  4 |  true   |      82 |        true        | decommissioning |   false
(1 row)
```

The command will report the progress of the decommissioning and—hopefully—
eventually report that all replicas have been moved:

```
id | is_live | replicas | is_decommissioning |   membership    | is_draining
----+---------+----------+--------------------+-----------------+-------------
  4 |  true   |       0 |        true        | decommissioning |   false
(1 row)
```

```
No more data reported on target nodes. Please verify cluster health
before removing the nodes.
```

During the decommission, you can also check the individual node in the replication
dashboard. You should see the replicas per store for the decommissioning node
reducing—Figure 14-8 shows an example.

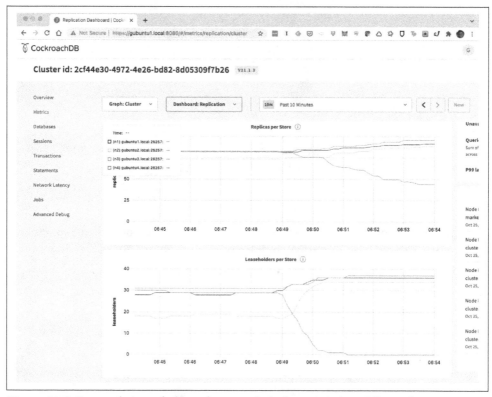

*Figure 14-8. Ranges being rebalanced as a node is decommissioned (large format version
(https://cockroa.ch/cockroachDB-figs))*

When the decommissioning process is complete, shut down the node. The node should be removed from the cluster once `server.time_until_store_dead` has passed.

Decommissioning can hang indefinitely if CockroachDB is not able to move ranges to other nodes. In this case, you could either add another node to allow the decommissioning to proceed or recommission the node. See the CockroachDB documentation (*https://cockroa.ch/3uVMBgO*) for more details.

Troubleshooting

An informal survey of the CockroachDB support staff revealed that the bulk of troubleshooting requests by CockroachDB users relate to development and coding or to cluster performance. For instance:

- My query is taking too long; how do I improve it?
- I have high CPU on a particular node. How do I troubleshoot that?
- Why am I experiencing transaction retry errors?
- How do I reduce read latency across my multiregion cluster?

It's good to know that CockroachDB users are generally concerned with these sorts of issues; this indicates that, by and large, CockroachDB itself is stable and reliable, and instead of struggling with cluster availability, users are primarily pursuing the never-ending goal of making the database run faster.

We discussed query performance in detail back in Chapter 8, and we'll dig deep into cluster performance in Chapter 15. Here, we'd like to examine a few of the situations that can cause nodes in the cluster to become unresponsive or unavailable.

With every release, the CockroachDB team resolves many issues and improves performance and stability. Each release also adds new functionality. Consequently, the types of issues that users encounter change with every release. The CockroachDB team maintains a Troubleshooting overview (*https://cockroa.ch/3DHWd2L*) that you should review if you encounter an issue not covered here.

Whatever the issue that you encounter, always do the following:

- Review the logs pertaining to the node concerned. Remember, there are multiple log channels, so make sure you've reviewed all the relevant files.
- Make sure there is free disk space in the log destination! Many a troubleshooting hour has been lost trying to find a problem that is not logged, only to belatedly realize that there was no space left to write any logs.

Clock Synchronization Errors

Einstein may have demonstrated that time is relative, but for a CockroachDB cluster, time needs to be—within reason—absolute. Any node that finds itself more than 500 ms (or the value of the startup parameter `--max-offset`) away from at least half of the nodes in the cluster will remove itself. You'll see an error something like this in the logs:

```
F211023 03:31:36.974367 81 1@server/server.go:322 [n1] 10 clock
synchronization error: this node is more than 500ms away from
 at least half of the known nodes (0 of 1 are within the offset)
```

This almost certainly means your time synchronization is failing and that you should review the setup of your NTP time synchronization service (see Chapter 10). Make sure that all nodes are using the same time servers and that time synchronization is enabled on all nodes.

If for some reason, you can't get tight enough time synchronization, you can increase the `--max-offset` parameter to allow greater clock drift. However, changing this parameter requires a complete cluster restart—it cannot be done using a rolling restart.

Do not increase this parameter capriciously. In fact, lower values for multiregion deployments are recommended (250 ms, for instance)—since it helps lower latency for global tables.

Node Liveness

All nodes in a cluster maintain and update a node liveness record, which is shared with other members of the cluster. Cluster members that fail to produce a timely liveness message may be removed from the cluster. Logs would typically show an error like this:

```
cockroach.gubuntu1.cockroachdb.2021-09-05T22_57_56Z.008851.log:W210905
22:58:05.686268 211 kv/kvserver/liveness/liveness.go:723 : [n1,liveness-hb]
91  failed node liveness heartbeat: ‹operation "node liveness heartbeat"
 timed out after 4.5s›: context deadline exceeded
```

Node liveness failures are most often the result of some other issue on the node concerned, e.g., nonliveness is a symptom, not a cause. For instance, nonliveness failures can be caused by:

- Running out of file descriptors or other OS limits
- Very heavy OS contention, particularly for disk I/O
- Network communication errors between nodes

Examine logs and monitoring data to try to determine the root cause of the problem. The CockroachDB Console records the last liveness record in the */reports/nodes* page (see Figure 14-9). CockroachDB support can be extremely helpful when trying to troubleshoot esoteric liveness issues.

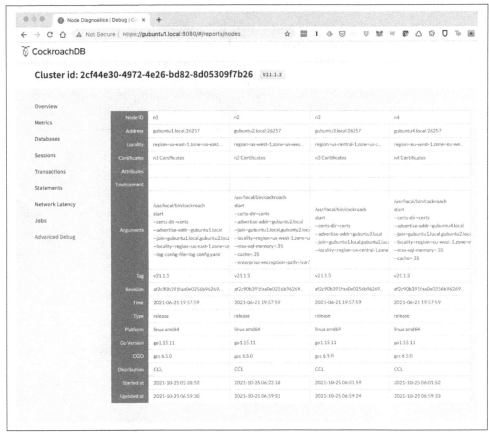

Figure 14-9. Liveness information in the DB Console (large format version (https://cock roa.ch/cockroachDB-figs))

Networking Issues

CockroachDB can handle network connectivity failures between isolated nodes, providing that there are a majority of replicas available. Nodes that are isolated from the cluster will show as SUSPECT and eventually DEAD on the CockroachDB Console and will fail their liveness checks.

As in many horror movies, CockroachDB nodes can come back from the dead, but luckily not as brain-eating zombies. As soon as network connectivity is restored, you should expect the node to return from the dead and rapidly return to full health.

If half or more of the nodes of the cluster lose connectivity, or if half the replicas in important system ranges are rendered unavailable by node failures, then the entire cluster will be unavailable, even if some nodes are still running correctly.

For instance, consider the situation shown in Figure 14-10. Earlier in the chapter, we added a fourth node to our three-node cluster. Now only two of those nodes are available. On a three-node cluster, we'd have under-replicated ranges but not unavailable ranges. However, with a four-node configuration, some ranges have two of the three replicas on the unavailable nodes—those ranges can now not be updated, and indeed, the correct status of those ranges cannot be determined. So the cluster is at best only partially available, but in practice, probably unresponsive (because some of the unavailable ranges will be mandatory system ranges).

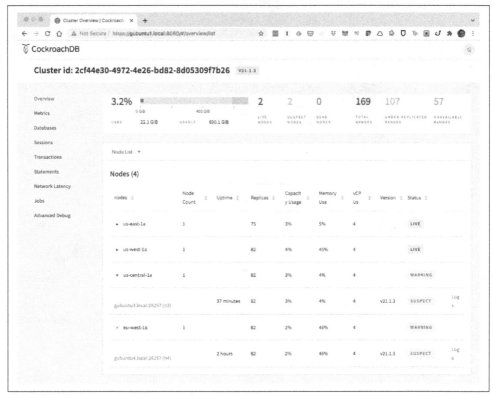

Figure 14-10. Unavailable ranges as a result of a network partition (large format version (https://cockroa.ch/cockroachDB-figs))

To allow two nodes to fail, we need a replication factor of at least five, and therefore, at least five nodes.

Loss of Client Connectivity

Making sure that the nodes that constitute the cluster can communicate is an obvious best practice. However, it's not much good if cluster nodes are all communicating, but client programs are failing to connect.

In an on-premise deployment, the load balancer serves as a single point of failure for client connectivity. This is not CockroachDB software, so there's more variation in configuration and less direct support from the CockroachDB team. A poorly configured load balancer might result in a complete failure of client connectivity. There should be redundant load balancers configured, and they should be configured to use DNS round-robin or similar configuration to ensure that client connections can continue if one of the load balancers fails. You should monitor the state of the load balancers just as you would monitor other components of the cluster.

Running Out of Disk Space

Although running out of free space on a disk device is an obvious failure, it's surprising how often it is not anticipated ahead of time and is not always easy to resolve. When disk space is exhausted on a device, processes wanting to write to that device will often block without any ability to signal their difficulty. If the logfiles are being written to the same device, then CockroachDB will be unable to even log the problem.

Resolving an out-of-space situation can also be difficult. Relatively large amounts of space must be freed up to allow normal operations to proceed while you reconfigure your system with more storage. This is why CockroachDB creates a "ballast file." The ballast file holds space in reserve and can be deleted quickly to get your system running again—see Chapter 10. You may want to think about the best size for your ballast file—CockroachDB defaults to 1% or 1 GB of space (whichever is smaller), which might not be enough to maintain availability while you provision more disk.

If you don't have a ballast file, look for large files within the device. The following command will let you browse through the directories on a device—run it from the top-level directory of the device:

```
du -k|sort -nr|less
```

If logfiles are being written to the device, they may be the first candidate for removal. A long-running server with no log purging can consume a large amount of storage.

Working with CockroachDB Support Resources

If you've worked in database administration for more than a few days, you know that a big part of the job is dealing with unexpected problems. It's not possible to anticipate everything that can go wrong in a distributed deployment, when each deployment may have unique combinations of hardware, software, and topologies. Indeed, one of the most powerful motivations for moving to a fully managed cloud database service such as CockroachDB Dedicated or Serverless cloud is to eliminate the potential problems caused by self-hosted deployment idiosyncracies.

Nevertheless, the CockroachDB team is ready to help you if you have any issues with CockroachDB under any deployment scenario. You should be aware of the following support resources and leverage them as appropriate:

- The CockroachDB documentation contains continually updated support and troubleshooting information (*https://cockroa.ch/3JlctrX*).
- CockroachDB maintains a community forum (*https://forum.cockroachlabs.com*) and a Slack channel (*https://cockroachdb.slack.com*) where you can ask questions of fellow users and CockroachDB support engineers.
- You can lodge an issue with CockroachDB support (*https://support.cockroa chlabs.com*).
- You can file an issue at GitHub (*https://cockroa.ch/3j4JbCY*) if you feel that there is an issue with the CockroachDB software that requires attention.

Summary

In this chapter, we've provided a quick overview of some of the routine tasks encountered running a CockroachDB installation. Most of these tasks are handled for you when you choose a CockroachDB Serverless or Dedicated cloud deployment. However, a self-hosted deployment does require some care and attention, and even a cloud deployment may require some administration.

Monitoring your CockroachDB deployment ensures that you are aware of the health of the system and have the necessary information required for forward planning. CockroachDB has its own built-in monitoring in terms of the CockroachDB Console but also integrates with popular monitoring frameworks such as Prometheus or Datadog. Logs are your best friends when trying to troubleshoot any anomalous behavior. CockroachDB logs are highly configurable, and we showed how to tailor log output to match your requirements.

Almost all clusters will need to be upgraded as new releases of CockroachDB software become available, so we showed how to perform a rolling upgrade of a CockroachDB cluster. A big part of any database administrator's job relates to handling unexpected problems. We outlined some of the most common issues in cluster availability and discussed how to proceed when trying to resolve issues that we can't anticipate.

Cluster Optimization

It doesn't matter what database, framework, application, or device you're responsible for—someone always wants it to be faster. This is probably one of the most persistent challenges for computer scientists. One can imagine after Alan Turing created his breakthrough decoding machine during World War II that his superiors said, "Well done Alan, but can it be faster?"

It's not surprising that performance optimization is such a perennial activity. It's always been important to provide users with responsive applications and to be able to maintain acceptable throughput for batch processes. However, in the modern era, performance has become even more important. In the internet era, poorly performing customer-facing applications lead to customers abandoning your online services, directly affecting the bottom line. In the cloud era, performance optimization is cost optimization—a poorly performing application will consume more cloud computing resources, which will increase your monthly bill.

Tuning Versus Firefighting

Performance optimization usually occurs in one of two forms:

Performance firefighting
A critical performance problem arises and must be addressed immediately.

Performance tuning
The system is optimized systematically to improve its performance and reduce the cost of operation.

The more performance tuning you do, the less performance firefighting you'll need to undertake. Nevertheless, for almost all database administrators, you'll need to know how to function in both modes.

In firefighting mode, you're typically trying to find something that has "gone wrong" —this might be a new SQL statement or transaction that is creating a drag on the cluster, a hardware or node failure, or a performance problem caused by a change in application load.

In tuning mode, you are systematically working through the layers of the database cluster and making sure that workloads are optimized and that software and hardware components are correctly configured. It's generally best in tuning to work "down" through the layers of the database stack. Way back in Chapter 2, we introduced these layers; Figure 15-1 summarizes these levels.

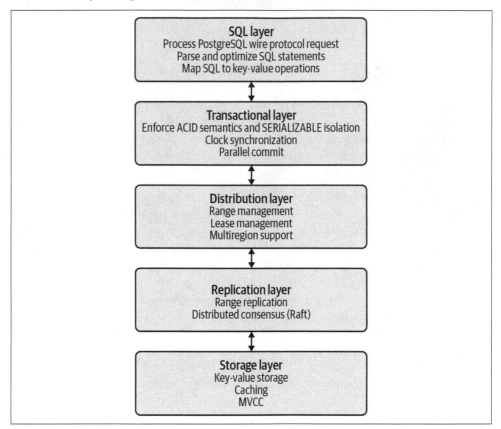

Figure 15-1. CockroachDB software layers

The load on each layer is determined by the configuration of the layer above. Therefore, there's no point in tuning a lower layer until you have completed tuning the higher layer. For instance, there's no point looking at increasing the sizes of your nodes unless you have made sure that you have all the necessary indexes. Adding an index is a simple and quick activity that requires no downtime or additional cost.

Depending on your configuration, adding nodes to an existing cluster might be a time-consuming and expensive process.

Therefore, in this chapter, we'll work through the layers of the application when discussing cluster optimization. Even when firefighting, it makes sense to look at each layer of the cluster in turn, because a lot of problems that require firefighting involve changes to workload, which is the highest layer.

Workload Optimization

By far, the biggest influence on cluster performance is the workload that the application generates. Poorly tuned SQL can generate orders of magnitude higher logical and physical resource demands than well-tuned SQL. In particular, without effective indexing, it's unlikely that any workload will be scalable and optimized.

We devoted Chapter 5 to the design of a performant database schema, Chapter 6 to effective application implementation, and Chapter 8 to SQL tuning. In an ideal world, applications would arrive perfectly tuned before encountering production. In the real world, untuned SQL statements, unexpected data distributions, and higher than expected contention scenarios often lead to application tuning issues only becoming apparent in the production system.

During application development, the tuning process involves ensuring that individual SQL statements and transactions are optimized and correct. In production, the tuning process is somewhat different—we are looking for SQL statements and transactions that appear to be consuming a higher than expected proportion of system resources and looking for ways that these might be resolved.

Detecting Problem Workloads

When faced with a database that is "slow," we generally look first at the workload on the system. After all, "slowness" for a database probably relates to one or more SQL statements that are performing below expectations, so we might first want to find those SQL statements. Secondly, a typical cause of poor performance is the introduction of a new or unique SQL statement that is causing problems.

What Is Slow?

The end consumers of database servers are rarely concerned with the performance of individual SQL statements as such. They are far more concerned with the performance of mission-critical transactions performed by the SQL layer. These transactions generally perform SQL operations but often also execute web services or CPU-intensive logic. A "slow" application can therefore be slow as a result of a slow database but could also be slow due to application layer code efficiency, network latency, or a variety of other issues.

Where possible, application logging or instrumentation should be able to distinguish between slow database response and other causes of poor performance. Unfortunately, this is not always true, and all too often, managing application performance involves a lot of finger-pointing and trial-and-error tuning at multiple levels.

The best way to avoid these issues is to implement application monitoring and instrumentation that can at least break down response time between database requests and other sources.

The CockroachDB Console is usually the first port of call when trying to examine workload. The Sessions page shows currently active sessions (Figure 15-2).

Figure 15-2. CockroachDB Console Sessions screen (large format version (https://cock roa.ch/cockroachDB-figs))

Clicking on a particular session shows us the currently executing statement together with a few additional bits of information (Figure 15-3).

Figure 15-3. CockroachDB Console Sessions details screen (large format version (https://cockroa.ch/cockroachDB-figs))

Another way to get currently executing queries is by querying the `system.crdb_internal.cluster_queries` table:

```
defaultdb> \set display_format=records

defaultdb>
SELECT node_id, current_timestamp AT time ZONE 'UTC'- START run_time,
 user_name, QUERY, phase
  FROM SYSTEM.crdb_internal.cluster_queries
  ORDER BY START
LIMIT 10;

-[ RECORD 1 ]
node_id   | 1
run_time  | 00:02:06.264411
user_name | root
query     | SELECT v.type, u.city, sum(r.revenue)
              FROM rides AS r JOIN vehicles AS v
                ON ((r.vehicle_city = v.city)
                AND (r.vehicle_id = v.id))
                JOIN users AS u ON (u.id = r.rider_id)
              GROUP BY v.type, u.city ORDER BY 3 DESC
phase     | executing
```

If you find an anomalous SQL statement is causing a drag on the cluster, then you do have the option to kill it, either by using the "Cancel query" button on the statements page or the "Cancel query" or "Cancel session" statements. However, be careful with these options. Generally, we only cancel SQL statements that are ad hoc—SQL statements that have been directly issued by a human being using the SQL prompt or from a business intelligence tool such as Tableau. Canceling a query that is being run programmatically may lead to unpredictable application behavior and might even make things worse if the application retries the failed statement. If possible (and it's not always possible), try to terminate the application process that is running the problem SQL.

While long-running SQL statements that are currently executing are often a problem, just as often it's SQL statements that are frequently running at a volume that dominates the workload. To see performance statistics aggregated for each SQL, we can use the Statements page of the CockroachDB Console (Figure 15-4).

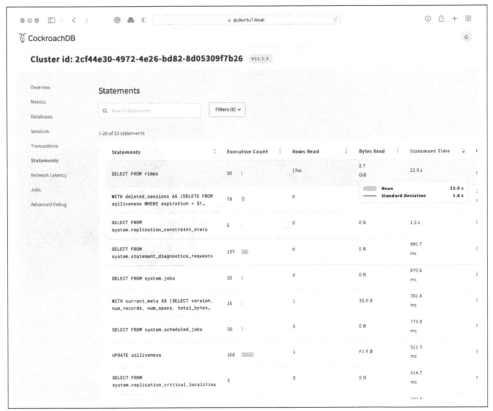

Figure 15-4. CockroachDB Console Statements screen (large format version (https://cock roa.ch/cockroachDB-figs))

Drilling into a statement lets us see the full SQL text, as shown in Figure 15-5.

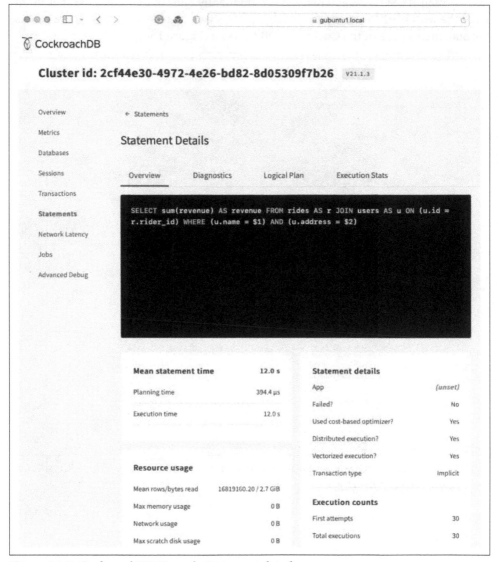

Figure 15-5. CockroachDB Console Statement details

We can also see the execution plan, as illustrated in Figure 15-6.

Figure 15-6. CockroachDB Console Statement Explain screen (large format version (https://cockroa.ch/cockroachDB-figs))

We can sort the DB Console Statements page by absolute time, contention time, network time, or rows processed. If we find that one statement is dominating overall execution time or has high contention, we will move into tuning the SQL using the techniques from Chapter 8. (We'll recap these in a moment.)

You can use the `crdb_internal.node_statement_statistics` table to look at statements executed on a particular node. This table lets you hunt for statements matching various criteria, including text matches for the SQL:

```
defaultdb> \set display_format=records
defaultdb>
SELECT KEY, count, service_lat_avg,
       count::float * service_lat_avg sum_service
  FROM crdb_internal.node_statement_statistics
 ORDER BY count::float * service_lat_avg DESC
 LIMIT 10;

-[ RECORD 1 ]
key            | SELECT sum(revenue) AS revenue
    FROM rides AS r JOIN users AS u ON (u.id = r.rider_id)
```

```
    WHERE (u.name = $1) AND (u.address = $2)
count          | 48
service_lat_avg | 12.680283943604165
sum_service    | 608.6536292929999
```

When dealing with transaction contention-related issues, it can be advantageous to focus on transactions that are experiencing retries or high contention times. The Transactions page on the DB Console can do this (Figure 15-7).

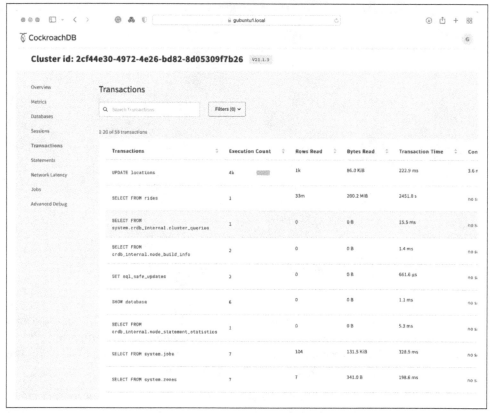

Figure 15-7. CockroachDB Console Transactions screen (large format version (https://cockroa.ch/cockroachDB-figs))

You can sort the transactions by each metric to identify the culprit. Drilling into the transaction shows all of the SQL statements in the transaction together with retry counts and contention wait times (Figure 15-8).

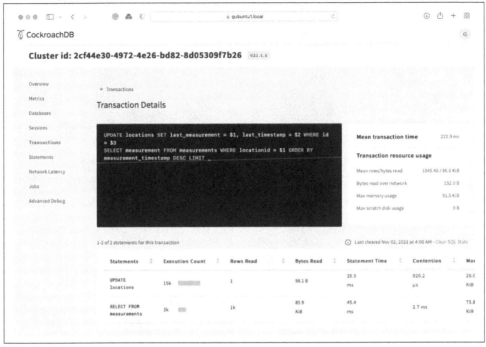

Figure 15-8. CockroachDB Console Transaction Details screen (large format version (https://cockroa.ch/cockroachDB-figs))

This information can be retrieved from SQL using the `crdb_internal.node_transaction_statistics` table.

Review of Workload Optimization Strategies

Having identified problematic statements or transactions that are affecting cluster performance, what next?

Well, we spent more than a couple of chapters covering the nuances of schema design, SQL tuning, and transactional implementations throughout Chapters 5–8. These are the foundational practices for a robust CockroachDB application.

However, when faced with a badly performing CockroachDB database, you don't usually have the luxury of going back to the drawing board and redesigning your application. Usually, you're looking for relatively quick fixes that can improve performance without major application redesign. Let's look at a few ideas.

Indexing

It's great to see a poorly performing SQL statement and realize that a new index will save the day. For instance, earlier we identified a worrisome statement in Figure 15-5. Here's the statement:

```
SELECT SUM(revenue) as revenue
  FROM rides r
  JOIN users u ON
       (u.id = r.rider_id)
 WHERE u.name = $1
   AND u.address = $2
```

And in Figure 15-6, we saw that the statement's execution plan looked like this:

```
distribution: full
  vectorized: true

  • group (scalar)
  | estimated row count: 1
  |
  └── • hash join
      | estimated row count: 14
      | equality: (rider_id) = (id)
      |
      ├── • scan
      |     estimated row count: 15,767,943 (100% of the table;
      |     table: rides@primary
      |     spans: FULL SCAN
      |
      └── • filter
          | estimated row count: 1
          | filter: (name = 'Michael Jimenez')
          |     AND (address = '13579 Campbell Camp')
          |
          └── • scan
                estimated row count: 1,050,096 (100% of the table;
                table: users@primary
                spans: FULL SCAN
```

This is a classic unindexed "bad query"; both the initial lookup and subsequent JOIN are based on full table scans. The initial query against the users table is based on NAME and ADDRESS—columns that almost certainly should be indexed if this query is to be run regularly.

The unindexed JOIN between rides and users represents a coding error more than an indexing error. Both tables have primary keys that are prefixed with the CITY column—which allows the MovR application to be optimized for a multiregion deployment. The JOIN clause should have been expressed as follows:

```
FROM rides r
JOIN users u ON
    (u.id = r.rider_id AND u.city=r.city)
```

Although you would be technically correct to throw this SQL back to the developer (especially if *you* were the developer!), in an emergency, you might consider creating an index simply on `rider.rider_id`. This would immediately reduce the footprint of the SQL. Once the SQL `JOIN` condition was correctly recoded, this index could be removed.

Keep in mind, however, that creating indexes puts a substantial load on the cluster during the index creation process and can have a significant impact on write performance when in place.

For more information about indexing and schema design, see Chapter 5. For effective application design strategies, see Chapter 6. For SQL tuning strategies, see Chapter 8.

Ad Hoc or Analytic Queries

CockroachDB is primarily intended to support transactional workloads. However, all databases are subject to analytic-type queries. Sometimes these queries are used to satisfy reports that are part of an application, but sometimes users will perform ad hoc analytic queries for business intelligence purposes.

Queries that aggregate large amounts of information can impact transactional statements by overwhelming cluster resources and by increasing contention. Full table scans of massive tables might create I/O overloads, smother memory caches, and overwhelm inter-node network traffic. Sorts in analytic queries can also require large amounts of disk I/O and/or memory.

If analytical statements really must be run on base tables, then the use of `AS OF SYSTEM TIME` can reduce the latency and contention involved in these statements. By using `AS OF SYSTEM TIME`, we avoid the chance that a statement that reads active ranges might need to be retried. By adding just a short delay—`AS OF SYSTEM TIME '-1m'` for instance—we can obtain a dramatic reduction in the SQL statements contention footprint.

Cluster Balance

In the iconic 1980s movie, *The Karate Kid*, Sensei Miyagi advises his pupil, "In all things have balance." Nowhere is this advice more pertinent than in a distributed database.

The ability to scale workloads across multiple machines is predicated on the ability to distribute load equitably across the cluster. If there's a single node that is doing more work than other nodes, then that node may become the limiting factor on performance, and efforts to scale the system by adding more nodes could be ineffective.

The DB Console provides many views that can be used to determine if a cluster is balanced. For instance, in Figure 15-9, we see a cluster in which one node appears to be almost completely idle, while another node is very busy and the remainder are somewhere in between. This is a cluster that is wasting the resources of the idle node and may see a bottleneck form on the busiest node.

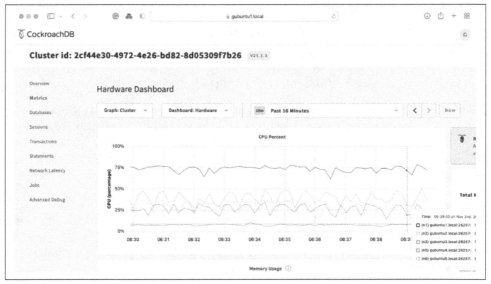

Figure 15-9. CockroachDB Console CPU by node (large format version (https://cock roa.ch/cockroachDB-figs))

I/O is another strong indicator of overall balance. In Figure 15-10, we see a cluster in which I/O on three of the five nodes is significantly higher.

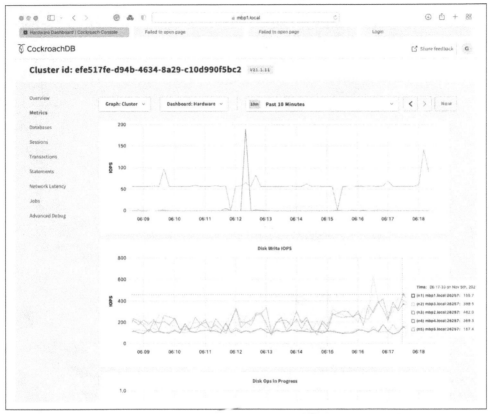

Figure 15-10. CockroachDB Console I/O by node (large format version (https://cock roa.ch/cockroachDB-figs))

Causes of Imbalance

Imbalances in cluster load are usually caused by one of the following factors:

- "Hot" ranges
- Incorrectly configured load balancing
- Changes in cluster topology

Let's look at each in turn.

Hot Ranges

Hot ranges are ranges that are heavily hit by specific queries.

In the replication dashboard, you might see one node with significantly higher query rates than the others, such as in Figure 15-11.

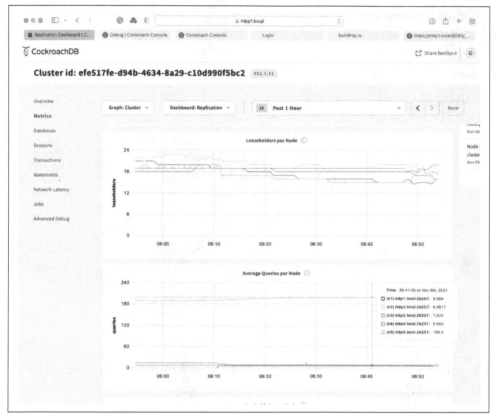

Figure 15-11. CockroachDB Console queries per node (large format version (https://cockroa.ch/cockroachDB-figs))

If the range is being updated as well as read, you'll see high I/O on the leaseholder and replicator nodes, such as in Figure 15-12.

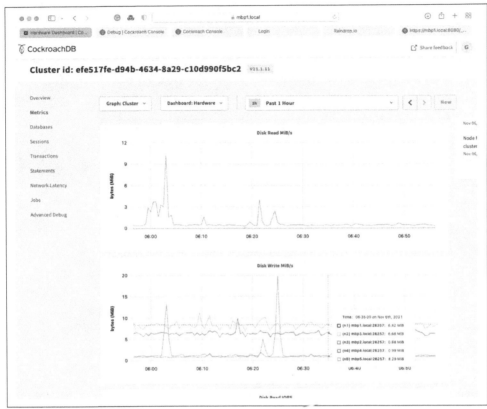

Figure 15-12. CockroachDB Console disk writes per node (large format version (https://cockroa.ch/cockroachDB-figs))

In the logs, you might see messages like this:

```
I211106 06:50:33.731061 244 kv/kvserver/store_rebalancer.go:240
  [n5,s5,store-rebalancer]
3280  considering load-based lease transfers for s5 with 199.88 qps (mean=44.41,
upperThreshold=144.41)
I211106 06:50:33.783731 244 kv/kvserver/store_rebalancer.go:288
  [n5,s5,store-rebalancer]
3281  ran out of leases worth transferring and qps (199.85)
is still above desired threshold
(144.41); considering load-based replica rebalances
```

The first step is to identify the hot ranges. We can get hot ranges from the console at the *status/hotranges* endpoint (*https://<nodeAddress>:8080/_status/hotranges*), as shown in Figure 15-13.

Figure 15-13. CockroachDB Console hot ranges endpoint (large format version (https://cockroa.ch/cockroachDB-figs))

You could download this data and analyze it programmatically. For instance, the following JavaScript code will take the output of */status/_hotranges* and print the top 10 ranges in the cluster:

```javascript
const fs = require('fs');

async function main() {
    const unsortedRanges=[];
    let ranges = await fs.readFileSync('hotranges.json','utf8');
    let rangeJson=JSON.parse(ranges);
    Object.keys(rangeJson.hotRangesByNodeId).forEach((node)=>{
        let hotRanges=rangeJson.hotRangesByNodeId[node];
        hotRanges.stores.forEach((store)=>{
            store.hotRanges.forEach((range)=>{
                unsortedRanges.push({node,storeId:store.storeId,
```

```
        rangeId:range.desc.rangeId,
        queriesPerSecond:range.queriesPerSecond});
                });
            });
        });
        unsortedRanges.sort((a, b) => a.queriesPerSecond > b.queriesPerSecond && -1
    || 1);
        for (let ic=0;ic<10;ic++)
            console.log(unsortedRanges[ic]);
    }

    main();
```

Alternatively, you can use the `cockroach debug zip` command to extract a full diagnostic debug file. Inside that file, the script `hot-ranges.sh` will print out the hottest ranges on the cluster:

```
$ cockroach debug zip cockroachDebug.zip --host=mbp1.local \
 --certs-dir=cockroach/certs
establishing RPC connection to mbp1.local:26257...

writing cockroachDebug.zip
requesting data for debug/events... writing: debug/events.json
requesting data for debug/rangelog... writing: debug/rangelog.json
….
writing: debug/pprof-summary.sh
writing: debug/hot-ranges.sh

$  /tmp unzip cockroachDebug.zip
Archive:  cockroachDebug.zip
  inflating: debug/events.json
  inflating: debug/rangelog.json
….
  inflating: debug/hot-ranges.sh
$  /tmp cd debug
$  debug bash hot-ranges.sh
./nodes/2/ranges/230.json:    "queries_per_second": 1690.8093415717535,
./nodes/2/ranges/4.json:    "writes_per_second": 274.54947854147895
./nodes/3/ranges/4.json:    "writes_per_second": 272.13645921782273
```

Once we've found the hot ranges, we can look at the `crdb_internal.ranges` table to see what tables and keys are associated with the range:

```
defaultdb> \set display_format=records

SELECT table_name, start_pretty, end_pretty , replicas, lease_holder,
       round(range_size / 1048576) mb
  FROM crdb_internal.ranges
WHERE range_id = 230;

-[ RECORD 1 ]
table_name   | tweet_likes
start_pretty | /Table/77/1/500/31
```

```
end_pretty   | /Table/77/1/1000/21
replicas     | {1,2,4}
lease_holder | 2
mb           | 14
```

Now that we've found the hot range, we can try a few things. In order of descending difficulty, they are:

- Configure CockroachDB to split ranges more aggressively based on load
- Split the ranges manually
- Redesign the application to avoid the hot ranges

In this example, we've found that the hot range belongs to the `tweet_likes` table. Looking at the DB Console, we see that the most active statement against that table is this one:

```
UPDATE tweet_likes
   SET tweet_likes = tweet_likes + _
 WHERE (tweeter = $1) AND (tweet_id = $2)
```

It increments a tweet count for a specific tweet. Now, as we know, some Twitter users are more popular than others, and at any given point in time, some tweets are going viral and getting lots of "likes." So it's these viral tweets from key influencers that are causing hotspots.

By default, CockroachDB will split ranges based on load, providing that `kv.range_split.by_load_enabled` is set to `true`. So if it's not already set to `true`, you probably want to do so now:

```
SET CLUSTER SETTING kv.range_split.by_load_enabled=true;
```

The setting `kv.range_split.load_qps_threshold` defines when a range will be split. By default, it splits when it exceeds 2,000 queries per second (QPS). In our output, it looks like that hot range is at about 1,690 QPS. Maybe we should lower that value so that ranges will split at a lower query rate—say 400 QPS:

```
movr> SET CLUSTER SETTING kv.range_split.load_qps_threshold = 400;
```

If this still fails to break up the hot range issue, we could try manually splitting the ranges. To do this, you need insight into what individual rows are being hit, which requires some application instrumentation or analysis of data. For instance, if we have good reason to believe that Twitter user 50 is responsible for our hotspots, we could issue a command like this to split up their tweets into separate ranges:

```
movr> ALTER TABLE tweet_likes SPLIT AT VALUES (50,1),(50,2),(50,9),(50,20);
         key         | pretty |       split_enforced_until
---------------------+--------+-------------------------------------------
 \325\211\272\211    | /50/1  | 2262-04-11 23:47:16.854776+00:00:00
 \325\211\272\212    | /50/2  | 2262-04-11 23:47:16.854776+00:00:00
```

```
\325\211\272\221 | /50/9  | 2262-04-11 23:47:16.854776+00:00:00
\325\211\272\234 | /50/20 | 2262-04-11 23:47:16.854776+00:00:00
```

Note that we've created some pretty small ranges here. But as vendors of expensive disks like to say, "Disk is cheap." We might even have one range with a single tweet—that tweet gets so many likes that we wanted to isolate its I/O from all other tweets.

Manual splitting doesn't tend to work very well as a reactive strategy; if the automatic splitting hasn't solved the problem, it's most likely a problem that can't be solved by splitting. That might be because the hotspot is either a single row that is "atomic" and can't be split any further or the hotspot is moving (based on an incrementing ID or timestamp), and no stable split point can be found.

Manual splits, therefore, often are a *preemptive* technique: Suppose Twitter user 50 is going to appear in the World Cup Finals tomorrow; you may wish to create some preemptive splits around them, so you don't have to wait for the auto-splitter to notice when the traffic starts.

Unfortunately, there are times when the application design creates hotspots that cannot be resolved by server configuration. If all sessions in an application read and/or write from a single row, then we have few options unless we can change the application design. Sometimes, these sorts of global counters can be partitioned into multiple rows and aggregated when needed. There's also the case—outlined in some detail in Chapter 5—where using monotonically increasing primary keys leads to hot ranges. The use of UUID-based identifiers is the most effective solution here.

In a production scenario, it's not usually possible to change the primary key on a hot table. However, you could try implementing hash-sharded indexes on monotonically incrementing keys—this procedure is also outlined in Chapter 5.

Load Balancing

Failures in load balancing are a common cause of imbalanced workload. Although any node in the cluster can serve as a gateway node for handling queries, it's important that the gatekeeper responsibilities be distributed evenly across the cluster; otherwise, the dedicated gateway node may become overloaded. Figure 15-14 shows an example. A workload has been initiated in which the supplied connection string listed only the first node in the cluster (gubuntu1.local). Although gubuntu1 allocates work to other members of the cluster (particularly, the leaseholders of the ranges involved), the responsibilities of performing the gateway functions are sufficient to unbalance the workload.

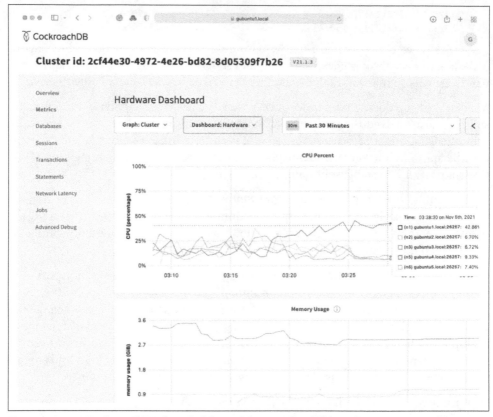

Figure 15-14. CockroachDB leaseholders and query load (large format version (https:// cockroa.ch/cockroachDB-figs))

A similar effect can occur if a load balancer is misconfigured. In Chapter 10, we described how to configure load balancers for on-premise and other deployments. It's important that the load balancer configuration always is up-to-date with the node topology. For instance, if you add a node to a self-hosted cluster behind a `haproxy` load balancer, you should modify the *haproxy.cfg* file to include that new node, and restart the load balancer.

Changes in Cluster Topology

As nodes are added or removed from the cluster, rebalancing of ranges may cause a transitory imbalance in load. These are generally not a frequent or serious concern, but if you have a node that has sporadic connection issues, then you might see the disruption in workload balance as the cluster copes with the disconnection and reconnection.

Figure 15-15 shows how query balance is affected by rebalancing operations. During a period in which some nodes of the cluster were unavailable, ranges were redistributed, resulting in a temporary period of imbalance.

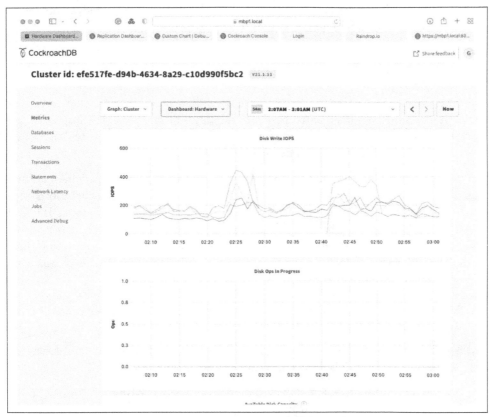

Figure 15-15. Cluster performance during rebalancing (large format version (https://cockroa.ch/cockroachDB-figs))

Admission Control

A well-provisioned CockroachDB cluster may still encounter performance bottlenecks at the node level, as stateful nodes can develop hotspots that last until the cluster rebalances itself. When hotspots occur, they should not cause failures or degraded performance for important work.

Admission control is designed to prioritize work to avoid these issues. When admission control is enabled, CockroachDB sorts request and response operations into work queues by priority, giving preference to higher-priority operations. Internal operations critical to node health, such as node liveness heartbeats, are high priority. The admission control system also prioritizes transactions that hold locks, to reduce contention by releasing locks in a timely manner. Admission control is disabled by default. To enable admission control:

- Set the `admission.kv.enabled` cluster setting to true for work performed by the KV storage system.
- Set the `admission.sql_kv_response.enabled` cluster setting to true for work performed in the SQL layer when receiving KV responses.
- Set the `admission.sql_sql_response.enabled` cluster setting to true for work performed in the SQL layer when receiving responses from Distributed SQL.

We recommend enabling admission control on all layers if you decide to use admission control. The Overload dashboard displays metrics relevant to the admission control system. It is available from the Metrics section of the DB Console. The dashboard displays indicators relevant to the admission control system, such as CPU utilization, storage engine health, and status of the admission control system. Figure 15-16 shows the Overload Dashboard.

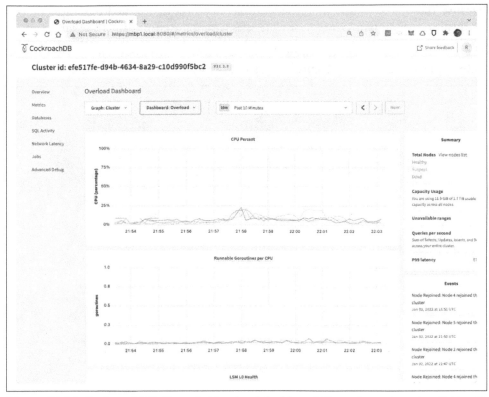

Figure 15-16. CockroachDB Console Overload dashboard (large format version (https://cockroa.ch/cockroachDB-figs))

Network

We've waxed lyrical about the advantages of distributed databases throughout this book. However, it's important to recognize that a distributed database system adds additional latencies to database operations. Many operations involve multiple nodes —but the time taken to transmit information between the nodes of the cluster adds to overall execution time.

Network latency is a factor in almost all database requests, but in a monolithic database like MySQL or PostgreSQL, the only network latency we need to consider is that between the client and the database server. In a distributed system such as CockroachDB, we have to add in the network time for all the communication between the nodes. You may recall from Chapter 2 how a transaction involves network communication between the client, transaction coordinator, leaseholders, and replica nodes (see Figure 2-12).

Because there is so much more network latency in a distributed SQL system, the motivation to maintain low network latencies within the cluster is particularly high.

The DB Console provides a view of the latency between the nodes in a cluster on the Network Diagnostics page. Figure 15-17 shows an example.

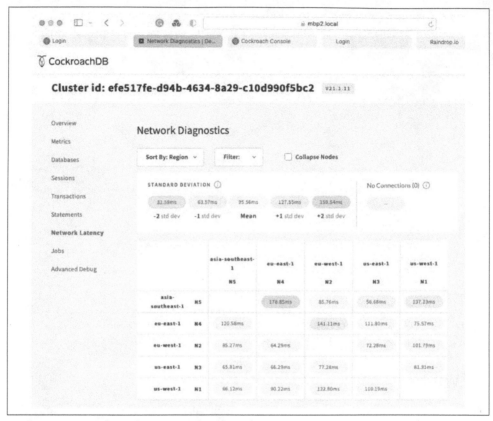

Figure 15-17. CockroachDB Console Network Diagnostics

The expected network latency between nodes in a cluster is dependent on your topology. The latency between nodes in different geographic regions is bound to be higher than nodes in the same data center.

For nodes within a private data center, we'd generally expect latencies under 10 ms. For nodes located in the same continent, 30 to 80 ms are typical. Between continents, latencies of several hundred ms are not unusual. Cloudping (*https:// www.cloudping.co/grid*) maintains a real-time report on latencies between AWS data centers that might give you an idea of the sorts of latencies experienced in the real world.

For nodes within the same region, using a private network between nodes can help reduce network latency by avoiding any disruption of inter-node communication by wider network activity. In this scenario, each node is started with `--listen-addr` instead of `--advertise-addr` to denote the private network IP address or fully-qualified domain name (FQDN) of each node. Nodes use the private network (*https://cockroa.ch/3x0GxGH*) to communicate with each other and communicate with clients over the public network. Setting up a private network is probably not warranted on performance grounds alone, but if one is present, you might as well use it.

In a multiregion deployment, there's probably going to be a limit to what you can do to reduce latency between regions—although we know of one case in which IP routing had been configured in such a way that regions B and C couldn't talk to each other directly, and their packets were transparently routed through region A. This showed up as higher-than-expected latency on the network matrix for those regions.

More generally, you can *avoid* cross-region traffic in the following ways:

- `REGIONAL BY ROW` tables can be used to locate rows in the regions in which they are most likely to be accessed, thus reducing the chance that cross-region lookups will be needed. This is particularly important for rows that are frequently updated and which might otherwise require cross-regional consensus.

- `GLOBAL` tables are perfect for relatively static tables that are read from every location.

- Reading from regional tables can be enhanced by using "follower" reads (e.g., a `SELECT` with `AS OF SYSTEM TIME`). Nonvoting replicas of data are maintained outside the core region, and if a `SELECT` uses `AS OF SYSTEM TIME`, these slightly "stale" copies can be read locally.

See Chapter 11 for more details on optimizing multiregion performance.

Memory Optimization

As with virtually all database systems, CockroachDB uses memory to avoid disk I/O. There are broadly two areas of memory that each node configures:

- The KV store cache keeps copies of blocks of KV store data in memory, avoiding disk I/Os when data is read from the store. Its size is defined by the `--cache` startup parameter.

- The SQL cache includes sort and hash areas and intermediate data sets. Its size is defined by the `--max-sql-memory` startup parameter.

It's not easy to size these caches precisely, so most of the time, we recommend assigning about 35% of total system memory to each cache. These values are not the default settings, so it's important that when you configure a production node, you explicitly allocate the memory areas, as in the following fragment of a system start file:

```
ExecStart=/usr/local/bin/cockroach start --certs-dir=certs
--advertise-addr=gubuntu2 --join=gubuntu1,gubuntu2,gubuntu3
--locality=region=us-west-1,zone=us-west-1a
--max-sql-memory=.35 --cache=.35
```

Key-Value Cache

We can measure the effectiveness of the KV store cache by examining the metrics `rocksdb.block.cache.hits` and `rocksdb.block.cache.misses`. These metrics reflect the number of times a wanted piece of data was found in the cache and the number of times it was not found, resulting in a disk I/O:

```
defaultdb> SELECT *
FROM crdb_internal.node_metrics
WHERE name IN ('rocksdb.block.cache.usage',
 'rocksdb.block.cache.hits',
 'rocksdb.block.cache.misses')
;
  store_id |            name             |     value
-----------+-----------------------------+---------------
         5 | rocksdb.block.cache.hits    | 5.8032604e+07
         5 | rocksdb.block.cache.usage   | 6.7350942e+07
         5 | rocksdb.block.cache.misses  |        396948
```

Note that these metrics are currently still prefixed with *rocksdb* even though they now record statistics from the newer PebbleDB KV store. Also, remember that this query picks up statistics for just one node.

High relative values for `rocksdb.block.cache.misses` might indicate that a larger cache might reduce I/O, although only trial-and-error modifications to cache sizes will prove that hypothesis. Nevertheless, if you have a system that appears to be overloaded with read I/Os, then increasing the cache size—possibly in conjunction with increasing the memory footprint of the node itself—might be effective.

max-sql-memory

The max-sql-memory setting controls the size of the memory area used to store temporary result sets for multistage SQL operations, for sort and hash areas relating to joins, ordering, and grouping. Unlike the information in the KV cache, the SQL cache is transitory for a statement. Once a SQL statement completes, the information is discarded. If the amount of memory required by a SQL statement exceeds the amount available, then the SQL might fail with an error like this:

```
pq: sql: memory budget exceeded: 282746880 bytes requested,
8434251776 bytes in budget
```

Even if your application is not reporting this error, it still could be that max-sql-memory is insufficient because some memory operations will "spill" to disk rather than fail. In the DB Console Statement Details page—the statistic "max scratch disk usage" will reveal the amount of disk used when memory is exceeded.

The amount of memory needed in max-sql-memory will depend largely on the complexity of the SQL your system must accommodate. You can see the memory requirements for individual SQL statements using EXPLAIN ANALYZE:

```
movr> EXPLAIN ANALYZE
SELECT v.TYPE,sum(revenue) FROM rides r
JOIN vehicles v ON (v.city=r.city AND r.vehicle_id=v.id )
GROUP BY v.type
ORDER BY 2 desc;
                       info
------------------------------------------------------------
  planning time: 1ms
  execution time: 54.9s
  distribution: full
  vectorized: true
  rows read from KV: 10,697,726 (1.8 GiB)
  cumulative time spent in KV: 1m31s
  maximum memory usage: 86 MiB
  network usage: 326 MiB (26,104 messages)
```

This statement should need only 86 MiB of SQL memory.

Theoretically, if you have a workload that performs only simple single-row lookups, you won't need much SQL memory, and you might get better performance from allocating that memory to --cache. On the other hand, if there are a lot of complex analytical queries, you might need to increase -max-sql-memory. If in doubt, best to leave the two memory areas at the recommended settings of 35%.

Host Memory

Whatever changes you make to memory configuration, it's absolutely critical to ensure that the OS itself does not run out of memory.

In a self-hosted deployment, you can use the `vmstat` command to show available memory:

```
$ vmstat -s
    16398036 K total memory
    10921928 K used memory
    10847980 K active memory
     3778780 K inactive memory
     1002340 K free memory
        4236 K buffer memory
     4469532 K swap cache
           0 K total swap
           0 K used swap
           0 K free swap
```

You should pay attention to active memory, which represents memory currently allocated to a process, and `used swap`, which indicates how much memory has been swapped to disk. If active memory is approaching total memory, you may be about to experience a memory shortage.

Used swap should generally be zero. Indeed, the CockroachDB team recommends completely disabling virtual memory on production machines (*https://cockroa.ch/3K2Ky0V*).

Disk I/O

A lot of tuning and optimization measures are designed to reduce disk I/O overhead. Even in the age of fast SSD devices, disk I/O remains far slower than memory or CPU operations and typically competes with network time as the biggest drag on distributed SQL performance.

Disk I/O is inevitable. We can reduce some large amount of read disk I/O through memory caching, but any busy CockroachDB database will generate significant I/O. I/O itself is not a problem unless it becomes a bottleneck.

The "Disk Ops in Progress" chart is one place we might see an indication of a disk I/O bottleneck (Figure 15-18). If there are significant operations "in progress," then it probably means that the disk on that node is becoming overloaded.

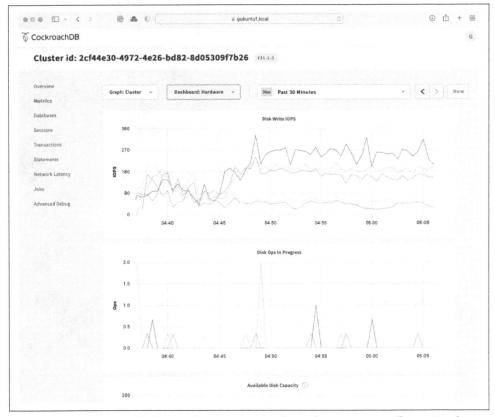

Figure 15-18. CockroachDB Disk Ops in progress (large format version (https://cock roa.ch/cockroachDB-figs))

On a self-hosted cluster, you can look at raw OS statistics to determine if I/O is problematic:[1]

```
$ iostat -xm -o JSON sdc 5 2 |jq
        {
          "avg-cpu": {
            "user": 45.97,
            "nice": 0,
            "system": 3.63,
            "iowait": 1.81,
            "steal": 0,
            "idle": 48.59
          },
          "disk": [
            {
```

---

1 You might need to install the sysstat and jq packages to run this example.

```
        "disk_device": "sdc",
        "r/s": 0.4,
        "w/s": 49.2,
        "rkB/s": 15.2,
        "wkB/s": 2972,
        "rrqm/s": 0,
        "wrqm/s": 0.4,
        "rrqm": 0,
        "wrqm": 0.81,
        "r_await": 15.5,
        "w_await": 42.55,
        "aqu-sz": 2.08,
        "rareq-sz": 38,
        "wareq-sz": 60.41,
        "svctm": 0.87,
        "util": 4.32
    }
  ]
}
```

aqu-sz represents the length of the disk queue. Values close to 0 indicate that the device is under no stress; values above 1 indicate that the disk is frequently busy. The r_await statistic indicates the average time to service a read I/O request in milliseconds. Values greater than 10 ms may indicate that the device is either overloaded or under-configured.

If you determine that the I/O subsystem is struggling, then you have a couple of options:

- Reduce the amount of I/O
- Get faster disks
- Allocate more disks

Reducing the amount of I/O is largely the result of workload tuning (indexes, etc.) that has been the subject of many previous portions of this book. We might also see if allocating more memory to cache can help.

Otherwise, we are looking at increasing I/O bandwidth by using faster or more disks. On a cloud system, we can potentially change our disk type to higher I/O-provisioned devices. On a self-hosted on-premise system, we can look at upgrading our disks from (for instance) mid-tier MLC SSD devices to higher-speed SLC or Peripheral Component Interconnect (PCI) devices. We discussed the considerations for choosing disk devices in Chapter 9.

It's also possible to improve I/O bandwidth by increasing the number of physical disk devices attached to a host. Multiple disks can either be striped (RAID0) to provide greater throughput or the CockroachDB node can be launched with multiple --store flags. We discussed the pros and cons of each approach in Chapter 9.

The other obvious way to address an I/O bottleneck is to distribute the I/O load across a larger number of nodes...which is the subject of our next and final section.

Scaling Out

We started this book by describing the objectives of the CockroachDB database. To paraphrase Chapter 1, a core design goal of CockroachDB is *scalability*—to allow cluster performance to scale predictably as the number of nodes increases.

We'd be the last to recommend that you solve all performance problems by adding nodes to a cluster. While adding nodes will often—though not always—resolve performance problems, it's not always the most cost-effective or fastest option. On-premise, adding nodes costs money and usually takes a significant amount of time. In the cloud, adding nodes adds directly to the cost of your cluster. If you can resolve a performance problem by adding an index or taking another cost-effective measure, that's preferable to adding nodes. Furthermore, there are some performance issues—those relating to hot ranges in particular—that cannot be resolved by simply adding more nodes.

However, when you've done your best to optimize your workload and node configurations, scaling out your CockroachDB cluster is exactly what you're supposed to do. There are CockroachDB clusters running with hundreds of nodes in production, so you're definitely not traveling into uncharted territory.

We described the process for adding additional nodes to the cluster in Chapter 14. Most of the time, once the new node is added, performance throughput will adjust automatically.

In general, we want to ensure that all nodes in the cluster are roughly equivalent in terms of hardware capacity. However, because the sweet spot for price-performance changes over time (even for cloud-based VMs)—you may find yourself tempted to add new nodes that exceed the capacity of existing nodes. That is perfectly fine, but over time you should endeavor to upgrade the older nodes in the cluster to the new node configuration. Indeed, the process of "repaving" a cluster involves periodically and systematically upgrading nodes in the cluster to a new configuration.

Summary

In this chapter, we've looked at some of the ways to improve the performance of a running cluster. There are typically two modes in which we approach cluster performance—systematic tuning and "firefighting." Both modes are valid, but we'd encourage as much systematic tuning as possible to avoid the sort of performance crises that typically lead to firefighting.

The most important factor in cluster performance is workload. Therefore, our first step when evaluating cluster performance is to ensure that there are no anomalous or poorly tuned workloads.

Balancing workload across all nodes of the cluster is critical. Imbalance is usually caused either by a misconfiguration of load balancing or "hot" ranges. We discussed how to address these issues.

Network latency and disk I/O are major factors in almost all database workloads. We need to ensure that neither of these resources is a bottleneck.

Once we've confirmed that our workload, network, and node configuration are optimal, then it's time to consider scaling the cluster by adding new nodes to the cluster. Although we don't recommend scaling out as a universal panacea for all performance issues, it's what CockroachDB was designed for and definitely not something to be nervous about.

This is the last chapter in the book. We hope you find it a useful reference for working with CockroachDB. Remember, though, that there are myriad resources available to you. In particular, the CockroachDB documentation set is constantly being expanded, and there is a rich community of fellow CockroachDB users, most of whom are more than ready to collaborate. Good luck, and feel free to reach out!

Index

portability, 14
Postgres, 72
PostgreSQL, 80
    CDC slots, 210
    DDL (Data Definition Language)
        extracting, 204-205
    wire protocol, 20
pre-relational databases, 4
prepared statements, 165-167
PRIMARY KEY, 98
primary keys, 123
    3NF (third normal form), 123
    attributes, ordering, 131
    DDL conversion, 205
    design, 127
    hash-sharded, 130-131
    tables, 97
    UUID (universal unique identifier), 128
primary regions, 42
PrivateLink (AWS), 359
PRIVILEGE channel, logging, 377
privilege management, 374
programming languages
    Java, 74-75
    Node.js, 73-74
    Python, 75-76, 77-78
projection, 173
Prometheus, 386-388
protected timestamps, 48
protocols
    gossip, 40
    wire protocol, 20
Python, 75-76

Q

QLC (quad-level cell), 294
QUEL language, 8
queries
    anti-joins, 83-83
    arrays, 89
    common table expressions, 86-87
    correlated subqueries, 85
    cross joins, 83
    distribution, 251-253
    FROM clause, 81
    group operations, 84
    horizontal partitioning and, 136
    JOINS, 82
    lateral subqueries, 85-86

ORDER BY clause, 87-88
partition elimination, 136
SELECT list, 81
set operations, 83-84
standard view, 103
subqueries, 85-85
WHERE clause, 86
window functions, 88-89
with JSON, 91-92
query optimizer, 275

R

RAC (Real Application Clusters), 10
Raft, 40, 43
    leaseholders and, 44
    Raft leader, 20
    Raft log, 44
Raft logs, 340
ranges, 22
    splits, 41
RANK() window function, 89
RDBMS (relational database management system), 8
    clustered systems, 10
read/write conflicts, 37
recurring backup, 348
RECURSIVE clause, 87
redaction flag in log entries, 396
redundancies, 122
region topologies, 299
regional by row tables, 42, 137
regional tables, 42
    regional by row tables, 42
regions
    cluster regions, 42
    multiregion deployment, 315
relational data models, 120
relational model
    constraints, 6
    implementing, 7
    joins, 6
    keys, 6
    operations, 6
    projections, 6
    relations, 6
    rows, 7
    tables, 7
    third normal form, 6
    transactions, 7

T

About the Authors

Guy Harrison is CTO at ProvenDB and a software professional with more than 20 years of experience in database design, development, administration, and optimization. He is the author of *Next Generation Databases* (Apress), *MongoDB Performance Tuning* (Apress), *Oracle Performance Survival Guide* (Prentice Hall), *MySQL Stored Procedure Programming* (O'Reilly), and many other books and articles on database technology.

Jesse Seldess is VP of Education at Cockroach Labs, where he leads the documentation and training teams. He has nearly 20 years of experience in technical documentation and has built teams from the ground up at Cockroach Labs and AppNexus (now Xandr).

Ben Darnell is the cofounder and chief architect at Cockroach Labs, where he built the distributed consensus protocols that underpin CockroachDB's transactional model. He started his career at Google and then went on to a series of startups where he saw firsthand the need for better scalable storage systems.

Colophon

The animal on the cover of *CockroachDB: The Definitive Guide* is an Australian bush cockroach. There are more than four hundred species of native cockroaches that live in the bush, which tend to be more visually appealing than their American or German counterparts.

A striking example of an Australian bush cockroach is the Mardi Gras cockroach (*Polyzosteria mitchelli*), also known as Mitchell's diurnal cockroach. This wingless, flat insect has a blue-black body with yellow stripes along its back, and is primarily found in the arid regions of western and south Australia.

Native cockroaches feed on pollen, bark, and tree leaves. Some species have even adapted to eating decomposing wood, akin to termites. Native cockroaches are an important part of their ecosystem, serving as a valuable source of food for invertabrates, mammals, frogs, and reptiles. To repel such predators, certain species release a pungent odor when in danger.

The cover illustration is by Karen Montgomery, based on an antique line engraving from *Insects Abroad*. The cover fonts are Gilroy Semibold and Guardian Sans. The text font is Adobe Minion Pro; the heading font is Adobe Myriad Condensed; and the code font is Dalton Maag's Ubuntu Mono.

O'REILLY®

Learn from experts.
Become one yourself.

Books | Live online courses
Instant Answers | Virtual events
Videos | Interactive learning

Get started at oreilly.com.

CPSIA information can be obtained
at www.ICGtesting.com
Printed in the USA
JSHW022009190422
25102JS00003B/5